Math Instruction for Students with Learning Problems

SUSAN PERRY GURGANUS

College of Charleston

PEARSON

Boston ● New York ● San Francisco

Mexico City ● Montreal ● Toronto ● London ● Madrid ● Munich ● Paris

Hong Kong ● Singapore ● Tokyo ● Cape Town ● Sydney

Executive Editor: Virginia Lanigan
Series Editorial Assistant: Matthew Buchholz
Senior Marketing Manager: Kris Ellis-Levy
Production Editor: Annette Joseph
Editorial-Production Service: Omegatype Typography, Inc.
Composition Buyer: Linda Cox
Manufacturing Buyer: Linda Morris
Electronic Composition: Omegatype Typography, Inc.
Cover Designer: Elena Sidorova

For related titles and support materials, visit our online catalog at www.ablongman.com.

Between the time website information is gathered and then published, it is not unusual for some sites to have closed. Also, the transcription of URLs can result in typographical errors. The publisher would appreciate notification where these errors occur so that they may be corrected in subsequent editions.

Many of the designations used by manufacturers and sellers to distinguish their products are claimed as trademarks. Where those designations appear in this book, and Allyn and Bacon was aware of a trademark claim, the designations have been printed in initial or all caps.

Library of Congress Cataloging-in-Publication Data

Gurganus, Susan Perry.
   Math instruction for students with learning problems / Susan Perry Gurganus.—1st ed.
     p.   cm.
   Includes bibliographical references and index.
   ISBN 0-205-46089-5
   1. Mathematics—Study and teaching.   2. Learning disabled children—Education.   3.
Mathematics—Remedial teaching.   I. Title.
   QA11.2.G87 2007
   371.92'647—dc22
                                             2006046818

Printed in the United States of America

10 9 8 7 6 5 4 3 2 1   10 09 08 07 06

To my husband, Al, who encouraged this project from its inception and whose love and understanding during the long hours of research, writing, and revising were constant.

Brief Contents

Contents

ASSESSMENT AND INSTRUCTION

Preface

This book is for current and future educators who want to learn more about mathematics and effective methods for teaching mathematics to students who have great difficulty learning and doing mathematics. You might be an elementary teacher with students struggling to learn math concepts, a special education or remedial teacher attempting to address specific mathematics disabilities, or a secondary mathematics educator seeking information on how to teach students who have mathematics learning problems. The purpose of this book is to provide the following:

1. Information about the current mathematics standards for all students within the contexts of mathematics reform, high-stakes assessment, special education mandates, and societal change
2. Specific approaches for assessing and teaching mathematics to students with learning problems, including methods of informal assessment, research-supported instruction, problem solving, and functional applications
3. Guidance in developing deeper understanding of the "big ideas" of mathematics to facilitate more effective instruction with struggling students
4. Numerous resources including website links, journals and organizations, concrete materials, commercial programs, and other resources for teaching mathematics
5. Most importantly, the stimulus and positive approach for teaching mathematics to students who have difficulty learning

ORGANIZATIONAL OVERVIEW

Whether you are a practicing teacher, teacher candidate, or college instructor, this book has been organized to be user friendly. You can move through the book in a number of ways, depending on your interests and purpose.

The first part of the book sets the foundation for mathematics teaching. Chapter 1 reviews mathematics reform movements, outlines the current national mathematics standards and their implications for students with disabilities and their teachers, provides an overview of mathematics curriculum K through 12, and provides some "attitude adjustment" activities to get the reader thinking mathematically. The second chapter examines the foundations of mathematics, including concept development in young children, theories related to mathematics learning, and learner characteristics.

Chapters 3 through 7 build on the previous chapters to develop the most effective teaching methods for students with mathematics learning problems:

■ Chapter 3 examines how mathematics learning is assessed for various purposes: identification of mathematics learning problems, standardized assessment for accountability, and classroom-based assessment for teacher decision making. Strategies are provided for the most efficient and effective informal methods.

■ Chapter 4 presents the heart of this text—guidelines for effective mathematics instruction with students with learning problems. Ten guidelines are described and expanded for teachers of students in all grade levels. This chapter also addresses lesson and unit development.

■ Chapter 5 explores problem-solving instruction. While the reader will learn about problem solving throughout the book, this chapter focuses on effective problem-solving sequences and heuristics across grade levels.

■ Chapter 6 further expands on effective instruction by exploring the materials and other resources that enhance mathematics teaching and learning. This chapter includes sections on using manipulatives, technology, and curriculum programs.

■ Chapter 7 addresses functional, applied mathematics. Readers will explore real-life applications of mathematics and integrating mathematics with literature, science, and other school subjects.

There has been a long-running dilemma among mathematics educators about the content of "how to teach mathematics" courses and their texts. How much time should the instructor devote to teaching (or re-teaching) actual math concepts versus the strategies for teaching those concepts? Many teacher candidates and teachers are deficient in mathematics concept understanding themselves. To begin to address these deficiencies, this book infuses mathematics content within the methodology, deliberately sampling across grade levels and content strands throughout the text.

To supplement that content is a more intensive study of mathematics content in the final section of the book, organized by strands from a "big ideas" perspective. The term *big ideas* is used across the curriculum to denote those most critical, underlying concepts of the content area. "Big ideas are those concepts, principles, or heuristics that facilitate the most efficient and broadest acquisition of knowledge. They are the keys that unlock a content area for a broad range of diverse learners" (Kame'enui & Carnine, 1998, p. 8).

The big idea strands central to mathematics presented here are:

A. Number Sense and Place Value—the understanding of numbers and how they are represented and related, and the system of assigning value to digit positions. This strand also includes an overview of data analysis.
B. Whole-Number Relationships—how the operations on numbers are related; the interdependency of addition, subtraction, multiplication, and division; and their properties.

C. Spatial Sense—the ability to visualize relative positions in space in mathematics applications such as measurement, geometry, and graphing.

D. Rational Numbers—including fractions, decimals, percentages, and other expressions of numbers. Related concepts include equivalence, proportion, ratio, and probability.

E. Functions—relations that involve one-to-one and one-to-many correspondences. Concepts explored in this strand include variables, rates of change, linearity, exponentiality, and quadratic functions.

So the choice is yours: read straight through, work through the numbered chapters, study the big ideas strands, alternate chapters with strands, or select topics of interest. Each chapter includes instructional features to assist your reading. Chapters begin with a series of questions to provoke thinking. All chapters include "Try This" activities embedded in places where exploration will enhance your understanding. There are special boxes and figures with elaborated examples, illustrations of concepts, and multicultural connections. Each chapter closes with a summary and resource list. This book was written to provoke thinking, learning, and an enjoyment for mathematics that will be shared with students who currently struggle to learn.

Supplements for Students and Instructors

■ **Instructor's Manual with Test Bank.** The instructor's manual includes sample syllabi and course assignments with rubrics; sample professional development outlines; chapter outlines with teaching notes and class activities; and a test bank with multiple-choice and essay-type items.

■ **Companion Website (www.ablongman.com/gurganus1e).** The Companion Website includes solutions to the problems that appear throughout the text, as well as other features for students and instructors.

Acknowledgments

I am grateful for the confidence of my editor, Virginia Lanigan, and her willingness to take on a new author and unusual project. Her guidance, encouragement, and experience made this book possible.

Thanks also to my colleagues at the College of Charleston who offered expertise and reviewed sample chapters: Linda Edwards for her keen understanding of early childhood and her experience as a writer; Michael Skinner for reviewing the theoretical material and statistical representations; Robert Fowler for recommendations on the technology sections; Ann Wallace for her collaboration on multiplication approaches; and the entire staff of the Addlestone Library, College of Charleston, for their tireless assistance and invaluable support services. Special thanks goes to former graduate student, friend, and master mathematics teacher, Melinda Del Mastro, for her assistance with the strand on functions.

I also thank my reviewers: K. Alisa Lowrey, University of South Carolina; Margo A. Mastropieri, George Mason University; Sandra Luna McCune, Stephen Austin State University; Kendall McLeod, Kelly Mill Middle School; and Mary Ellen Sullivan, Mount Saint Vincent.

Thanks to my graduate student assistants—Whitney Pickens, Betsy Parker, and Allison Grooms—for attending my mathematics methods classes and taking critical notes, tracking down sources and permissions, and maintaining chapter files.

Finally, thanks to the students in my mathematics methods courses for the past four years. You will find your names embedded in word problems throughout this book. Together we found that teaching and learning about mathematics is incredibly fun!

SPG

Chapter 1

Chapter Questions

1. How are teachers' and students' attitudes toward mathematics related to learning?
2. What mathematics reforms have influenced the current mathematics curriculum?
3. What national standards have an effect on state and local mathematics curricula?
4. What mathematics topics are emphasized in K through grade 12 classrooms?
5. How have the national standards affected state and district testing programs?
6. What are the roles of general, remedial, and special educators in providing mathematics instruction?

Mathematics in Today's Schools: The Context for Learning Challenges

Angela Smith has been hired immediately after graduation as a special education teacher at Maple Street Middle School. The principal has just informed her that she is to support regular mathematics classes for three periods of the day and will teach special pull-out mathematics classes two periods each day. Leaving the principal's office, Angela feels panic as she struggles to recall the mathematics programs reviewed over only a two-week period in her special education methods course.

Joseph Lopez has just met with his new principal at Hilltop High School and was informed that a total of 20 students with learning, emotional, and communication disabilities will be in his two Geometry classes and three Algebra I classes. Joseph recalls accommodations for physically, visually, and hearing disabled students but cannot imagine what he should plan for students with other learning problems.

Chris Johnson feels fortunate to have a teaching position at Pine Grove Elementary School in October after relocating to Pine Grove to be closer to her family. But the meeting with the principal has left her puzzled. What is a remedial mathematics support teacher?

In a meeting of new teachers in the district, Angela expresses her anxiety about teaching a subject she is not very strong in herself. Joseph talks about his love of everything mathematical but uncertainty regarding student needs. Chris feels confident that her five years of elementary teaching will be beneficial for instructional planning but is not sure about how to work effectively with so many other teachers. ■ ● ▲

Angela, Joseph, and Chris are facing the challenges of new teaching positions that will involve mathematics instruction or the support of mathematics instruction for students who are struggling to learn mathematics skills and concepts. In a fairly short period of time they must understand their instructional roles, get to know students, review the district mathematics curriculum standards, and develop long- and short-range instructional plans in cooperation with other teachers. All three teachers have doubts about their abilities to meet the needs of students with learning problems within the mathematics curriculum. But they all have many strengths and demonstrate professional attitudes about developing new skills. How important is the teacher's attitude toward collaborating with other teachers, working with challenging students, and teaching mathematics? These professional dispositions are as important as content and pedagogical knowledge and skills for successful instructional programs.

There is some evidence that teacher candidates in elementary and special education are generally weak in mathematics content and are anxious about the responsibility of teaching mathematics (Timmerman, 2003; Kimmel, Deek, & O'Shea, 1999). Many of their own experiences with math in school were not enjoyable and their teachers rarely emphasized concept understanding or meaningful applications. When asked about memories of math class, many teachers and teacher candidates did not hesitate to mention the following negative teacher behaviors (Gurganus, 2005; see also Oberlin, 1982; Martinez & Martinez, 1996):

- modeled their dislike for math
- never showed students "why"
- verbally abused students for errors
- insisted on following the text page by page
- gave lots of homework every night
- didn't give feedback on student work
- didn't show how the topic was relevant
- told students they must work all problems their way
- made students correct all mistakes
- used lots of worksheets
- skipped the applications and hands-on activities
- treated math as a set of facts and operations to memorize
- withheld instruction (I'm only going to explain this once.)
- isolated learners (There will be no talking.)
- used extra math work as punishment

One teacher recalled her third-grade teacher who administered a multiplication test each day before recess. All students scoring less than 100% on the one-minute test were required to stay in from recess and write the facts over and over until the class returned. There were quite a few students who didn't have recess for weeks. This teacher never taught multiplication as a concept or explained how multiplication is related to addition. She didn't even show students strategies and relationships such as the commutative property ($2 \times 3 = 6$ and $3 \times 2 = 6$). Students were expected to memorize 100 facts on their own.

Great teachers also influence attitudes toward mathematics. One seventh-grade teacher was responsible for both mathematics and science. She frequently integrated mathematics skills into science activities such as preparing graphs showing the development of a chicken from an egg. She taught rules only after students had explored several examples of a problem. The entire class had an inquiring-mind philosophy that would be called "guided discovery learning" today.

Teachers and teacher candidates should explore their own experiences with and feelings about mathematics if they are to be effective mathematics teachers for students with learning problems. The following range of statements can assist teachers and teacher candidates in identifying their current views about teaching mathematics.

1. I avoid teaching math at all costs. I don't do well in math and I'd hate to teach my students the wrong way.
2. I really dislike math but if you give me a good textbook with lots of practice problems, I can muddle through.
3. I wish I knew more about teaching math. If I knew more effective ways of teaching it I wouldn't feel so intimidated.
4. I trained (am training) as a special education teacher, not a math teacher. In fact, we didn't have a single course on how to teach math in my training program.
5. Math is just another subject in school. I do (plan to do) the lessons and assign the work. I will spend extra time drilling what I know will be on the end-of-year tests.
6. I'm okay in math and try to learn more by going to workshops and reading journals. I want to learn more.
7. I'm a whiz at math but I'm not sure how to get the concepts across to students.
8. I enjoy (look forward to) teaching math and understand the concepts fairly well. I use (plan to use) a lot of hands-on and problem-solving activities in my classes. I still want to learn more.

MATHEMATICAL DISPOSITIONS

One strategy for in-service or pre-service teachers to get into a more mathematical frame of mind and actually enjoy some interesting aspects of mathematics is to engage in games and other activities based on mathematical concepts. These are also great for beginning the school year with students. Figures 1.1 through 1.5 illustrate several different types of activities including puzzles, number patterns, everyday math, and dominoes. Other activities can be found in mathematics journals, professional books, and on teacher websites.

What teacher dispositions are critical for promoting student learning of mathematics? Some are certainly global, important for all teachers: a keen personal interest in learning and growing; reflective teaching; a view that all students can learn but each student is an individual learner; high but realistic expectations of learners; flexibility in adapting instruction, materials, and assessment to varying contexts; and the ability to create a positive yet goal-oriented classroom environment. Some dispositions are more specific to mathematics content: genuine interest in mathematical concepts and connections; a persistence with

Figure 1.1
Picture Puzzlers

1. How many 2 by 1 by 1 blocks (length by width by height) make up this structure if at least one face of each block is visible? How many 1 by 1 by 1 blocks would be required to make the same structure?

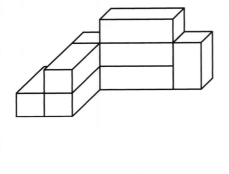

2. Here is a pattern for making a cube (three-dimensional shape with six squares for sides—such as a die). The thin "tabs" are to be folded for gluing. Using a piece of graph paper, design another pattern for a cube. Or try another shape, like a pyramid or tetrahedron.

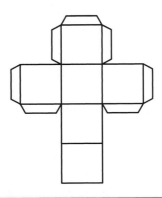

Figure 1.2
Fun with Fibonacci Numbers

Fibonacci numbers are numbers of the following sequence: 1, 1, 2, 3, 5, 8, 13, 21 . . . where successive numbers are the sum of the two preceding numbers. This sequence of numbers or patterns formed by this sequence appears naturally in the environment. Find a leaf, stem, pinecone, or seashell with the spiral pattern shown here. Look for this pattern elsewhere in nature or art.

Draw your own spiral on a piece of graph paper following these directions.

1. Select one square near the center and trace it.
2. Trace in one square to the right.
3. Trace in a square that is 2 blocks by 2 blocks (2 x 2) above the two previous squares.
4. Trace in a square that is 3 by 3 to the left.
5. Trace in a square below that is 5 by 5.
6. To the right, trace in the next square, 8 by 8.
7. Above, trace in a square 13 by 13.
8. Continue as long as you have room on the paper.
9. Beginning in the first square, connect the corners of each square in the same sequence with a looping spiral, like that of a nautilus shell.

That spiral is a Fibonacci pattern!

Figure 1.3
Other Number Patterns

1. Predict the number that would come next. What is each pattern?

   2, 3, 5, 7, 11, 13, 17, 19, _____, _____
   1, 4, 9, 16, 25, _____, _____
   1, 3, 4, 7, 11, 18, _____, _____

2. Using the hundreds chart (1 to 100) in the appendix, explore the concepts of multiples and factors (prime and composite numbers):

   > circle 2 and strike through all multiples of 2
   > circle 3 and strike through all multiples of 3
   > continue with 5, 7, 11, 13, 17.
   > (The number 1 is neither prime nor composite.)

   Circle all numbers not crossed out. These are prime numbers and don't have factors other than one and themselves. This process is called the "Sieve of Eratosthenes" after the Greek mathematician (275–195 B.C.E.) given credit for this simple method for identifying prime numbers (Wolfram, 2002).

   (See the solutions at the Companion Website, www.ablongman.com/gurganus1e.)

Figure 1.4
Math All around Us

1. Take a walk around your neighborhood and make a list of all the mathematics applications you spot.

2. Look through a newspaper and make a list of all the mathematics applications (obvious and hidden). Some examples of obvious applications: weather charts, stock market, sports statistics, grocery sales. Hidden applications: probability of events, statistics within an article, graphs, reports on science and technology.

Figure 1.5
Dominoes: A Common Game with Powerful Math Concepts

Obtain a set of 28 dominoes or copy and cut out a set from a public domain website. Study the dot patterns and count up the groupings. The pieces are sometimes called bones, the dots are called pips. Any group of bones with a common end is called a suit and bones with identical ends are called doublets.

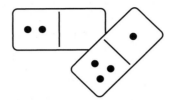

Make up a game for two players or follow the rules below for a simple game. (More complex rules can be found in the encyclopedia or books on dominoes.)

• Place all pieces facedown and shuffle them around.
• Draw for the lead by selecting the piece with the highest number and reshuffle. Each player then draws seven bones.
• The lead player usually plays his highest domino first. The object of this game is to have the fewest pips left in hand.
• The second player must play a piece that matches one end of a piece on the table. Doublets are played crosswise. Players who cannot make a match must draw another bone.
• The player who matches all bones in his hand calls "Domino" and earns the number of points as there are pips in his opponent's hand.

finding solutions to problems; the willingness to consider multiple processes or multiple solutions to the same problem; and an appreciation for mathematics-related applications such as those in music, art, architecture, geography, demographics, or technology.

Student Dispositions

What about the mathematics dispositions of students? There is quite a bit of research on the strong relationship between attitudes and achievement in general. Research on the student's view of his or her own learning and success (Weiner, 1985) indicates that students who have self-perceptions of low ability or make "I can't" statements usually debilitate their own success. An early study by Collins (1982) of children with high or low efficacy beliefs related to mathematics ability found that children who had the stronger belief in their efficacy, regardless of ability, solved more problems, chose to rework unsuccessful problems, and eventually solved more problems successfully. Other studies have confirmed the power of belief in one's abilities. Bouffard-Bouchard (1990) found that regardless of ability level, students with higher efficacy beliefs showed greater strategic flexibility in searching for solutions, achieved higher performances, and were more accurate in self-evaluations. Schunk (1989) studied children with severe deficits in mathematics in a program of self-directed learning. Children's learning was influenced by cognitive modeling, strategy instruction, performance feedback, and learning goals. Again, children with similar ability differed in performance on the strength of their perceived efficacy.

A student's perceived self-efficacy is the "belief in one's capabilities to organize and execute the courses of action required to produce given attainments" (Bandura, 1997, p. 3). Perceived self-efficacy may influence motivation, thought processes, course of action, level of effort, perseverance, and, ultimately, level of accomplishment. High self-efficacy and improved performance result when students set short-range goals, apply specific learning strategies, and receive performance-contingent rewards (Pintrich & De Groot, 1990). Self-assurance from efficacy beliefs may be the key factor that combines with capability to enable students to manage difficult tasks. The opposite disposition, learned helplessness, results when students view their failures as insurmountable and out of their control. Helplessness is accompanied by passivity, loss of motivation, depression, and declining performance.

The most influential sources of efficacy information are experience, vicarious experience, and verbal persuasion (Bandura, 1997). Students who experience success begin building positive beliefs in their abilities. However, easy successes are not helpful; experience with success in challenging tasks that require perseverance and even involve setbacks along the way lead to stronger efficacy beliefs. Vicarious experiences, or viewing models by which to compare one's capabilities, can positively or negatively influence self-efficacy beliefs. Teachers should be cautious in using comparative models so that students focus on the instructive elements for self-improvement and not simply make an evaluative comparison. Finally, verbal persuasion, more frequently termed performance feedback, can also promote or undermine self-efficacy beliefs, depending on its use. Good persuaders must cultivate students' beliefs in their capabilities, structure activities for success, and encourage students to engage in self-evaluation, not merely voice positive encouragers.

A critical goal for teachers providing mathematics instruction is to foster positive student dispositions toward mathematics learning. Desirable student dispositions include:

- seeing the world mathematically
- willingness to take risks and explore multiple problem solutions
- persistence with challenging problems
- taking responsibility for reflecting on one's own work
- an appreciation for the communicative power of mathematical language
- willingness to question and probe one another's thinking about ideas
- willingness to try different tools for exploring mathematical concepts
- having confidence in one's abilities
- perceiving problems as challenges (NCTM, 2000; Martinez & Martinez, 1996)

Teachers know that students' attitudes toward math can range from enthusiasm, interest, and confidence to dislike, rigidity of thought, avoidance, anxiety, and even phobia. What makes the difference? In addition to success with difficult tasks and positive performance feedback, as described previously, there is evidence that teachers' beliefs about their instructional efficacy predicts levels of academic achievement, regardless of level of student ability (Ashton & Webb, 1986). Teachers with a high sense of instructional efficacy tend to view all students as teachable, believe they can overcome negating community influences through effective teaching, devote more classroom time to academics, maintain an orderly classroom, encourage struggling students, hold high expectations, and encourage student self-direction (Bandura, 1997). Teachers working with students with mathematics learning problems should choose significant and interesting topics, focus on understanding, have high but reasonable expectations, help students set and monitor learning goals, and acknowledge student achievements.

Encouraging Students with Learning Problems

Students who struggle with learning mathematics may comprise, by very rough estimates, 6 to 25 percent of the K–12 school population. Students with specific disabilities as identified under the Individuals with Disabilities Education Act (IDEA, 2004) include those with specific learning disabilities in mathematics, cognitive or developmental disabilities, emotional disabilities, communication disorders, traumatic brain injuries, and some severe health impairments such as attention deficit hyperactivity disorder (ADHD). Other students with disabilities who do not qualify under IDEA but may need individual provisions for learning include students with physical disabilities and health impairments (such as ADHD). Students who are learning English as a second or other language (ELL, English Language Learners) may have related mathematics learning problems. Other students, such as those with cultural differences, scarce resources at home, or highly mobile families, may also have significant learning problems.

For these students with challenges learning mathematics, positive dispositions are a critical foundation for achievement. Teachers have the responsibility for creating classroom contexts that foster positive dispositions. Some concrete methods for promoting positive dispositions in students towards mathematics include:

- Seek out student interests and plan activities that make connections with those interests. For example, one entire class was interested in playing softball. They challenged other fourth-grade classrooms and kept statistics on every aspect of their games.
- Personalize math lessons by using student interests, names, real events, and student-created problems. Some teachers name classroom "discoveries" after students: "the Sally Brown proof."
- Allocate just two or three minutes at the beginning of each mathematics class to warm-up activities with familiar material. Begin with success!
- Create classroom procedures that allow students to take risks and make mistakes without punishment or humiliation.

- Encourage students to set personal goals in mathematics and keep track of their progress through individual portfolios or graphs.
- Check for student understanding when introducing new concepts and adjust explanations and examples until students demonstrate strong understanding. Check understanding by watching students work and by listening to their explanations, not through testing at this initial learning phase.
- Analyze students' mathematics knowledge and understanding for gaps that will hinder new learning. Plan remedial instruction that will fill those gaps by connecting concepts, not with isolated skills.
- Communicate clearly with students the "why" of mathematics for the year. What new learning will they accomplish? Why will it seem they are working on some of the same topics as last year? How will this learning be beneficial in the long run? Listen to students' explanations of their views of mathematics.
- When students have accomplishments, guide them in making explicit connections with their efforts.
- When students hit roadblocks, teach specific strategies for learning skills or procedures.
- Model positive dispositions—about mathematics and about working collaboratively with other teachers for student learning.

The combination of positive teacher and student dispositions towards mathematics learning will provide a critical component for success with mathematics instruction.

MATHEMATICS REFORM

Most educators will point to the 4 October 1957 launching of the Soviet satellite *Sputnik I* as the flash point for reform initiatives in mathematics and science education in the United States. However, reform initiatives have been proposed throughout the history of education in this country—whenever the purpose of public education and the results of educators' efforts have been debated. The 1878 call for pragmatism by Charles Sanders Peirce, the 1893 Committee of Ten's high school curriculum proposals, early 20th century John Dewey's progressive education initiatives, and the visionary writings of James Bryant Conant in the 1950s and 1960s on school reform, national goals, professionalizing teachers, and comprehensive high schools were all major reform efforts that had an impact on mathematics instruction (Parker, 1993).

It has been only since the 1980s, however, that reform efforts have been truly national in scope with intense public scrutiny. The 1983 report *A Nation at Risk: The Imperative for Educational Reform*, ironically initiated as justification for dismantling the Department of Education in the Reagan administration, was the catalyst for national educational reform (NCEE). Citing dismal performance data on the achievement of students in the United States as compared with those of the rest of the industrialized world, the report called for more rigorous high school studies. It initiated higher standards for college admission, a nationwide system of standardized achievement testing, more homework, longer school days and years, career ladders and other incentives to attract better qualified teachers, and more state and local financing for school reforms. Dozens of other national reports on various aspects of education followed in the next few years. Most called for increased standards for students, better teacher preparation, and accountability to the community.

The reform initiatives of the mid-1980s represented a convergence of attention on standards-based curriculum development, accountability, and needs of employers in a technological world. For educational evaluation, they represented a shift from the traditional focus on input measures such as per-pupil spending and teacher–student ratio to outcome measures of student achievement. These initiatives spurred the 1989 and 2000 NCTM curriculum standards for mathematics, the Goals 2000 challenges (1990), the Trends in International Mathematics and Science Studies (since 1995), and the No Child Left Behind (NCLB) Act of 2001.

Although the reform documents mention students with disabilities only in general terms, the impact on these students has been significant. The 1997 reauthorization of the Individuals with Disabilities Education Act (IDEA), with its 1999 regulations, made mandatory the inclusion of students with disabilities in state and district assessments and the related standards-based curricula. The 2001 NCLB Act and 2004 IDEA required special education teachers to be highly qualified in the content areas, such as mathematics, that they teach.

NATIONAL MATHEMATICS STANDARDS

Leadership in reorienting reform efforts to focus on curriculum, instruction, and assessment standards for mathematics was provided by the National Council of Teachers of Mathematics (NCTM) in 1986 when it established the Commission on Standards for School Mathematics and involved all constituent groups in the development of national standards (Romberg, 1993). The *Curriculum and Evaluation Standards for School Mathematics* were published in 1989, the *Professional Teaching Standards* in 1991, and *Assessment Standards for School Mathematics* in 1995. The driving vision statement for the standards was "All students need to learn more, and often different, mathematics and . . . instruction in mathematics must be significantly revised" (NCTM, 1989, p. 1).

The 1989 curriculum standards were organized into four sections, matching the four planning groups: K–4, 5–8, 9–12, and evaluation. Each of the three grade-level spans included processes as the first four standards: problem solving, communication, reasoning, and connections. Nine or ten curricular areas followed within each span. The evaluation standards included three related to general principles of assessment, seven on student assessment, and four concerned with program evaluation. Since 1989, most states have revised their curriculum frameworks to reflect the NCTM standards.

Criticism of the standards and their development process was immediate. The standards were developed primarily through expert opinion and consensus, rather than research review. The product, therefore, was plagued by vague constructs, pedagogical dogma, and idealistic goals. The curriculum standards were criticized for being, on the one hand, an idealistic vision for promoting conversations about mathematics education while, on the other, attempting to establish clear expectations for student achievement by the end of each grade-level span.

Special educators cited the complete absence of references to students with disabilities, especially egregious given the increasing diversity of the K–12 student population in the 1990s (Hofmeister, 1993; Mercer, Harris, & Miller, 1993). They also questioned the fundamental process of directing change by standard setting rather than through validated, replicable, and affordable educational interventions that have been demonstrated to work with specific students. Also of concern was the emphasis on broad-based thinking skills rather than domain-specific ones. Further, they challenged the rigid adherence to an extreme constructivist paradigm where students invent their own knowledge and spend little time practicing routine skills, where teachers pose open-ended problems and provide opportunities to explore and converse, but don't directly instruct (more on these theoretical debates in Chapter 2).

The NCTM standards have undergone review and revision since 1989, headed by The Commission on the Future of the Standards, a process that resulted in the 2000 *Principles and Standards for School Mathematics* (NCTM). The writing group appointed by the commission circulated a discussion draft of the revised standards in 1998, and equity was one of nineteen issues raised during this input period. How can the document better address the needs of special student populations? Basically the issue concerned whether either curriculum or instruction should vary to meet the differing needs of various groups of students. *Should we be concerned with meeting individual needs?* In response, the equity section of the new standards document (pages 12 to 14), defined equal access to high-quality curriculum and instruction for all students as "reasonable and appropriate accommodations [should] be made as needed to promote access and attainment for all students," not identical instruction. "Some students may need further assistance to meet high mathematics expectations," such as "increased time to complete assignments or oral rather than written assignments." They "may need additional resources such as after-school programs, peer mentoring, or cross-age tutoring." What was not stated is revealing: these students have access rights to the curriculum and many are served with Individualized Education Programs (IEP) or "504" plans that require accommodations and collaboration with other educators.

In response to criticism of the earlier standards, another document, *A Research Companion to NCTM's Standards*, was published in 2003. This support document mentioned students with disabilities in only a few paragraphs in its entire 413 pages. In the chapter on implications of cognitive research, Siegler included a section on individual differences where he described three types of mathematics students: good, not-so-good, and perfectionists. The "not-so-good" type is slower, less accurate, uses less advanced strategies, and performs poorer on tests. In the last two paragraphs Siegler cited Geary's (1994) term "mathematical disabilities" as describing about 6 percent of students. This group is described as similar to the not-so-good group, but their problems are a result of a combination of limited background knowledge, limited processing capacity (working memory), and limited conceptual understanding. According to Siegler, these difficulties "need to be addressed," but he cited none of the research on mathematics instruction for students with disabilities. Other authors in this edited work briefly addressed specific concerns for students with disabilities such as an over-reliance on prescriptive methods rather than formative assessment, equity issues for large-scale assessment (Wilson & Kenney, 2003), and providing an opportunity to learn that takes into account prior knowledge and student engagement needs (Hiebert, 2003).

The NCTM documents collectively seem to have drawn a line, a parameter that excludes any detailed discussion of students with special needs with the exception of those with gifts. The emphasis in the research document is on the fidelity of classroom instruction with what the new standards are recommending. The authors of the 1989 standards found that teachers were not actually changing their traditional instructional methods. The current document clearly identifies the most important factor in learning as the opportunity to learn and regards any individual differences as the result of poor teaching.

The instructional focus for the revised standards appears to present a better balance of teacher guidance and student discovery, between concept understanding and skill mastery. Further, the consistency of the content strands across grade levels is an improvement. However, a confusing dichotomy of purpose remains. Is this a document of idealized visions to promote discussion among mathematics educators or a requisite set of student expectations?

The 2000 standards document was revised into four grade-level bands: PreK–2, 3–5, 6–8, and 9–12. The reorganized standards include six principles, five process standards, and five content standards, applied across all grade levels (see Figure 1.6). The new document begins with these sentences:

> Imagine a classroom, a school, or a school district where all students have access to high-quality, engaging mathematics instruction. There are ambitious expectations for all, with accommodation for those who need it. Knowledgeable teachers have adequate resources to support their work and are continually growing as professionals. The curriculum is mathematically rich, offering students opportunities to learn important mathematical concepts and procedures with understanding. (p. 3)

This vision is compelling and challenging, especially for teachers of students with learning problems or specific mathematics disabilities. While the standards do not address special-needs learners' instructional considerations, the emphasis on "all students" should be inclusive. The equity principle comes closest to assuring access and high expectations for all students:

> Excellence in mathematics education requires equity—high expectations and strong support for all students. . . . Low expectations are especially problematic because students who live in poverty, students who are not native speakers of English, students with disabilities, females, and many nonwhite students have traditionally been far more likely than their counterparts in other demographic groups to be the victims of low expectations. . . . mathematics must be learned by *all* students. (pp. 12–13)

Other specific references to students with disabilities are found solely in the principles section of the 2000 document. The equity standard reminds educators that

---

Figure 1.6
NCTM Principles and Standards for School Mathematics

Principles

Mathematics instructional programs:

equity	—should promote the learning of mathematics by **all** students.*
curriculum	—should emphasize important, meaningful mathematics through curricula that are coherent and comprehensive.
teaching	—depends on competent and caring teachers who teach **all** students to understand and use mathematics.
learning	—should enable **all** students to understand and use mathematics.
assessment	—should include assessment to monitor, enhance, and evaluate the mathematics learning of **all** students and to inform teaching.
technology	—should use technology to help **all** students understand mathematics and should prepare them to use mathematics in an increasingly technological world.

Content Standards

Number and Operations: deep and fundamental understanding of, and proficiency with, counting, numbers, and arithmetic, as well as understanding number systems and their structure.

Algebra: study of relationships among quantities, including functions, ways of representing mathematical relationships, and the analysis of change.

Geometry: study of geometric (2- and 3-dimensional) shapes and structures and how to analyze their characteristics and relationships.

Measurement: the assignment of a numerical value to an attribute of an object or to a characteristic of a situation.

Data Analysis and Probability: how to formulate questions, collect and organize data, describe and analyze data, and display data in ways useful for answering questions.

Process Standards

Problem Solving: engaging in a task for which the solution method is not known.

Reasoning and Proof: expressing patterns, structure, or regularities in real-world and symbolic objects and situations through conjecture, argument, logic, and justification.

Communication: sharing ideas and clarifying understanding.

Connections: making connections among mathematical ideas and with applications outside mathematics.

Representation: creating, selecting, using, and translating mathematical ideas in various forms.

Source: Reprinted with permission from *Principles and Standards for School Mathematics,* copyright 2000, by the National Council of Teachers of Mathematics. All rights reserved. Standards are listed with permission of the Council of Teachers of Mathematics (NCTM). NCTM does not endorse the content or validity of these alignments.

*The emphasis on "**all** students" is made here, not in the NCTM document.

---

high expectations and access are not enough, that some students will require further assistance and accommodations *without inhibiting the learning of others* [emphasis added] (NCTM, 2000, p. 13). Teachers are challenged to understand the strengths and needs of their students, accommodate differences, and confront their own beliefs and biases about what students are able to learn.

The 2000 standards document specifically stated its intentions to supply guidelines and goals by which local districts and materials producers can orient curriculum, teaching, and assessment efforts for decades to come (p. 6). These standards have subsequently influenced mathematics standards in most states. Some states have adopted the NCTM content standards and grade-band structure, while others have designed their own or modified the NCTM structure. For example, Colorado, Illinois, Massachusetts, and Washington State adopted the NCTM content standards. Arizona's 2003 mathematics standards combined geometry and measurement into one content standard and added structure and logic, articulating the standards by specific grade level rather than bands of grade levels. California also applied the NCTM content standards to each grade level, combined geometry and measurement, and added mathematics reasoning.

Traditionally, teachers have used the district- or state-adopted textbook as a guide for organizing the scope and sequence of mathematics study. The NCTM curriculum standards are beginning to influence textbook content because textbooks tend to lag at least ten years behind major curriculum changes. According to a survey by the National Center for Education Statistics (2003), of the twenty states selecting or recommending mathematics textbooks by 2002, all twenty based their selections on state content standards. Although most elementary texts are still organized by math topic (e.g., multiplication), integrated concepts aligned with NCTM content and process standards are beginning to appear within chapters and unit activities. Middle grades texts were evaluated by Project 2061, using specific standards-based criteria (American Association for the Advancement of Science, 2000). Of the twelve textbook series reviewed, only two included in-depth mathematics content. High school texts are either integrated or topical (e.g., algebra, geometry), based on the district's or state's approved coursework. Topical texts are beginning to include some integration across the standards but, by design, emphasize narrower applications. The teacher's materials for all current texts include curriculum matrices that reference NCTM and state standards, but the actual alignment with those standards is not always strong. (A more in-depth view of general mathematics texts is in Chapter 6.)

Special education and remedial mathematics teachers should be familiar with their state's curriculum and assessment standards across *all* grade levels. They need to know the content addressed in regular classrooms where their students are working, the gaps in learning their students may possess, and be able to reference general education content for individual learning goals. Students with mild to moderate disabilities are most often engaged with mathematics instruction in general education classes and must take all state and district-mandated tests. Even those students receiving mathematics instruction in separate special education or remedial settings must have access to the general curriculum.

General education mathematics teachers should also be familiar with the full K–12 span of the standards, regardless of their grade-level teaching assignments. The eighth-grade teacher initiating a unit on statistics must understand how the concepts were developed from the earliest grade levels, recognize gaps or advances in learning among students, and prepare students for future concept development.

▲■▲●▲■▲●▲■▲●▲■▲●▲■▲●▲■▲●▲■▲

TRY THIS
Locate your state mathematics standards and compare them with the NCTM standards.
▼■▼●▼■▼●▼■▼●▼■▼●▼■▼●▼■▼●▼■▼

SCOPE OF THE MATHEMATICS CURRICULUM

This section will provide an overview of the NCTM process and content standards.* Educators first studying the standards may feel overwhelmed with the amount of content addressed within each grade-level span. State frameworks that dictate standards for each grade level exacerbate this situation. However, a longitudinal view will show how the same topics are developed over several years in a spiral and interconnected pattern. For example, the concepts of multiplication and division are introduced in the PreK–2 band, but fluency with these operations isn't expected until the 3–5 band. Multiplication and division skills are used in grades 6–8 with problem solving and algebraic equations and in grades 9–12 with vectors, matrices, and other advanced applications. It is critical to keep in mind that deeper study of a few topics is more important for student learning than covering dozens of discrete topics at a surface level. Less is more!

Process Standards

The process standards address ways of acquiring and using knowledge and are developed across the entire mathematics curriculum. They also can be applied across other content areas and real-world problems. These processes are the "verbs" of math. The role of the teacher is to provide settings, models, and guidance for these processes to develop and to assess student skills in using these processes. The process standards are applied at every grade level and across all five content areas.

    Problem solving is a major focus of the mathematics curriculum; engaging in mathematics *is* problem solving. Problem solving is what one does when a solution is not immediate. Students should build mathematical knowledge through problem solving, develop abilities in formulating and representing problems in various ways, apply a wide variety of problem-solving strategies, and monitor their mathematical thinking in solving problems. Problems become the context in which students develop mathematical understandings, apply skills, and generalize learning. Students frequently solve problems in cooperative groups and even create their own problems. Problem solving is addressed

*Reprinted with permission from *Principles and Standards for School Mathematics*, copyright 2000, by the National Council of Teachers of Mathematics. All rights reserved. Standards are listed with permission of the Council of Teachers of Mathematics (NCTM). NCTM does not endorse the content or validity of these alignments.

Conjectures are estimations based on education or experience. A mathematical *argument* is a connected series of statements (premises) intended to support another statement (conclusion).

throughout this book, with Chapter 5 focusing on specific types of mathematics problems and their strategies.

Students should learn to **reason and construct proofs** as essential and powerful aspects of understanding and using mathematics. These processes involve making and investigating conjectures, developing and evaluating arguments, and applying various types of reasoning and methods of proof. Reasoning skills are critical for science, social studies, social skills, literature, and most other areas of study.

Communication skills are an integral part of mathematics activities. Students must understand and use the language of mathematics—in listening, speaking, reading, and writing. Mathematics communication involves specialized vocabulary and new symbol systems, and becomes a tool for organization and thinking. More than ever, students and teachers are "talking about math" with each other. Many new mathematics assessments require students to explain their thoughts and processes for solving problems in writing. Some mathematics teachers and mathematicians have tremendous understanding of mathematics concepts, yet have difficulty with communication skills. They can't convey concepts on a level others will understand, or effectively use communication devices such as analogies and examples. Communication must be modeled with a full range of curriculum applications.

Making **connections** fosters deeper mathematics understanding and assists learning. Students are encouraged to make connections among different mathematics topics, across other content and skill areas, and into the "real" world. When introducing new concepts, it is critical that teachers assist students in making connections with previous, understood concepts. Linking prior knowledge results in more efficient and generalizable learning.

Students are taught to make and apply **representations** across all mathematics topics. Representations assist with organization, recording, communication, modeling, predicting, and interpreting mathematical ideas and situations. Examples of representations are graphs, diagrams, charts, three-dimensional models, computer-generated models, and symbol systems.

TRY THIS

Select items from one state's mathematics assessment instrument. Evaluate the process standards required. For example, the following test item requires all five process skills—problem solving, communication, connections, reasoning, and representation:

Which of the following could be the lengths of the sides of a triangle?

  A) 1, 2, 1   B) 2, 3, 1   C) 3, 5, 4   D) 7, 15, 7

Source: North Carolina End-of-Grade Mathematics Grade 4 Sample Items, 2003. Permission to reprint from the North Carolina Department of Public Instruction/State Board of Education, Accountability Services, North Carolina Testing Program.

For solutions to the problems presented in this book, please visit the Companion Website at www.ablongman.com/gurganus1e.

Content Standards

The five content standards* are also applied across all grade levels. The process standards discussed in the previous section are critical for the development of each of the content standards. Each content standard will be "unpacked" in the following sections, tracing the development across the four grade-level spans and examining the most essential concepts.

Number and operation.   Many teachers, parents, and students erroneously consider number and operation, typically called arithmetic, to be the full extent of school mathematics. Understanding number and operation is essential for progress in the other four math content areas; work with the other content areas in turn enhances number and operation understanding. Topics in this standard are the real number system, place value, and the operations and properties for the number system.

Our base ten number system derives from Hindu (Indian) number notation and includes ten symbols: 0, 1, 2, 3, 4, 5, 6, 7, 8, and 9. These numerals are often called the Arabic number system because Persian mathematicians transmitted the system to the Western world. It can be helpful to examine a concept chart of the real number system (see Figure A.1, page 250) and to manipulate number charts (see Appendix) to better understand numerical relationships and patterns. Concepts such as zero, negative numbers, primes, factors, square roots, and place value took centuries to develop; it is worth the time to explore these concepts with students to develop deeper and more connected understandings of number systems.

Numbers are ways for identifying units (things), or sets (groups of things), or their parts and relationships. Some numbers represent only names or labels of things and have no inherent meaning, such as telephone numbers or social security numbers. These are nominal (name) numbers. Other numbers designate something's position in rank or order within a set—ordinal numbers. Examples of ordinal numbers are class rank, days of the month, and results of a foot race. Ordinals are expressed in words (tenth) or by using a suffix (10th). Numbers that are used to quantify a set are called cardinal numbers. I have 12 library books. The children picked up 14 pennies and 3 nickels. All four arithmetic operations can be performed with cardinal numbers.

The natural numbers, or the whole numbers beginning with 1, are typically called counting numbers. Including zero and negative or opposite numbers results in the set of integers. Including all the numbers in between integers (expressed as fractions or decimals) yields all rational numbers. The term *rational* comes from ratio, such as 1 to 2 (1/2) or 3 to 3 (3/3 or 1). Other types of numbers are irrational (cannot be written as a terminal or repeating decimal), prime (the only factors are 1 and itself), composite (have more than two positive whole number factors), and perfect squares (4, 9, 16, 25, . . .). There are many other special, less useful but interesting, types of numbers such as perfect, complex, Fibonacci, Lucas, random, sociable, untouchable, and weird.

*Reprinted with permission from *Principles and Standards for School Mathematics*, copyright 2000, by the National Council of Teachers of Mathematics. All rights reserved. Standards are listed with permission of the Council of Teachers of Mathematics (NCTM). NCTM does not endorse the content or validity of these alignments.

Number sense is a complex concept dealing with our innate ability to individualize objects and extract numerosity of sets. It is the intuition about numbers (estimations, comparisons, simple addition and subtraction) and understanding of the meaning of different types of numbers and how they are related and represented and the effects of operating with numbers. Number sense is an ability that is further developed through experience. Students in early grades formalize early number sense through learning number symbols, working with larger numbers, and becoming fluent in basic number facts. As they progress to higher levels, students develop abilities in estimation, representation, analyzing relationships, and working with more complex numbers.

The base-ten number system allows for the manipulation of numbers of all sizes and types by using only ten number symbols. Without a **place value system,** we would have to memorize the name and symbol for each possible unit. The first place value systems of 20 or even 60 digits taxed memory and computational abilities—even with special notations for places. Different number systems are still used today, as in New Guinea, where there are 33 numbers with corresponding body parts. Of course the most common system in this technological age is the binary system—using only two values (often named 0 and 1) for digital transmissions.

Place value means that the symbol for a number, say "4," has the value or meaning of 4 units when positioned in one place; 40, or 4 tens when positioned in the second place; and 400, or 4 hundreds if positioned in the third place. It would mean 4/10 if placed immediately to the right of a decimal point. Place value is difficult for children for several reasons. It requires good spatial perception, new language, and multi-step cognitive manipulation. In addition, it requires an understanding of multiplicative properties of number (multiples of 10) usually before multiplication has been introduced.

The previous exercise simulates the feeling of learning about number systems for the first time. How many young children make up numbers and keep on counting? "eighteen, nineteen, tenteen, eleventeen. . . ." Children who don't understand place value have memorized numbers such as 27 and 84 in their sequence, not realizing that the digits within those numbers have special meaning because of their positions within the numbers. These children may also be on cognitive overload: "How can I possibly remember more than twenty or thirty numbers?" Further, the right-to-left order of values and algorithms dependent on place value compared with the left-to-right order of reading numbers can be confusing for some students.

The four **operations**—addition, subtraction, multiplication, and division—are interconnected forms of calculations with real numbers. These operations are used with integers, fractions, decimals, and within algebraic equations. In the simplest sense (with whole numbers), they are ways of counting up and back. Addition is counting on; subtraction is counting back. Multiplication is counting on by groups, and division is

TRY THIS

Use a base-five number system (using 0, 1, 2, 3, and 4 instead of inventing new symbols) to count up to 30.

Hint: After the digit 4, regroup: 0, 1, 2, 3, 4, 10, 11, 12, 13, 14, 20. Now try these addition and subtraction problems:

22 + 14 =

43 − 14 =

Explain why regrouping is used and how it works.

Algorithm refers to a set of instructions or procedures to solve a problem.

counting back by groups. Subtraction of integers is the same as adding the opposite. Division of fractions is multiplying the reciprocal. There are more complicated computational algorithms to deal with larger and more difficult numbers.

What is critical knowledge about operations? Students should understand the effect of each operation on different types of numbers. They should become computationally fluent, able to use efficient and accurate methods for computation (but not necessarily the teacher's method). An important related skill is estimation—both for solving problems where exactness is not required and for determining the reasonableness of exact answers. Students should be able to employ a variety of tools and strategies in performing computations and explain the processes used. Students who simply memorize facts and algorithms by rote, rather than understand the concepts and connections, will be less able to apply computations and adjust strategies in problem-solving situations.

Numbers also have special properties that assist with operations, such as the identity, distributive, and commutative properties. Many students memorize these properties without understanding their meaning or use. It is much more powerful to have students "discover" these magic rules and be able to depend on them. Students who don't understand these rules of math may think math is a haphazard endeavor or make up their own, sometimes faulty, rules.

For more information and teaching strategies on number sense, operations, and properties of whole numbers, see content strands A and B.

Patterns, functions, and algebra.

In the 1989 standards document, the K–4 standards included patterns and relationships, the 5–8 standards included patterns and functions as one standard and algebra as another, and the 9–12 standards listed algebra, functions, and geometry from an algebraic perspective. Combining these areas into one standard emphasizes the K–12 development of similar and interrelated concepts.

Children are encouraged to look for **patterns** in numbers, geometry, measurement, and data collections. Detecting patterns is critical for understanding common concepts and connections in mathematical relationships. As students gain the ability to use symbols they can manipulate more complex patterns. One of the most important skills for problem solving is the ability to recognize patterns—of relational elements within problems and relative to similar problems.

Patterns also form the foundation for understanding function and sequence. Even a seemingly simple concept as sequence becomes increasingly complex in the mathematics curriculum. Counting leads to counting by multiples which leads to concepts of exponential growth, proportional growth, recursive sequences, and related functions.

Extensions of working with patterns, **functions** include variables that have a dynamic relationship: changes in one will cause a change in the other(s). Functions can be depicted with equations, tables, spreadsheets, graphs, and geometric representations. One of the most powerful functions is the proportion, first introduced in the study of rational numbers and operations and continued through algebra. For example, a field trip for a class of 30 students will cost $4 per student and we need to find out the cost for k students. We can easily see which numbers to treat with which operations by setting up the proportional equation: $30/k = 4/c$.

Algebra is the study of abstract mathematical structures involving finite quantities. It involves the symbolic representation of quantitative relationships and the subsequent

A *recursive sequence* is a sequence of numbers in which there is a rule for getting the next number based on values of previous numbers, such as with Fibonacci and Lucas sequences (Wolfram, 2002).

manipulation of various aspects of the representation. The earliest experiences children have with algebra are with open sentences and missing numbers. For example, "If there are ten books in this stack and two are yours, how many belong to me?" translates into: $10 - 2 = \square$ or $2 + \square = 10$. The equals sign becomes less a symbol for an answer (doing something) and more a symbol for equivalence. While it has been taught abstractly and by rote in the past, algebra today is taught using manipulatives, technology, and other representations.

Students' work with number, operation, property, patterns, functions, and geometry complements algebraic understanding. Elementary students develop fluency in working with symbols, numbers, operations, and simple graphing. Middle school students develop concepts of linear functions, geometric representations, and polynomials. And high school students explore other types of functions including rational, exponential, and trigonometric. Deeper understanding of the algebraic characteristics of our number system allows students to explore structures and patterns, pose and solve problems in a number of ways, and develop foundations for the next level of mathematics study.

Geometry and spatial sense.

Concerned with properties of space and objects in space, geometry is one of the most appealing topics for students. The world of space and objects becomes a playground for exploration. Geometry has so many real-world applications. Take, for example, building a simple backyard shed. Consider a few of the mathematical challenges: the shed should be parallel to an imaginary line drawn straight back from the house, the roof should be the same pitch as the roof on the house (rise over run), a 10′ by 12′ shed will require how many linear feet of siding, how many square feet of roofing, and so on. One problem solved leads to three more questions.

Geometry is fundamentally based on three undefined terms: point, line, and surface. An understanding of these terms is necessary for understanding other terms and concepts: angle, parallel, congruence, polygons, circles, and solids. Measurement, proportion, functions, and algebraic concepts are also important for the study of geometry.

Geometric ideas are useful for representing and solving problems in mathematics and other fields (science, architecture, geography, engineering, sports, the arts, and social sciences). Geometric experiences involve analyzing and manipulating the characteristics and properties of two- and three-dimensional objects and using different representational systems, methods, and tools such as transformations, symmetry, visualization, spatial reasoning, graphing, and computer animations to solve problems. Like the study of algebra and the number system, geometry involves analyzing patterns, functions, and connections and developing and using rules (theorems or axioms) within the system to solve problems or develop more complex relationships.

Students in grades K–2 study properties of two- and three-dimensional shapes and explore relative positions, directions, and distances using these shapes. Grade 3–5 students begin using coordinate systems, transformations, and other means for analyzing the properties of shapes. They use geometric models to solve problems. Middle school students create and critique inductive and deductive arguments involving geometric concepts and use coordinate geometry to examine properties of shapes. They use geometric models to extend number and algebraic understandings. By high school, students are testing conjectures, using trigonometric relationships, and applying geometric models to solve problems in other disciplines.

For more information and teaching strategies on pattern, function, and algebra, see content strand E.

Theorems are assertions that can be proved true by using the rules of logic. *Axioms* (also termed *postulates*) are simple and direct statements generally accepted as true without proof.

A *deductive argument* is a series of premises that guarantees the truth of the conclusion. An *inductive argument* is a series of premises leading to a conclusion that is probably, but not absolutely, true.

Measurement.   Imminently hands-on yet elusively abstract, measurement skills and concepts can be engaging but challenging to teach. What can be measured? Time, energy, space, and matter. Each of these physical aspects of our world has its measurable aspects, their respective measurement tools, and units of measure (see Figure 1.7). Some textbooks and curriculum frameworks classify money as a measurement topic; however, money is not measured but counted (unless all quantification is considered a form of measurement). Measurement is a critical topic for other mathematics applications and is related to many other topics outside mathematics. Both customary (U.S.) and metric systems are referenced in the standards (the customary system reinforces fraction concepts and metrics reinforce the base-ten place value system and decimal concepts).

Young children develop the concept that objects have various attributes, some of which can be measured. They develop the language to express measurement ideas such

For more information and teaching strategies on geometry and spatial sense, see content strand C.

Figure 1.7
Measurement: Subjects, Tools, and Units

Category	Subject	Example Tool	Example Unit
Time	long periods	calendar	months
	short periods	clock	hours
	shorter periods	stopwatch	seconds
	tempo	metronome	beats per bar*
Energy	atmospheric	pressure barometer	millibars
	electric	electric meter	kilowatts
	temperature	thermometer	degrees
	earthquake	seismograph	moment magnitude
	hearing	audiometer	decibels, Hertz*
	atomic radiation	Geiger-Müller tube	particles per minute*
Space	length	meter stick	centimeters
	height of elevation	altimeter	meters
	capacity	tape measure	cubic feet
	distance	odometer	miles
	angle	protractor	degrees
Matter	volume (capacity)	flask	milliliters
	mass (weight)	scale	pounds
	density (liquid)	hydrometer	specific gravity units*

When we want to measure something, there may be a standard unit (as above), more than one unit (e.g., meters or yards), or a unit and scale can be created.

---

*The items indicated are actually ratios of measures. Scientists tend to focus on mass, length, and time and ways they combine. For example:

speed = distance (length) / time (short periods)
density = volume (three-dimensional space) / mass

Vectors represent quantities with both magnitude and direction such as force, velocity, and acceleration.

● ● ● ● ● ● ● ● ●
For more information
and teaching strategies
on measurement, see
content strand C.
● ● ● ● ● ● ● ● ●

as longer or more. They begin to associate specific attributes with units and tools of measurement and make simple measurements fairly accurately. Elementary students gain experience with a variety of tools and measurement concepts, in both metric and customary systems. They work with formulas for perimeter, area, and volume of various shapes. By the secondary grades students gain experience with derived attributes (ratios of measurements), conversions, formulas, precision, and error concepts.

Data analysis, statistics, and probability.   A group of four- and five-year-olds was recently observed "doing" data analysis using probability and statistics. They were discussing their ice cream choices for the monthly parent's night. On the wall was a chart, a pictograph, with little white, brown, and pink ice cream cones depicting their predictions the previous day of their parents' preferences for vanilla, chocolate, or strawberry ice cream. (Chocolate was by far the winner.) That day the children were sharing results of asking their parents about their favorite flavors. As the new graph evolved, the children exclaimed about the prevalence of vanilla. These young children made predictions, collected data, represented data on a graph, and analyzed those data. They discussed their findings in ways that were mathematically powerful. Like the other content strands, data analysis, statistics, and probability are developed across all grade level spans.

Data are quantifications of aspects of the world. It seems that everything is quantified: sports scores, weather records, income levels, test scores, stock market trends, population patterns, and political views. Data analysis and the application of statistical methods are used across the curriculum. Students are taught how to collect and record data, to represent data in various forms, and to interpret and use data. Students are taught to describe their data collections with frequency charts, measures of central tendency, and various graphs and charts. Higher-level concepts include variability, significance, correlation, sampling, and transformations.

The study of probability assists us in making more accurate estimations with problems involving uncertainty. Probability helps answer the question, "How likely is some event?" Applications range from educational assessment, business, politics, and medicine to scientific phenomena. Students engaged in probability activities will use their knowledge of number and operations, variables and algebraic equations, problem-solving skills, measurement and graphing, and logical reasoning. Ultimately, skill with probability and statistics should enable students to make more informed decisions in all aspects of their lives.

● ● ● ● ● ● ● ● ●
For more information
and teaching strategies
on data analysis and
statistics, see content
strands A and E.
● ● ● ● ● ● ● ● ●

▲ ■ ▲ ● ▲ ■ ▲ ● ▲ ■ ▲ ● ▲ ■ ▲ ● ▲ ■ ▲ ● ▲ ■ ▲ ● ▲ ■ ▲ ● ▲ ■ ▲ ● ▲ ■ ▲ ● ▲ ■ ▲ ● ▲ ■ ▲ ● ▲ ■

TRY THIS
Select a test item from a state or district mathematics test and analyze the content knowledge required. For example, the following item requires facility with number and operation, geometry, and possibly measurement concepts.

Draw a rectangle and a triangle that have the same area. Label the dimensions. Show that the areas are the same.

▼ ■ ▼ ● ▼ ■ ▼ ● ▼ ■ ▼ ● ▼ ■ ▼ ● ▼ ■ ▼ ● ▼ ■ ▼ ● ▼ ■ ▼ ● ▼ ■ ▼ ● ▼ ■ ▼ ● ▼ ■ ▼ ● ▼ ■ ▼ ● ▼ ■ ▼

HIGH-STAKES TESTING AND IMPLICATIONS FOR STUDENTS WITH LEARNING PROBLEMS

Today's elementary and secondary students are undergoing more mandated assessments than any group in the history of education in the United States. In 2001, forty-nine states required statewide assessments in mathematics, as compared with forty-five in 1994 and thirty-four states in 1984 (CCSSO, 2002). The outcomes of these measures have more implications for the students, teachers, schools, and districts than ever before. Some high-stakes assessments are used to determine student placement, promotion, and graduation; teacher assignments and bonuses; and overall school ratings and benefits. Perhaps the most serious effect may be the "teaching to the test" syndrome that is occurring in many classrooms.

What are the implications for students with specific disabilities and other learning problems? According to the 1999 regulations of IDEA (and reauthorized in 2004), students with disabilities must have the necessary supports to "be involved and progress in the regular curriculum" and to participate in state and district assessments of student achievement (§300.347). These regulations were adopted because too many students with disabilities were being excluded from testing programs and therefore not provided the same access to the general education curriculum as their peers. Often these students weren't expected to meet the general education mathematics standards, so they couldn't enroll in courses required for college or technical training, although they may have had the ability. The No Child Left Behind Act of 2001 also required the "participation in such assessments (high-quality, yearly student academic assessments) of all students." (Section 1111 (3) (C) (i))

Now with new opportunities for participation come the challenges. What testing accommodations are fair for students with disabilities or language differences that adhere to the same performance standards? Can a student who is working on standards one or two grade levels behind his peers be expected to take a grade-level test? How can districts apply standardized scores to students who have taken off-grade level tests? Are standardized tests the best measure of student understanding and skill? Should teachers and schools be penalized for differences in student performance that are disability or language related? The questions are endless, but the issues are found in every town's newspapers.

For teachers responsible for preparing students with disabilities for mandated assessments, the most important considerations will be understanding the assessment requirements and determining needed accommodations. Assessment requirements include administration dates, formats, and conditions, in addition to the test content emphasis. Most state and district assessments are administered in the late spring and may take an entire week. If the mathematics portion is last or is scheduled later in the day, students may not do as well. Some tests allow and even encourage calculator use for portions of mathematics tests, but students should have been using the same calculators throughout the year if this is the case. For test content, teachers should ask to review test development materials and, if permitted, previous forms of tests.

Formats for mathematics assessments vary considerably from state to state and may even differ from formats within the state's adopted textbooks. In recent years, more states

Test *accommodations* are changes in the way tests are administered or changes in the testing environment, not in the construct being measured. *Modifications* usually are not allowed on high-stakes tests because they change the construct being measured (National Center on Educational Outcomes, 2005).

have incorporated open-ended and performance items into their assessments in addition to multiple-choice items (CCSSO, 2002). In the 2003–2004 academic year, states gave a total of ten norm-referenced mathematics tests, sixty-six criterion-referenced tests, and five augmented norm-referenced tests that included mathematics subtests (some states administering more than one statewide test each year or different tests for different grade levels). The NCLB Act requirements have caused criterion-referenced tests to be much more prevalent (CCSSO, 2005). For example, in 2001, Arizona students in grades 2 through 8 were given the *Stanford Achievement Test* (ninth edition), a norm-referenced test of multiple-choice items. Students in grades 3, 5, 8, and 10 were also given the *Arizona Instrument to Measure Standards* (AIMS), a criterion-referenced test with multiple-choice, short response, and extended response items. Now Arizona administers only the AIMS. Teachers should expose students to the question formats that will be required on these summative assessments throughout the school year when specific, corrective feedback can be provided.

Different testing accommodations are permitted in different states. In addition to students with IEPs, accommodations are provided in many states for students with 504 plans (for students who are disabled, but do not qualify under IDEA), students with limited proficiency in English (ELL), and an emerging group of students with "emotional anxiety" about test taking. A few states make accommodations available for all students as needed (Thurlow, Lazarus, Thompson, & Robey, 2002). The most common accommodations for mathematics assessments are extended time, separate setting, and portions read aloud. Since these state-level assessments are now required for all students, state policies on accommodations have become more specific, but educators are not always trained in implementing them. It is important for the accommodations selected to actually match student needs, not be applied to all eligible students. Inappropriate accommodations may actually cause lower performance. And like the use of calculators, accommodations used on high-stakes tests should have been used for other assessments throughout the school year.

TODAY'S MATHEMATICS CLASSROOMS: A CASE FOR COLLABORATION

During a staff development meeting of first-year teachers in January, Angela Smith, Joseph Lopez, and Chris Johnson met again to compare experiences. They all agreed that mathematics classes today are not like their own experiences in school. "We had to sit in rows, not speak, and solve long algorithms exactly like the teacher modeled," shared Chris. "Our third-grade teacher took away free time if we could not pass the timed one-minute fluency tests," complained Angela. "I remember going to the blackboard to show proofs in front of the whole class and feeling superior if I had a solution and no one else understood it," recalled Joseph.

"Our elementary mathematics classes are working on topics such as algebra and statistics that we weren't introduced to until late middle school," reported Chris. "These students are working in small groups on teacher-posed problems and are allowed to use any method that works as long as they can justify their solutions. My role as a remedial teacher has been to build up gaps in prior knowledge, teach explicit strategies, and provide alternative examples when students are not making critical connections. I have been working closely with all the school's teachers to get to know the curriculum demands."

"At the middle school I have actually been a co-teacher with three of the mathematics teachers," Angela shares. "I had no idea how advanced the concepts had become—algebra, statistics, and integrating geometry with everything. The students love the hands-on work and working in small groups and, surprisingly, they are not off-task. Perhaps that's because they have two teachers but also because the math they're working on is interesting to them—we use sports, current events, music, space travel—whatever is interesting for these students has powerful mathematics applications. Our goal is concept understanding and making connections, not just working problems."

"I have been surprised how much I enjoy working with the students who struggle with mathematics," exclaims Joseph. "It has been a challenge for me to figure out what they already understand and how I should present the next concept in these college-prep classes. The special educators have been so helpful in showing me how to design good assessments of student learning and multiple examples for new concepts. I was worried I would have a group of students working out of middle school workbooks, but we've been able to work on the same concepts with the extra time in the mathematics support classroom. These students are actually going home and challenging their parents with interesting mathematics problems. Imagine that!" ■ ● ▲

Angela, Chris, and Joseph have highlighted the critical features of today's mathematics classes. Today's teachers and students work together in classrooms with more diversity. Students with disabilities, language and cultural differences, varying socioeconomic backgrounds, and a range of abilities learn in mixed groups. Schools and teachers are under increasing pressure to demonstrate that all their students are performing according to grade-level standards. The mathematics curriculum is more standardized across classrooms because of national and state standards and state-level testing programs. Today's mathematics teachers must provide high-quality instruction to very diverse students in a climate of reform and accountability.

Students in these classes are using more hands-on materials and technologies to understand concepts. They are working in groups and discussing concepts among themselves, coming up with alternative solution strategies and defending their reasoning. Teachers pose problems that lead students to make mathematical connections across concepts. The curriculum is challenging, with advanced topics introduced earlier, but relevant to students' interests. And teachers are working collaboratively so that all students will be successful in learning.

The roles of educators responsible for mathematics instruction are changing. General education mathematics teachers serve more diverse students and work with more support personnel than ever before. Special educators provide a broader array of support services including full co-teaching within general math classes and support teaching in pull-out programs. Remedial teachers sometimes specialize in mathematics and offer a range of pull-out, co-teaching, and after-school services, working with the total mathematics program in the school. With the increase in decision making at the school-building level, program models may be extremely varied and creative as they are planned by parent and teacher partnerships.

These changing roles and responsibilities may require additional teacher training. General education mathematics teachers should have training in methods for designing instruction and accommodations for students with learning differences (disabilities, language, culture, giftedness) and collaborating with other professionals, not just an overview of student characteristics. Special educators should have training in specific mathematics pedagogy that is applicable across the grade levels, including planning mathematics assessments, providing research-based interventions, working collaboratively with mathematics teachers, and locating and using mathematics resources. The NCTM's position on the mathematics training of elementary teachers calls for mathematics specialists in each school who have a minimum of nine semester hours studying "fundamental ideas of elementary school mathematics" (Lott, 2003). However, elementary and secondary teachers responsible for mathematics instruction should have basic knowledge of the full PreK to 12 curriculum.

All teachers responsible for mathematics instruction or the support of that instruction should take advantage of professional development opportunities in mathematics pedagogy and individual student program planning. Administrators should provide support for professional development and establish a truly collaborative atmosphere within schools in which professionals can share resources, conduct joint planning of units and assessments, and monitor instructional effectiveness and mathematics achievement of all students. By working together in supported collaborative teams, teachers can meet the mathematics learning needs of all students.

CHAPTER SUMMARY

- Teacher and student dispositions about mathematics have a powerful effect on student achievement.
- The educational reforms of the 1980s were catalysts for today's initiatives in curriculum standards and accountability for student achievement.
- The 1989 NCTM standards were criticized for lacking a research base, not addressing diverse student needs, emphasizing discovery learning of broad concepts over explicit instruction of skills, and lacking cross-grade cohesiveness.
- The 2000 NCTM curriculum standards were organized into six principles, five content areas, and five

process standards and were articulated across four grade-level spans. These standards have affected state-level mathematics standards, assessments, and textbook selection.
- District and/or state-level high-stakes assessments are having a significant impact on students with learning problems and their teachers. Teachers need to understand assessment requirements and accommodation issues.
- General, remedial, and special education teachers' roles are evolving to better meet the individual needs of students with mathematics learning problems.

RESURCES

For additional resources on developing positive attitudes about mathematics:

Garland, T. H. (1998). *Fibonacci fun: Fascinating activities with intriguing numbers.* Upper Saddle River, NJ: Dale Seymour Publications.

Mirra, A. (2004). *A family's guide: Fostering your child's success in school mathematics.* Reston, VA: National Council of Teachers of Mathematics.

Tang, G. (2001). *The grapes of math.* New York: Scholastic, Inc.

Zaslavsky, C. (1998). *Math games & activities from around the world.* Chicago: Chicago Review Press.

Additional resources on the NCTM standards:

National Council of Teachers of Mathematics: www.nctm.org.

Mathematics Standards by State:

www.edexcellence.net/institute/publication (search term: math standards).

For interesting reading on the evolution of number systems and symbols:

Dehaene, S. (1997). *The number sense: How the mind creates mathematics.* New York: Oxford University Press.

Pappas, T. (1994). *The magic of mathematics.* San Carlos, CA: Wide World Publishing.

Chapter 2

Chapter Questions

1. What skills and concepts are
    precursors for math learning?
2. What developmentally
    appropriate practices with young
    children lead to mathematics
    concept development?
3. What broad learning theories are
    most applicable to mathematics
    learning?
4. What is constructivism and how does it
    relate to mathematics teaching and
    learning?
5. Do theories of mathematics disabilities
    inform identification and instruction?
6. What are the general characteristics of
    students with learning problems that will affect
    mathematics teaching and learning?

Foundations of Mathematics Learning

Zachary reaches out and selects a red block from among a group of brightly colored wooden blocks. He pulls it in to his chest for a better grasp. Next he moves it up with both hands to his mouth and gnaws on a corner before dropping it. That block loses Zachary's attention when he notices a mobile of animals circling above his head. He reaches up and tugs at the lion. The mobile dances away from his grasp, swinging back and forth over Zachary's head.

Kristy is outside in the backyard with three of her friends from preschool. They are stacking plastic blocks into walls with a gap for the door. Kristy decides the walls need a roof so that they can hide inside. She finds some fallen palm branches and creates a roof. Only two of the children can fit inside so they decide to make the house larger. Kristy's friend suggests that they make windows and use those blocks for more walls.

David loves helping his mom bake cookies. He measures the flour into a big pan. She adds soft butter and sugar. He asks his mom how many chocolate chips they should add. "Do we count them all first?" After they drop the dough onto a cookie sheet, his mom says, "The oven's ready." David asks, "How does it know how hot to get for our cookies?" ■ ● ▲

Anyone who claims that mathematics is simply a subject in school or is the formal study of numbers and operations should watch Zachary, Kristy, and David. Children are born cognitively programmed to be curious about their world. Zachary is analyzing three-dimensional objects in space, studying their properties, and considering a theory of pendular movement. Kristy and her friends are studying volume and surface area. David is formulating new rules about when to count or measure and when to estimate. All three children are observing and interacting with elements in their world and adding to their growing understanding about them. These are mathematics and problem-solving pursuits. These activities are critical for normal cognitive development that will lead to more formal math and problem solving experiences in school.

PRECURSORS OF MATHEMATICS LEARNING

What concepts and skills are developed during early childhood that form the foundation for mathematics learning in school? How are these concepts and skills developed? Read the following descriptions that describe milestones in the first five years in the life of a child named Jessica. Think about the concepts and skills Jessica is developing, how they are developed, and how they may be related to later, more complex, mathematics.

At **3 months** Jessica is lying on a carpet in the den of her home surrounded by blocks and toys. When her dad picks up a ball she follows it with her eyes and smiles. She is starting to reach for objects close by.

At **6 months** Jessica is rolling over and picking up her blocks. Of course they go right into her mouth. Her mom sits her up and gives her a green block. Jessica can hold it with either hand. When her older brother reads a book with Jessica, Jessica looks at the pictures and makes vocalizations.

When Jessica turns **one year** old her parents and brother give her a party. Jessica can pick up her new toy animal with her thumb and one finger. She can put one block on top of another and when her brother hides a block behind himself, Jessica points for it, vocalizing in words, "there" and "mine." Jessica is walking with a bit of help.

At **eighteen months** Jessica can bring toys to others when asked for them by name. She loves exploring new things like the cardboard boxes that came with the new dishes. She also enjoys scribbling with her crayons on large sheets of paper. When her brother reads books, Jessica can name things in the pictures using words like "baby" and "doggy."

When Jessica is **two years old** she enjoys turning the pages in a book when her dad reads and can describe the pictures using short phrases such as, "boy threw it" and "dog running." She can recall events in the past such as playing with a friend or visiting a relative. She can run over to her toy box and find each toy when her mom asks her for it by name. She loves to listen to music and beat on an old pan. She can lace large beads onto a string. Jessica is aware of general times of the day such as naptime and dinnertime.

At **thirty months** Jessica can use crayons more deliberately, making lines and circles to cut out with scissors. She can put a simple puzzle together and take it apart again. Jessica also understands the concepts of today and tomorrow, and the prepositions in and under. She loves to hear the same story over and over.

Shortly after her **third birthday,** Jessica begins describing objects: red car, fuzzy bear, big chair. She understands many size and location words like big, small, over, and behind. Many of Jessica's sentences begin with question words: why and how. She can manipulate clay and blocks to create representations of real things. When asked to count eight crayons, Jessica holds out her fingers and counts while touching each crayon—1, 2, 3, 4, 5, 1, 2, 3.

Between the ages of two and six or seven, Jessica is in what Piaget called the preoperational stage (1952). From **age two to five** she is very quickly learning language—new words and the syntax and morphemes that are common. But most everything Jessica learns is through her experience with her world. She explores in her room—toys, puzzles, books, games—pretending she is teaching her stuffed animals and telling them stories. She explores in her back yard—swinging, playing in the sandbox, and kicking a ball with her older brother.

By **age five or six** Jessica is able to classify objects by color or shape, she can understand that one thing might have more than one name (dog, terrier), and she is beginning to learn symbols such as numbers and letters in her world. Jessica is cutting and pasting and drawing. She is counting out crayons for her friends when they visit. And she loves to make patterns with her blocks on the floor, making up rules as she plays. Jessica uses over 2,000 words in five- to six-word sentences. She knows left from right, can identify coins, and is beginning to relate special times of day to times on the clock.

Before exploring the contributions of these informal activities to later mathematics learning, the next section discusses the importance of environmental stimulation on brain development.

TRY THIS

Which of the above descriptions have direct relationships to later formal mathematics learning?

For solutions to the problems presented in this book, visit the Companion Website at www.ablongman.com/ gurganus1e.

Brain Development

At birth, the human brain is comprised of 100 billion neurons with one quadrillion rather unorganized synaptic connections (Sprenger, 1999). Synaptic connections are the pathways for signal transmission within the brain and between the brain and other parts of the body such as muscles and sense organs. Shortly after birth, the infant's brain begins to form a proliferation of synapses—many more than are extant in the mature brain. The period of synaptic overproduction is followed by a period of reduction (or pruning). This reduction process is experience-dependent and generally occurs up to the point of sexual maturity, when the number of synaptic connections is approximately that of the adult. The period of overproduction of synapses has been correlated with the initial emergence of a new skill or behavior, but skills and behaviors continue to develop during the reduction and mature periods (Bruer, 1998).

Neuroscience has not linked specific types of early childhood experiences to the development of synapses, rather any typical interaction with the environment should provide enough stimulation to form more efficient connections for later learning. What has been established, however, is that impairments in sensory systems (vision, hearing, touch) and language development can cause long-lasting effects on brain functioning, especially impairments that occur during critical developmental periods (Bruer, 1998).

Critical periods of development vary for specific functions of sensory systems and represent subtle and gradual changes in the brain's elasticity. For specific sensory system functions (e.g., ocular dominance in vision), there appear to be three phases within the critical period of development: rapid change during which the mature processing level is reached, sensitivity to deprivation during which the system is still plastic enough to be affected by lack of stimulation, and a compensatory phase during which therapy can remediate the loss (Daw, 1995).

The type of learning that results from exposure to rich, complex environments and new experiences is different—it results in new synapse formation. This ability to form new connections persists throughout the lifetime. This is the type of brain plasticity that allows learning from experience, formal schooling, and continuous development.

> *Ocular dominance* is the tendency of nerve cells in the cerebral cortex to be activated by the images from one eye rather than stereoscopic integration from both eyes.

Concepts and Skills Developed during Early Childhood

Young children like Jessica are inquisitive, eager to explore their immediate environments. They want to touch objects around them to learn more about them. What do they feel or taste like? What happens when they are dropped or rolled? Do they make sounds or movements? Are other significant people interested in these objects? Each exploration adds to a newly forming view of the world, a schema about the properties of objects and other surroundings. These explorations facilitate the child's development of early concepts critical for later formal learning, as in mathematics. This early concept development can be linked directly to important foundations for mathematics learning.

One of the earliest concepts is that of **identity,** that a person or object has identifying features. A young child recognizes his or her family members. Later the child recognizes toys and other familiar objects. Objects in the child's environment have permanence—the child can depend on seeing these people and objects again, even if they are temporarily out of sight. Identity is an important concept for the more complex ideas of number identity and the identity of physical properties. For example, adding zero to other numbers does not change the value of those numbers. Breaking a piece of clay apart does not change its fundamental composition.

Another early concept is **labeling** or naming. As soon as children begin to recognize speech as language, they begin associating names and labels with people and objects. Expressive language typically begins with canonical syllables, followed by the names of concrete objects in the child's narrow immediate environment (Lamb, Bornstein, & Teti, 2002). Then meaningful toys, food, and personal care items gain names or labels (by twelve months). Pacifiers, toy animals, bottles, foods, and other everyday objects have identifying labels. As the child grows older and his world gets larger and larger, more objects gain labels and labels become more specific. Chairs, table, refrigerator, swing set, sand box, street, neighbors, other children, preschool teachers, and so forth. Labeling continues into formal mathematics with the identification of shapes and their properties, types of numbers and sets, visual representations such as charts and graphs, and various measurement tools.

> *Canonical syllables* are combinations of vowels and consonants into syllables such as ma-ma and da-da, at about six to eight months.

As children are exposed to more than one type of chair or several different cars, they begin noticing the similar and different aspects of those objects, between ages four and five. They are observing **properties of objects** and are **classifying** objects by those properties. They are **comparing** objects based on observable attributes. This car is red but those are blue and green. This is the biggest chair and that one is the smallest. Making observations, recognizing properties of objects, and classification are critical skills not only for later mathematics learning but for other formal studies as well. For example, in mathematics students will compare numbers (these numbers are even, they are all divisible by two) and shapes (these squares are all rectangles but not all rectangles are squares). In science they will be asked to classify living and nonliving things and compare their properties.

Typically between the ages of four and five, children realize that numbers are used to **count** things (Sophian, 1998). Previously, numbers have been used like labels: "I am three years old." "We live at 42 Oak Lane." As children use numbers to count, they are engaging in a very complex activity. That's why counting skills take a while to develop. Children must recall the names for numbers, their **sequence** (**seriation**), assign a number to each object counted (**one-to-one correspondence**), keep track of the objects counted, and realize that the last number they count is the total number of the entire group of objects (cardinal number). How many fingers do you have? How many blocks are on the table? How many crayons are in your box? How many red ones? Counting games, poems, and songs assist children to develop counting skills. Counting leads to associating numbers with their written symbols, counting larger numbers, counting by twos or fives, and every higher math concept.

Another concept that begins early is that of **cause and effect.** Children learn these relationships by using their senses to explore the environment, to observe actions and re-actions, and to actually cause reactions. For example, pushing a ball across the floor may cause it to hit the wall and come rolling back. Blowing toward a mobile causes it to move. Crying causes someone to pick the child up. Smiling causes other people to smile back. In formal mathematics study, cause and effect are critical concepts. Adding numbers together results in a larger number. Multiplying a whole number by a percentage (less than 100%) or simple fraction will result in a smaller number. Cause and effect are closely related to the later concepts of operations and functions.

In his classic experiments with young children, Jean Piaget (Piaget & Inhelder, 1969) described the development of cognition through children's interactions with science- and math-like tasks. Some tasks were related to identity and seriation, concepts described above. Others involved **conservation**—knowing that changing the form doesn't change the amount of liquids or malleable objects such as clay. Pouring liquid from a wide container into a tall thin container doesn't change the amount of liquid. Rolling a ball of clay into a thin rope doesn't change the amount of clay. Subtracting four from each side of the equation $3 + 2 = x + 4$ won't change the balance of the equation. What we perceive can sometimes be faulty unless we make careful observations. The concept of conservation is applicable to specific mathematics conversions. Making careful, informed observations is central to the work of mathematicians and scientists. Closely related to the development of conservation and observation skills are perspective taking, flexibility of thought, problem solving, and concept manipulation.

Development of Cognitive Structures Related to Mathematics

As children develop cognitively from pre-lingual and pre-symbolic stages to the use of language and symbols to manipulate concepts, their abilities related to later mathematics learning are also developing. Some of the most critical cognitive abilities for mathematics learning are memory, language skills, and the ability to make mental representations of number and space.

Young children begin using their **memory** abilities as they interact with the environment and recall those experiences. Infants will respond to familiar faces and music. Children enjoy retelling stories and singing songs over and over again. As they begin noticing environmental print, children begin to understand the role of letters and numbers as abstract representations for familiar things. Names of streets, stores, candy, and numbers on houses and roads begin to take on meaning. Children ask to be taught to write their names and memorize the markings. Some children are so delighted with their new skills that they make markings everywhere—on books, walls, and under furniture.

With formal schooling, memory tasks become more challenging. Children must recall the written character for letters, numbers, and other symbols used in writing and mathematics. They are required to remember math facts and the sequences for performing operations with numbers. In problem solving, children are encouraged to recall a similar problem type or situation. Memory tasks are more successful when children learn through concept understanding rather than by rote memorization. New concepts should be connected to real-life experiences of children so that cognitive structures are formed in long-term memory.

Language development is critically integrated with mathematics development. Children use language to express relationships, assign labels, manipulate concepts, and communicate understandings with others. Language becomes the mediation tool for performing more difficult mathematics tasks, as can be seen in native language comparison studies (see, for example, Miura & Okamoto, 2003). Teachers use carefully selected language to ask questions and explain new concepts.

Children with language delays may have corresponding delays in mathematics development. Cognitive abilities of symbolic thinking, temporal–sequential organization, verbal memory, and rate of language processing are language abilities directly related to mathematics tasks (Jordan, Levine, & Huttenlocher, 1995). Nonverbal mathematics tasks, such as the manipulation of objects without verbal requirements, are generally developed earlier than verbal tasks (story problems) and are less sensitive to socioeconomic differences. Jordan, Levine, and Huttenlocher examined the calculation abilities of young children (kindergarteners and first graders) and found that children with language impairments performed as well as their peers on nonverbal calculations but significantly worse on story problems (presented orally) than the non-impaired group.

Younger children with language disabilities should concentrate on the cardinal aspects of number—number represents the number of objects in a set—and work with small quantities until those are firm concepts (Grauberg, 1998). They should not be discouraged from using compensatory strategies such as finger counting (Jordan, Levine, & Huttenlocher, 1995). Additional nonverbal activities can build concept understanding while the verbal aspects are strengthened. Some students may benefit from a delay in writing number symbols or using tallies of number symbols until number and quantity concepts are secure.

The ability to make **mental representations** is critical for later mathematics learning but very difficult to assess in young children. Infants can distinguish between sets of objects with one and two, three and four, and even eight and sixteen objects depicted (Sophian, 1998). This skill requires interpretation of two visual images as different, but researchers have not been able to determine whether a sort of nonverbal counting takes place or a visual subitizing. Toddlers (about age two) can distinguish between sets with different numbers of objects and relative magnitude of sets (e.g., a card with eight dots looks like it has more dots than a card with three dots), especially when the number of objects is not close enough to need counting (Ginsburg, 1982). Young children (about three years old) can recognize that adding objects to a set will result in more, and removing objects results in fewer.

The act of actually counting objects develops later because it becomes a bridge between the concrete (objects visualized) and abstract (objects matched with numbers). Although some children at 18 months can count up to three objects, it is not a firm one-to-one correspondence counting or view of magnitude, just labeling. Many five-year-old children can "count" to 20 but mostly by rote and often in number chunks. When asked for the number after 18, they may have to "hear" 15, 16, 17, 18, to recall "19." Around age five children begin associating numbers by their relative magnitudes. Counting by tens may also be learned first by rote (without meanings of number or magnitude) and may not be a reflection of understanding until first or second grade.

Other important mental representations for children are those spatial aspects of mathematics that are, in fact, closely related to number concepts. Infants view quantities as overall amounts and relative amounts rather than discrete numbers (Mix, Huttenlocher, & Levine, 2002). Although some spatial tasks are closely related to number concepts (number lines, graphs, measurement in units), others seem to be less connected (flipping an object mentally, interpreting relative positions in space). Mental representations include the characteristics of objects (shape, size, color), relative positions of objects (distance, over, behind), rotations of objects as the same object (flips, turns), composition and decomposition of objects, recognition of symbols (equals sign, minus sign, numerals), spatial orientation, interpretation of drawings (map of classroom, graph of buttons), and even some concepts of time.

These concepts are developed through guided interaction with a rich environment and should not be required on a purely abstract level until concepts are formed—possibly not until the second grade in formal schooling. Some children will be ready and even eager by age three or four to use symbolic notations because older siblings do that, and parents may think it a sign of giftedness. But overemphasizing work at the abstract level using primarily paper and pencil tasks with four-, five-, and even six-year-olds may actually disrupt and delay stronger concept development that should develop from informal understanding at the concrete level (Pound, 1999).

Importance of Informal Mathematics Knowledge

Baroody and Ginsburg (1986) termed the knowledge that children develop in everyday settings prior to attending formal schooling "informal knowledge." Most preschoolers arrive at school with important mathematical competencies, such as a sense for numbers and counting that are foundational for formal mathematics learning if understood by educators. Even with older children, the everyday, informal knowledge that is developed through experience can be tapped for enhancing formal mathematics learning.

Seo and Ginsburg conducted an interesting study of the types of informal mathematical activities in which four- and five-year-old children were engaged in natural settings (2004). The researchers classified observable activities by their mathematics characteristics:

- Classification activities involved sorting, grouping, or categorizing objects.
- Magnitude activities were statements made about global magnitude of objects, direct or side-by-side comparisons, or judgments without quantification.
- Enumeration activities involved saying number words, counting, subitizing, and even reading and writing numbers.
- Dynamics involved putting things together, taking them apart, or making other transformations such as turning and flipping.
- Pattern and shape activities included identifying or creating patterns or shapes and exploring the properties and relationships of shapes. (Seo & Ginsburg, 2004, pp. 93–94)

After coding 15-minute videotaped segments of ninety children, the researchers concluded that most children (88%) engaged in mathematical activities naturally and that about forty-three percent of the time observed was spent in math-like activities. Very significant in their findings was the conclusion that there were no income level or gender differences in these activity levels. In general, children engaged in pattern and shape activities the most, and classification the least, and were capable of achieving quite complex levels of performance. For example, some children demonstrated estimating the number in a set without counting and transforming a rhombus shape into a trapezoid.

Both quadrilaterals because of their four straight sides, a *trapezoid* is a quadrilateral with two parallel sides; a *rhombus* is a quadrilateral with both pairs of opposite sides parallel (also called a rhomb or diamond).

Informal mathematics knowledge is also important for older students. It may be harder to extract informal from formal learning and some misconceptions may be more rigidly held by older students, but teachers need to assess prior knowledge in whatever form for better connections to new mathematics learning. For exam-

TRY THIS
Visit a child-care center or preschool and observe children ages three to five. Using the Seo-Ginsburg categories, note the informal mathematics activities in which children are engaged.

ple, Jamie is a student in Mrs. Banks' third-grade class and was taught in previous grades that applying multiplication to whole numbers would result in larger numbers. This concept was confirmed with Jamie's experiences grocery shopping with her mother. If one apple costs 20¢, then four apples cost 80¢. Buying a six-pack of soda for $2.50 was cheaper than buying six sodas at the individual price of 50¢. Mrs. Banks is attempting to explain why $6 \times \frac{1}{2}$ would result in a smaller number. She could begin with Jamie's understanding that six sodas $\times$ 50¢ would result in a $3.00 purchase. Shown another way, that would be $6 \times \frac{1}{2}$ of a dollar, or 3 dollars.

Misconceptions of older students are often caused by inadequate concept development through a wide enough range of examples during formal instruction or by limited informal experiences. For example, if a child had only cube-shaped blocks to play with, he could not compare other three-dimensional shapes and their properties. Viewing a diagram of a pyramid would be confusing for this child.

Signs of Learning Problems in Young Children

When should parents, teachers, and other caregivers be concerned about the development of young children in areas related to later mathematics learning? The early childhood literature has rarely addressed developmental delays and learning problems in mathematics to the extent needed by today's preschool educators. The message has been that young children develop at different rates and that is natural. But with the explosion of young children born drug-exposed and in poverty in the 1990s and 2000s and their significant learning and behavioral needs, early childhood educators must address these needs and provide early interventions. Even special education research with young children has not made strong connections with later mathematics learning difficulties for children younger than six or seven.

With the caveat that young children develop at individual rates but with the reality of early experiences in cognitive development being most effective, early childhood educators should be concerned when observing these characteristics in three- and four-year-olds:

- Language: problems with naming objects, following simple directions, rhyming, recalling number words 0 to 10, or using language to express needs or thoughts.
- Social/emotional: not making choices, following simple rules, engaging in play with other children, or sticking with a task or activity; easily frustrated or angry; overly egocentric as compared with peers.
- Sensory/motor: avoids hands-on tasks; clumsy and immature large motor skills as compared with peers; excessively disorganized; over- or under-reacts to environmental stimuli; awkward pencil, crayon, or scissors grip for age.
- Cognitive: Cannot count objects to 4 or 5, cannot name colors and simple shapes, does not recall simple words or directions, cannot sort objects by one attribute, cannot make simple comparisons, cannot offer a simple reason for an action.

DEVELOPMENTALLY APPROPRIATE MATHEMATICS FOR YOUNG CHILDREN

The term "developmentally appropriate practice," or DAP, was applied to the concept of planning children's activities in preschool settings according to age appropriateness by Bredekamp (1987) in the first National Association for the Education of Young Children (NAEYC) monograph on early childhood programming. DAP relates to the developmental appropriateness of activities based on age, individual growth patterns, and cultural factors. Individual development involves aspects of cognitive, physical, social, and emotional development as well as familial and other environmental influences.

Activities in preschool and early school settings (homes, child care centers, and schools for ages birth through seven or eight) can range along a continuum from developmentally inappropriate to developmentally appropriate (Hart, Burts, & Charlesworth, 1997). Practices on the developmentally inappropriate end would include teaching through lecture; requiring rote memorization of isolated facts; forcing paper and pencil tasks too early; designing curriculum into isolated formal school topics of math, science, and social studies; administering standardized tests as a means of measuring learning; applying whole-group learning goals; and requiring children to sit at desks for most learning experiences. In contrast, developmentally appropriate practice builds on the child as the source for learning activities. Children have options in the learning environment, activities integrate curriculum areas, the environment includes hands-on explorations, and teachers are able to guide children in flexible ways depending on developmental needs.

Developmentally appropriate practice does not preclude important mathematics learning, however. Young children can develop concepts and attitudes that will have a significant impact on their formal mathematics learning. The NAEYC and NCTM developed a joint position statement* about appropriate mathematics experiences for children ages three to six (2002). Their ten recommendations have been illustrated here with elaborated examples:

1. *Enhance children's natural interest in mathematics and their disposition to use it to make sense of their physical and social worlds.* For example, observe children playing with objects for exploration. Children naturally sort, classify, and compare objects such as blocks, balls, and other toys. Their curiosity in the world around them should be encouraged through enriched environments and prompting by others.

2. *Build on children's experience and knowledge, including their family, linguistic, cultural, and community backgrounds; their individual approaches to learning; and their informal knowledge.* Before age two, most children develop the general concepts of shape and number. Between two and six or seven they should have experiences that develop classification, comparison, counting, locating parts in wholes, ordering, using initial mathematics language, measuring informally, making simple graphs, and using simple mathematics symbols. Number systems and mathematics language may be influenced by linguistic differences. For example, Asian-language children are more likely to show larger numbers in a base-ten system than non-Asian children, who tend to use numbers as a one-to-one collection of objects (Miura & Okamoto, 2003). Asian languages represent numbers in exact base-ten references, whereas non-Asian languages do not always emphasize the number system structure and may actually reverse the order of spoken and written language (fourteen for 14 in English; three and forty for 43 in German).

Experience with counting, ordering, and classifying is influenced by opportunities to engage with a wide variety of materials and activities. For example, the four-year-old who helps her father with cooking family meals and setting the table may develop concepts of number, spatial relationships, and measurement earlier than her peers. A five-year-old

---

*Ten recommendations, adapted, with permission, from Early Childhood Mathematics: Promoting Good Beginnings: A joint position statement of the National Association for the Education of Young Children (NAEYC) and the National Council for Teachers of Mathematics (NCTM) (2002).

child who travels with his mother and older sister on the subway develops concepts of value of money, time, distance, and spatial navigation.

3. *Base mathematics curriculum and teaching practices on knowledge of young children's cognitive, linguistic, physical, and social–emotional development.* Although generalizations about child development can assist teachers in planning experiences, exact timelines based on these generalizations should not be imposed. One child may be using a pencil or crayon to draw representations of objects while another child's fine motor skills are not as developed so she uses larger implements and cut-outs. One child perceives a drawing as representing real objects while another child the same age cannot make that connection yet. New learning experiences should be based on each child's current developmental level but work to gradually scaffold the child's understanding to a higher level.

4. *Use curriculum and teaching practices that strengthen children's problem solving and reasoning processes as well as representing, communicating, and connecting mathematics ideas.* The five process standards for mathematics learning, described in Chapter 1, also apply to young children. Using developmentally appropriate activities, teachers should ask questions, set up learning experiences, and scaffold understanding so that children can form the foundations for these processes. Consider the following preschool setting.

> Mr. Sanchez is sitting at a low table with three children—Amy, Jennie, and Bart. His goal for the interaction is to have the children count buttons and make representations of their findings. Mr. Sanchez asks the children how many buttons they are wearing today. Amy counts five, Jennie three, and Bart finds eight on his clothing. Mr. Sanchez asks comparison questions such as, "Who has the most buttons? Who has the smallest number?" This is to encourage the children to use their mathematics vocabulary. Bart exclaims that he has the same as Amy and Jennie together but this notion confuses the girls. His buttons are not like theirs at all. Mr. Sanchez explains to the children that they are going to create a graph showing the number of buttons using the chart paper and crayons. Each child draws in his or her buttons in a column over his or her name while the other children help by counting the buttons drawn. The children are eager to add to their graph so they ask Mr. Sanchez if they can each question another child about buttons and draw those on the graph. What mathematics processes were involved in this activity? Was the activity developmentally appropriate for preschool children? Did the activity allow for differences in individual development? (See the Companion Website at www.ablongman.com/gurganus1e.) ■ ● ▲

5. *Ensure that the curriculum is coherent and compatible with known relationships and sequences of important mathematics ideas.* The national curriculum standards encourage developing the big ideas of mathematics rather than teaching isolated facts. A recommended sequence, or learning paths, for concept development between the ages of three and six is found in Figure 2.1. The close connections among the mathematics content areas are especially evident in this age span.

6. *Provide for children's deep and sustained interaction with key mathematical ideas.* Rather than occasional and haphazard mathematics-related events or planned formal mathematics lessons covering dozens of topics, the standards call for a balanced

● ● ▲ ▼ ● ■ ● ■ ● ▲ ▼ ●
Scaffolding is used in education to refer to the supports provided by the teacher during the learning process so that students are able to participate in complex tasks they could not perform independently. Also called contingent instruction.
● ● ● ● ● ● ● ● ●

Continuum of Mathematics Concept Development in Young Children

Content Standard	Specific Concept	Examples from Early (age 3) through School-Age (age 6) Activities
Number and Operation	Counting items in a collection	3 years: counts 1 to 4 items
		6 years: counts up to 100 items, can use counting by two's and groups of 10
	Labels amount with a cardinal number	3 years: labels totals of 1, 2, and 3 items
		6 years: labels patterned (die) and unpatterned collections up to 6 items without counting
	Adds and subtracts with one-digit numbers	3 years: adds or subtracts with 1 and 2 objects
		6 years: adds or subtracts numbers to 10 using counting on or counting back strategies
Geometry and Spatial Sense	Identifies two- and three-dimensional shapes	3 years: matches and names simple 2-D and 3-D shapes by size and orientation
		6 years: names a variety of 2-D and 3-D shapes and can describe basic features
	Uses shapes	3 years: uses shapes to create a simple picture
		6 years: uses shapes in more complex combinations to create pictures
	Describes locations spatially	3 years: describes the location of objects using under, behind, and other simple words
		6 years: builds or draws simple maps of immediate environments
Measurement	Identifies measurable attributes	3 years: recognizes measurable attributes (short, big)
		6 years: uses simple units and processes of measurement
	Uses attributes	3 years: compares and sorts by attribute
		6 years: uses standard and nonstandard tools to measure
Patterns, Functions, Algebra	Recognizes patterns	3 years: notices and copies simple repeating patterns
		6 years: discusses number patterns
Data Analysis	Organizes by attribute	3 years: sorts and counts objects, compares groups
		6 years: classifies and organizes objects based on various attributes
	Represents data	3 years: helps make simple pictographs
		6 years: organizes and compares numerical representations using bar graphs

Source: Adapted, with permission, from "Learning Paths and Teaching Strategies in Early Mathematics" in Early Childhood Mathematics: Promoting Good Beginnings: A joint position statement of the National Association for the Education of Young Children (NAEYC) and the National Council for Teachers of Mathematics (NCTM) (2002).

approach with young children. Present concepts in a logical sequence and provide in-depth experiences including extensions by families or caregivers. This approach requires planning and focusing on the big ideas, especially in the areas of number and spatial sense.

An example of a shallow mathematics event would be for the teacher to have students count their raisins before making cookies. This counting experience is not connected to deep mathematics concepts and does not promote the processes. If the class is preparing to make cookies and the teacher wants to build number sense, a stronger, big ideas approach would be to ask students to predict the number of raisins in their boxes, then count them in any way they want to count. Then the teacher would ask thought-provoking questions such as, "Why did you count your raisins by two?" "Why didn't each box have exactly the same number?" "If our batch of cookie dough will make 24 cookies and we use three boxes of raisins, how many raisins do you predict will be in each cookie?" "Will each cookie have exactly the same number?" Extensions of this number sense activity could be planned around a graphing activity or another pictorial representation.

7. *Integrate mathematics with other activities and other activities with mathematics.* Activities with young children lend themselves to concept integration. Concept integration leads to stronger understanding and generalization. Children's literature, music, games, science explorations, social skills, social studies, and even classroom routines have many opportunities for the integration of mathematics concepts if planned at the appropriate level and with appropriate depth, not just random activities. One first-grade teacher plans weekly themes around which she constructs activities that support the entire curriculum. The first week of February was "snowflakes" and activities included reading *The Snowy Day* by Ezra Jack Keats, singing a song created by the class called "I'm a Little Snowflake," and studying the shapes and symmetry of cut-out snowflake designs. For science concepts, the class predicted the freezing and melting rates of ice and for social studies they read about the first person to photograph snowflakes, Wilson Bentley. For writing they created a group book called, "The Lonely Snowflake" using new words such as cold, dark, white, and night (and one student wanted to learn to spell the word *hexagon*).

8. *Provide ample time, materials, and teacher support for children to engage in play, a context in which they explore and manipulate mathematical ideas with keen interest.* With young children, play can be the best context for assessment, problem-solving, and concept development. The teacher's responsibility is to provide an environment with space and materials for exploration and to carefully observe and listen to children during these play activities. Teachers should ask questions that will stimulate children's making connections, building extensions, and developing new understandings. For example, a classroom for three-year-olds has many baskets of objects for play. One basket contains connecting blocks, another has assorted containers, and a third is full of multicolored geometric shapes. Individual children are playing with the objects, making up stories and names for their play. The teacher asks two children playing with the blocks whether they think the blocks will fit inside the containers. This question prompted the children to begin counting blocks into containers and comparing their results. The children viewed

this activity as the "fill up" game, but the teacher heard the children using predicting, counting, volume, and comparing words and concepts.

9. *Actively introduce mathematical concepts, methods, and language through a range of appropriate experiences and teaching strategies.* Beyond play activities, teachers need to plan specific learning experiences for young children with mathematics objectives in mind. Typically these activities also have motor, language, and social skills objectives for individual children. For example, a mathematics objective appropriate for most five-year-old children is, "children will count by fives from 0 to 20 (for some children to 50)." The planned activities for this objective could involve music, art, games, money, or time. The teacher should plan explicit activities and assessments for the objective, make deliberate plans for new vocabulary and skill development, and assure that each child is learning something new, extending or revising previous understandings of number. But the activities are still individualized and developmentally appropriate, not paper and pencil tasks at the symbolic level. Appropriate mathematics learning at this level cannot be left to chance.

10. *Support children's learning by thoughtfully and continually assessing all children's mathematical knowledge, skills, and strategies.* Assessment strategies at this level also must be individually relevant and developmentally appropriate. The most authentic and informative assessments are careful observation, children's products over time, open-ended questions, and performance assessments in real contexts such as play. For the example of counting by fives, the teacher should listen to each child count by five in another time and setting, using nickels, analog clocks, or objects. The assessment should take place in a natural setting, not formalized into a testing format. Authentic and natural assessments can, therefore, occur continuously as they are embedded within day-to-day activities. These informal assessment strategies are still planned and documented; they are just more developmentally appropriate and valid for young children.

When Zachary, Kristy, David, and Jessica begin formal mathematics instruction, will their teachers tap their informal mathematics knowledge to make linkages to formal learning? Will they have had the rich, developmentally appropriate experiences in preschool settings that provide strong concept understanding for more formal mathematics learning? What will their teachers in the early grades believe about how students learn mathematics? The following sections review the major theories of learning and discuss the constructivist philosophy as it applies to mathematics learning and students with learning problems.

THEORIES ABOUT LEARNING APPLIED TO MATHEMATICS

Why discuss theory when classroom practice is paramount for student achievement? Professional practice in the classroom without a theoretical grounding would be like a medical doctor prescribing medications at random or like governmental policy makers recommending program frameworks based on intuition. Those practices could not be defended, nor can instructional practices based on whim, fad, or habit. Theory provides a basis for the development of new practice, evaluating current practice, and guiding professional decision making.

Theories are organized sets of testable principles about particular events. They provide broad conceptual frameworks that serve a number of purposes including structuring research and designing classroom practice (Gredler, 1997). While we have a 120-year history of empirical educational research, only since the mid 1950s has most research been instructionally relevant. Most formal instructional approaches are grounded in behavioral, cognitive, and/or socio-cultural theories of learning. The following sections will provide brief overviews of these perspectives, with an emphasis on contributions to mathematics instruction. These theories attempt to explain how children learn most effectively, what instructional designs are most efficient, and under what conditions learning can be optimized. Teachers, as professionals, must consider the theoretical basis of their practice in order to make instructional decisions.

Behavorist Theories

Behaviorist, or **operant learning theories,** posit that behavior is the response of an organism to stimuli in the situation. All behaviors are learned and existing behaviors can be replaced by new behaviors (Skinner, 1963). Learning is behavioral change; learning is functionally related to changes in environmental conditions or events. The focus of behaviorist theories is on observable behaviors—those that can be observed and changed through manipulation of antecedents and consequences. For example, the teacher who wants to increase a student's success in calculating a set of math problems might work three or four problems with the student (*antecedent*) before allowing the student to work independently. Then the teacher would check the student's work immediately, affirming correct responses and suggesting reexamination of incorrect ones (*consequence*).

The most powerful means for increasing desirable behaviors is the use of reinforcement, the manipulation of specific stimuli after the learner's response. Reinforcement takes the form of either presentation of a desired stimulus (positive) or removal of an undesirable stimulus (negative). Behaviorists are not as concerned with mental processes, because they cannot be directly observed or measured (Engelman & Carnine, 1982). According to a behavioral perspective, instruction is primarily teacher-directed. The teacher analyzes the curriculum for its component tasks and learning hierarchies, evaluates the student's present level of performance within the curriculum, develops behavioral objectives to drive instruction and assessment strategies, and applies prompts and reinforcers throughout the learning process.

While many professionals view behaviorism as most cogent in influencing social behaviors, this theory was developed to explain how we learn in general and has been translated into many academic applications. For example, precision teaching, task analysis, behavioral objectives, shaping techniques, instructional feedback, direct instruction, stages of learning, the functional analysis of the learning environment, curriculum-based assessment, and the design of computer-assisted instruction were heavily influenced by behaviorist theories of learning. All of these methods can be applied to mathematics instruction and most mathematics curricula include behavioral aspects. The effectiveness of these behavioral-based interventions is well documented.

Cognitive Theories

Cognitive learning theory is concerned with thinking processes during learning. A developmental (biological) approach to cognitive learning theory is found in the work of Jean Piaget, although its roots can be traced to late nineteenth-century Gestalt psychologists in Germany. Piaget's research was actually focused on how logic develops in children, but his work on cognitive structures and the influences of the environment on cognitive development have placed his work within the realm of learning theory (Gredler, 1997). Cognitive theorists assert that children learn through thinking about their interactions with the environment. Learning is a process of forming and reforming mental schemas or cognitive structures, based on personal interactions and observations. To consider the classic example, a child may see two different-sized glasses with what appears to be the same amount of juice in each glass. The child's impression is based on viewing the level of juice in each glass. However, the teacher encourages the child to pour the juice into other containers. After several experiments, the child, if developmentally ready, comes to realize that the size and shape of the containers must also be considered and the best way to compare the amount of juice is to use two similar containers.

According to Piaget, children move through a universal sequence of developmental stages in their logical-thinking skills: sensori-motor, preoperational, concrete operational, and formal operational (1952). Cognitive theorists also classify knowledge into four types: social-arbitrary, like the names of objects or social rules; physical knowledge, that which derives from personal experience; logical knowledge, concepts and conclusions that come from thinking about personal experiences; and social-interactive, or understandings of people and interactions gained by interacting with others.

In his later years, Piaget devoted less time to stage theory and more to construction theory and the mechanisms of learning, especially the processes of equilibration in cognitive development (Bidell & Fischer, 1992; Fosnot, 1996). Rather than learning by stimulus-response in a rather passive role, the active learner assimilates new information or stimuli and accommodates or adjusts and adapts it with previous learning. Learning is the active reconstruction and self-regulation by the learner of a revised understanding. This Assimilative Base Model was more applicable to educational settings, especially with the shift in research at the Genevan School in 1976 from the study of structures to the study of strategies children use to learn (Gallagher & Wansart, 1991).

The teacher's role, according to Piagetian theorists, is one of facilitator for interactions with rich environments. The concepts contributed by cognitive psychologists have visible translations in classroom practice for mathematics: hands-on learning, discovery learning, the use of discrepant events, developmentally appropriate practice, readiness, individual differences, and the developmental and spiral nature of the curriculum.

A cognitive theory with different origins and applications is **information-processing theory**. The various parts of this framework for how cognitive processes work during learning can be attributed to a number of sources such as Broadbent's multistage memory (1958); Atkinson and Shiffrin's multistore, multistage theory of memory and control processes (1968); Gagné's conditions for learning (1985); and other work on perception, attention, motivation, memory, metacognition, and knowledge types. But its roots as a

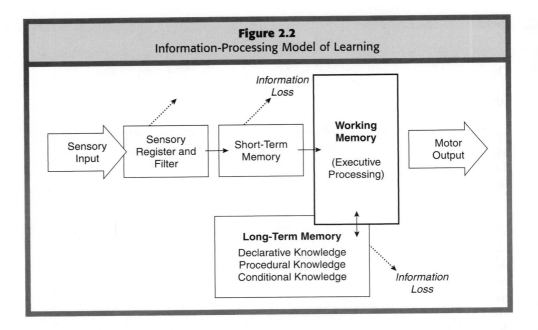

Figure 2.2
Information-Processing Model of Learning

learning model can be found in post World War II computer development. In the information-processing model, thinking processes are compared with computer functions—sensory input is received, filtered, organized, transformed, stored, and finally retrieved and used. Concepts of short-term, working, and long-term memory; executive functioning; perception; attention; and mental structures are important components that have direct applications in the teaching–learning setting (see Figure 2.2). For example, the teacher may use a concept map of the various units of measure to enhance student understanding of how aspects of the concept relate (connections) and to assist with later recall (long-term memory). As each new piece of the larger concept of unit of measure is explored, the teacher can refer back and add to the concept map.

In an information-processing paradigm, the teacher is concerned with the organization and presentation of information as well as assisting the student in becoming a more independent and strategic learner. The student is actively attending to and processing information. This processing includes making connections with previous learning, directing one's own thinking and executive functions, and drawing on previous learning to solve problems or transfer skills, all critical for mathematics learning.

Socio-Cultural Theories

Like behaviorist and cognitive perspectives, socio-cultural theories regard the interaction of learner with environment as critical for learning. Socio-cultural views differ in the emphasis they place on personal interactions and cultural and historical effects on learning. An educational researcher gaining renewed analysis is Russian psychologist Lev Vygotsky, whose work spanned only fourteen years (1924–1938). Central to Vygotsky's writings were the role of culture and social interactions in the learning process. The signs and symbols of a culture (and they vary considerably across cultures)—especially oral language—are the means of social behavior and individual thought development (Vygotsky, 1924/1979). One aspect of communication studied by Vygotsky was the concept of private speech and its role in developing mental functions, self-regulation, and problem solving (Berk & Winsler, 1995).

Communication between teacher and student is also critical to the learning process by creating a *zone of proximal development* in which the student is encouraged to achieve what he could not accomplish alone (Vygotsky, 1934/1986). We see direct applications of this concept in scaffolding techniques and reciprocal teaching. Vygotsky believed that the very nature of the content being taught influences the development of complex mental functions.

A classroom example from this perspective is the teacher working with a small group of kindergarten students on concept development. The teacher shows the students a cardboard triangle and asks them to describe what he is holding. After lots of ideas—some factual, some experiential, and quite a few imaginative, the teacher asks the students to compare the triangle with a cardboard quadrilateral. The students say that the quadrilateral is bigger and a different color than the triangle (but are not using the terminology yet). The teacher rephrases his questions to include: How many sides do you count on this shape? On the other shape? How many corners? The teacher carefully uses language such as, "The shape with three sides and three angles is called a triangle." After several of these exchanges, the questions are more difficult and the students are offering more observant and sophisticated responses, even posing questions of their own. They are guided to find the same shapes in the classroom.

One of Vygotsky's chief interests was neurophysiology and the study of disabilities affecting learning. He viewed the problem of disabling conditions as primarily social. The disability alters the individual's relationship and interactions with other people, leading to social deprivation and defective development (Gindis, 1995). Vygotsky classified disabilities as primary, an impairment of biological origin, and secondary, distortion of higher cognitive functions caused by social factors. Training, according to Vygotsky, should focus on restoring alternative but equivalent means of communication and cultural development—a very early conceptualization of learner accommodations.

Direct applications in the mathematics classroom of socio-cultural theories include modeling, peer tutoring, cooperative learning, apprenticeships, reciprocal teaching, interactive dialog, scaffolding, and accommodations. In this view many individuals serve as teacher during the learning process.

Interrelated Theories

Behavioral, cognitive, social, and information-processing theories contributed to the formation of **Cognitive-Behavior Modification Theory** (CBM) (Harris, 1982; Leon & Pepe, 1983; Lloyd, Forness, & Kavale, 1998). The principles of behavioral intervention, including task analysis, cuing, and reinforcing feedback, were derived from behavioral theories. From social learning theory, affective aspects such as attitude and motivation were acknowledged, along with the importance of modeling, especially cognitive modeling. The concepts of metacognition, knowledge construction, and self-regulation were contributed from information-processing and cognitive theories (Meichenbaum, 1977). CBM theory incorporated the roles that cognitive processes, behaviors of student and teacher, interaction with the environment, and dialog with others play in the complex and dynamic process of learning.

Since the mid-1990s, CBM terminology has been applied almost exclusively to interventions involving behavior rather than academics. Most likely this shift was due to the terms *behavior* and *modification* within CBM, too externally directed to reflect a balanced theory. Interrelated theoretical perspectives, even those with clear behavioral roots and contributions, are currently under the cognitive theory umbrella: cognitive information processing, meaningful learning, schema theory, metacognitive theory, situated cognition, and interactional cognitive theory. This shift also can be seen in Gagné's conditions of learning (1985). Gagné's work from the 1950s and 1960s for training the military focused on breaking tasks into components, teaching prerequisite skills, ensuring mastery, and sequencing tasks to ensure transfer, from a behavioral perspective. His work with mathematics problem solving in the 1970s and 1980s illustrated that learning tasks are not single, simple, or sequential processes and that learning is not merely associative. He identified five varieties of learning: verbal information, intellectual skills, motor skills, attitudes, and cognitive strategies. These varieties reflected the outcomes of learning, or new capabilities of the learner. Gagné further identified internal and external conditions of learning, such as prerequisites, expectations, practice, and feedback that have direct applications in effective classroom instruction.

Metacognitive processes are highlighted in many current cognitive theories and are particularly critical for mathematics learning. Metacognition refers to one's awareness of thinking and the self-regulation that accompanies this awareness (Flavell, 1978). Jacobs and Paris (1987) described three components of self-regulation. Planning involves goal setting, selecting strategies, and activating one's resources for the task. Evaluation is an active and continuous determination of understanding. Finally, monitoring involves checking one's progress and selecting alternative strategies as needed.

There is a great deal of research on the importance of metacognition in mathematics applications, especially problem solving (see for example Montague & Bos, 1986; Montague, 1997). Students with weak or delayed metacognitive skills spend less time planning, are not as aware of task demands, do not recognize their own errors as readily, and do not change strategies flexibly as needed. There is also a developing body of research supporting efforts to explicitly teach metacognitive skills for mathematics learning such as goal-setting, self-talk, self-monitoring, schema development, and strategy selection and implementation (Case, Harris, & Graham, 1992; Miller & Mercer, 1993; Jitendra & Hoff, 1995).

Another theory that is closely related to mathematics learning is the **multiple intelligences** (MI) theory of Howard Gardner (1983). While his theory was initially developed to dispute the 80-year-old notion that intelligence was a concept that could be measured in isolation and related in a single score, it has evolved to be a pragmatic view of the multifaceted potential of learners. Most of Gardner's eight intelligences relate in some way to mathematics learning: linguistic, logical-mathematical, spatial, bodily-kinesthetic, musical, naturalist, interpersonal, intrapersonal. Gardner asserted that all of us possess all eight intelligences (and possibly more), no two individuals exhibit the same intelligences in the same proportions, the intelligences work together in complex ways, and each can be developed to at least adequate competency (Gardner, 1993, 1999). Gardner also emphasized that certain experiences in the development of our intelligences can be crystallizing (turning points or catalysts in learning) or paralyzing (shut down or prevent learning).

Multiple intelligences theory posits that the development of intelligences is influenced by the interaction of heredity and early training. Gardner asserted that each intelligence has at its core an information-processing device unique to that intelligence; for example, phonological and grammatical processing for language, and tonal and rhythmic processing for music. At its core the logical-mathematical intelligence has pattern perception.

An example of how multiple intelligence theory may be applied in the classroom is for the teacher to create a learning environment that allows students with differing strengths to participate and learn through their strengths and build up weaker areas. In one mathematics classroom, students are studying data collection and analysis. The teacher plans to use concrete objects (bodily-kinesthetic), graphs and charts (spatial and logical-mathematical), and real-life surveys (interpersonal) for data collection and representation. Students are asked to describe and discuss their findings (linguistic) and make connections with other math concepts (logical-mathematical). If students are to develop multiple intelligences, they should be exposed to experiences in all areas.

Gardner's theory of multiple intelligences and its classroom applications have been criticized for lack of empirical support, lack of evidence that the specific "intelligences" can be distinguished from one another, and overall lack of supportable applications (Willingham, 2004). Even Gardner questioned trivial applications of this theory to classroom practice, emphasized that the intelligences are not fungible (development in one area will not substitute for that of another), and offered only general suggestions about possible entry points for individual students for topics under study. Other than promoting the diversification of materials and activities, which most experienced educators do anyway, MI theory does not offer research-based applications for specific groups of students.

Multiple intelligence theory should not be confused with learning-style (modality or sensory-channel) theories that are primarily process-oriented and also lack research support, or with the various personality theories, such as the Myers-Briggs model, that only indirectly relate to classroom practice (Armstrong, 1994). Unfortunately, many current mathematics textbooks offer teaching to student **learning styles** (LS) as a primary method for differentiating mathematics instruction for students with learning problems. Developed at St. John's University in the 1970s and embraced by the National Association of Secondary School Principals, the Dunn and Dunn Model of Learning-Style Preferences as an approach to increasing academic achievement has received very little research support. Yet, possibly because of the "intuitive, gut feeling factor," it has persisted in influencing curriculum development. In meta-analyses of studies of modality-based instruction, Kavale and Forness found effect sizes of .144 (slightly higher than chance) in a 1987 review of 39 studies. The research conducted by the Dunns and their colleagues and students has been criticized as lacking rigor, requisite description, and independent replication (Kavale, Hirshoren, & Forness, 1998; Snider, 1992).

What is problematic about using a learning styles approach to instruction? First, the approach is based on a faulty premise that the cause of learning problems is a mismatch between the student's learning style and the instructional method. Second, the LS approach grew out of the unsupported perceptual-motor and other processing deficit theories of the 1960s. Third, LS advocates claim that students can be assessed for preferred learning styles and should be taught in a matching teaching method. For example, Carbo (1988) suggested that global/tactile/kinesthetic learners who were poor readers should be taught with holistic reading methods and not phonics, that phonics instruction is for students who can already discriminate easily among sounds. Emphasizing holistic methods with younger and remedial students is contrary to virtually all other academic intervention research. Fourth, other instructional methods, such as direct instruction, cognitive strategy training, and mnemonic strategies, have achieved much higher gains (effect sizes from .75 to 1.62) than learning styles matching. Finally, attempting to implement instruction matched to each student's preferred style would be difficult at best. When little or no achievement gains could be expected, it would be hard to justify the extra effort. Kavale and Forness (1987, p. 237) reminded educators that "all modalities are strongly involved in the learning process, and academic achievement without the inclusion of all modalities is virtually impossible (for a child without sensory deficits)." A learning styles approach to teaching and learning underestimates the significance of learning problems and offers only surface-level, simplistic instructional interventions.

CONSTRUCTIVISM

"I'm a constructivist teacher." "I use a constructivist approach in my classroom." "My methods follow constructivist theory." Statements like these are heard frequently among educators today. Like other educational jargon (outcome-based education, whole language, new math), constructivism has taken on multiple meanings, an almost political flavor, and frequent confusion about its relationship to teaching and learning activities.

Constructivism is not yet one theory and may be best described as a philosophy about learning. Its constructs are not new; they date back to 18th-century psychology and science. But its application to teaching is a relatively recent phenomenon. Virtually every journal and text in mathematics, science, and even special education in the past few years has addressed some aspect of constructivism.

A perusal of published articles and conference proceedings on constructivism will reveal that few authors agree on how to define constructivism, delineate its key elements, or apply it to classroom teaching and learning. This section will provide a working definition, discuss briefly a few versions of constructivism, and describe the most common elements of this philosophy as it relates to educational settings. Finally, the implications for mathematics teaching, especially for students with disabilities, will be examined.

Figure 2.3
Constructivist Continuum

	Exogenous	Dialectical	Endogenous
Theoretical Non-Constructivism			Theoretical Radical Constructivism
	Direct Instruction	Guided Discovery	Pure Discovery
Teacher:	Directive	Supportive	Peripheral
Learner:	Engaged	Interactive	Self-regulated
Content:	Explicit skills	Skills, concepts, relationships	Concepts, relationships

What Is Constructivism?

Constructivism is a philosophy about learning that has implications for teaching. Constructivists view learning as the active construction of knowledge by the learner influenced by (to varying degrees) interactions with the environment, communication with other people, and the learner's own cognitive processes. The influences of Piaget, Vygotsky, Bruner, and even Dewey are evident in this description. Radical constructivists (see, for example, von Glaserfield, 1991) claim that knowledge is not absolute or universally prescribed; rather it is *only* that which is constructed by each person. Social constructivists (Prawat & Floden, 1994) emphasize personal interactions and the importance of language in influencing the construction of knowledge and understanding.

Perhaps a more useful way for educators to consider the variations of constructivism is with Moshman's (1982) endogenous, exogenous, and dialectical types as depicted in Figure 2.3 (see also Martin, 1998; Mercer, Jordan, & Miller, 1996). The endogenous constructivist, like the radical, assumes that knowledge is developed entirely within the learner; the teacher's role is facilitator of holistic, self-regulated learning. The other extreme, the exogenous constructivist, believes that all learning requires teacher direction and explicit, controlled instruction. In the centrist position is the dialectical constructivist who views instruction as a collaborative activity with a balance of implicit and explicit methods.

The following list synthesizes the most common elements of a constructivist philosophy about learning (Davis, Maher, & Noddings, 1990; Harris & Graham, 1996; Reid, Kurkjian, & Carruthers, 1994; Poplin, 1988; Brooks & Brooks, 1993; Fosnot, 1996; Wheatley, 1991; Martin, 1998; Driscoll, 2005):

1. All knowledge is personally constructed.
2. Cognitive structures are activated during the process of construction and are under continual development.
3. Children are inherently active, self-regulating learners.
4. Children construct knowledge in developmentally appropriate ways within a social context.
5. The starting point for learning is the child's prior knowledge and experiences; the best predictor of learning is prior learning.
6. Real understanding occurs only with full participation in learning.
7. Learning is a socially situated activity that is enhanced in functional, meaningful, and authentic contexts.
8. Learning is facilitated by disequilibrium, dialog, and reflection.
9. The curriculum should be relevant, student-centered, and problem-based.
10. Good teaching involves knowing students, posing problems, scaffolding student understanding, allowing risk-taking, promoting exploration and interaction, and encouraging higher-order thinking.

Constructivism has been contrasted with traditional teaching, behaviorism, reductionism, didactic teaching, direct instruction, objectivism, and process–product approaches. However, direct instruction, traditional teaching, and didactic methods can all be constructivist. Process–product research studied specific teacher behaviors that had a positive influence on student learning, including many constructivist-compatible techniques.

Reductionism is a paradigm about an approach to content that has most frequently been contrasted with constructivism. Constructivists view themselves as holistic, approaching the curriculum from the top-down, from the larger and interconnected concepts that are more than the sum of their dissected parts. They define reductionists as those educators who reduce concepts to their simpler, most understandable parts through task and concept analysis. However, as Kronick (1990, p. 7) has clarified, "if we were to reconceptualize bottom-up information as being relational rather than fixed, then it would become as meaningful as top-down information."

Objectivism, based on behavioral and cognitive theories of learning, holds that knowledge is external and that personal knowledge is developed through experiences with external content and instruction. The radical constructivist would insist that the only real knowledge is internal and personally constructed.

We could attempt to describe non-constructivist learning and teaching: the learner is a passive recipient of irrelevant information transmitted by an uninvolved teacher. In the real classroom, that stereotype should be hard to find. It appears that approaches to teaching and learning take on constructivist characteristics when the student is an active learner; the curriculum is relevant, meaningful, and challenging, but connected to students' previous learning; and the teacher arranges an environment conducive to learning and actively facilitates and monitors learning.

How Is Constructivism Related to Mathematics Learning?

Constructivist philosophy is particularly relevant for mathematics learning and teaching. Mathematics is inherently related to a philosophy promoting active, hands-on learning; student interactions; scaffolding of higher-order understanding; meaningful and authentic contexts; and developmental, spiraling, and interrelated content.

For example, the mathematics standards discussed in Chapter 1 call for addressing the larger, interrelated concepts (big ideas) of the content rather than teaching thousands of isolated and often unrelated facts and concepts. Some big ideas of mathematics include number, proportion, dimension, function, scale, and place value. The mathematics standards also emphasize a problem-solving approach and higher-order thinking skills. Processes of mathematics include estimation, data collection and analysis, classification, inferring, and communication. These concepts and processes require active construction by students.

As will be discussed in later chapters, assessment in mathematics in today's schools is moving away from forced-choice, single-answer questions toward problem solving and performance approaches that require demonstration or communication of processes, cross-curricular experiences, and higher-order applications. This type of assessment more closely resembles real-world problems and requires instructional approaches that promote active, interrelated learning.

Is Constructivism Relevant for Students with Learning Problems?

A critical aspect of the teaching–learning context is consideration of individual learner differences. However, individual differences are virtually ignored by constructivist proponents (Case, 1992). Students who have difficulty learning have the most problems with indirect, inductive approaches espoused by the more radical constructivists. For example, examine the experiences of poor readers with radical whole language programs (Harris & Graham, 1994). These students rarely figured out the code for reading without explicit instruction in symbol-sound associations.

It is true that all learning is constructing meaning, and constructivist philosophy posits the personal nature of the construction process. But the subsequent attempts to translate philosophy into instructional methods appears to promote a one-size-fits-all approach. Again, Kronick is especially compelling (1990, p. 6): "The obduracy with which holists reject the role that individual differences play in learning failure flies in the face of their concern about the distinctiveness of individuals and about learning as a transactional construct." Learners come to us with widely varying previous experiences and understandings. They require different approaches in constructing new understandings—some need very explicit instruction, others need to see several examples and be involved in discussions or hands-on activities, and still others seem to make constructions in purely abstract ways almost in isolation. What may be most important is that teachers be able to determine prior understanding, provide necessary environmental and instructional scaffolds, and assess whether new learning is occurring with all students. Many of the elements of constructivist teaching and learning are, in fact, very appropriate for students with disabilities and other learning problems.

Knight (2002) maintained that intensive–explicit instruction and constructivist approaches are compatible and may actually support the limitations of each other. For example, intensive–explicit instruction has been criticized for being reductionist, separated from meaningful applications, and not promoting generalization. Constructivism has been criticized for overlooking the needs of students with learning problems and leaving students with gaps in essential learning. According to Knight, intensive–explicit instruction could take place within authentic, holistic learning environments that would promote generalization while still building background knowledge, essential skills, and competence within a discipline.

A Balanced View

Some researchers and educators have called for a retreat from the extreme, fringe elements of theoretical perspectives, such as radical constructivism, that seem to dominate the professional literature to support nonpolemic, coherent, integrated instruction based on individual student needs and contextual circumstances (Harris & Graham, 1994; Mercer & Pullen, 2005; Dixon & Carnine, 1994; Mather & Roberts, 1994). Trent, Artiles, and Englert (1998, p. 296) charged that, "our inability to transcend extreme views has precluded widespread understanding of how common threads run across various instructional models and paradigms." Advocates of what has been termed a functionalist or pragmatic approach urge teachers to identify individual student needs and then borrow concepts and methods from whatever perspective offers the most likelihood of resulting in effective instruction (Berliner, 1989). The instructional method must be adjusted based on the changing roles of teacher and student, nature of the content, and the student's stage of learning within the content.

The best teachers are able to provide instruction to students with a range of abilities and previous experiences in a way that is coordinated yet affords each student the opportunity to learn and be challenged. One elementary teacher with twenty-five students of varying abilities was able to plan and provide instruction in a unit on measurement that challenged all the students at their instructional levels. Some students were learning to estimate distances in feet, others were making accurate measurements to confirm estimates, and others were making conversions to meters. All the students were solving realistic problems at their content level. The teacher was able to pose questions at each student's level and to provide learning opportunities that would increase understanding to the next level as well as interconnections. The teacher also assessed each student's responses frequently to ensure concept understanding and made immediate adjustments as needed. This teacher had the content knowledge expertise and the pedagogical repertoire grounded in learning theory necessary to promote successful learning.

Why consider learning theory? Theory grounds and gives direction for professional practice and research. Professional practice should be based on sound theoretical approaches confirmed by research.

TRY THIS

Select a research article in a professional journal in mathematics or special education. Read the introductory section carefully for the theoretical basis of the study. Which theories described above contributed to the study? Which learning factors were studied?

THEORIES ABOUT MATHEMATICS DISABILITIES AND STUDENT CHARACTERISTICS

Theories also provide a framework for the study of individual student characteristics, including specific disabilities, and the educational needs of those students. It has been estimated through very scant study that approximately five to seven percent of children and youth in school have specific mathematics disabilities (Geary, 2003; Gross-Tsur, Manor, & Shalev, 1996; Badian, 1983). These disabilities generally emerge in the early grades, although they tend to be identified later than those in reading, and continue throughout school and into adult life. It is also estimated that co-morbidity with reading disabilities is somewhere between 17 and 50 percent (Badian, 1983; Ostad, 1998; Gross-Tsur et al., 1996). Mathematics disabilities have not received the attention that reading has garnered, but with more attention on mathematics testing, curriculum standards, and problem-solving skills curriculum-wide, there has been a significant increase in research and intervention in recent years.

Specific Mathematics Disabilities

Early work on specific mathematics difficulties by Russell and Ginsburg (1983) found that children with mathematics difficulties had generally adequate informal knowledge of mathematics, basic understanding of base-ten concepts, differing abilities (that confounded the researchers) related to number fact retrieval and use, and could solve more concrete word problems but had difficulty with complex ones. These findings were initial glimpses into a complex and multidimensional view of mathematics disabilities.

Children with mathematics disabilities typically demonstrate grade-level skills in some areas of mathematics but deficits in others (Geary, Hamson, & Hoard, 2000; Jordan & Montani, 1997; Russell & Ginsburg, 1984). The most consistently identified deficit is in the ability to quickly and accurately recall basic facts from long-term memory. It has been theorized that this retrieval deficit is due to problems representing information from semantic memory or difficulty with inhibiting irrelevant associations during the process (Geary, 2003).

Several researchers (Geary & Hoard, 2001; Jordan & Montani, 1997) have theorized that children with low mathematics achievement but average reading ability have problems with working memory capacity. Children with average mathematics achievement but low reading scores do not typically demonstrate working memory problems. Children with low achievement in both reading and mathematics have the most significant deficits but are still able to perform some skills at grade level.

Geary (2003) theorized three subtypes of mathematics disabilities. The **procedural** subtype is recognized by use of immature procedures, frequent errors in carrying out procedures, poor concept understanding, and sequencing difficulties. These students' performances in mathematics are similar to those of younger students. The **semantic memory** subtype is characterized by problems retrieving math facts and filtering erroneous numbers. This subtype appears to represent a cognitive difference and seems to occur with phonetic-specific reading disabilities. The **visuospatial** subtype typically demonstrates difficulties representing mathematics concepts spatially and misinterpreting spatial information such as models, diagrams, graphs, or measurement estimates. Research into specific mathematical domains and disabilities is extremely limited but should increase with renewed emphasis on mathematics skills and this theoretical groundwork.

Characteristics of Students' Mathematics Learning Problems

About 23 percent of fourth-grade students and 32 percent of eighth-grade students scored below basic on the 2003 National Assessment of Educational Progress Mathematics Assessments (National Center for Educational Statistics, 2003). Although scores have improved since 1996, when 37 percent of fourth graders and 39 percent of eighth graders scored below basic, between one-fourth and one-third of students could not meet grade-level standards in mathematics on the 2003 assessments.

Those students with mathematics disabilities identified under the Individuals with Disabilities Education Act (IDEA, 2004) typically are classified under the categories of specific learning disabilities, mild to moderate cognitive disabilities, emotional disabilities, language impairments, and other health impairments (such as ADHD), where the disability has been identified as having a significant impact on learning. Students with these identified disabilities may be served anywhere on the continuum of placement options, but most are served in regular classrooms or in limited but intensive pull-out programs.

Other students who perform below standards on state or district mathematics tests sometimes have individual intervention plans depending on district or state policies. The No Child Left Behind Act (NCLB, 2001) made no provisions for meeting the needs of individual students who do not meet standards, other than the option to transfer schools if their overall school does not meet criteria for adequate yearly progress. Students from low-income families may qualify for supplemental after-school or Saturday services under the NCLB provisions for Title I schools. Some of these students are served in remedial mathematics programs funded through a variety of sources and others are served primarily in the regular classroom.

Students who have problems learning mathematics or fail to meet grade-level standards are usually identified between third and fifth grade, much later than those identified for reading problems, and are referred for special education services or other remedial programs. Special education and remedial teachers find that these students' basic concept and skill development generally one to two years behind their peers upon identification. Even with interventions, the achievement gap for many students with identified disabilities continues to widen. These math achievement problems are usually due to a combination of teaching and student factors including language, cognitive, metacognitive, motor, social and emotional factors, habits of learning, and previous experiences.

1. *Language problems.* Most students with mild disabilities have primary or secondary language problems. A language disorder, according to the American Speech-Language-Hearing Association, is "impaired comprehension and/or use of a spoken, written, and/or other symbol systems" (ASHA, 1993, p. 40). The disorder may involve form, content, or function of the language. Even if a student does not have an identified language disorder, he or she may exhibit language deficiencies related to his or her disability.

In mathematics class, language problems are evident when students have trouble using symbols of math, expressing math concepts to others, and listening to mathematics explanations. Problems also appear with reading or writing word problems and writing and expressing math "sentences." Language can provide the bridge between the concrete representations of math and the more abstract and symbolic forms. As students advance in math learning, they also use language to think—they manipulate concepts and ideas through language (oral or inner) without having to rely on concrete materials.

Unfortunately, some students have few opportunities to talk about math. Teachers who limit lessons to lecture, demonstration, and worksheets are limiting their students' language development and related math progress. Students should be responding frequently and discussing math problems and concepts with each other and the teacher. Students whose parents continue the dialog at home will have additional benefits.

2. *Cognitive factors.* Most students with mild to moderate disabilities have cognitive factors that impede learning. These may be perceptual, memory, attention, or reasoning factors. Perception involves taking in information from the environment and processing that information for storage or use. It's not just seeing the symbols for numbers but seeing and copying them. It's not just hearing the oral number sequence but hearing it and continuing the sequence. It's not the seeing or hearing alone, it's the discrimination and interpretation of visual and auditory input. Perceptual problems show up with difficulties keeping place on a worksheet or within a column of numbers, differentiating numbers or symbols that are close in form, copying shapes or symbols, following directions with algorithms or graphs, recognizing patterns or sequences, and understanding oral directions or drills.

Memory problems can affect long-term, short-term, or active, working aspects. Memory capacities, in the information-processing model, serve to store and retrieve information needed to interact with the environment. Long-term memory is the background knowledge and prior experience to which new information is added in various forms. Inefficient organization and integration of information going to long-term memory will cause problems with retrieval later. Short-term memory is the briefest register of new information, most of which is filtered and discarded. Active working memory is where new information is organized, filtered again, and the destination for previous learning to be retrieved for active use during a learning or problem-solving situation. The student's processing depth, organization, attention, and integrative abilities affect how well these capacities work (Swanson & Sáez, 2003).

Attention is a regulator for learning. It is concerned with alertness, mental effort, shifting attention, focus, and self-regulation. Students with attention problems either lack organized executive processing abilities or fail to apply efficient strategies and controls. In the mathematics classroom, attention problems are evidenced by difficulty sustaining focused attention during a lesson or while solving a problem, inability to filter out irrelevant parts of problems, and failure to complete work.

Reasoning is a higher-order cognitive ability that is essential for math success. It involves various forms of conceptualization, deductive and inductive thought, working in the abstract, and solving problems. Students who have trouble with tasks involving reasoning have trouble seeing patterns and relationships, use faulty logic, typically accept things at face value rather than questioning and analyzing, and can't explain the "why" behind a math process.

3. *Metacognitive factors.* Metacognition is an awareness of the skills, strategies, and resources that are needed to perform a task and the ability to use self-regulatory mechanisms, including adjustments, to complete the task (Borkowski & Burke, 1996). Sometimes called "thinking about one's own thinking," metacognition is the process involving being aware of and monitoring the use of executive and cognitive strategies. Students with metacognition problems have trouble selecting and using effective learning strategies. They don't monitor their own use of strategies and have difficulty with generalization across time and setting. For example, a student may have trouble deciding how to solve a non-routine word problem. Even if the student attempts the problem, he doesn't monitor the process or results. (Does this make sense? How can I change what I attempted?) Further, he can't draw on experiences with similar problems because they don't appear similar in his conceptualization of the problem.

4. *Motor factors.* Motor problems with written work are most evident in younger students but even adolescents with no physical disabilities can struggle with number and symbol formation. Motor skills, like perceptual ones, involve more than one process. They may involve memory of the symbol along with its actual formation (visual and motor memories). They may involve visual perception and transfer (copying). Or they may involve integration of fine muscles with task demands. Indicators of motor problems are highly visible: poorly formed symbols, little control of spacing, excessive time for a task, and avoidance of written work.

5. *Social and emotional factors.* Sometimes overlooked in the academic realm, social and emotional factors can cause as many learning problems as cognitive ones. The range of these factors is as diverse as the students served. Some students have trouble with peer or adult relationships, causing problems in cooperative learning settings or seeking assistance. Others have self-concept and self-esteem problems that lower motivation, task persistence, and effort. Impulsive students make careless errors and don't take the time to understand the deeper concepts and connections. Students with extreme anxiety—either toward mathematics or school in general—tend to avoid the source of their anxiety or perform at much lower levels than their abilities.

6. *Habits of learning.* A combination of environmental, cognitive, social, and emotional factors, habits of learning are formed from an early age but certainly can be modified throughout the lifespan. "Habits of learning" refers to how individuals view and participate in learning, their self-discipline and self-motivation, goal setting, engagement in learning activities, and acceptance of challenges. Habits that could interfere with math learning include avoidance, learned helplessness, impulsivity, little curiosity, poor assignment completion, disinterest, and working for the "right answer" rather than understanding. Even students with high mathematics abilities have habits, such as the drive for perfection, that can interfere with strong concept development and flexible problem solving.

7. *Previous experiences.* A student's prior knowledge and previous experiences with mathematics are the best predictors of future success. Many of these experiences have been influenced by the factors described above. However, previous instructional experiences also can have a significant impact on achievement. If previous teachers did not explain

concepts well, use effective teaching methods, or allow time for mastery and success, students' mathematics learning will be affected. If the curriculum and materials used weren't aligned with math standards, learning might be superficial or limited. And if the student wasn't able to develop the deep concept understanding that comes from good teaching and sound curriculum, his or her math achievement will suffer.

Students who have been served in separate special education settings for part or all of the school day may be affected by factors such as instruction from teachers without specific mathematics training, being "pulled out" of the regular classroom during critical instructional time, or having less than adequate time devoted to mathematics instruction. Students who changed schools frequently may have gaps in learning. Students with few opportunities for learning at home due to poverty or parent background may demonstrate significant delays. Those students whose primary language is not English may experience difficulties with the language demands of mathematics instruction.

The beginning of this chapter introduced Zachary, Kristy, David, and Jessica, young children interested in the world around them. All of these children were involved in excellent preschool programs that offered rich environments with well-trained teachers. One of these children is going to be evaluated for a specific mathematics disability in second grade after spending a frustrating year in first grade unable to add and subtract, write numbers, or draw diagrams like the other first graders. This student's reading ability is progressing as expected but mathematics has become a source of failure, confusion, and anxiety. Although this child had a strong foundation in preschool, the formal pencil and paper tasks in math class have not been effective for continued progress in concept development. The student evaluation team must plan assessments that will provide information on specific learning problems and plan for more effective interventions. The next chapter will explore assessment strategies for identification of problem areas, planning instruction, and monitoring student progress in mathematics.

> **TRY THIS**
> Observe students with mathematics learning problems in special, remedial, or general education settings and note the factors described above. Examine work samples and interact with the students if possible.

CHAPTER SUMMARY

- Research connecting brain development and learning underscores the need for rich learning environments from the earliest years.
- Young children develop many informal mathematics concepts that lead to formal learning including: identity, labeling, properties, classifying, comparing, sequencing, counting, determining cause and effect, and conservation.
- Essential cognitive abilities for mathematics learning are memory, language, and making mental representations.

- Delays in language, social/emotional, sensory/motor, and cognitive domains may indicate later problems with formal mathematics learning.
- The NAEYC and NCTM issued a joint position statement on early mathematics experiences that included ten guidelines for developmentally appropriate practice with young children.
- Current theories of learning tend to incorporate aspects from several older theories from the behaviorist, cognitive, and social-cultural domains. Current learning

theories most applicable to mathematics learning for students with learning problems include information processing, conditions of learning, and metacognition.

- Constructivist philosophies of mathematics teaching and learning can be consistent with effective instruction for students with disabilities if they promote active learning in authentic mathematics contexts and consider the backgrounds and needs of individual learners.

- Mathematics disabilities are theorized to take the forms of procedural, semantic, and visuospatial subtypes.

- Students with mathematics learning problems have varying learning characteristics in the areas of language, cognition, metacognition, motor, social and emotional development as well as habits of learning and previous experiences that have an impact on mathematics learning.

RESOURCES

Charlesworth, R. (2005). *Experiences in math for young children*. Clifton Park, NY: Thomson Delmar Learning.

Coates, G. D., & Kerr, J. (1997). *Family math for young children: Comparing*. Berkeley, CA: Lawrence Hall of Science.

Copley, J. V. (2000). *The young child and mathematics*. Reston, VA: NCTM and NAEYC.

Copley, J. V. (2004). *Showcasing mathematics for the young child: Activities for three-, four-, and five-year-olds*. Reston, VA: NCTM and NAEYC.

Koralek, D. (Ed.). (2003). *Spotlight on young children and math*. Washington, DC: National Association for the Education of Young Children.

Overholdt, J. L., White-Holtz, J., & Dickson, S. (1999). *Big math activities for young children*. Clifton Park, NY: Thomson Delmar Learning

Prairie, A. P. (2005). *Inquiry into math, science, and technology for teaching young children*. Clifton Park, NY: Thomson Delmar Learning.

Chapter 3

Chapter Questions

1. What are the purposes of assessment?
2. What do the NCTM standards recommend regarding mathematics assessment?
3. Which of the standardized assessment tools in mathematics are most useful?
4. How can teachers select or create alternative assessments?
5. How are higher-order processes in mathematics best assessed?
6. How can general, special, and remedial educators collaborate to implement assessment cycles?

Mathematics Assessment of Students with Learning Problems

Ms. Boswell, a fifth-grade teacher, and Mr. Hernandez, the mathematics support teacher for students with mild disabilities, are meeting before school begins for the year.

Hernandez: Can you tell me a little about the assessment in your classroom for mathematics? How do you determine students' levels of instruction and progress in learning?

Boswell: Well, during the first week of school each year I administer the textbook's accompanying assessment. That generally tells me which students have not mastered fourth-grade concepts and skills. I follow the text chapters in order, giving the chapter tests for a grade.

Hernandez: What do you do for those students who have not mastered the fourth-grade standards?

Boswell: I've been struggling with that and perhaps you can give me some ideas. I tried to do a week of review for all students but some students are still way behind.

Hernandez: I could assist by providing some targeted instruction for students with gaps just prior to each unit of study if you can help me identify the gaps and outline the unit prerequisites.

Boswell: That's a great idea! Would you want to do this during your pull-out time or come into the classroom and work with a larger group than those identified for your program?

Hernandez: Let's start with a pull-out, more intensive model and see how the students respond to that.

Boswell: OK, then my chapter tests will also indicate students who have not mastered material to the level necessary for the next concepts. Do I move ahead or hold everyone back while I reteach?

Hernandez: That's a critical point. You could provide extension or application activities in the same content area for those who have met mastery while we can jointly plan some reteaching with other students. Or I could come in prior to the chapter tests and work with students in the class you've identified as needing extra assistance. Those who still don't meet mastery could spend extra time with my pull-out program.

Boswell: Let's try the extension and application approach first because I believe those students need deeper connections made, then we can assess the results. ■ ● ▲

● ● ● ● ● ● ● ● ●
For solutions to the problems presented in this book, visit the Companion Website at www.ablongman.com/gurganus1e.
● ● ● ● ● ● ● ● ●

What assessment activities are described in this conversation? How are they related to mathematics standards and instructional planning? How might assessments in the general education and special education or remedial setting differ? This chapter will examine the broad purposes of assessment, mathematics assessment standards, and specific methods for mathematics assessment of students with learning problems.

PURPOSES OF ASSESSMENT

Yogi Berra stated the essence of assessment in one profound sentence: "You can observe a lot by watching" (Berra, 1998, p. 123). Of course the most informative and valid assessment is that which is closest to the day-to-day instructional events in a classroom. However, with the current atmosphere of reform and accountability, the assessment demands on teachers and students are not so simple. Teachers should first consider the purposes of mathematics assessment.

All students in elementary and secondary schools today are subjected to more assessments than at any time in the history of public education. Assessments specific to mathematics achievement include classroom-based, teacher-administered instruments to determine learning needs and the effects of instruction, such as pre- and post-unit tests, chapter tests, lesson assessments, and other informal measures. Other, more formalized assessments are district- and state-mandated annual assessments of achievement, such as end-of-grade, end-of-course, or annual assessments of individual student achievement. Some students undergo special assessments for qualifications for accelerated or remedial programs, special education eligibility, or early childhood screening.

Assessments for Students with Disabilities

Students with disabilities undergo assessments related to their special education services as well as all regular education assessments. Many of these assessment activities measure achievement in mathematics. Special education assessments include the multidisciplinary team assessment to determine eligibility for special education, annual assessments for IEP reviews, and periodic reevaluations for program eligibility.

According to IDEA (§§ 300.301-300.305)* a full and individual evaluation is conducted for **initial and reevaluations** for student eligibility for services. (Reevaluations are

*According to the regulations published 14 August 2006, to be finalized in 2007.

conducted when conditions warrant but at least every three years; these may simply involve a review of existing assessment data.) "A variety of assessment tools and strategies [must be used] to gather relevant functional, developmental, and academic information about the child, . . . including progress in the general curriculum." Further, the child must be assessed "in all areas related to the suspected disability, . . . the evaluation [being] sufficiently comprehensive to identify all of the child's special education and related service needs, whether or not commonly linked to the disability category. . . ." The variety of assessment tools and strategies for students with mild disabilities usually includes formal (standardized) and informal (nonstandardized) assessments of academic progress.

Assessments for the **annual evaluation and development of IEPs** are also mandated by IDEA. Section 300.305 requires the IEP team to consider the results of individual evaluations and classroom-based, local, and state assessment results in developing the IEP. The IEP must include statements of "the child's present levels of academic achievement and functional performance, . . . how the child's disability affects the child's involvement and progress in the general curriculum, . . . any individual appropriate accommodations that are necessary to measure the academic achievement and functional performance of the child on State and districtwide assessments, . . . when periodic reports on the progress the child is making toward meeting the annual goals . . . will be provided [to parents]." (§ 300.320). IEP-related assessments may include both formal and informal types of assessment.

Academic assessment addresses skills and concepts in subject areas such as reading, mathematics, and science. *Functional* assessment measures students' functioning within a context, such as social skills for cooperative groups or the range of skills needed to use public transportation. *Developmental* assessment refers to comparing a student with developmental milestones of a normative group in areas such as language development or motor skills.

Response to Intervention

Students suspected of specific learning disabilities may now be evaluated through alternative methods (other than IQ-discrepancy criterion) such as a "systematic assessment of the student's response to high quality, research-based general education instruction," termed response to intervention, or "the assessment of achievement skills . . . by examining the strengths and weaknesses in achievement," sometimes called achievement pattern analysis (see the justification section of the *Federal Register*, 14 August 2006, beginning on page 46646).

The **response to intervention** (RTI) approach to identification of students with learning disabilities is applied in general education settings with some assistance from special educators. Fuchs and Fuchs (2005) described a four-step process that includes (1) screening all students using brief screening tools in reading and mathematics (or screening students scoring at or below the 25th percentile on previous years' tests); (2) implementing classroom instruction for an 8-week period that includes evidence-based curricula and instructional methods (with documentation of sound implementation) along with monitoring student responsiveness weekly; (3) for nonresponders, implementing an 8-week supplementary, diagnostic instructional trial with weekly monitoring; and, for those students not responding at this level, (4) providing an individual, comprehensive evaluation with all legal safeguards, including a multidisciplinary evaluation team process. Some criticisms of the RTI approach have been that it has received very little field-testing; some models focus exclusively on reading achievement; some models do not include timelines, thus delaying needed services; some models do not include any comprehensive evaluation phase to rule out other disabilities or causes of low achievement;

Identification of specific learning disabilities using a *discrepancy method* typically involves comparing standard scores on ability measures such as intelligence tests with those on achievement measures such as a standardized mathematics test. A significant difference between scores is usually 15 to 20 points when standard score comparisons are used, supported by other evidence of unexpected underachievement.

students with dual exceptionalities (gifted learning disabilities) may be overlooked at the initial screening phase; and this approach is not sufficient for periodic reevaluations (see for example, National Joint Committee on Learning Disabilities, 2005; Vaughn & Fuchs, 2003). Other concerns with using the RTI approach include over-identification of disadvantaged, minority, and English language learners; the paucity of research-based approaches implemented with fidelity in general education classrooms in areas such as mathematics; time and resource demands on general educators; and assessment issues such as personnel training and reliability and validity of informal curriculum-based measures. Large-scale efficacy studies, best-practices guidelines, and personnel training criteria are not available even as school districts are implementing a number of RTI models.

Purposes of Broader Assessments

State and district assessments include norm- and criterion-referenced tests and usually include assessment of mathematics achievement. IDEA requires students with disabilities to be included in these assessment programs, with any individual accommodations or modifications to be documented in the IEP (§300.320). (Students who cannot participate in regular assessments—about one to two percent of students—should undergo alternative measures to determine progress toward academic and functional goals.) The No Child Left Behind Act of 2001 required state-approved mathematics and reading assessments for all public school students in grades 3 through 8 and once in high school.

Teacher-developed assessments are generally curriculum-based and include tests, observations, student work sample analysis, portfolio reviews, and other informal methods. These assessments inform students, teachers, and parents of students' academic progress and some are used for grading purposes. IDEA requires that the parents of a child with a disability be informed of their child's progress concurrent with the school's quarterly report cards, with the same regularity as with other students' progress reports (§300.320).

In addition to these student-centered purposes, assessment also **informs teachers** about the success of their instructional strategies or specific curriculum programs. Most effective teachers build in some type of assessment with each lesson to determine if the lesson objectives were met or whether the lesson should be extended or modified. For example, a lesson objective might be "to identify six polygons by their mathematical names." An easy, immediate, and effective assessment would be to hold up polygons and have students name them or hold up response cards. Lesson-specific assessment is curriculum-based, quick, and provides immediate feedback for students and teachers.

Curriculum programs are often **field-tested** in school districts with participating and control classrooms each measuring student progress for comparison. Well-developed programs should provide the results of these field tests in their supplementary materials. However, most curriculum programs, unless developed at universities, have not been submitted to rigorous field-testing. One intent of the No Child Left Behind Act (2001), according to Secretary Paige in 2002, was to require rigorous standards for educational research, the identification of instructional methods that really work (not fads), and the application of research-based instruction in the classroom (Yell & Drasgow, 2005). Federally funded instructional programs under this Act must be based on sound scientific research. However, even programs that offer "research results" rarely provide separate data on the performance of students with disabilities or other special learning needs.

Another purpose for student assessment in many states is to **rate teachers, schools, and districts** for a range of benefits and penalties: merit pay, federal and state funding, administrator assignments, student assignments, eligibility for special programs, governance restrictions, and political agendas. Since the 1997 reauthorization of IDEA, many previously exempted students now must participate in these high-stakes assessment programs and more attention is being directed toward assessment (and related instructional) issues involving students with disabilities. Congress clearly intended for school districts to include all students with disabilities in assessment programs and to provide them an educational program as close to the general education curriculum as possible. According to Thurlow, Elliott, and Ysseldyke (1998), students with disabilities should be included in accountability systems because including their scores gives a more accurate picture of education, comparisons among states would be more accurate, and the students would benefit from educational reforms and higher expectations. The accountability reports behind these broad assessment programs now must document the progress of all students including those with disabilities. Schools whose students consistently fail to meet state standards are deemed not making "adequate yearly progress" and face public identification, student transfers, and other censures under the NCLB Act provisions (2001).

Some students may qualify for assessment accommodations under state or district policies. Accommodations are changes in test presentation or response format that do not alter the construct under consideration (Tindal & Fuchs, 1999). They must be selected for individual students so that testing will still be valid and that the student will not be unfairly assisted or handicapped by the alterations. They should be used in the classroom on a regular basis, not just on formal tests.

The most common accommodations for mathematics tests are extended time, separate setting or small group setting, and portions read aloud (Bielinski, Ysseldyke, Bolt, Friedebach, & Friedebach, 2001). There is some evidence that accommodations can increase students' scores on standardized tests by .5 to 1 standard deviations and can also affect the scores of non-disabled students, indicating that the performance tasks by all students need refining and that the accommodated scores may not be comparable (Elliott, Kratochwill, & McKevitt, 2001). However, results of accommodation studies have not been consistent. One study found that reading math questions to students with reading disabilities did not affect test validity (Johnson, 2000). Another large-scale study of 1,250 accommodated students (extended time) and 1,250 nonaccommodated students on Florida's ninth-grade mathematics test found that the use of accommodations contributed little to overall test performance (Cohen, Gregg, & Deng, 2005). The two groups differed in mathematics performance on the state test, but the differences were attributed to student competency. The authors emphasized that accommodations equalize testing access or demonstration of knowledge but do not substitute for appropriate instruction.

TRY THIS

1. Interview a teacher about the types of mathematics assessments he or she uses for mathematics.
2. Find and analyze state and district scores for mathematics achievement under the NCLB Act.

With wide-scale use of accommodations in mathematics assessments, it will be important for IEP committees to establish protocols for identifying appropriate accommodations for individual students. Systems such as the *Dynamic Assessment of Testing Accommodations* (see Fuchs, Fuchs, Eaton, Hamlett, & Karns, 2000) and the *Assessment Accommodations Checklist* (Elliott, Kratochwill, & Schulte, 1998) can assist committees in making accommodation decisions.

ASSESSMENT STANDARDS

The NCTM 2000 *Principles and Standards for School Mathematics** included assessment as a principle of mathematics programs. "Assessment should support the learning of important mathematics and furnish useful information to both teachers and students" (p. 22). But the document scarcely mentioned assessment beyond the introductory three pages although assessment and instruction are interdependent.

The 1995 NCTM document *Assessment Standards for School Mathematics* outlined four purposes of assessment: to monitor student progress, to make instructional decisions, to evaluate student achievement, and to evaluate programs. According to this document, assessment should:

- reflect the mathematics that all students need to know, be able to do
- enhance mathematics learning
- promote equity
- be an open process
- promote valid inferences about mathematics learning
- be a coherent process

All mathematics assessments, according to the 1995 document, involve four interrelated phases: plan assessment, gather evidence, interpret evidence, and use results (see Figure 3.1). Consider a mathematics example while reviewing these phases, a middle school unit on linear equations.

Linear functions are functional relationships (where values of one term or magnitude depend on the values of another) that, when graphed, form a straight line, as in $y = 5x$.

Planning assessment first requires teachers (or districts and states) to translate the broad curriculum standards into grade, classroom, and individual goals relevant for their students. Learning goals include aspects of factual information, conceptual understanding, skills, problem solving, applications, processes, and even mathematical dispositions. These goals should be clear and specific for instructional and assessment purposes. For example, in the NCTM standards linear functions are within the patterns, functions, and algebra content standard. In earlier grades students have used objects and representations

---

*Reprinted with permission from *Principles and Standards for School Mathematics*, copyright 2000, by the National Council of Teachers of Mathematics. All rights reserved. Standards are listed with permission of the Council of Teachers of Mathematics (NCTM). NCTM does not endorse the content or validity of these alignments.

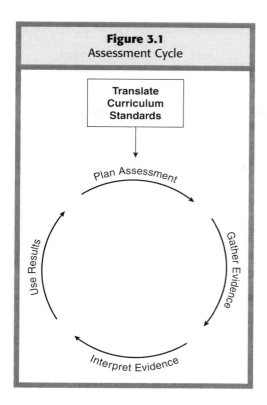

Figure 3.1
Assessment Cycle

Translate Curriculum Standards

Plan Assessment

Gather Evidence

Interpret Evidence

Use Results

for symbols and have developed the concepts of variable, change, properties of operations, and equivalence. The goal for the middle grades is to "recognize and generate equivalent forms for simple algebraic expressions and solve linear equations."

Assessment tasks and schedules can be planned that inform both teachers and students. The variety of methods includes selected-response quizzes, student-constructed responses, open-ended questions, performance tasks, observations, conversations, and portfolios. The collection method selected should take into account learning goals, age and experience of students, and purpose of assessment. Prior to a unit on linear equations, teachers should conduct simple but direct assessment of prerequisite concepts (properties of operations, function of variables, and equivalence) as well as a selection of unit concepts (generating equivalent forms for expressions and solving linear equations).

Next, teachers should implement the assessment plan and **gather evidence** for individual students on a schedule that will be frequent enough to impact instruction but not take excessive amounts of instructional time. Assessment that is embedded within instruction best meets these criteria. The pre-unit assessment on linear equations may indicate some students require a review or re-teaching of prerequisite skills and concepts. Other students may be able to solve simple equivalent equations already. Assessment during the unit, embedded within lesson activities, should show individual student progress, even those students with more advanced goals for the unit. The post-unit or summative assessment should confirm students' mastery of concepts and skills and readiness for the next unit of study.

The **interpretation** stage of the assessment cycle reminds teachers of validity, quality, and ethical issues. Can valid interpretations be made with the types of collection methods used? Does the evidence from a variety of sources converge to support inferences? Are teachers able to interpret assessment results? Do students and parents also understand results? Are assessment results useful for planning instruction? For the assessment types described in the previous phase, the teacher should consider whether the skill and concept domain of linear equations was sampled adequately and whether any assessments were unclear or not reflective of student understanding because of language, format, item selection, or other factors.

Using assessment results to make instructional decisions also has multiple purposes. Teachers can examine the effects of instruction and the learning environment on student knowledge and skills. Individual student needs can be pinpointed and addressed. And students can view their own progress toward goals. Formative types of assessment, such as day-to-day monitoring of student performance to inform instructional decisions, and summative assessments, such as year-end or end-of-course evaluations, should be linked to provide a coherent and integrated decision base. For the linear equation example, the pre-unit assessment informs the teacher of necessary remedial instruction or the need for individual student goals. The formative assessments within the unit inform the teacher whether a lesson's objectives were achieved or whether re-teaching with an alternative approach would be in order. The post-unit assessment provides information for future instructional units and skill maintenance. Most importantly, students who could not solve equations at the beginning of the unit will see that they now have new skills and understandings about these functions.

Teachers should consider the real purpose of each assessment or evaluation activity in their classrooms. For those mandated assessment activities, how well is the curriculum aligned with assessment instruments? How much decision-making authority do teachers have? Can the results be useful in other ways? For grading purposes, what measures will be fair to students? Do students understand which assessments are formative and which are summative? And for instructional assessments, what methods will prove to be informative yet efficient?

STANDARDIZED TOOLS FOR INDIVIDUALIZED MATHEMATICS ASSESSMENT

Standardized tests are administered and scored under uniform conditions and are either group- or individually-administered, depending on the purpose and design. Tools that have been standardized are developed with a national scope, typically have norm-referenced scoring, and usually have a limited number of items per construct. Group-administered standardized mathematics assessments include screening tools, district and state achievement tests such as the *Metropolitan Achievement Test* (MAT-8) and the *California Achievement Test* (CAT-5), and qualifying examinations such as the *Scholastic Aptitude Tests*.

Individually administered mathematics assessments are generally used in special education and remedial programs for initial and reevaluation testing and the annual review process.

Group- and individually-administered instruments can be classified as norm-referenced and/or criterion-referenced tests. **Norm-referenced tests** (NRT) compare a student's performance with that of his or her peers and provide derived scores such as age- and grade-equivalents, standard scores, and percentiles. **Criterion-referenced tests** (CRT) compare a student's performance with academic criteria or learning objectives derived from the grade-level curriculum. Results from CRT translate more readily into instructional goals. Standardized assessments can also be classified by purpose: achievement, diagnostic, predictive, aptitude, interest, or screening. Most **general achievement tests** include sections on specific academic areas such as mathematics. These tests cover such a broad range of skills that they can give only a general level of achievement and should be followed by more specific **diagnostic** or alternative measures. Diagnostic tests should yield specific strengths and weaknesses about the student's mathematics learning and provide enough information for the teacher to plan appropriate instruction. Figure 3.2

Figure 3.2
Group-Administered Standardized Achievement and Diagnostic Tests

Test	Version	Type	SB	Subtests	Response Mode
California Achievement Test (5)	1993	NR, CR, SCR	✓	Computation Concepts and Applications	MC (Supplemental OR)
Iowa Tests of Basic Skills (M)	1996	NR, CR, SCR	✓	Computation Concepts and Estimation Problem Solving and Data Interpretation	MC
Metropolitan Achievement Test (8)	2001	NR, CR, SCR	✓	Concepts and Problem Solving Computation	MC
Stanford Achievement Test (10)	2004	NR, CR, SCR	✓	Problem solving Procedures	MC, OR
Stanford Diagnostic Mathematics Test (4)	1995	NR, CR, DIAG	✓	6 subtests in concepts and applications 9 subtests in computation	MC, OR

NR = norm-referenced
CR = criterion-referenced
SCR = screening
DIAG = diagnostic
SB = standards-based

MC = multiple choice
OR = open or constructed response

provides a synthesis of the most commonly used standardized group tests. Figure 3.3 offers an overview of selected standardized assessment instruments that are individually administered and that target mathematics achievement in part or all of the tests.

Figure 3.3
Individually Administered Standardized Achievement and Diagnostic Tests

Test	Version	Type	Subtests	Response Mode
Diagnostic Achievement Battery (3)	2001	NR, SCR	Calculation Reasoning	OR
Diagnostic Achievement Test for Adolescents (2)	1993	NR, SCR	Calculation Reasoning	OR
Kaufman Test of Educational Achievement-NU (Comprehensive Form)	1997	NR, SCR	Applications Computation	OR
Peabody Individual Achievement Test-Revised-NU	1998	NR, SCR	Concepts and Computation	MC
Wechsler Individual Achievement Test (2)	2001	NR, SCR	Numerical Operations Mathematics Reasoning	OR
Woodcock-Johnson Tests of Achievement (3)	2001	NR, SCR	Calculation Math Fluency Applied Problems Quantitative Concepts	OR
BRIGANCE Diagnostic Comprehensive Inventory of Basic Skills-Revised	1999	CR, DIAG	Number Computation Word Problems Applications Vocabulary	OR
Comprehensive Mathematical Abilities Test	2002	NR, DIAG	Basic Calculations Mathematical Reasoning Advanced Calculations Practical Applications	OR
ENRIGHT Diagnostic Inventory of Basic Arithmetic Skills	1983	CR, DIAG	Computation—144 arithmetic skills in 13 sections	OR

Figure 3.3
(Continued)

Test	Version	Type	Subtests	Response Mode
KeyMath-Revised-NU	1998	NR, CR, DIAG	3 subtests in concepts 5 subtests in operations 5 subtests in applications (break-out of 43 domains)	OR
Monitoring Basic Skills Progress (2)	1998	CR, DIAG	CBM with 6 levels of computation (30 versions each) and grades 2 through 6 concepts and applications (30 tests each).	Primarily OR
Test of Early Mathematics Ability (3)	2003	NR, SCR, DIAG	Informal concepts: relative magnitude, counting, calculation Formal concepts: numbers and symbols, number facts, calculation, base-ten	OR
Test of Mathematical Abilities (2)	1994	NR, SCR	Vocabulary Computation General Information Story Problems Attitude	OR
NU = normative update only, not a revision	NR = norm-referenced CR = criterion-referenced SCR = screening DIAG = diagnostic		MC = multiple choice OR = open or constructed response	

Group-administered instruments.   The group-administered instruments listed in Figure 3.2 have been revised since the first NCTM standards (1989) and all claim to be aligned with those standards. The only diagnostic instrument on this list—the *Stanford Diagnostic Mathematics Test*—can be administered to individual students. All teachers should be familiar with the interpretation of scores of these group-administered instruments, as well as their limitations in reflecting student achievement or diagnosing learning problems.

Individually administered instruments. Of the individually administered instruments in Figure 3.3, only the 2002 *Comprehensive Mathematics Abilities Test* claims alignment with state and local curriculum standards. These tests vary widely in purpose, content, and processes measured.

The *BRIGANCE Diagnostic Inventories* are among the most popular criterion-referenced tests used for curriculum-based assessment, developing instructional objectives, and monitoring student progress. The *Comprehensive Inventory of Basic Skills-Revised* (1999), recognized by its green cover, includes twenty-three subtests (154 specific assessments) and is appropriate for PreK through grade 9. Math subtests include grade placement (computation and problem solving), numbers, number facts, computation of whole numbers, fractions and mixed numbers, decimals, percents, time, money, measurement and geometry, and metrics. The *Inventory of Essential Skills* (red) is appropriate for grades 4 through 12 and measures mathematical achievement in thirteen areas, including functional math.

The *Comprehensive Mathematical Abilities Test* (2002) was developed in alignment with new content standards. The core subtests include computation, problem solving, and interpreting charts, tables, and graphs. The supplemental subtests, used for higher-level students, address algebra, geometry, rational numbers, time, money, and measurement.

The *ENRIGHT Inventory of Basic Arithmetic Skills* is a criterion-referenced test but is limited to arithmetic skills. Four types of tests are basic facts, broad survey-type placement tests, skill placement tests for error analysis, and skill tests for monitoring instruction. This test is based on 233 identified common errors in computation in seven clusters: regrouping, process substitution, omission, directional, placement, attention to sign, and guessing.

The *KeyMath-Revised* is a comprehensive diagnostic instrument (K through 9) that includes thirteen subtests: rational numbers, geometry, numeration, addition, subtraction, multiplication, division, mental computation, time and money, interpreting data, problem solving, measurement, and estimating. Students respond orally to teacher questions and visuals presented on an easel with the exception of paper and pencil computation subtests.

The curriculum-based measurement instrument *Monitoring Basic Skills Progress* (Fuchs, Hamlett, & Fuchs, 1998), offers computer-based or paper and pencil versions of repeated measures for computation and applications. The computation section requires the student to compute twenty-five survey items at a given level. The teacher has thirty versions at the same level for the repeated measures. The concepts and applications section includes twenty-four items at a given grade level (grades 2 through 6) with thirty versions for repeated measures. Most items are open response format and content ranges from measurement, geometry, and data analysis to number concepts, vocabulary, and word problems.

The *Test of Early Mathematics Ability* (TEMA-3) is unique in addressing the mathematics concept understanding of young children ages three to nine. The subtests address both informal and formal (school) concepts and skills: numbering skills, number comparison, numeral literacy, mastery of number facts, calculation skills, and concept understanding. Also included is the companion book *Assessment Probes and Instructional Activities*. After administering the test, the examiner can probe areas of concern and begin interventions. The kit includes cards, blocks, and tokens that are used during the assessment process.

The *Test of Mathematical Abilities* (TOMA-2) assesses very different mathematical skills than the other tests discussed. The general information subtest is the only one that must be administered individually; however, large-group assessment should not be used with students with disabilities due to potentially confusing directions, reading demands, and the need to monitor ceilings to prevent frustration. Other subtests are math-related vocabulary (students write out definitions to terms), story problems (multiple-choice responses), computation, and attitude toward math (responses on a Likert-type scale).

Problems with standardized instruments.   Standardized assessment instruments save development time and provide normed comparisons, either with other students or with a standard curriculum, but teachers and parents should be aware of their drawbacks. Many of these tests were field tested without students with disabilities in the normative group. Formal tests are costly—in materials, administration time, and scoring effort. There may be content validity problems with tests assuming differing grade-level objectives or placing differing emphases on topics than are reflected by students' actual curriculum. Because most group-administered standardized instruments require closed-end responses, these tests tend to measure lower level knowledge and skills. And many formal tests have experiential or cultural biases, especially in mathematics applications problems, language demands, or sections on "common knowledge."

Standardized instruments that require multiple-choice or limited responses don't allow probing or diagnostic interviews that are so valuable in assessing students' cognitive processes and concept understanding. Almost none of the individually administered instruments are aligned with the mathematics standards promoted by NCTM. Even the more recent instruments that claim alignment with NCTM standards have validity problems. Finally, the more emphasis test scores receive, the more teachers feel compelled to shape the curriculum to match tests, regardless of stated instructional goals. This "teaching to the test" results in narrowing the content in which students are engaged.

TRY THIS

Examine one of the instruments listed above for alignment with NCTM or state curriculum standards.

ALTERNATIVE MATHEMATICS ASSESSMENT OF STUDENTS WITH LEARNING PROBLEMS

Reforms in mathematics and special education are driving what has been termed a paradigm shift in assessment practices (Reschley, 1997; Herman, Aschbacher, & Winters, 1992). Reforms in mathematics education, driven by the 1989 NCTM standards and 2000 revisions, have shifted the emphasis to **what** is taught (more authentic tasks with higher-level cognitive demands) and **how** it is taught (to a more constructivist and interactive orientation) (Lajoie, 1995). Reforms in special education include the emphasis on access and achievement within the general education curriculum and assessments that yield information for instruction, not simply classification (IDEA, 1997, 2004).

In general, remedial, and special education settings, assessment practices are shifting away from psychometrically sound but pedagogically limited standardized instruments to more direct but robust curriculum-based, authentic performance tasks. Mathematics content is addressed at the level of conceptual understanding, not merely knowledge of facts and procedures. Alternative assessments in mathematics also address student attitudes, communication skills, cognitive strategies, use of technology and manipulatives, and contributions to group efforts. These alternative measures are typically more valid (closer alignment with curriculum and instruction), less intrusive, easier to interpret, and more flexible than standardized ones. However, teachers need significant training in developing and using the variety of informal assessment alternatives effectively. Alternative assessments can also be time-consuming, difficult to develop, biased, and lack reliability and validity. Further, only limited research has been conducted on the efficacy of these procedures.

Terminology for these alternative assessments is still evolving and somewhat confusing, and tends to differ by discipline. In mathematics education, the terms *authentic, alternative,* and *performance assessment* are often used interchangeably (Wilson, 1995). **Authentic assessment** was first promoted as an alternative to standardized testing by Archbald and Newmann (1988) and described an assessment that is worthwhile, significant, and meaningful. The NCTM Standards (1989) furthered the concept through an emphasis on worthwhile or essential mathematics tasks. Authentic assessment "refers to the situational or contextual realism of the proposed tasks" but is not synonymous with performance assessment (Wiggins, 1998, p. 20).

Lajoie (1995) offered the following principles for authentic assessment:

1. provides us with multiple indicators of learning
2. is relevant, meaningful, and realistic
3. is accompanied by appropriate scoring and scaling procedures
4. serves to improve instruction
5. considers biases
6. is an integral part of the classroom
7. differentiates between individual and group performance (pp. 30–31)

Performance assessment was defined by the Office of Technology Assessment (U.S. Congress, 1992) as "testing methods that require students to create an answer or product that demonstrates their knowledge or skills" (p. 5). The term was selected because it was less emotionally charged than other terms such as *direct, appropriate,* or *authentic*. It was described as a continuum of formats from simple student-constructed responses to collections of work over time. These formats include portfolios, computations, writing samples, interviews, demonstrations, and investigations. Performances require student construction of responses and allow for observation of behavior and illumination of thinking processes (Coutinho & Malouf, 1993). It is possible for a performance assessment not to be authentic but it is unlikely that an authentic assessment would not also be a performance assessment (Meyer, 1992).

In special education, the term *curriculum-based assessment* has been used to describe the informal assessment of student performances in the curriculum through a variety of direct measures. Curriculum-based assessment is a form of performance assessment and can certainly be authentic. As students with disabilities are required to participate in the general education curriculum and meet the same curriculum standards, they will be engaged in more of the alternative assessment formats.

The following sections provide more specific guidelines for developing, administering, and interpreting the most prevalent alternative assessment methods for mathematics. Those descriptions are followed by a section on assessment techniques that are used across formats.

Curriculum-Based Assessment

The assessment model for directly measuring the curriculum being taught is called **curriculum-based assessment** (CBA). "CBA includes any procedure that directly assesses student performance within the course content for the purpose of determining that student's instructional needs" (Tucker, 1985, p. 200). "CBA is a criterion-referenced test that is teacher constructed and designed to reflect curriculum content" (Idol, Nevin, & Paolucci-Whitcomb, 1996, p. 1). "CBA can be characterized as the practice of taking frequent measure of a student's observable performance as he or she proceeds through the curriculum" (Jones, Wilson, & Bhojwani, 1998, p. 172). Deno (2003) described CBA as very broad, "any information-gathering practices that occur when obtaining information about student performance in the curriculum" including worksheets, oral reading, or performance on a unit test (pp. 4–5).

CBA can be used to screen new students, set and measure annual IEP goals and objectives, establish a baseline for classroom interventions, and monitor the effectiveness of daily instruction. It is also used as part of a multidisciplinary team evaluation to provide additional evidence to supplement the broader formal achievement tests. Reliability must be established through intra-observer agreement, and validity comes from analysis of the content match.

Two general types of CBA have been identified (Fuchs & Deno, 1991; Rivera & Smith, 1997). **Curriculum-based measurement** (CBM) is a repeated measure of the general outcome of the unit of instruction. It is a broader survey measure to establish initial instructional goals and objectives, measure global performance outcomes, monitor skill maintenance, and conduct summative evaluations (see Figure 3.4). **Mastery measures** are the more specific probes of students' progress within objectives. Also frequent and direct, mastery measures evaluate students' progress in only what has been taught (see Figure 3.5). According to Deno and Fuchs (1987), these types differ in two ways: the scope of target instructional objectives measured and goal of measurement.

Curriculum-based measures.   Curriculum-based measures (CBM) are developed using the following procedures:

1. *Identify the annual goal or broad area of assessment for a unit of study.* For example, *computation with fractions* is a typical unit of study in the upper elementary grades. Goals should be derived from the general curriculum standards considering individual student needs.
2. *Conduct a task analysis of the skill area.* With computation of fractions, students must know that fractions are symbols that represent parts of objects or sets (or quotients, ratios, operators, or measures) and are expressed with denominator and numerator. Students must also be able to manipulate the forms of fractions (mixed numbers, reduction to lowest terms) and recognize these forms within applications (word problems, measurement). The skills within the target area are addition and subtraction with common denominators; addition and subtraction with different denominators; computation of products of combinations of various forms of fractions;

• Convert to mixed numbers.

$$\frac{5}{2} = \qquad \frac{9}{4} = \qquad \frac{6}{3} =$$

$$\frac{31}{3} = \qquad \frac{2}{3} =$$

• Convert to improper fractions.

$$3\frac{2}{3} = \qquad 6\frac{1}{4} = \qquad 10\frac{2}{7} =$$

computation of quotients of combinations of various forms of fractions; and application of these concepts to problem solving. (See content strand D for more on rational numbers.)

3. *Develop test items for each task within the skill sequence.* Test items are usually arranged in order of difficulty so that testing can be stopped when students are unable to answer several problems. Some assessors recommend using three or four items per instructional objective with mastery of 75 to 80% required on that objective by the end of the unit. However, this requirement may make the survey instrument too long. Create multiple forms so the measure can be repeated. See Figure 3.4 for an example of a portion of a teacher-made survey instrument.

4. *Administer and interpret the CBM instrument.* While most mathematics tests can be administered to groups of students, individual administration has several advantages. The teacher can stop the student who is experiencing increasing frustration as the problems become more difficult. The teacher can ask students to explain how they solved specific problems, getting an insight into conceptual understanding and strategy use. And teachers can move directly into a probe with several more items when the student begins to have trouble with a certain type of problem. But CBMs can be designed to be effective in small group or computer-based administrations.

Chart individual student results using a progress graph that includes baseline results and data for the intervention over time. The graph in Figure 3.6 shows correct and incorrect items on a fractions and decimals applications instrument. Each version of the CBM included thirty items. The results on this graph indicate a plateau about the fifth or sixth week of intervention, indicating the need for better feedback or a change in instruction. After an instructional change, the student's steady progress continued.

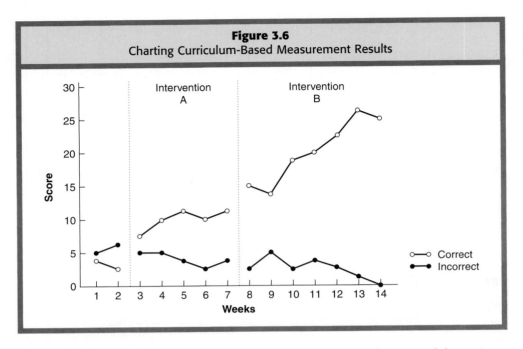

Figure 3.6
Charting Curriculum-Based Measurement Results

5. *Follow up unclear results with probes or begin instruction.* An advantage of alternative assessment is the flexibility in probing student responses, not allowed on most standardized tests. For example, a student may have added two fractions with like denominators correctly but had trouble with subtraction with like denominators. The single item on the survey was $\frac{7}{8} - \frac{5}{8} = \frac{1}{8}$ (student response) and the teacher could not interpret how the student worked the problem. He could probe by asking the student to explain her work or give the student three or four additional problems. Those strategies should quickly answer questions about the student's understanding. When an instructional level has been determined, instruction should begin immediately with skill monitoring using randomized versions of the CBM survey at weekly or biweekly intervals. The repeated measure of the global outcome, when charted, will show progress towards the learning goal.

Mastery-based measures.   Mastery measures for monitoring instruction are also developed directly from the curriculum being taught. A good mastery probe should be efficient (quick and easy), effective (yields good and useful information), and frequent (at least weekly). A similar assessment sequence is followed:

1. *Identify the specific instructional objectives in a lesson or short sequence of lessons.* For example, converting mixed numbers to improper fractions and reversed.
2. *Develop several items that measure the objective(s).* These items can be paper-and-pencil, oral response, or performance/observation items. However, they should reflect only the instructional objective being taught. For the probe illustrated in Figure 3.5, the student was given eight very specific problems measuring a range of fraction

items. The instructional objective for this probe is "the student will compute conversions between improper and mixed number forms of fractions for 7 of 8 (87.5%)."

3. *Administer and interpret the probe.* Individual administration allows for better analysis and additional probing as needed. But even with paper-and-pencil or group probes, students should be given feedback on their performances as soon as possible. Mastery levels can be defined in terms of accuracy (number or percent correct), fluency (number of correct digits per minute), or ratings on a qualitative rubric or checklist. It is beneficial for the teacher and student to maintain a record of the student's progress, either with selected work samples, narrative descriptions, or by charting results.

4. *Re-teach or continue to the next skill.* If students have difficulty with the probe items, re-teaching is in order, usually with a different approach or elaborated examples. If students reach mastery on the probe, instruction on the next skill area can proceed. But it is critical for long-term retention to recycle skills and concepts in maintenance checks. The goal of this assessment-guided instruction is not simply skill mastery but concept understanding and application.

Performance Tasks

Other forms of curriculum-based assessment are the variety of performance tasks designed by teachers to reflect student learning within the curriculum. **Open-ended or constructed-response performance tasks** can be designed for individual or group assessments and can assess narrow mathematics skills or interconnected mathematics concepts. These performance tasks can allow for the evaluation of the process as well as the answer or finished product and offer a vehicle for examining higher-level mathematics understanding. Teachers can use tasks in more formal ways such as on unit tests or informally as part of the classroom's instructional activities.

To develop and implement a system of performance tasks, the teacher should follow the following steps:

1. *Consider the types of student response(s) needed to assess critical areas within the curriculum.* Responses can be individual or group-based; short (minutes) or conducted over time (weeks); written, oral, or performance; and involve few or many materials.

2. *Find or create tasks that reflect the critical knowledge, skills, and concepts in the curriculum.* Stenmark (2002) outlines eight criteria for good tasks: essential (a big idea of mathematics), authentic, rich, engaging, active, feasible, equitable, and open (more than one solution or approach). Sources for tasks or ideas for tasks include textbooks, journals, life situations, books of problems, and released state test items (usually available on the web). Some sample tasks:

   a. An open-ended task after a unit on measurement and geometry would be the problem of painting the classroom walls. Students would be asked to estimate, then calculate the area of the painted surfaces and compute the amount of paint needed (Type: group, three days, written in chart form and oral report, measurement tools and chart paper).

   b. A creative performance task would be for fourth-grade students to create comic books to teach younger students math concepts such as how to round numbers to the nearest 10. (Type: individual or pairs, one week, written document, craft paper and crayons.)

    c. Examples of shorter tasks include asking a student to demonstrate the concept of even number using manipulatives or to set a specific time on a clock. (Type: individual, short, performance, manipulatives or clock).

    d. Word problems that are multi-dimensional and allow for alternative solutions also meet the criteria for open-ended tasks. For example, a baseball player has a batting average of .250 after playing in twenty games this year (average of 3 at-bats per game). Chart two different ways he can bring his average up to .300 over the next ten games.

    e. Many state-level mathematics tests now include open-ended questions that require students to show their work and justify their solutions. For example, *write out a real-life problem that would be answered by solving this equation:* $20x + 4 = 150$. Students need significant practice and specific, corrective feedback with this type of test item.

3. *For the selected task types, create evaluation rubrics.* Using the same rubric for tasks of a similar type allows for comparison over time and concepts. Rubrics should be understandable by students and described before the performance task. They should have clear descriptors that discriminate between levels of performance. Rubrics should be checked for content validity (the important concepts are emphasized in the correct proportion), bias, and feasibility (see, for example, Figure 3.7). Rubrics can be global (rubric is general enough to be used for all tasks of the same type), or task-specific. There is more discussion on rubric development in the next section.

4. *Establish a system for using constructed-response tasks.* Teachers using these tasks for the first time should begin with simple tasks that assess important concepts. Evaluate the use of the performance tasks in terms of time and effort, information about student learning, and alignment with curriculum and assessment standards. Once confident with development and evaluation procedures, teachers should revisit the total assessment system for the class and make decisions about which types of assessment should be used for what purposes, with what frequencies, and for which students. For example, short performance tasks could be built into lessons while longer group tasks could be used for unit assessment.

Constructed-response performance tasks have great promise for assessing what is important in mathematics learning. However, research on their effectiveness is limited because of the varying definitions of performance assessment, formats, and evaluation methods. Woodward, Monroe, and Baxter (2001) developed performance assessments to accompany the *Everyday Mathematics* (Bell, Bell, & Hartfield, 1993) text for classrooms including students with learning disabilities in mathematics and at-risk students. The researchers used an augmented global rubric (the typical 0 to 4 scale was augmented with specific descriptors between levels (e.g., $0, -1, 1, +1, -2, 2 \ldots$) to evaluate student progress over five months. The performance assessment tasks were able to illustrate significant student differences such as the complexity of explanations, organizational methods, and strategy use and were sensitive enough to show incremental progress by all the

Figure 3.7
Evaluative Rubric: Task-specific
Performance: Measuring Surfaces and Recording Area Data in Cooperative Groups

Performance	Excellent (3)	Good (2)	Needs Improvement (1-0)	Comments
Accurate use of rulers and tape measures.	Measures within 1/8 inch.	Measures within 1/4 inch	Measures within 1/2 inch or inaccurate.	
Accurate computation of area using formulas.	Notes indicate correct application of length × width forumula; correct computations.	Correct use of formula but some computations incorrect.	Incorrect use of formula and/or computations	
Representation of data in chart form.	All parts of chart labeled and data entered correctly	Parts of chart incorrectly labeled or some data entered incorrectly.	Chart incorrectly labeled and/or data entered incorrectly	
Cooperative group work.	All members contributed to group results and discussions were about math concepts.	All members contributed to group results but needed more group discussion.	Most members contributed to group results and needed more group discussion.	
Totals				

students. However, students with learning disabilities still performed well below their peers, even with ad hoc tutoring and peer mediation.

Portfolios

A portfolio is a collection of representative permanent products from the student's work. These products may include samples of written work, audiotapes or videotapes of reports or demonstrations, unit projects (or photographs of projects), CBM graphs, rubrics and results of performance tasks, student journal entries, and summaries of student performance. Three basic types of portfolios have been identified (Columba & Doglos, 1995): showcase portfolios, with the student's best work samples; teacher-student or working portfolios, to enhance communication; and teacher alternative assessment portfolios, solely for evaluation.

Evaluative portfolios are usually developed throughout a school year to document long-term progress and to use as a communication tool with students and parents. The types of products and performance criteria should be predetermined and made clear to students. Usually a checklist or evaluative rubric is used to judge performance standards.

Figure 3.8
Example Mathematics Portfolio Contents

Example Mathematics Portfolio Contents

- Cover letter and/or summary
- Table of contents
- Investigations
- Nonroutine problems
- Journal entries and essays
- Book review
- Draft and revised versions of a complex problem
- Photographs of large charts or models
- Student explanation of procedure and why it works
- Group reports or investigation results
- Informal assessment results
- Corrected work samples
- Student-created charts or tables
- Performance task at end of unit of study with reflection
- Work from another subject area that includes math concepts
- Teacher checklist of performance
- Math autobiography

Figure 3.8 illustrates possible items to include in an evaluative portfolio for mathematics (Koca & Lee, 1998; Stenmark, 2002).

Some issues to consider when implementing a portfolio evaluation system are:

- Will the portfolio be used for evaluation of student performance or program evaluation?
- Will the portfolio be specific to mathematics achievement or interrelated content areas?
- Who should determine the content of the portfolio?
- How often and by what means should portfolios be reviewed?
- How can scoring rubrics be developed that are understood by students and have reliability and limited bias?
- How should portfolios be graded and weighted?
- How can portfolios best reflect student learning of mathematics concepts and use of the processes: reasoning, problem solving, communication, representations, and connections?

Portfolios can assist students in understanding their own progress and in realizing the importance of the learning process, not just the correct answer or product. They help teachers and students better integrate instruction and assessment and communicate about student progress. Students can gain greater responsibility for their learning, especially with portfolios that allow student choice and encourage reflections.

Teachers should be aware of potential disadvantages including increased time requirements for planning and evaluating portfolios, potential subjectivity or bias, logistics of maintaining portfolios over time, and decisions about portfolio contents that reflect an appropriate balance of the curriculum (Koretz, 1994). Very little research has been conducted on the impact of portfolio assessments on learning by students with disabilities or other learning problems. Studies of implementation of the state-wide portfolios in Vermont and Kentucky indicated issues with equitable scoring, reliability and validity, standardization, teacher training, and actual impact on instruction (Koretz, 1994; Kahl, 1992).

A growing number of states are using portfolio assessments for the required alternate assessment of students not able to participate in regular state assessment programs. As of 2000, the date by which IDEA regulations for state-wide assessment of all students was required, twenty-six states indicated they were using portfolio systems or had plans for the development of those systems for alternate assessments (Thompson & Thurlow, 2000). In many cases the IEP team, composed of both regular and special educators, develops the portfolio protocol for item selection and evaluation of individual students.

Assessment Strategies

There are several useful strategies available to the teacher conducting any of these alternative assessments. Teachers of mathematics will find these strategies essential in their assessment "toolboxes."

Error analysis is the process of examining student errors for clues to misconceptions or erroneous strategies. Identifying a pattern of errors can be especially enlightening. Error analysis should not be used to make sure students are "doing" their math algorithms the one way they were taught, but to uncover misunderstandings and faulty procedures. Figure 3.9 shows a student work sample with a discernable pattern of errors. Error analysis can also be conducted with formal assessments as long as the test protocol is followed.

Figure 3.9
Error Analysis

23	14	21
× 2	× 2	× 5
26	18	25

32	45	34
× 3	× 4	× 3
36	48	312

25	33	40
× 3	× 4	× 5
215	312	40

Figure 3.10
Diagnostic Interview

Ms Walker is interviewing Leah about her work (Figure 3.9) to determine Leah's understanding of multiplication procedures.

Ms Walker: Leah, would you explain how you solved the first problem, 23 times 2?

Leah: I'm not sure I did it right.

Ms Walker: That's OK, I just want to see what you understand and what I need to explain more.

Leah: OK, first I looked at the 3 times 2 and I know that's 6 so I wrote it down. Then I just brought down the 2 and wrote that underneath.

Ms Walker: Can you tell me how you worked this one, 34 times 3?

Leah: It was the same way. First I said 4 times 3 is 12 and wrote that down. Then I brought down the 3 left over.

Ms Walker: I think I see. Leah, you really know your multiplication facts well, you don't have to stop and figure those out. And you know the rule about starting problems on the right, in the one's column. But I think I need to show you what to do with larger numbers. Watch while I work a couple of examples, then I want you to help me.

Leah: I really want to get these right, thanks for helping me.

Bryant and Maddox (1996) proposed using reading miscue analysis with written word problems as part of the assessment of mathematics word problem solving.

If teachers are stumped by students' written work, the **diagnostic interview** (sometimes termed clinical interview or think-aloud) can provide clues to difficulties and misunderstandings. In this technique a student is asked explain how he solved a problem or asked to "think out loud" while working a problem. This procedure is not the dreaded "being sent to the board" but is usually conducted individually or with small groups in a nonthreatening and nonpunitive atmosphere. Students will quickly realize that probing will lead to clearer instruction and better understanding and success (see Figure 3.10).

Ericsson and Simon (1993) traced the history of **think-aloud techniques** in psychology, cognitive science, and educational applications for assessment, instruction, and research methods in their text *Protocol Analysis: Verbal Reports as Data*, an elaboration of their theory on verbal thinking-aloud protocols as data, first published in 1980. The theorists credited Watson (1920) for the first documented analysis of thinking-aloud activity, published after a decade of work refuting introspection research methods. "A good deal more can be learned about the psychology of thinking by making subjects think aloud about definite problems, than by trusting to the unscientific method of introspection" (Watson, 1920, p. 91).

Research supports the use of think-alouds in mathematics to determine student concept understanding and metacognitive approaches of students with learning problems. For example, Lowenthal (1987) used interviewing to probe mathematics error patterns. Ginsburg (1997) demonstrated the use of clinical interviews to trace the mathematics concept understanding of individual students receiving the same instructional experiences over time. Think-alouds were used by Montague and Applegate (1993) to study the mathematics problem solving approaches of students with learning disabilities. And Gurganus and Shaw (2005) demonstrated the use of think-aloud protocols to probe "big idea" mathematics concept understanding of students with learning disabilities.

Taking the diagnostic interview a step further and attempting to instruct the student during the assessment process to measure potential for change are approaches called **dynamic assessments** (Swanson, 1994). Included in this model are measures that are more sensitive to thought-process measurement (e.g., math thinking and problem-solving skills) such as microgenesis—repeated observations and interviews of individual children working on a set of problems over a relatively long period of time (Kuhn & Phelps, 1982) and teaching experiments that involve working within Vygotsky's zone of proximal development to guide (scaffold) a student to a higher level of understanding and then assessing transfer to near and far problems (Campione, Brown, Ferrara, & Bryant, 1984). Dynamic assessments may augment initial assessment methods by providing a measure of the student's potential to learn through a given intervention method. They can answer questions not only about the nature of a student's learning problems but about appropriate interventions.

Jitendra, Kame'enui, and Carnine (1994) employed dynamic assessment techniques to compare student learning in two mathematics curriculum programs. Their techniques included close observation of student problem solving, facilitative questioning, and instruction in think-aloud procedures for problem solving. Dynamic assessment techniques allowed the researchers to identify learners who had the correct answer but lacked concept understanding and those who understood concepts but lacked mechanical skills, evidence that would have been misinterpreted in traditional assessments.

Another assessment strategy mentioned in the previous sections is the use of an evaluative **rubric**—a device for assessing qualitative aspects of student work. Used most commonly with analysis of written language, a rubric is typically a list of task components with benchmarks and a rating scale for each item. Rubrics are useful with performance-based assessments, portfolios, and cooperative group efforts. Students should be familiar with the rubric that will be used to assess their work and can, with practice, develop their own rubrics.

Teachers should be aware of the different rubric types before developing or using rubrics. The holistic rubric gives a single rating for the entire product, whereas the analytical rubric divides the product into essential components (Arter & McTighe, 2001). For example, some rubrics for state-wide mathematics constructed response items include holistic ratings using scales from 0 (does not address task) to 4 (all parts of the question are answered accurately and completely). The North West Regional Educational Laboratory (2000) offers a five-trait rubric for scoring problem-solving efforts, with each trait rated on a four-point scale. Traits include conceptual understanding, strategies and reasoning, computations and execution, communication, and insights. Analytical rubrics are more formative, while holistic rubrics are more appropriate as summative tools.

Figure 3.11
Generic Rubric

Level	Performance Description
4—Exceeds expectations	Response is complete and comprehensive, addresses all parts with integration of concepts evident. Includes strong arguments that are supported with evidence.
3—Meets expectations	A good solid response but less complete regarding connections and arguments.
2—Needs improvement	One or two problems with response: not complete, lacking support, lacking connections, or unclear communication.
1—Below standard	Omits significant portions of response, has major errors.
0—Well below standard	Does not attempt or responses do not match problem or question.

Additionally, teachers should consider whether to use generic or task-specific rubrics. Generic rubrics can be used across similar performances and may benefit student understanding and allow for comparison across time (see Figure 3.11). Task-specific rubrics must be developed for each task but can yield more specific content learning information and can be easier to evaluate (see Figure 3.7).

Arter and McTighe (2001) offer a useful rubric development process:

a. Gather samples of student performance that illustrate a skill or performance.
b. Sort the samples into groups and consider why they were grouped in this manner (e.g., strong, average, weak). List the reasons.
c. Cluster the reasons into traits or dimensions of the performance. (This is where some traits listed are holistic and others more analytical.)
d. Write a "value-neutral" definition of each trait. For example, the statement, "response includes specific mathematics terminology in correct contexts" is value-neutral, while the statement, "response uses appropriate terminology" is not.
e. Find examples of student work that illustrate each score.

Semilogarithmic graph paper is used to graph exponential growth over time. The horizontal scale is linear (units of time) but the vertical scale is logarithmic, with the distance from 1 to 2 being much larger than that from 2 to 3 and so forth.

It is important that rubrics reflect curriculum standards (criteria) and discriminate among student performances. Teachers can pool their expertise of the curriculum and establish rubric reliability by working together to develop these tools.

Charting student work is an effective strategy for documenting progress and encouraging students' involvement in their progress. Younger students tend to understand bar graphs or pictographs more easily than line graphs. Some teachers, especially those trained in applied behavior analysis and precision teaching, prefer to use semilogarithmic graph paper, but those graphs can be confusing for students and parents. Students can be taught to graph their progress using standard arithmetic graph paper or they can be

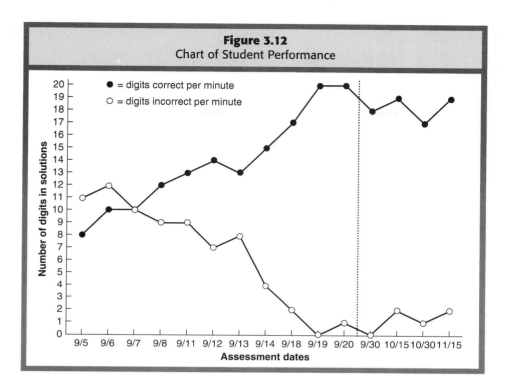

Figure 3.12
Chart of Student Performance

taught how to enter data and create charts with spreadsheets. After all, data collection, analysis, and graphical representations are important mathematics skills.

The protocol for depicting performance data in graph form is to list scores or percents on the ordinate (vertical axis), labeled with the measurement system as in Figure 3.12. Time, usually days or weeks, is represented on the abscissa (horizontal axis) and labeled accordingly. Performance rates and accuracy cannot be represented on the same graph; however, indicating correct and incorrect responses (accuracy) on the same graph is very useful. Teachers who want to be more scientific in their interventions plot baseline data (performance before the intervention), intervention data, and maintenance or generalization data, all clearly delineated with vertical lines on the graph.

Another strategy for designing teacher-made CBAs is the development of a **table of specifications** (Tyler, 1949). These tables provide a way to plan instruction and match assessment methods systematically. The content to be taught is subdivided and listed down the side of the table; student behaviors (e.g., response modes) are listed across the top; and the number or weighting of test items or tasks are within the cells. For purposes of instruction, these behaviors can follow the instructional sequence. For assessment they usually indicate how the skill performance or concept understanding will be observed. An example of a table of specifications for telling time is depicted in Figure 3.13. A partner table could be developed that analyzed the assessment tasks by state process and content standards.

There has been a lot of criticism of this two-dimensional "content-by-process" matrix in the mathematics education literature, claiming that it is a behaviorist approach and is

Figure 3.13
Table of Specifications for Telling Time on Analog Clock

Objectives	Teacher Observation of Student Performances	Oral Responses to Questions	Paper and Pencil Tasks
Count by fives		✓	
Identify parts of clock		✓	
Identify morning (a.m.) and afternoon, evening (p.m.) activities		✓	
Tell and set time to nearest hour	✓	✓	
Tell and set time to nearest half hour	✓	✓	
Tell and set time to nearest quarter hour	✓	✓	
Tell and set time to nearest minute	✓	✓	✓
Identify times of day for specific activities, including a.m. or p.m.		✓	

State Content Standards:
Number and operations
Spatial Sense
Measurement

Required State Processes:
Representations
Communication
Connections

reductionist in nature (Romberg & Wilson, 1995). Critics view this matrix as unnaturally linear and hierarchical. However, methods of organizing content and processes such as matrices and concept maps promote better understanding of interrelated concepts and more valid curriculum-based assessment strategies. Matrices or webs should be robust enough to allow for concept overlays and interconnections.

Classroom Assessment Systems

Teachers who are committed to using assessment within the instructional cycle should develop their own **assessment systems.** Systematizing assessment activities ensures their implementation and consistency and saves planning and instructional time. The features of a system will depend on caseload, the amount of direct contact with students, the

Figure 3.14
Assessment of Goals and Objectives from IEP

Performance Strengths: Student is fluent in number combinations (addition, subtraction, multiplication, division facts); demonstrates mastery of addition and subtraction of multi-digit problems; expresses fractions in lowest terms,; converts between percent and decimal forms; names place values for whole and decimal forms.

Annual Goal: Student will compute with rational number forms (whole numbers, fractions, decimals, and percents) for isolated problems and in applications at 80%, as measured by district CBM.

Estimated Instructional Period	Short-Term Objectives*	Date of Mastery	Maintenance Checks	Planned Applications
9/11 to 9/25	Given multiplication problems up to three digits (whole numbers and decimals), student will compute 18 of 20.	9/25 90%	10/10—88% 11/15—	January unit on sports applications of math, calculator applications
9/26 to 10/10	Given division problems with one- or two-digit divisors, student will find quotient for 9 of 10.	10/10 95%	10/16—90% 11/15—	January unit on sports applications
10/11 to 10/30	Given 20 addition and subtraction problems with simple, improper, and mixed fractions, student will solve and express solutions in lowest terms (90%).	11/6 85%	11/15—	Word problem applications in December; February unit on measurement
11/1 to 11/15	Given 20 multiplication and division problems with the range of fraction types, student will solve and express solutions in lowest terms (90%).			Word problem applications in December; February unit on measurement
11/16 to 11/30	Student will convert between fraction, decimal, and percent forms for 18 of 20 problems.			Consumer math unit in March
12/1 to 12/20	Given one- and two-step word problems involving fractions, student will solve 8 of 10.			Application of previous concepts and skills

* Short-term objectives (benchmarks) are required only for those students with alternative assessments under IDEA 2004, but many states and districts consider them critical for determining short-term progress.

assessment conducted by general and special education teachers, access to technology, and other setting-based variables. General guidelines are offered here:

1. *Use the IEP or other curriculum goals and objectives as a framework for assessment activities.* On a chart or computerized form, list each student's goals on separate pages followed by the list of objectives (or benchmarks) for each goal (see Figure 3.14). Following each objective there should be periodic notations of progress

2. *Establish a schedule of CBA, collecting data on each student at least once a week.* If well planned, this assessment should take only about two to five minutes for short, skill-specific probes and about ten to fifteen minutes for constructed-response performance tasks. If not carefully planned, assessment can eat up instructional time and yield little useful information. For example, one teacher instituted a one-minute timed fluency test at the beginning of class. There were several problems with her system: she used the same test every day and students memorized the answers; the test took only one minute but preliminary activities, checking, and recording consumed almost fifteen minutes; and the tests were the same for her eighteen students and unrelated to their instructional objectives. Computer programs can randomize items and chart progress. Efficient classroom management should take care of time issues.

3. *Set up an assessment center.* Include graph paper, timers, student folders, calculators, and assessment probes and performance tasks on large file cards. Teach students to chart their own progress, either on graph paper or with computer programs.

4. *Build in assessment items that resemble those of state- and district-wide assessments.* If students must select responses in a multiple-choice format or write out narratives to explain their answers, they should be practicing those tasks when corrective feedback is allowed.

5. *Conduct maintenance checks routinely.* Deliberately schedule assessment points for previously learned skills and concepts. About a month after a unit on fractions, when working on geometry objectives, conduct a fraction review and brief assessment. Integrate objectives from one unit into the next; for example, fractions are used in measurement. Observe facility with fractions while students measure.

ASSESSING HIGHER-ORDER PROCESSES

Recent reforms in mathematics education have important implications for assessment practices. As noted in the assessment standards of NCTM, assessment must be an integral part of the instructional cycle and reflect the mathematics content proposed in the standards. Therefore, mathematics assessment should measure students' process skills in problem solving, reasoning, communicating, forming connections, and making representations as well as measuring progress within the five content areas. Traditional forms of assessment tend to measure specific subskills of (limited) content areas but not the higher-order processes.

Mathematizing is the activity of interpreting, organizing, and constructing meaning of situations with mathematical modeling (Freudenthal, 1973).

Jan de Lange (1995) asserted that there are different levels or depths of assessment, just as there are different levels of understanding. **Lower level assessment** is the target of most traditional assessment. Objects, definitions, technical skills, standard algorithms, and simple multiple-step problems are addressed at this level. For example, "compute the average of a group of data" is a lower-level task for fifth-graders. **Middle level assessment** requires students to relate two or more concepts or procedures. An example would be to apply the concept of volume from instruction about cubes to a new three-dimensional figure such as a rectangular prism. The most difficult, **higher level assessment,** involves mathematical thinking and reasoning, communication, attitudes, interpretation, reflection, creativity, generalization, and mathematizing. These constructs are extremely difficult to assess. For example, students would be asked to make decisions on the method of data collection for a problem, how to best represent the data, and to interpret the data including making reasoned predictions.

Higher-order processes and thinking skills also are difficult to describe and observe. Resnick (1987) identified nine features of higher-order thinking: nonalgorithmic; tends to be complex; often yields multiple solutions; involves nuanced judgment; involves the application of multiple, sometimes conflicting, criteria; often involves uncertainty; involves self-regulation of thinking; involves imposing meaning or structure on disorder; and requires much mental effort. For example, a group of teachers in a school have been given the authority to alter grade-level patterns, teacher allocations, administrative and support personnel structure, book adoptions, schedules, and other district-imposed guidelines. Their problem is extremely complex and will require collecting data from a number of sources, establishing negotiated goals, understanding new parameters, and predicting the results of various sets of decisions. For middle school students, a higher-order task would be to use surveying methods to determine the position of a future baseball diamond on school grounds.

Frameworks or taxonomies can assist educators in planning to meet state standards while addressing higher-order processes. The 1954 Bloom's Taxonomy of Educational Objectives was revised in 2001 to provide both cognitive process and knowledge dimensions (Anderson & Krathwohl, 2001). In order of increasing complexity, cognitive processes are now verbs: remember, understand, apply, analyze, evaluate, and create. Four categories of knowledge move from concrete to abstract: factual, conceptual, procedural, and metacognitive. An example of an instructional objective within the taxonomy for mathematics is, "The student will convert fractions to decimal form." The task is primarily *procedural* and the cognitive process is at the *understand* level unless the student is asked to apply the skill in context. A higher-order objective would be, "The student will create a word problem that illustrates the use of rate." This task is *metacognitive*, requiring the student to consider how to approach the task, and is at the *create* level.

Alternative means of developing mathematics assessments for higher-order processes must consider the purpose of assessment, the complexity of the processes, qualitative aspects of the instructional cycle, and the ongoing nature of learning. Another useful framework is the SOLO (Structure of the Observed Learning Outcome) taxonomy, concerned with describing the structure of students' responses within the learning cycle during a problem-solving session (Biggs & Collins, 1982) depicted in Figure 3.15. Applied with both open and closed response formats, SOLO assessments pose problems within real contexts and use a range of response modes such as mapping, clinical interviews, written explanations, and pre-coded rubrics (Romberg, Zarinnia, & Collins, 1990).

The research literature on SOLO applications indicates more use with secondary content areas and in higher education settings. For example, college chemistry faculty found SOLO useful for identifying areas of difficulty and following student progress in

Figure 3.15
Structure of Observed Learning Outcomes (SOLO) Taxonomy

SOLO Level	SOLO Descriptors	Mathematics Problem-Solving Example
Unistructural	Single relevant feature Generalizations on basis of one aspect Premature closure	Solves one part of a multi-faceted problem, ignores other information.
Multistructural	Lists relative features Makes generalizations based on few aspects independently of each other Some inconsistency	Focuses on isolated parts of problem but ignores interconnections.
Relational	Considers data as a whole Uses and interrelates all information Induces conclusions from data available Seeks consistency Seeks to control variables	Uses all information in problem in interrelated ways to solve problem.
Extended Abstract (contextual)	Integrates ideas into disciplinary concepts Uses deductive logic to relate specific to general Recognizes alternative approaches Can extend structures under consideration and look for more abstract features	Uses alternative approaches and integration of explicit and abstract concepts to solve and perform checks on problem solution.

Source: Adapted from Evaluating the Quality of Learning: The SOLO Taxonomy by Biggs, J. B., & Collins, K. F., pp. 24–25, Copyright 1982, with permission from Elsevier.

understanding concepts (Hodges & Harvey, 2003). They used this analytical tool to guide intervention design and for better informing students of their progress. Lake (2002) described SOLO's use with college-level students to evaluate their understanding of mathematical concepts needed in social sciences studies. He adapted the taxonomy into a pedagogical template for developing needed concepts.

The SOLO taxonomy has promise for evaluating higher-order skills and making essential links to instruction in many more settings. For example, a team of middle-school mathematics and support teachers applied the SOLO taxonomy in evaluating students' performances on the culminating problem in a unit on data analysis and statistics. Students were required to work in small groups to select a problem, collect data, analyze the data, interpret their findings, and offer a solution. Problem choices included determining the most reasonable entrance fee for the holiday carnival, determining the best location for the class garden, or ordering healthy snacks to restock the school vending machine. Those groups using all the information provided, gathering important additional information including information from other fields of study, integrating data in various ways, and interpreting the results with supporting evidence would be working at the relational to extended abstract levels on the taxonomy.

An example of using the SOLO taxonomy to evaluate individual students' work on performance items would be to present upper elementary students with the problem, "develop a drawing to show a net (two-dimensional pattern) for a three-dimensional solid with the volume of between 650 and 700 cubic units." Students demonstrating relational and extended abstract thinking would have alternative approaches to the problem, perform solution checks, and apply number, algebraic, measurement, and geometric concepts to the problem. They would also communicate the problem solving processes employed and recognize generalizable patterns and rules for the problem.

Regardless of the lesson or assignment, teachers should use mathematics processes as a filter for evaluating student responses. Was students' mathematics language accurate and specific? Could students represent mathematics concepts in flexible ways? Did students employ a sound problem-solving process that included studying the elements of the problem and reasonableness of solutions? Were students able to make connections with prior learning in mathematics or other areas? Were student reasoning and generalizations based on logical, deductive, and supported argument? When developing instructional units, teachers should deliberately plan to teach and assess these higher-order processes.

TRY THIS

Exercises in Assessing Higher-Order Processes

1. Analyze the following assessment task. What level of assessment is involved? In this interdisciplinary unit, what mathematics content standards are addressed? What process standards are addressed? What response mode is required? How should the groups' performances be evaluated?

   Assessment Task for Middle School Students: Students have been involved in a unit of study on the parts and functioning of computer processors, leading to the culminating activity of putting a computer together from a package of parts. In small groups they must identify the parts, assemble them into a working processor, connect the processor to a monitor and keyboard, and test the functioning of the computer (speed, memory, input, output). The group must prepare and complete a chart of functions.

2. Given the following criteria, develop an assessment task that would be appropriate for younger elementary students. Describe the response mode and scoring procedure.

   Content areas addressed: patterns, geometry, and measurement
   Processes addressed: problem solving, communication, and making representations
   Level: Grades 2 to 3

COLLABORATION FOR ASSESSMENT

Ms. Boswell and Mr. Hernandez meet again after the first unit of study on number theory:

Boswell: Thank you for working with that group of students before the chapter test. Four of the five still didn't meet mastery but they did better than I expected.

Hernandez: Did you have an idea they did not understand the concepts earlier?

Boswell: They had most of their homework correct but they didn't do well on the workbook activities in class. I couldn't figure out how they could do the same problems correctly for homework but not in class.

Hernandez: When I was working with that group I noticed some confusion with the terms. Three students used the terms whole, rational, and integer interchangeably. They didn't seem to understand the difference. I drew a diagram and showed how each number type is related to the other. Then I had the students give examples of each type until I was sure they were making clear distinctions.

Boswell: Those students did very well on that part of the test. And more importantly, I will be using those terms all year as I explain other concepts.

Hernandez: Let's discuss the areas where students didn't reach mastery and explore more the reasons for that. If necessary I can do some dynamic assessment, evaluating their understanding and doing some instruction at the same time.

Boswell: That would be wonderful! While you work with that group, I'll do some extension activities into number theory with the other students. ■ ● ▲

How did these teachers work together to plan and use assessment? What types of assessment were useful? How did collaboration contribute to student learning? As more students with learning problems are included in general education classrooms with differing levels of support services, it is critical that teachers collaborate on an individual student level to plan, conduct, and interpret evaluations for the purposes of informing instruction and planning student interventions. Teachers can pool their expertise—in mathematics content understanding, student characteristics knowledge, and experience with assessment—to design tools that will reflect learning. Collaboration activities that will benefit assessments include:

- Discuss the types of assessments and the overall assessment systems within each setting—general, special, and remedial education.
- For similar assessment tasks, consider developing common rubrics. This approach would have the advantages of being consistent for students and the opportunity for inter-observer reliability measures.
- Share and discuss assessment results of individual students in terms of strengths and weaknesses and needed interventions.
- Special and remedial educators may be responsible for offering alternative settings for assessments with special accommodations such as extended time, read aloud, or

small group administration. It is important that accommodations used on district and state-wide tests are also used for regular classroom assessments and that the tests be administered within the specified parameters of the accommodations.

Assessment has many purposes within mathematics education. It can assist teachers in understanding student learning needs. It can inform communities of the mathematics performance of their children as compared with others. The most important purpose is that which informs teachers and students of progress and instructional success—designed and administered by teachers within the instruction-assessment cycle.

CHAPTER SUMMARY

- Primary purposes of assessment include initial evaluation for special education eligibility, annual evaluation for IEP planning, state and district performance assessment, teacher-developed assessments for instructional planning, and high-stakes assessment for decisions about individuals and schools.
- The NCTM assessment standards recommend an assessment process that involves setting learning goals and planning assessments, gathering evidence, interpreting evidence, and making instructional decisions.
- Standardized assessment tools include norm- and criterion-referenced instruments that can be administered in group or individual settings. Not all these tools are aligned with the NCTM or state curriculum standards.

- Two primary types of curriculum-based assessment are curriculum-based measurement and mastery measurement.
- Alternative assessments include performance tasks and portfolio assessment.
- Assessment strategies and tools for informal measures are error analysis, diagnostic interviews, dynamic assessment, evaluative rubrics, and charting. Teachers should plan assessment systems that are effective and efficient.
- Higher-order assessment is more challenging but can yield important information about students' mathematics processes.
- Teachers should work together to pool their assessment expertise.

RESOURCES

Arter, J., & McTighe, J. (2001). *Scoring rubrics in the classroom: Using performance criteria for assessing and improving student performance.* Thousand Oaks, CA: Corwin.

Ashlock, R. B. (2002). *Error patterns in computation: Using error patterns to improve instruction* (8th ed.). Upper Saddle River, NJ: Merrill Prentice Hall.

National Center on Educational Outcomes (University of Minnesota). This center studies the participation of students with disabilities in national and state assessments, standards-setting efforts, and graduation requirements. Available at: education.umn.edu/nceo.

National Council of Teachers of Mathematics (1999 to 2003). *Classroom assessment for school mathematics, K–12 series.* (by grade band by various authors). Reston, VA: NCTM.

Romberg, T. A. (Ed.) (2004). *Standards-based mathematics assessment in middle school: Rethinking classroom practice.* New York: Teachers College Press.

Thurlow, M. L., Elliott, J. L., & Ysseldyke, J. E. (1998). *Testing students with disabilities: Practical strategies for complying with district and state requirements.* Thousand Oaks, CA: Corwin.

Effective Mathematics Instruction for Students with Learning Problems

Chapter Questions

1. What overall principles should guide mathematics instruction?
2. How should teachers plan to deliver the most effective instruction?
3. How can teachers design effective mathematics curricula for students with varying needs?
4. How can teachers collaborate to provide the most effective instruction for students with mathematics learning problems?

Entering Mr. Martin's classroom, we see students working at desks arranged in four rows of three. The students are filling in math worksheets and Mr. Martin is doing paperwork at his desk. All the students are working on the same "add or subtract" worksheet. Two students are drawing pictures in the margins, three students are slowly adding each problem using their fingers, one student has finished and is trying to get the attention of another student, and the other four students have their hands raised. ■ ● ▲

This special education classroom serves students with mild disabilities who have mathematics goals and objectives on their IEPs. However, the students' mathematics abilities vary considerably. Are the students learning mathematics required by the general education curriculum? Are their individual needs being met in this setting? Is math time simply busy-work time for this teacher?

Special education teachers who are not familiar with mathematics content or methods but are responsible for mathematics instruction typically teach mathematics the way they were taught or follow the lessons in a basal textbook. Modeling one's teaching after the most effective teachers in one's experience certainly can have benefits. However, in reflecting back on best teachers, teacher candidates may not realize all the behind-the-scenes work involved in planning, assessment, and other decision-making related to the instruction of the range of students in a class.

Textbooks offer clues about sequence, activities, assessment, and extensions, but may not provide information on underlying concepts and connections; adaptations, examples, and problems appropriate for diverse students; or sequences that consider prior learning, review, and generalization. Over-reliance on a text results in ignoring student interests, differences, and needs; emphasizing rote learning; diminishing professional decision-making; skewing the importance of various content topics; and neglecting other, more powerful methods and technologies.

Special education and remedial teachers responsible for mathematics instruction or even the support of mathematics instruction within the regular mathematics classroom should be familiar with and skillful in curriculum, instruction, and assessment in mathematics across the grade levels for which they are certified. The Division for Learning Disabilities (DLD) identified twelve knowledge and skill competency areas in mathematics that teachers of students with learning disabilities should demonstrate (Graves, Landers, Lokerson, Luchow, & Horvath, 1993). These include: knowledge of the K–12 mathematics curriculum, knowledge of a variety of instructional techniques and activities in mathematics, understanding the use of manipulatives and in encouraging students to voice understanding of mathematics concepts, understanding of providing a balanced mathematics program, and knowledge of current research in mathematics instruction.

This chapter will build on the previous discussions of curriculum reform, models of instruction, early concept development, curriculum scope, and assessment of mathematics learning. Guiding principles and specific methods and adaptations for effective mathematics instruction will be explored, enhanced by "try this" opportunities. Take the time to explore these applications, preferably with students. Immediate application will deepen your understanding of the methods and mathematics concepts addressed. Attention is also given to lesson and unit planning and teacher collaboration for instruction.

This chapter on instruction is not a how-to or recipe file of teaching ideas and activities for discrete topics, such as how to teach long division or how to provide practice for finding the area of quadrilaterals. There are many other resources that offer those instructional suggestions, including journals and websites. The purpose of this chapter is to highlight research-based instructional methods that can be applied across grade levels and curriculum topics in mathematics. Embedded examples and activities allow for specific applications. The content strands located after the chapters in this book offer more content-specific concepts and teaching strategies.

PRINCIPLES OF MATHEMATICS INSTRUCTION

Instructional principles serve as broad guidelines for planning and providing instruction. They are reminders of the big picture that is frequently forgotten in the day-to-day activities of teachers. They provide benchmarks for purposeful and reflective teaching. The following principles of mathematics instruction represent a synthesis of professional experience and research (Figure 4.1). The first three principles establish a foundation for teaching and learning: ponder **underlying concepts and connections,** link **prior knowledge** to new learning, and activate **positive attitudes.** The next four apply to planning instructional formats: present concepts in **problem-solving contexts,** establish an effective **sequence of instruction,** consider the appropriate degree of **explicit instruction** for the content, and plan for **variety within structure.** The final three principles enhance instruction: remember the importance of **language** for learning, recognize the power of **strategies,** and ensure **transfer of learning.**

1. *Ponder the underlying concepts, connections, and big ideas of whatever content or procedures are being addressed.* While planning units of study, teachers should review the deeper mathematics concepts and connections related to unit objectives. For example, a unit addressing the addition and subtraction of fractions is built on the understanding of parts of a whole or set, what portion is represented by numerator and denominator, the use of factors, and basic addition and subtraction

---

Figure 4.1
Principles of Mathematics Instruction

1. Ponder the underlying concepts, connections, and big ideas of whatever content or procedures are being addressed.

2. Employ techniques to link prior knowledge of your students with new concepts.

3. Activate positive attitudes in the learning environment.

4. Present new mathematics concepts in realistic, meaningful, problem-solving contexts.

5. Establish an effective and cognitively appropriate sequence of instruction.

6. Consider the appropriate degree of explicit instruction for the content.

7. Develop lessons that offer variety within structure.

8. Remember the importance of language for math learning.

9. Recognize the power of strategies to transcend topics and create independent learners.

10. Ensure that mathematics instruction includes transfer-of-learning activities.

---

concepts as reciprocals. A student who does not understand the concept of the denominator representing the whole or set will not understand why denominators must be represented in the same terms in order to apply addition or subtraction algorithms. Another student who cannot manipulate factors with understanding will not be able to set up addition and subtraction problems or reduce their results to lowest terms.

It really is like the forest and the trees. It is better to keep the forest in mind—the nature of the total forest system—and to address several connective aspects than to address the characteristics of each tree, flower, grass, animal, stream, rock, and other inhabitant of the forest. Understanding mathematics is not understanding each fact, procedure, and concept in an isolated form but understanding the collective relationships. And, fortunately, it is easier to learn mathematics through relationships and broader concepts than by learning isolated facts.

For more information on fractions, see content strand D.

What are the most important concepts or big ideas of mathematics? Kame'enui and Carnine (1998) defined big ideas as "those concepts, principles, or heuristics that facilitate the most efficient and broadest acquisition of knowledge" (p. 8). They "represent major organizing principles, have rich explanatory and predictive power, help frame questions, and are applicable in many situations" (p. 95). The focus on big ideas is a reaction to the over-proliferation of narrow instructional objectives and explosion of knowledge in the sciences. The NCTM standards and related state frameworks provide a guide for prioritizing concepts. Examples of big ideas in mathematics include factor, multiple, volume, unit, and variable. For example, the concept of factor derives from multiplicative properties of number, a factor is a positive integer that divides exactly into another positive integer, with 1 being a factor of all positive integers (Sidebotham, 2002). Knowledge of factors assists simple division, reduction of fractions to lowest terms, solving algebraic equations, and factorizing expressions such as the difference of two squares ($a^2 - b^2$). The concept of factors is introduced in early elementary grades but is developed throughout the mathematics curriculum, thus a big idea.

Heuristics are strategies that are invoked when dealing with new and unfamiliar problems (Shoenfeld, 1992).

Teachers should consider six to eight concepts as the basis for the year's mathematics program. In an example of an upper elementary class, the major concepts and big ideas have been formulated as questions:

   a. How are whole numbers, fractions, decimals, and integers related?
   b. How are primes, composites, factors, and multiples used within number systems?
   c. How are the basic arithmetic operations related to each other?
   d. In what ways can we represent algorithms?
   e. By what attributes can we classify two- and three-dimensional shapes?
   f. How can we select an appropriate unit of measure for a given distance or amount and estimate the measurement?
   g. How can we collect, organize, represent, and interpret a set of data?

Teachers should share these broad questions with students and parents at the beginning of the school year with illustrations of activities in which the class will be

TRY THIS

Select another grade-level span and list the six to eight most important concepts or questions.

engaged. A periodic review of these goals is also helpful for keeping "the forest" in mind. Of course, similar broad goals are developed for IEPs of students with disabilities if they are not addressing the same goals as the general education class.

2. *Employ techniques to link prior knowledge of your students with new concepts.* We know that the learning process in the brain involves responses in a variety of neurological networks simultaneously (Sylwester, 1995). The networks are linked or synchronized through neural activity. Different neurological systems are responsible for various aspects of the learning situation—attention, spatial aspects, movement, language, and symbols. Initial neurological activity stimulates memory networks with related information to become active and follow a similar activity pattern. When enough information is synchronized between immediate (short-term attention) stimuli in the thalamus and limbic systems and related past experiences stored in the cortex, an overt response or reformed long-term memory develops. This response is enhanced if there is an emotional aspect to the learning experience or repetitive use of the connections. Frequent activation of the same networks results in physical changes in the brain such as more branching along dendrites and more efficient connections.

These neurological activities have direct implications for teaching. Each lesson should begin with review activities that stimulate previous experiences. Yesterday we converted mixed numbers into improper fractions; let's do a couple of these together to review. Yesterday our groups developed formulas to explain the relationship between the tall and short cylinders; would someone from each group review your results? Last week we measured long distances with meter sticks and yardsticks. Who can demonstrate how we did that?

New concepts should be introduced using direct connections to previous learning. Today we're going to change improper fractions into mixed numbers— reversing what we did yesterday. Today we're going to examine different aspects of cylinders—building on some of your ideas from yesterday. Today we're going to compare meters and yards using your measurements from yesterday. Today we're going to look at a new topic (data collection and statistical analysis) by finding out information from our friends. Who has seen surveys in newspapers, magazines, or on television? Tell me what you remember.

Some of the most powerful teaching tools for new concepts are well-developed examples. The class is introduced to the new concept of volume but the diagrams of cubes and cylinders in the math text are unfamiliar to many students. However, most students have had experience with swimming pools, gas tanks, milk cartons, or hot water heaters. Or the more abstract discussion of *space* could examine the dimensions of a room, an empty swimming pool, an empty refrigerator box, or a hamster cage. Now the new concepts of base, height, and edge have concrete references for students.

A related concept is that of *informal knowledge* (Baroody & Ginsburg, 1986). Informal knowledge is what children develop or construct on their own through interactions with the environment—personal experiences rather than formal instruction. Teachers should be aware that children come to the classroom with informal knowledge about mathematics that can be connected to concepts introduced through formal instruction. For example, when counting objects many children realize they can take shortcuts in counting such as counting on from a known number or counting by two's.

Students from different cultural or linguistic backgrounds may have different informal mathematics experiences and prior knowledge. Accurate and unbiased assessment of the mathematics background of these students is critical. Teachers should be aware of myths associated with cultural and linguistic differences:

- Myth one: Language differences are disabilities. In fact, language differences may hide giftedness and true performance levels.
- Myth two: Mathematics is a culture-free area of study. Language and culture are important factors in teaching and learning mathematics as described in section 8 below.
- Myth three: A student's ethnicity will indicate mathematics ability. A teacher cannot assume that an Indian-American student will be gifted in mathematics or that a Native-American student will not be competitive. Each student's background and abilities should be assessed without the bias of these stereotypes.
- Myth four: A student with a background of poverty will have little informal mathematics knowledge. Again, individuals will have different experiences that influence their informal knowledge. A child in an impoverished environment may have some important mathematics experiences such as careful budgeting, playing counting games, or mental mapping of the neighborhood.

Teachers should take care to plan examples and real-life problems that link to individual student experiences yet extend a student's world knowledge.

TRY THIS

Match each concept below with at least one necessary prior knowledge or informal experience.

1. coordinate graphing
2. probability
3. simple fraction
4. percentage
5. negative integers

3. *Activate positive attitudes in the learning environment.* As discussed in Chapter 1, student and teacher attitudes have a direct effect on student learning. Teaching strategies that can build positive attitudes towards math include: help students set goals, provide opportunities for early success, include relevant applications of concepts, help students see the relationship between effort and result, model positive attitudes, and establish a classroom environment that promotes positive views and common goals.

Having students set and monitor progress toward goals can have a significant effect on achievement in mathematics (see, for example, Fuchs, Bahr, & Rieth, 1989).

For solutions to the problems presented in this book, visit the Companion Website at www.ablongman.com/gurganus1e.

Goal setting is particularly difficult for many students with disabilities. Some instructional models such as Mercer and Miller's *Strategic Math Series* (1991–1994) include specific steps for goal setting. Students write personal achievement goals and chart their own progress toward those goals. This deliberate and visual type of goal setting has been linked to greater motivation toward learning and more success in reaching goals (Mercer & Miller, 1992). Self-monitoring and charting strategies also help students see the relationship between effort and success.

Motivation is the "why" behind behaviors and cognition. It is what focuses or energizes a student's attention, emotions, and activity (Mercer & Pullen, 2005). Motivators can be extrinsic or intrinsic, with a goal to promote more intrinsic, lifelong, self-motivated habits of learning. Students with poor motivation toward school in general or specific subjects such as mathematics have usually experienced repeated failure and/or poor teaching. Additional techniques that are effective in promoting positive motivation include: give students choices and opportunities to help with planning, employ a variety of instructional methods, make instruction personally relevant for students, challenge students (within reason), provide clear and frequent feedback, focus on student effort and improvement, treat errors as a normal part of learning, communicate positive expectations, plan for student success, and teach with energy and enthusiasm (Stipek, Givvin, Salmon, & MacGyvers, 1998; Olson & Platt, 1992; Mercer & Pullen, 2005).

TRY THIS
Visit a math class and note the affective elements in the learning environment. What teacher and student behaviors promote or detract from a positive learning environment?

Teachers have an enormous influence over the affective aspects of the learning environment. By sending verbal messages of high expectations and positive reinforcement, providing opportunities to learn while allowing risk-taking and making mistakes, arranging productive student groupings, and planning meaningful learning activities, teachers create atmospheres that support learning.

4. *Present new mathematics concepts in realistic, meaningful, problem-solving contexts.* Rather than teach isolated facts, rules, procedures, and concepts, use examples from students' experiences and areas of interest to illustrate the concepts involved and the *why* behind the computations. Mathematics classrooms, especially in special education settings, include too much rote learning isolated from meaningful context. Students with disabilities who have memory and strategic deficits are even more handicapped by these approaches. Meaningful contexts promote understanding of related concepts, provide clues to strategies, and are motivating. Adding meaning is not the only benefit for teaching through problem solving. Deeper understanding of concepts leads to better transfer of skills, solving unfamiliar problems, and success with higher-order thinking skills.

The debate over the context of teaching math concepts is not new. A 1949 text on structural arithmetic included the following view:

> Most of the progressive teaching of arithmetic stops at the periphery, with an attempt to dramatize the subject by surface embellishments of the examples. The child is supposed to find the examples exciting because they deal with cats and dolls instead of straight

numbers. But the cats and dolls are irrelevant to the principle and, . . . merely distract the child from the real issues. In our method, the learning of "pure" arithmetic itself becomes a drama . . . [the child] approaches each task in the spirit of discovery that is characteristic of the true mathematician. (Stern, 1949, pp. 287–8)

This shift to "pure" mathematics instruction was in reaction to the progressive emphasis on daily life applications and functional skills rather than "serious" mathematics. It was a call to rebalance the emphasis of mathematics in schools.

Even as recently as the mid-1980s, teacher education texts and teacher's guides emphasized mastering math facts and computations before making applications, arguing that these skills were prerequisites of applications and problem solving. Word problems in textbooks were simplistic and contrived to illustrate algorithms. Discrete chapters on isolated math concepts sent a strong message to students and teachers that mathematics concepts could be learned without connections. Current best practice calls for teaching computation and problem solving simultaneously—teaching for understanding at a deeper level through using problem-solving contexts. Problem solving is doing math.

What is meant by the *context* for presenting new math concepts? Using the example of introducing percents for the first time, how should this concept and the subsequent relationships be presented to students?

One approach would be to teach rules and procedures. Students would record and memorize **rules** such as "percent means per hundred and can be expressed in the form $\frac{n}{100}$," or **procedures** such as "to convert a percent to decimal form, move the decimal two places to the left." Lots of practice follows to ensure mastery of this knowledge. This approach lacks meaning, concept connections, and power for application and generalization.

Another approach, typical of textbooks, is to show a brief real-world example, such as an ad for sporting goods on sale (e.g., 20% off marked price). That example typically follows with rule and procedure instruction and practice as described above. Unless supplemented by the teacher, the brief example is not connected to the concept and the new concept is not connected to others.

Presenting the new concept of percents in a more powerful problem-solving context could involve a larger problem. For example:

> Our class has collected data from other fifth-grade classrooms about their prefer-
> ences for the community activity this year. We need to explore these data to find
> patterns and make conclusions that are understandable. Ms. Pressley's fifth-grade
> class has twenty-five students, with five voting for the activity at the senior center ($\frac{5}{25}$),
> eight voting for the park project ($\frac{8}{25}$), and twelve choosing the preschool project ($\frac{12}{25}$).
> Mr. Skinner's class has twenty-eight students with votes as follows: ten for senior
> center ($\frac{10}{28}$), nine for the park ($\frac{9}{28}$), and nine for the preschool ($\frac{9}{28}$). And our class has
> twenty-six students, with six for the senior center ($\frac{6}{26}$), eight for the park ($\frac{8}{26}$), and
> twelve for the preschool ($\frac{12}{26}$). First, I'd like each group to attempt to show these data
> in any way you can to help make them understandable and comparable.

Later the groups would be guided to use percent as a way of equalizing the data set comparisons for within-classroom as well as total group results. More explicit instruction in procedures using percents, including accurate terminology, would follow.

For more on percents, see content strand D.

This problem-solving approach lends itself to making the connection between prior fraction concepts and new percent concepts, as well as their representations in graph form and other applications. It incorporates the concrete materials and prior knowledge of the previous examples but develops a broader understanding of the concept of percents through different problem types. Through this activity and the ones that follow, students gain a deeper understanding of the concept *percent* and situations where percents can be used to solve problems. This approach will not only facilitate the understanding of percent, but also establish solid groundwork for related concepts of other rational number forms as well as metric systems.

Novice teachers typically teach mathematics concepts and skills in discrete content units (e.g., fractions, measurement, and geometry). Problem-solving contexts in these units can be used to introduce new concepts and provide meaningful and varied practice. Problems also provide necessary connections among mathematical concepts. As teachers gain experience with mathematics content and student characteristics, they are able to develop thematic or problem-based units that cross concept areas yet address those competencies required by district curriculum frameworks.

TRY THIS

With a class partner or colleague, work on one activity below:

1. Discrete content units of instruction. Select a specific grade level and describe a realistic problem-solving context for one of the following units of study: early fractional concepts, measurement of angles, division, coordinate plane graphing, or simplifying algebraic expressions.
2. Thematic units of instruction. Select a problem-based theme and list the math skills and concepts that would be developed through that theme as well as a realistic problem-solving context. Themes: analyzing sports statistics, building doghouses, conducting opinion surveys, or planning the location for a new road for a community.

5. *Establish an effective and cognitively appropriate sequence of instruction.* The sequence for teaching new mathematics concepts and skills derives from Bruner's modes of representation or ways of knowing (1966). Of course, Pestalozzi proposed the systematic use of objects to make number relationships clear around 1800. Many methods texts of the early twentieth century recommended the use of objects for mathematics instruction, but the cognitive sequence that included a representational stage had not been developed until Bruner's work (Bidwell & Clason, 1970).

In Bruner's model (Figure 4.2), the **enactive mode** works through actions with objects in the environment, through use of motor responses and not images or words. In mathematics this is translated into the **concrete level,** where students manipulate materials to represent concepts.

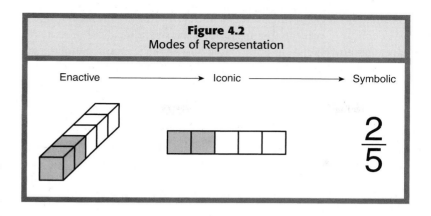

Figure 4.2
Modes of Representation

Enactive ⟶ Iconic ⟶ Symbolic

$$\frac{2}{5}$$

The **iconic mode** works through organized images or icons that represent objects. This has been called the **representational** or **semi-concrete level** in mathematics. Examples include using pictures, graphs, tallies, boxes, or other pictorial representations of math concepts.

Finally, the **symbolic mode** (also called abstract) works through rather arbitrary symbols to represent objects or concepts. In the symbolic mode, students use numerical and other math symbols to represent math ideas.

This concrete–representational–abstract (CRA) instructional sequence will ensure better understanding of mathematics concepts. Many students who have difficulty learning new math concepts and procedures have not had adequate experience with the concrete and representational levels of the sequence and bridging between levels that is provided by language (self-talk, communication with others, and teacher-directed scaffolding). Some teachers begin with concrete objects but move too quickly into representational and abstract forms. Others allow students to use concrete manipulatives far longer than needed for concept understanding. Many teachers omit the representational level altogether. Others, especially at higher-grade levels, work exclusively at a symbolic/abstract level. Textbooks begin at the representational level unless a manipulative set accompanies the text or the instructor's manual emphasizes the importance of the concrete level.

Even with higher-level topics such as algebra and trigonometry, students need to work with models and representations of concepts in ways that are familiar as bridges to the demands of the abstract level. With the spiral nature of the mathematics curriculum (topics revisited year after year at increasingly higher levels), a topic introduced at the concrete level one year may be continued at the representational level the next year and applied only at the abstract level in later years.

An example of moving through Bruner's modes of representation is developed here with the concept of volume of cubes. The concrete level would involve students manipulating interconnecting blocks. Each block represents a cubic unit. Combining

For more information on volume and measurement, see content strand C.

blocks to form larger blocks would result in cubes of differing dimensions, from which students could compute volume in a number of ways. The next level, representation, would involve diagrams depicting cubes labeled with dimensions. Students could use their concrete models of cubes to "see" the make-up of the diagrams or apply rules developed using the models to the dimensions indicated on the diagrams. Finally, students working at the symbolic/abstract level should be able to apply previous learning to a question such as, "What is the volume of a swimming pool with the dimensions 8 meters deep, 12 meters across, and 20 meters long?" They should use only the numbers and other mathematical symbols and formulas. Students who have trouble working entirely at the abstract level can fall back on drawing a diagram (representational) or making a model (concrete).

TRY THIS

Select one of the following math concepts and develop activities at each level of the instructional sequence: concrete–representational–abstract.

1. adding fractions with like denominators
2. introducing addition with regrouping
3. computing the areas of quadrilaterals
4. interpreting a set of data

6. *Consider the appropriate degree of explicit instruction for the content.* There is no question that direct, explicit instruction in mathematics is effective and efficient for students with learning problems. That is one of the most compelling outcomes of four decades of effectiveness research (see, for example, Vaughn, Gersten, & Chard, 2000). However, the nature of the content taught plays a role in how explicit the instruction should be in different portions of lessons or units of study.

A continuum of choices for the degree of directed, explicit instruction was discussed in Chapter 2 (see Figure 2.3). Generally speaking, the more factual the content, the more explicit and teacher-directed the instruction. Content that is more conceptual, procedural, problem-based, or requiring higher-thinking skills requires not so much explicit instruction but rather explorations that are carefully guided by the teacher (called guided discovery). For example, the teacher should provide explicit instruction in how to place a ruler for measurement and what to call the units of measurement. But for instruction about factors, more powerful learning would be developed if students could explore the number patterns for pairs of numbers using number lines or number charts (see Appendix) and be encouraged to describe patterns. Then the teacher would guide students to use specific terminology such as *factor* and *multiple*, and develop rules and procedures for finding greatest common factors. Students will see more connections, study the new concept in context, and be exposed to a variety of representations and examples with this less directive approach. More discussion on creating explicit and guided lessons is found later in this chapter.

7. *Develop lessons that offer variety within structure.* Effective teachers employ classroom routines to manage student behaviors and maximize instructional time. For example, one teacher writes two or three problems on the board before students enter the class. Students know that the expected routine is to enter the classroom, arrange materials for the class, and begin working on the problems. This routine allows time to greet students, note any absences, and begin circulating among students

to check their work. This procedure requires only two minutes but is invaluable in saving time, avoiding behavioral problems, and getting students mentally ready for class.

Many teachers also use a routine for the end of class with similar purposes. In the last two or three minutes, students may be responsible for arranging materials, beginning a homework assignment, summarizing main points, or solving a group problem. The important goals are providing closure, limiting opportunities for misbehavior, and maximizing instructional time.

Whether teachers are conducting a direct instruction or guided discovery lesson (discussed later in this chapter), the major part of instructional time can be structured for maximum effectiveness and efficiency. Typical parts include:

a. mental math practice (2–5 minutes)
b. brief review of previous lesson concepts (2–5 minutes)
c. model or demonstration of new concepts (5–15 minutes)
d. exploratory or practice opportunities with feedback (10–20 minutes); this step would be reversed with step c in a guided discovery lesson
e. lesson closure (1–3 minutes)

If working at the concrete level, teachers should allow more time for materials distribution and use. This lesson structure spans 25 to 50 minutes.

Providing variety within this structure keeps students and teachers interested and motivated. Teachers should vary the review formats, content of the mental math exercises, methods for modeling new concepts and skills, practice activities, student response modes, and homework assignments, as depicted in Figure 4.3. Nothing is more boring or dreaded than worksheets every day or homework assignments of fifty problems a night. There are so many interesting ways for teachers to present lessons and for students to apply concepts and practice skills.

> **TRY THIS**
> Choose one of the following practice activities and share.
> 1. List several ways for students to practice math facts.
> 2. Provide several alternatives to doing a set of problems for homework (e.g., long division, algebra equations, fraction-to-decimal conversions).
> 3. Brainstorm some alternatives to using a worksheet for in-class practice.

8. *Remember the importance of language for mathematics learning.* As with reading, mathematics learning involves the automatic recognition, comprehension, and use of a symbol system. This process has been called the language of mathematics. As with other languages, mathematics involves syntax (the structure of the language), semantics (comprehension aspects), and pragmatics (how the language varies within contexts). The language of mathematics allows us to manipulate difficult concepts and communicate with others. Language forms the bridge between the concrete representations of mathematics ideas (manipulatives and diagrams) to symbolic and abstract forms (formulas and mental manipulations).

Grauberg (1998) discussed specific language difficulties and provided suggestions for teachers and parents. She targeted the following areas as typical weaknesses of children with language impairments that will have a direct impact on mathematics learning:

- symbolic understanding: diverse use of number words, written symbols for number, place value and zero, relational signs, money, and time symbols
- organizational skills: understanding the decimal system, organizing quantities, organizing word problems, and spatial organization demands
- memory: learning the first 10 numbers, learning to count to 100 and beyond, learning number facts, and retrieval problems that occur with various topics
- relative concepts and vocabulary: concepts with variable points of reference, time, space, comparisons, and quantities
- auditory discrimination: discrimination between similar number words or forms of numbers (14, 14th, and 40)
- social interaction: listening to others, asking questions, participating in the back-and-forth nature of conversations, accepting suggestions, and being aware of the contributions of others

Students should be asked to express math sentences, concepts, and processes orally as they are working with math. They should be asked to read math sentences aloud, to explain the steps in a process, or share how they came up with a solution to a problem. Teachers should deliberately increase the verbal response rate of each student within learning contexts, whether they are in whole group or small group settings. Typical students benefit from time in cooperative group activities because each student has the opportunity to use more language and contribute more often. However, if not monitored closely by the teacher, these activities can mask nonparticipation of a reluctant student or other students may feel obliged to speak for that student.

The teacher's language is also directly related to student learning. Teachers should be cognizant of their math language used with students. They should build student understanding of terms by connecting language use with hands-on experiences, being consistent with terminology, and using math language redundantly as students gain understanding. Teachers who don't have a math background should make an extra effort to research the most current and appropriate terminology before delivering instruction to students. For example, students in the 1960s and 1970s "borrowed" and "carried." Today's teachers use the term "regrouping" for these place-value conversions.

Mathematics language is challenging for students—especially those with language-based disabilities. Teachers need to be aware that mathematics vocabulary often has confusing meanings for children (Thompson & Rubenstein, 2000; Rubenstein & Thompson, 2002). For example, some words have different meanings in everyday English and mathematics: right, foot, reflection (see Figure 4.4). Other math words have more than one meaning within mathematics: round, square, side, second. Teachers can explore word origins (see, for example, Rubenstein, 2000), use literature, and have children create their own definitions to enhance mathematics vocabulary learning.

Students whose primary language is not English or who use English dialects may have language-related problems when learning mathematics. Most importantly, assessment practices must yield information on individual mathematics concept understanding and linguistic background (Gutiérrez, 2002). Assessment must be authentic, taking into account the student's prior experiences with mathematics, facility with language, and cultural and parental attitudes about mathematics. Students' language and cultural differences should be viewed as resources rather than obstacles.

The NCTM (1998) recommended mathematics instruction in both first and second languages. Students benefit from heterogeneous groupings to promote cross-linguistic communication among students and the code switching that is required as students are able to consider concepts in two languages. Teachers should increase their focus on mathematics language, build on students' background knowledge and interests, and hold high expectations.

Teachers should stress the language of mathematics by restating questions in different ways, reinforcing new vocabulary through visual aids and other devices, and building on linguistic and mathematical prior knowledge. Mathematics tasks that involve reading, such as textbook examples and word problems, may be particularly challenging for students who are learning English. Strategies such as paraphrasing, explaining the

Figure 4.4
Confusing Mathematics Terminology

material to a partner, and drawing schematic diagrams may assist students in interpreting the important information and what is being asked. It is critical that students' reading levels not determine their mathematics levels and therefore block access to more advanced concepts.

It is not necessary for teachers to be fluent in several other languages to meet the needs of English language learners. However, teachers should be aware of how linguistic and cultural differences affect mathematics learning and the individual characteristics of the students they serve. Teachers who establish supportive learning communities that allow for high levels of interaction will allow them to listen to and observe students and scaffold mathematics concept understanding.

▲■▲●▲■●▲■●▲■●▲■●▲■●▲■●▲■●▲■●▲■●▲■●▲■●▲■

TRY THIS
Focus on the language demands of the following activities.
1. Read the following sentence aloud:

   To reduce a common fraction to its lowest terms, also called simplifying, consider the greatest common factor and divide both the numerator and denominator by that factor.

2. Simplify the expression and *explain* your process: $(2x^2 + 3y - 7y + 5y^2)/2y$

▼■▼●▼■▼●▼■▼●▼■▼●▼■▼●▼■▼●▼■▼●▼■▼●▼■▼●▼■▼●▼■▼

9. *Recognize the power of strategies to transcend topics and create independent learners.* A strategy is an individual's approach to a task, including how a student thinks and acts when planning, executing, and evaluating performance on the task (Deshler & Lenz, 1989). Strategies allow students to acquire, store, and use information in a variety of new settings, thereby gaining more control of their learning.

Strategies are most effective when they can be applied to a range of task demands. Strategies for mathematics include problem solving (Poylá, 1973; Montague, 1992), creating memory devices (e.g., simple mnemonic devices to remember sequences or number facts), algebra word problems (Hutchinson, 1993), and calculation strategies (Mercer & Miller, 1992). While many students appear to develop strategies naturally, students with learning problems generally need explicit instruction in how to select and apply strategies.

Simple mathematics strategies can be demonstrated and practiced within one or two lessons. For example, an alternative strategy for solving multi-digit multiplication problems is called lattice multiplication because the drawing resembles latticework (Broadbent, 1987). This strategy, thought to originate in fifteenth-century Europe, reduces the confusion of regrouping several times over the same column of numbers and limits the memory demands on the student (see Figure 4.5). A simple strategy such as lattice multiplication maintains fidelity to the underlying mathematics concepts but is limited to a narrow range of applications.

More complex strategies take longer to teach but can be applied to a wider range of situations. Examples include Mercer and Miller's DRAW strategy for solving computations (see Chapter 6) and the problem-solving strategies discussed in Chapter 5. More complex strategies empower students to select and evaluate procedures for mathematics situations, to monitor their own performance, and to be aware of their executive processes during learning.

Teaching cognitive and metacognitive strategies has been cited as one of the most effective instructional approaches for students with disabilities (Swanson, Hoskyn, Sachee-Lee, & O'Shaughnessy, 1997; Lloyd, Forness, & Kavale, 1998). Included in this

● ● ● ● ● ● ● ● ●
For more information on computation strategies, see content strand B.
● ● ● ● ● ● ● ● ●

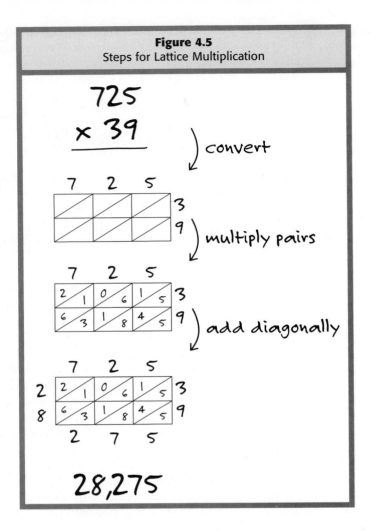

Figure 4.5
Steps for Lattice Multiplication

instruction are effective teaching techniques such as modeling (thinking aloud), providing guided practice with feedback, teaching for mastery, and teaching for generalization. Gradually the student assumes responsibility for practice, self-monitoring, and applying the strategy in actual learning settings. Students who have developed a repertoire of learning strategies are more successful in regular classroom placements (see, for example, Montague, 1997). Strategic learners eventually personalize strategies or develop their own strategies for dealing with instructional setting demands.

While this approach is generic and has been supported in a wide range of research, especially for students with disabilities, the most well known application is the **Strategies Intervention Model** (SIM) developed at the University of Kansas Institute for Research in Learning since 1977 (Deschler & Schumaker, 1986). One group of interventions in SIM is called **learning strategy interventions**. These interventions were developed to help students learn to deal successfully with secondary (content) setting demands. The learning strategies curriculum includes strategies for acquisition, storage, and expression or demonstration.

A more recent companion to the strategies are the **content enhancement routines**, used by teachers to enhance their delivery of content information in ways that promote understanding, recall, and strategic learning (Tralli, Colombo, Deshler, & Schumaker, 1996). Content enhancement routines include organizational routines (course organizer, unit organizer, chapter survey) and concept routines (concept mastery, concept anchoring, concept comparison). Using these routines results in strategic teaching.

TRY THIS

Some strategies are considered "mini-strategies" because they are relatively easy to develop and learn but can be applied in only limited contexts. Develop a mini-strategy for one of the following tasks:

1. remembering the order of operations in algebra
2. following an algorithm for long division
3. recalling the prefixes for the metric system (milli, centi, etc.)

---

10. *Ensure that mathematics instruction includes transfer-of-learning activities.* A baseball player knows that without follow-through with the bat, the ball will simply drop short. Without follow-through activities for mathematics learning, new concepts and skills will be isolated learning or even forgotten. According to the stages of learning model (acquisition–fluency–maintenance–application–generalization), critical aspects of follow-through are maintenance of skills over time, application of skills when appropriate in school-based or real-world situations, and generalization of skills to new problems or concepts.

The mathematics curriculum is cumulative and recursive, building on the same basic concepts over time to more advanced levels. However, students with learning problems may regress or forget concepts previously taught unless **maintenance** is an explicit goal. Ways to promote skill and concept maintenance are to build in periodic reviews and check points, teach for understanding rather than isolated skills, and teach memory and concept organization strategies. When gaps or losses are noted, skills and concepts should be re-taught.

Application of new skills and concepts in appropriate mathematics contexts is another goal of learning. When new concepts are taught, enough examples should be provided that students can view the range of applications. If concepts are taught in overly structured situations, their transfer power will be limited. For example when teaching the concept of factoring, the narrow view is to teach students to consider a number's factors as in the multiplication facts. Factors for 12 include 4×3, 2×6, and 1×12. This concept will have limited applications for students unless they explore related number theory and concepts (e.g., number patterns, divisibility, common factors, larger numbers, and strategies for representing numbers in multiple forms). When a student moves on to factoring polynomials, these concepts can be applied.

Generalization is similar to application but refers to a broader range of situations and novel contexts. These situations may be in other subject areas in school or in the world outside school. Mathematics concepts are necessary in many science and social studies contexts. Teachers should work together to identify and reinforce common concepts. Home, community, and work situations require mathematics skills ranging from the simplest computations to the more complex problem solving involving multiple concepts. Word problems and performance tasks can simulate these situational requirements. Chapter 7 describes incorporating these applications within a mathematics program.

In their research-based principles for high-quality and effective instruction, Kame'enui, Carnine, Dixon, Simmons, and Coyne (2002) described three that are particularly relevant for transfer of learning. **Conspicuous strategies** are those that are taught explicitly and that clearly connect the skill or concept with its use. **Primed background knowledge** refers to the importance of knowing students' prior knowledge and using that to build new concepts. Previous learning is constantly linked to new learning. **Judicious review** is defined as "the process of repeatedly considering material in sensible and well-advised ways" (p. 14). It is not mindless drill and practice but carefully selected review to cap off other effective instructional strategies. Teachers who design instruction that includes transfer-of-learning opportunities are more likely to see long-term student benefits.

TRY THIS

Select one of the following mathematics concepts and develop at least two appropriate applications (in later mathematics, in another school subject, or in the real world):
1. exponents
2. average
3. volume

PLANNING AND DELIVERING INSTRUCTION

The previous section provided global principles for providing mathematics instruction. Those guidelines can be used as planning tools for developing instructional sequences that would encompass a unit or portion of a unit of instruction. A planning matrix derived from the principles becomes a tool for instructional planning.

Planning with Principles in Mind

For more information on fractions and equivalence, see content strand D.

The ten principles of mathematics instruction are benchmarks for unit planning. This section provides examples of this planning at two grade-level spans: 3 through 5, and 9 through 12. Figure 4.6 illustrates a plan for a unit on equivalent fractions. (A blank planning matrix can be found in the Appendix.)

Figure 4.6
Application with Equivalent Fractions

Equivalent Fractions: 3rd to 5th grade levels

Principles in Question Form	Brainstorming Lesson Content
1. What are the "big ideas" that provide underlying concepts and connections?	Equivalency in broader terms Connections to other forms of equivalency (equations with whole numbers, expressions of the same in different terms)
2. What essential prior knowledge and skills do my students have?	Addition, subtraction, multiplication, and division concepts and fluency with facts; concept of factor; concept of simple fractions at concrete level
3. How can we promote positive attitudes in this unit?	Use materials of interest to students Play the Fraction Track Game (NCTM Illuminations)
4. What problem-solving context would be appropriate?	Measuring pieces of cloth for a quilt (we would use only 1/2's 1/4's, 1/8's, and 1/16's with this problem) Other possible applications: ribbons, buttons, tiles, diagrams
5. What sequence of instruction is needed?	Begin with cut out pieces to manipulate with representational drawings (rulers, number lines, and fraction strips), then teach with numbers and equations
6. How explicit should the instruction be for this content?	The unit should begin with guided discovery but provide more explicit instruction for the strategies involving comparing and changing fractions.
7. How can I provide variety within structure?	Vary materials and practice activities; maintain the structure of warm-up, model, practice, and apply.
8. What mathematics language is critical for understanding?	Fraction Equivalent Equal Set Greatest common factor (GCF) Proper fraction Improper fraction Numerator Denominator
9. What strategies would be helpful?	Develop strategies for: 1. compare two fractions and apply cross-multiplication 2. from one fraction, multiply or divide the numerator and denominator by the same number 3. to find the simplest form, divide numerator and denominator by the GCF
10. How can I plan for transfer-of-learning?	In the future unit on algebraic sentences, review equivalence and apply to the two sides of equations; solving those equations using concepts from rational numbers.

Notice that the NCTM process standards are all embedded in this planning chart—problem solving, reasoning, communication, connections, and representation.* This plan also reminds the teacher to consider the students' prior knowledge and interests, to brush up on the related concepts of equivalence, and to identify needed resources for instruction.

General education textbooks that introduce and "teach" equivalent fraction concepts and skills typically state the definition of equivalent fractions, provide one or two rules for finding equivalents, offer drawings of number lines or fraction strips, and provide practice with solving equations. What should the instructional sequence look like for the plan in Figure 4.6? The lessons could be designed as follows:

Lesson one. Introduce the problem. Seek student input to gauge understanding of mathematical concepts and language. "Today we need to cut out cloth pieces for the quilt we are making for our class volunteer. The pieces are quadrilaterals related proportionally to each other in size. Here are drawings of each shape with the dimensions for one size. For example, this rectangle is $2\frac{1}{2}$ by $3\frac{1}{4}$ inches. We need to make that size and double and triple sizes as well. What materials will we need?"

Lesson two. Ask students to solve the problem in small groups using materials and guidance from the teacher. "Here are the materials you listed yesterday for making each piece of the quilt." Model two or three examples eliciting student help. Assign each group three shapes to calculate and cut.

Lesson three. Discuss the students' findings. Ask which pieces were easiest and hardest to figure out. What strategies did students use? Can we develop strategies for doubling and tripling the dimensions of each shape and then for finding the exact measure on our rulers? Chart out students' recommendations on the board, point out patterns with fractional parts of inches.

Lesson four. Explain that the class will use the work from the previous lessons to develop some methods for comparing and reducing fractions. Make sure students are able to say the names of proper fractions ($\frac{1}{2}, \frac{2}{5}, \frac{7}{8}, \frac{10}{13}$) and describe what they mean. Why did the fractions $\frac{8}{16}, \frac{4}{8}$, and $\frac{2}{4}$ (write on board) all turn out to be the same as $\frac{1}{2}$? Ask for student explanations and listen to reasoning and language. One strategy for finding out if two fractions really represent the same number—are equivalent—is to write them side-by-side and cross multiply (see Figure 4.7). Ask yourself, is 1×8 equal to 2×4? If so, the fractions are equivalent.

Show two more examples using the same exacting language. Then pair students up to decide whether any of 10 sets of simple fractions on note cards are equivalent.

Lesson five. Review the method for deciding whether two fractions are equivalent. Ask for students to explain the method. Tell the students that they also need to know how to create a new fraction that is equivalent to one given. Sometimes they will need one with a

*Reprinted with permission from *Principles and Standards for School Mathematics*, copyright 2000, by the National Council of Teachers of Mathematics. All rights reserved. Standards are listed with permission of the Council of Teachers of Mathematics (NCTM). NCTM does not endorse the content or validity of these alignments.

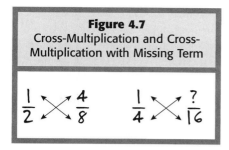

Figure 4.7
Cross-Multiplication and Cross-Multiplication with Missing Term

specific denominator, and sometimes they will need one with the lowest possible numbers—called the simplest terms.

If you have a fraction like $\frac{2}{4}$ and you want to rename it so it means the same but the denominator is a larger number like 16, you set up the fraction like we did before but there is one number missing in the numerator position (see Figure 4.7). For this we also cross multiply, saying $2 \times 16 = 32$, so $4 \times$ what number is 32? That's right, 8. Can anyone think of another method for finding the missing number?

What if we want to find the simplest fraction? For that we need to find the largest number we can think of that will divide into both the numerator and denominator. This is called the greatest common factor. How can we remember that? For $\frac{2}{4}$ that would be the number 2. What fraction would be left after dividing this way? Yes, $\frac{1}{2}$. You can check that by again using cross multiplication to see if the fractions are equivalent. Let's do a couple more together and then today we're going to practice with our individual white boards.

Lesson six. Begin with a review of the methods for comparing for equivalence, creating a new equivalent fraction, and finding the simplest fraction. Ask students to explain the methods. Listen for concept comprehension, clarity in method sequence, and language. Pose a new problem to check understanding.

Customize this sequence. How can the teacher address the needs of students with significant learning problems within this lesson sequence? One method is predicting or observing specific types of learning problems and building in adaptations and extensions that directly address those issues. Teachers employing a mastery learning model (see Bloom, 1971 and Guskey, 1997) use a pre-unit assessment that includes prerequisite skills and concepts as well as unit concepts to determine student learning needs, prior knowledge, and misconceptions. For the equivalent fraction example, typical problems might include:

a. Difficulty with new mathematics language: Use terminology clearly, consistently, and introduce only two or three new terms in one lesson. Use strategies to teach the difference between confusing terms such as GCF and LCM. For example, GCF can refer to pieces of a puzzle. The factor will be smaller or equal to either of the numbers. LCM can remind you of multiplying rabbits—the answer will be larger than both numbers.

b. Gaps in prior knowledge. Do a brief pretest or review session to determine prior knowledge. If necessary, teach mini-lessons to supplement skills.

● ● ● ● ● ● ● ● ●
For more information
on correlation, see
content strand E.
● ● ● ● ● ● ● ● ●

c. Poor alignment of written numbers and equations. Provide graph paper for recording equations.

d. Problems applying skills to a novel problem. When introducing the novel problem, ask for students to identify similarities. Review strategies that will be useful. Provide multiple examples for application.

e. Poor recall of sequence of operations. Teach mnemonic devices or other memory tools to assist recall. Allow the student to use alternative methods that make sense if they are mathematically valid (will hold up for future applications). Have peers tutor the steps with their own language.

TRY THIS

Analyze the abbreviated lessons above for effective instructional methods. How would you assess individual student learning? What other mathematics concepts are connected within this series of lessons?

Another planning example is appropriate for ninth- through twelfth-grade content in data analysis and probability—the concept of *correlation*. This plan incorporates strong understanding of the data analysis strand across the curriculum, terminology for data analysis that is consistent with that of algebra and geometry, and all five of the NCTM process standards.*

The sequence of instruction for developing the concept *correlation coefficient* (Figure 4.8) could be as follows:

Lesson 1. Lead a discussion and brainstorming session on everyday events or phenomena that are likely related. For example, hours studying and grades, or the amount of car repair costs and number of oil changes per year. Why might the two categories of data be related? How can we find out? Select one investigation that can be conducted by class members with relatively little time or cost. For example, collect data on students' hand and foot lengths. Collect the data and graph it as a whole class or in small groups. Discuss the findings. Use terminology clearly and expect students to use the terminology: x and y coordinates, scatter plot, variables, line, and positive or negative slopes.

Lesson 2. Using the previous lesson's graphs, discuss the conclusions that can be made about the data. Provide each group of students with a pre-designed data set. Have students graph the data either by hand or by using a computerized graphing tool. Each group's members should describe their graph. Introduce the term *correlated* and point out that the groups with graphs that formed a line or almost formed a line had variables that were correlated. We can't say that one variable causes the other but we can say they are negatively or positively correlated and to what degree, or not correlated.

Lesson 3. Today your groups will be plotting data using a technology tool that automatically calculates the regression line and a special statistic called the correlation coefficient. Use examples from the previous lesson to explain the meaning of various values of r (from -1 to $+1$). Model two examples for the class, then provide each group

*Reprinted with permission from *Principles and Standards for School Mathematics*, copyright 2000, by the National Council of Teachers of Mathematics. All rights reserved. Standards are listed with permission of the Council of Teachers of Mathematics (NCTM). NCTM does not endorse the content or validity of these alignments.

Figure 4.8
Application with Correlation Coefficients

Correlation Coefficients: 9th to 12th grade levels

Principles in Question Form	Brainstorming Lesson Content
1. What are the "big ideas" that provide underlying concepts and connections?	The relationship between two or more variables can be explored using tools such as graphing, equations, and charts and can inform us of important connections by which to make decisions. A correlation is a different relationship than cause-and-effect.
2. What essential prior knowledge and skills do my students have?	Graphing and interpreting linear equations Negative and positive integers Interpreting descriptive data
3. How can we promote positive attitudes in this unit?	Use examples of interest to students Use technology such as the regression plotting tool at http://illuminations.nctm.org/imath/912/LinearRelationships/index.html
4. What problem-solving context would be appropriate?	Analyzing data from surveys, census charts, or actual observations
5. What sequence of instruction is needed?	Collect data from surveys or publications, graph or chart data, interpret graphs (primarily at the representational level)
6. How explicit should the instruction be for this content?	Guided Discovery with the group graphs, the explicit modeling of coordinate plane graphing, and terms and technology use
7. How can I provide variety within structure?	Vary examples of data, vary representations—chart, graph, technology applications
8. What mathematics language is critical for understanding?	Graphing terminology (x and y coordinates, coordinate plane, scatter plot, slope) Terms related to measures of center and dispersion Linear equations represented in graph form Least squares regression lines Functions Predictions Positive and negative integers
9. What strategies would be helpful?	Strategies may be needed for: —modeling language that accurately describes correlations —recalling the possible values of the correlation coefficient r and how to interpret values
10. How can I plan for transfer of learning?	Skills will be transferred to extended use of the graphing calculator and trigonometric concepts.

a new set of data to graph and interpret. Have students report their findings by using the correct terminology and defending their conclusions.

Lesson 4. Guide student groups to conduct their own investigations, graphing and interpreting data, and reporting their findings back to the class. Allow for "what if" explorations with linear equations, predictions, and other extensions.

Customize this sequence. What problems might students with significant learning problems have with this lesson sequence?

a. Using mathematics terminology accurately. Use a strategic approach for helping students recall new terms such as *correlation*. "The word *relation* is within correlation and begins with an *r*." Introduce only two or three new terms within each lesson in the sequence. Make sure students are using the terms in their group work and reporting. Post key terms on a chart or bulletin board.

b. Working in small groups. Teach group work strategies explicitly, provide ground rules, plan assessments for group and individual performances.

c. Understanding number relationships in the band between -1 and $+1$. Draw a long number line on chart paper and label tenths and hundredths in different colors. Use this line when illustrating positive, negative, weak, and perfect correlations.

d. Creating an accurate graph. Use pre-labeled coordinate planes on graph paper or allow students to create graphs on white boards that are erasable. Provide prompting questions such as, "Along which axis is the x-coordinate found?" Repeat the same wording until students systematically graph each coordinate pair without assistance. Using a computer-generated graphing system solely may cause students to misunderstand the concepts being taught.

▲■▲●▲■●▲■●▲■●▲■●▲■●▲■●▲■●▲■●▲■
TRY THIS
For the lesson sequences on correlation, what other mathematics concepts are connected? How would you assess student learning? What resources would be required?
▼■▼●▼■▼●▼■▼●▼■▼●▼■▼●▼■▼●▼■▼●▼■▼

Lesson-Specific Planning

The sequences described in the previous section addressed units or parts of units of instruction, across a number of class periods. Teachers must also engage in lesson-specific planning and instructional delivery. In addition to the overall planning matrix for the unit or sequence of instruction, teachers should consider nature of content, student grouping patterns, and effective instructional strategies specific to the lesson objective(s).

Nature of content. While explicit or implicit content types help determine the use of direct instruction or guided discovery, the teacher also must consider whether the lesson objectives address discrimination, fact, rule, procedural, concept learning, or problem solving (Mastropieri & Scruggs, 1994). These different types of learning, first described by Robert Gagné (1970), emphasize the levels of skills needed for learning situations and require different instructional considerations.

Discrimination learning is simply discriminating one stimulus from another. Students have to discriminate letters, numbers, and other visual symbols, colors, shapes, objects, names, and so forth. Discrimination learning is an important foundation for other types of learning. To teach students to discriminate, teachers use examples and nonexamples, modeling, and prompts with feedback. For example, students may be discriminating rectangles from other two-dimensional shapes. The teacher would show lots of examples of rectangles as well as shapes that are not rectangles. Then students would be asked to identify examples as rectangles or not.

Factual learning is establishing a basic association that follows a stimulus-response pattern. For example given $7 + 4$, the response is 11. The perimeter of a polygon is the sum of its sides. One yard is the same as 36 inches. Sometimes factual learning should be fluent, sometimes it must be sequential, and other times it is a prerequisite for concept learning. Factual learning is usually accomplished through repetition, drill and practice, and mnemonic strategies.

Rule learning usually incorporates discrimination and fact learning but allows students to generalize learning to new examples. For example, to convert an improper fraction to a mixed number one divides the denominator into the numerator. Math rules are generally consistent, but other rules, such as phonics rules, may be unpredictable. For example the letter k is always silent before an n, but "when two vowels go walking"—the first says its name only 45 percent of the time (Lerner, 2000). Rules are also taught through examples, modeling, and repetitive practice.

Procedural learning is important for the execution of a sequence of tasks such as starting a computer program, applying a math algorithm, or solving a multi-step mathematics problem. It often involves discrimination, fact, and rule components. Procedures are taught by modeling, providing application activities, and giving corrective feedback. In mathematics there is usually more than one effective procedure for achieving a solution.

Concepts can range from very simple (shape) to complex (fractals). Concept understanding is difficult to measure, even at the simplest levels. Students may demonstrate understanding by giving examples or nonexamples, identifying the concept in a novel situation, or using the concept in an analogy or broader concept. Some concepts are quite concrete: linear measurement, percents, frequency distributions, and area. The most difficult concepts are abstract: dimensions, probability, proof. Concept understanding is developed through the use of examples and nonexamples, rules, guided experiences, models, analogies, and concept maps.

A final content type is **problem solving.** In the mathematics standards, problem solving is a primary goal of instruction. Problem solving situations in today's curriculum are realistic, complex, and frequently require interdisciplinary approaches. Problem solving is usually taught through strategic approaches; lots of practice and analysis of problem types; cooperative group work; and instruction in estimation, alternative procedures, and strategies (Reid & Stone, 1991).

Student grouping approaches.   Mathematics topics lend themselves to various student groupings for learning activities. Students solve problems, conduct investigations, and present data collection findings in groups. The most common peer-mediated instructional approaches are cooperative learning and peer tutoring, both of which take on several versions.

Cooperative learning involves small student teams, usually of varying ability, working together on a common problem or task. Groups may include two to five or six students and tasks can be short-term (a few minutes) or long-term (over the course of a unit). Some examples of cooperative group activities are: constructing a model replica of a significant building, researching local views on a new road, contrasting various geometric properties, developing an alternative algorithm, and creating a new word problem.

Extensive research on cooperative learning since the early 1970s has documented its effectiveness in groups involving students with special needs (Johnson, Johnson, & Maruyama, 1983; Slavin, 1984). In a review of 99 experimental studies, Slavin (1995) concluded that most studies demonstrated equal academic benefits for low, average, and high achieving students. He also cited generally positive effects on the acceptance of students with disabilities in integrated settings using cooperative learning, but cautioned that studies need to more carefully describe the activities and interactions being compared. Others have warned that cooperative learning sometimes leads to less effective learning than individual work and requires at least as much planning as traditional instruction (Levin & Druyan, 1993).

The format of cooperative learning models vary and include the jigsaw approach, group investigations, competitive teams, team-accelerated instruction, complex instruction, and structured dyadic methods (Olsen & Platt, 1992; Slavin, 1995). In each model, the teacher assigns student roles, structures the group process, facilitates student interactions, and evaluates group and/or individual performance. Some cautions have been noted. Slavin warned about the "free rider" effect in which some group members do all the work. This problem can be addressed with diffusion of responsibility strategies. Others are concerned about overemphasis on competition, content integrity, and stagnant student groupings—all of which should be addressed with careful planning and knowledge of students.

Peer tutoring, a cooperative and structured dyadic method, involves one student assisting another in the acquisition or reinforcement of specific skills. Students may be of the same or different ages and students with disabilities can be the tutor or tutee, or take turns in each role. Peer tutoring may be an informal pairing of students for a one-session skill review or a highly structured class-wide system. Peer tutoring has been demonstrated to be effective with students with disabilities in increasing academic performance and improving social acceptance and school behaviors (Eiserman, 1988; Scruggs, Mastropieri, & Richter, 1985). Fundamentally, peer tutoring seeks to increase the amount of academic learning time and active responding in a guided learning situation.

Potential problems with peer tutoring must be acknowledged. These include overuse of some students as tutors, lack of training of tutors in appropriate techniques, using peer tutoring for activities and instruction that should be provided by the teacher, and failing to monitor the success of the peer tutoring effort (Olson & Platt, 1992). With the new emphasis on after-school programs for remediation and new early reading programs, peer tutoring is being used in more settings than ever. For peer tutoring to be successful, tutors should be trained and know what is expected, parents should understand the benefits of the arrangement for their children, and cooperating teachers should hold the same philosophy about the program.

An example of a research-based class-wide peer-tutoring program is the Peer-Assisted Learning Strategies (PALS) program developed at Vanderbilt University (Fuchs, Fuchs, Mathes, & Martinez, 2002). Implemented with both reading and mathematics content, the PALS program incorporates the instruction of effective learning strategies with frequent responses, immediate corrective feedback, increased academic engaged time, and social support. In mathematics, the PALS approach addresses both basic skills and higher-order cognitive strategies (Fuchs et al., 1997).

Effective instructional techniques. Research over the past thirty-plus years has consistently supported several generic instructional techniques that are effective with students with disabilities and other learning problems. The body of research from which these findings are drawn has been called the "effective instruction literature."

A variable closely linked to increasing achievement is the amount of **academic learning time.** Academic learning time is the time within the allocated time for a particular subject that is actually used actively engaged in learning (Wilson, 1987). Factors that can steal academic learning time include poor classroom management procedures, teaching material already mastered, poor preparation, student off-task behaviors, external interruptions, scheduling problems, and ineffective practice and response methods. Many studies on allocated and engaged learning time have indicated the serious eroding of learning time to nonacademic activities or learner disengagement. For example, in studies on pull-out resource models, only about 80 percent of available time was typically allotted to academic learning (Pemberton & Smith, 1994) and of the allotted time, only about 44 percent was spent actively engaged in relevant instruction (Haynes & Jenkins, 1986). Percentages for regular classrooms and self-contained special education classrooms were even lower.

Even more significant for student achievement than academic learning time is **active responding time** (Greenwood, Delquadri, & Hall, 1984), or the time that students spend making active, overt responses. Strategies that promote overt responding and active learning include: choral responding (oral and with response cards), guided note-taking, sharing pairs strategies, rapid-paced questioning, guided cooperative group sessions, guided practice, and the elimination of time wasters and passive learning activities. Teachers should hone their questioning skills so that students are called on equally and randomly, corrective feedback is immediate, and questions scaffold students' understanding.

When beginning discrete segments of instruction, the teacher should provide some type of **advance organizer.** An advance organizer is material that is presented "in advance of and at a higher level of generality, inclusiveness, and abstraction than the learning task itself" (Ausubel & Robinson, 1969, p. 606). Advance organizers may be verbal, nonverbal, or written. They serve to prepare students for the learning task, increase comprehension and understanding, and ensure attention and readiness for learning. Some examples include: outline on board, statement of lesson objective, review of previous lesson, handout with parts missing, incomplete concept map, picture, even a quick pre-test. In a direct instruction lesson, the teacher may state the lesson objective explicitly; "Today we are going to classify three-dimensional objects by their major characteristics." For a guided discovery lesson the advance organizer might be more general, "By the end of the lesson today you will demonstrate a new way to solve a math problem." And for a lesson with student grouping, "Today we're going to work in our number groups, but before we get into our groups, let's look at our problem today and review group procedures."

Another critical feature of good instruction is **modeling.** Whether it is demonstrating how to push the keys using an overhead projector calculator, showing students the steps of an algorithm, or "thinking out loud" the mental processes of solving a word problem, modeling is an important step in the acquisition of a new concept or skill. Models help students visualize their goals and see the steps required to reach those goals.

In most direct instruction lessons, modeling is followed by increased involvement of students in a **guided practice** phase. Students practice a new skill together with the teacher. The teacher closely monitors student responses, prompts the new skill, and provides immediate, corrective, and supportive **feedback.** Guided practice ensures correct practice, immediate feedback, and more successful independent practice later. Generally teachers require a high level of success during guided practice (between 80 and 90 percent) before allowing students to work independently.

Types of Mathematics Lessons

Whether a teacher is planning a mathematics lesson for a large group, small group, or individual student, he or she must decide on the degree of explicitness, as highlighted in principle six previously. Most mathematics lessons are designed as either explicit, direct instruction; guided discovery; or a combination, although some teachers may attempt a pure discovery approach. A related consideration for lesson planning is the nature of the instructional objectives. Is the lesson addressing lower-level discrimination and association tasks or higher-level concepts and processes?

Direct instruction.   The instructional approach with the most research support for students with disabilities is the **Direct Instruction** model (Lloyd, Forness, & Kavale, 1998). Developed by Bereiter and Engelmann (1966) to enable disadvantaged children to master early language, reading, and math concepts, the model has since evolved into a generic approach. The direct instruction approach is known by its teacher-directed, systematic instruction (Gersten & Carnine, 1984) that involves explicit strategies, mastery learning, teacher-directed presentation and modeling, relevant and varied practice, error correction, independent practice, and cumulative review. Within each lesson the teacher employs effective methods such as advance organizers, corrective feedback, active student responding, and formative assessment of student learning. The teacher makes instruction extremely explicit in this model; students are informed of instructional objectives, expected mastery levels, individual performance, and generalization expectations.

This model has also been translated into commercial curriculum programs in reading and math (Reading Mastery, Corrective Reading, and Corrective Mathematics—published by Science Research Associates). These materials include scripts for the teacher to use during instruction and are organized for choral responding, immediate and positive correction, and rapid pace. The materials developed by the authors of Direct Instruction are often referred to as "capital" DI lessons. Teachers who develop their own lessons using DI components are using (lower-case) direct instruction methods. An example of a direct instruction lesson is featured in Figure 4.9. More

Figure 4.9
Direct Instruction Mathematics Lesson

Lesson objective:	Students will write equivalent forms for 2 of 3 fractions.
Curriculum standard:	Content standard: number and operation; State standard 1.5.2: students will identify equivalent fractions.
Opening:	1. Review concepts from previous class session on doubling and tripling the dimensions of shapes for the class quilt. Review the names of common proper fractions ($\frac{1}{2}$, $\frac{2}{5}$, $\frac{7}{8}$, $\frac{9}{16}$) and their meanings. Review the concept of mixed numbers ($2\frac{1}{4}$, $5\frac{3}{4}$, $4\frac{1}{3}$).
	2. Today we will identify equivalent fractions and work on procedures for finding those to make our calculations easier. Equivalent fractions are another name for the same amount.
Body:	3. Explain that there are three methods that will assist students in identifying equivalent fractions. The first begins with one fraction ($\frac{1}{2}$) and generates other equivalent fractions. The second method is for evaluating whether two given fractions ($\frac{1}{2}$ and $\frac{2}{4}$) are equivalent. We will study the third method—reducing a fraction to its lowest terms—in a later lesson.
	4. Demonstrate the first method by showing the multiplication of both numerator and denominator by the same number. For $\frac{1}{2}$, multiply both parts of the fraction by 2, 3, 4, 5, and 6 with the resulting equivalent fractions. Show these equivalent parts using fraction bars. Repeat with $\frac{1}{3}$ and $\frac{1}{5}$, eliciting student assistance. Let's call this method "fraction expansion of equivalent terms."
	5. Demonstrate the second method by showing two equivalent fractions ($\frac{1}{2}$ and $\frac{2}{4}$) and the cross-multiplication procedure. Repeat for more nonequivalent and equivalent fractions ($\frac{1}{3}$ and $\frac{2}{5}$; $\frac{3}{4}$ and $\frac{6}{8}$; $\frac{2}{7}$ and $\frac{3}{8}$). Let's call this method "cross-checking for equivalent terms."
	6. Assign small student groups three sets of fractions to find equivalents (fraction expansion) and check (cross-checking for equivalent terms). After each group's work, report on their findings by demonstrating one fraction for the class.
Close:	7. Review concept of equivalent fractions and the two methods for identifying.
	8. Assign each student three fractions to match with at least four equivalent forms. Tomorrow we will study the third method for working with equivalent fractions and apply all three methods to our quilt problem.
Evaluation:	Students' independent work.
Materials:	Overhead transparencies of two methods; fraction bars (overhead and student versions), practice problems on task cards.
Special provisions:	Anticipate problems with following sequence of steps—have students create posters showing both algorithms.

discussion on the Direct Instruction approach and the SRA mathematics materials can be found in Chapter 6.

Guided Discovery Learning.　Another lesson-specific approach particularly relevant to mathematics teaching is the **guided discovery learning** approach (Shulman & Keislar, 1966). While the origins of learning by discovery certainly cannot be established, the discovery learning movement in education has roots with Montessori (1912), Piaget and Inhelder (1969), and Bruner (1960).

Pure discovery learning, often called an indirect teaching method, literally means allowing students to "discover" associations, concepts, or rules through their own exploration and inductive processes (Glaser, 1966). This approach to mathematics learning is supported by radical constructivists, as was discussed in Chapter 2. Needless to say, with the exception of young children exploring their immediate environs, this method is ineffective and time-consuming for most students and teachers.

The early views of discovery learning have been challenged and modified into a more structured **guided discovery** approach (Shulman & Kieslar, 1966). Research comparing pure discovery learning with guided discovery has resulted in consistently more effective learning through teacher guidance (Mayer, 2004). Guided discovery includes many of the same effective techniques as the direct instruction approach but it differs in several critical aspects. The teacher does not immediately make the lesson objectives explicit; rather, students are encouraged to explore, usually with carefully selected materials, and come up with understandings and connections on their own. Students usually work in pairs or small groups during these explorations and discussions. After the initial discovery phase, the teacher employs skillful discussion techniques to ensure the lesson objectives are addressed. The content focus for a guided discovery lesson is on concepts, rules, and associations rather than facts and is particularly relevant in mathematics instruction. Contrast the guided discovery lesson depicted in Figure 4.10 with the lesson using the direct instruction approach in Figure 4.9.

Limited but promising research has been conducted on the effectiveness of guided discovery approaches for students with mild disabilities. One study compared disabled and nondisabled students' science achievement in direct instruction and discovery teaching conditions (Bay, Staver, Bryan, & Hale, 1992). After lessons on displacement, floatation, variables, and prediction, both groups (direct and discovery) learned equally well as measured by a posttest. However, the discovery-teaching group retained more learning after two weeks and students with learning disabilities in the discovery group generalized better than those in the direct instruction group. The authors concluded that areas of science (and related mathematics) such as process skill development, conceptual understanding, and problem solving have many implicit qualities and may be best taught through a discovery learning method. Even Rosenshine (1986) acknowledged that direct instruction may be most appropriate for explicit content (computation, decoding, rules) and suggested that other methods should be used for implicit, less structured content such as composition, literature analysis, and complex concepts.

The teacher planning and delivering an effective mathematics lesson is like the orchestra conductor preparing for a practice session before a special concert. The long-range planning has taken place with each unit outlined, like the orchestra's seasonal

Figure 4.10
Guided Discovery Mathematics Lesson

Lesson objective: Students will create an accurate line graph depicting a set of real data.

Curriculum standard: Content standard: statistics, data analysis, and probability.
State standard 5.2.7: create various graphs and interpret data.

Opening: 1. Review unit organizer on graphing data from the first day of the unit. Review previous class session on types of graphs.

2. The lesson in the next two to three days will involve graphing actual data.

Body: 3. Brainstorm with students everyday events or phenomena that are likely related. For example, hours studying and grades, the amount of car repair costs and number of oil changes a year, grades and SAT scores. Ask why the two might be related. How can we find out the exact relationship?

4. Today your groups are going to investigate the relationship between hand and foot lengths or arm and leg lengths. I want you to collect data from at least 25 students and present your findings in a graphical form of your choice. You will be exploring and discussing your data in your group, graphing it in any form you select, and discussing your graphs with the whole class in tomorrow's class.

5. Allow students time to collect data and begin graphs, completing work the following day.

6. Have each group show and explain their graph and results. Ask each group to interpret the relationship of related data (coordinate pairs) and resulting graphs. Draw on group results to discuss the concepts: x and y coordinates, line slope, positive or negative slopes, and correlation. Emphasize the graphing process on the coordinate plane, graphing another set of data on overhead or chart for the entire class.

7. Explain that graphs that formed a line or almost formed a line showed variables that were correlated. We can't say that one variable caused the other but we can say they are negatively or positively correlated and to what degree or not correlated. Demonstrate graphing one additional set of data with a different slope.

Close: 8. Assign individual students sets of data to graph and interpret.

Evaluation: Individual graphs with oral or written interpretations.

Materials: Data sets, tape measures, example graphs, graph paper (chart and individual sizes).

Special provisions: Anticipate problems with new vocabulary in step 6; develop visual or mnemonic devices to connect concepts to meanings. Students with trouble hand graphing should use larger graph paper or computerized graphing.

schedule. The students have been enrolled and introduced to the classroom routines, the teacher learning each student's interests, strengths, and needs—like the conductor selecting and orienting each musician to the overall plan with strengths and needs of individual musicians clearly identified. Now the teacher is ready to plan one lesson based on a clearly defined objective for the group and possibly some individual objectives, like the conductor planning the last practice session before the concert.

The following steps outline the process for planning a mathematics lesson that encompasses only one or two class sessions:

1. Identify the primary lesson objective, derived from the long-range or unit plan. For example, an elementary objective for a unit on fractions might be "learners will reduce 4 of 5 improper fractions to their lowest terms and verbally explain their procedure for one problem." For secondary students studying linear equations, "learners will solve for the variable in 4 of 5 simple equations and answer three oral questions about the arithmetic properties as applied in solutions."
2. Consult the unit planning matrix for the lesson's focus within the sequence, stage of learning, mathematics language, strategies, and other elements for planning.
3. Consider any individual student needs such as modified curriculum objectives or classroom management issues.
4. Decide the best strategy for assessing learner outcomes regarding the lesson objective. Assessment of lesson objectives should be embedded as much as possible within lesson activities.
5. Make a decision about the degree of explicitness of instruction for the lesson—direct instruction or guided discovery.
6. Consider the nature of the content in planning instructional techniques.
7. Design an appropriate instructional sequence, incorporating advance organizer, modeling, frequent student responses, student motivators, guided practice, and independent practice.
8. Make decisions about student grouping patterns during the lesson components.
9. Pull together materials and other resources to support the lesson activities.
10. Teach the lesson and reflect—make notes on learner problems with understanding and the effectiveness of various aspects of the lesson.

DEVELOPING A STUDENT-CENTERED MATHEMATICS CURRICULUM

The international studies on mathematics achievement conducted under the International Association for Evaluation of Education Achievement analyzed students' opportunities to learn mathematics. Analyses by McKnight and colleagues (1987) and Travers and McKnight (1985) showed wide variation in mathematics curricula among U.S. schools and found that curriculum differences were more important in explaining student achievement differences than instructional time, homework, class size, or teacher training (Wilson & Blank, 1999). More recent studies confirmed the critical role of curriculum focus in student achievement and added two related variables: teacher preparation and teaching practices (Grissmer & Flanagan, 1998).

By 1998 almost all states had developed new content standards based on the 1989 NCTM standards calling for focusing mathematics content on a smaller number of areas with greater depth and understanding. However, international studies found most U.S. teachers attempted to address sixteen to eighteen different topics in a year, while teachers in Japan spent 67 percent of their time addressing only four topics: geometry; congruence and similarity; functions, relations and patterns; and equations and formulas (Wilson & Blank, 1999). U.S. teachers spent 17 percent of their time on fractions and between 2 and 6 percent of their time on each of seventeen other topics.

Many teachers find they have plenty of ideas for teaching mathematics and a basic understanding of the general mathematics curriculum, but struggle with long-range planning. How can they organize units of study that will address the five content strands, incorporate the five processes of mathematics, and prepare students for the state or district tests at the same time? How can they address the needs of students of varying mathematics abilities and achievement levels within the same units of study? And, most importantly, how can a mathematics curriculum be student-centered while addressing national standards? This section offers several long-range planning examples for various grade levels and settings, regardless of the textbook or other materials.

Unit Planning in Mathematics

Teachers engaged in long-range planning through the use of instructional units have several options regarding the type of unit to design. The first decision should be whether units are planned for whole-class or small-group configurations. Planning common units for the whole class saves time, channels resources, and can still meet the individual needs of students and allow for small-group instruction. However, units of study may be planned for small groups or individuals when the whole group is too diverse in learning needs. In this case the teacher must plan for effective use of independent work time by students not engaged directly with the teacher—either in guided exploratory activities or independent practice.

A second decision is the type of unit. Mathematics units are most commonly planned by content topic (e.g., fractions, measurement, geometry), integrated theme (e.g., ocean study, baseball, architecture), or problem situation (e.g., community service project, planning a garden). Examples of these unit types for different grade level spans are found in the next sections.

Finally, teachers should consider a unit-planning approach that involves students and brings forward the big ideas, connections, and key processes within the unit. In addition to the planning matrix that accounts for effective mathematics instructional elements, a content unit organizer is helpful. *The Unit Organizer Routine* (Lenz, Bulgren, Schumaker, Deshler, & Boudah, 1994) provides such a tool. By introducing students to unit concepts, relationships, sequences, and processes through a unit map and using the unit map as a guide and review tool throughout the unit, students are more aware of unit connections, learning goals, and expectations (see Figure 4.11). On field tests, students of teachers who used the *Unit Organizer Routine* consistently scored an average of 15 points higher on unit tests than students of teachers who used it only irregularly (Boudah, Lenz, Bulgren, Schumaker, & Deshler, 2000).

Figure 4.11
Unit Organizer Routine

The Unit Organizer

NAME _____
DATE _____

④ **BIGGER PICTURE**

⟵——————— Making Representations ———————⟶

② **LAST UNIT/Experience**
Graphing Linear Equations

① **CURRENT UNIT**
Two-Dimensional Shapes

③ **NEXT UNIT/Experience**
Graphing Data

⑧ **UNIT SCHEDULE**

Days

1	Shapes around us
2–6	Properties of Polygons—explore
7–10	Coordinate Mapping
11–12	Properties in depth
13–15	Transformations
16–17	Properties of Circles
18–19	Comparing Properties
20–25	Culminating Project

⑤ **UNIT MAP**

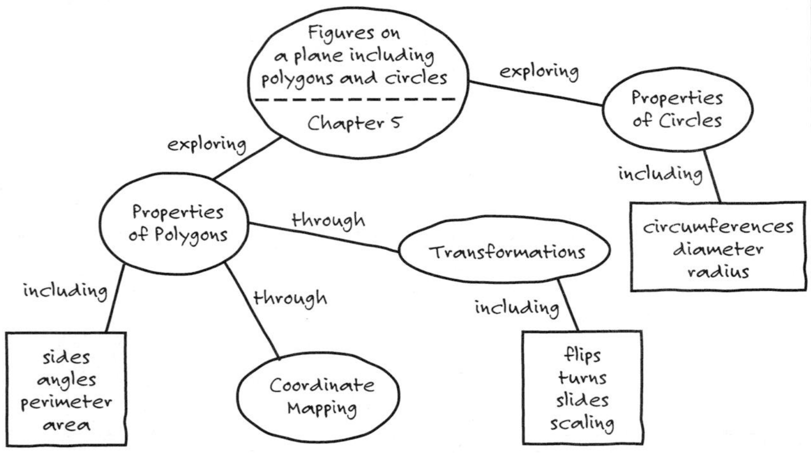

is about

Figures on a plane including polygons and circles

Chapter 5

exploring → Properties of Circles

including → circumferences diameter radius

exploring → Properties of Polygons

through → Transformations

including → flips turns slides scaling

including → sides angles perimeter area

through → Coordinate Mapping

⑦ **UNIT SELF-TEST QUESTIONS**

1. By what properties do various polygons differ?

2. How can a specific polygon drawn onto a coordinate plane be transformed?

3. How are the properties of circles related to those of polygons?

⑥ **UNIT RELATIONSHIPS**

compare
categorize
transform

This is a unit graphic organizer designed to focus student and teacher attention on the critical content related to math concepts using the Unit Organizer teaching device used in *The Unit Organizer Routine* (Lenz, Bulgren, Schumaker, Deshler, & Boudah, 1994). Unit device reprinted by permission. The unit organizer device is an instructional tool developed and researched at the University of Kansas Center for Research on Learning (Lenz, Bulgren, Schumaker, Deshler, & Boudah, 1994). It is a research-based tool that has been found to be effective with diverse student populations when used as designed. It is not effective if simply distributed to students. For more information on professional development on content enhancement routines including *The Unit Organizer Routine,* contact the University of Kansas Center for Research on Learning (785-864-4780; www.kucrl.org).

Figure 4.12
Topic-Driven Curriculum Plan

Week	Content
1–2	Review of number patterns, place value, and math games
3–5	Number and Operations I
6–8	Measurement
9	Applied Problem
10–13	Number and Operations II
14–17	Geometry
18	Applied Problem
19–22	Number and Operations III
23–25	Patterns, Functions, and Algebra
27	Applied Problem
28–30	Data, Probability, and Statistics
31	testing week
32–35	Number and Operations IV
36	Applied Problem

Teaching an elementary class by content units. The elementary mathematics class is typically an hour a day for the entire year of 36 weeks. Figure 4.12 provides an example of a long-range curriculum plan based on mathematics topics.

In the above example, each nine-week period includes two content-specific units capped with an application week. For the applied problem, the teacher should pose a multifaceted problem involving concepts from both units previously studied. Students could work in small heterogeneous groups or as a whole class. For example, after students worked through units on factors and measuring area, the teacher presents the following problem:

> Our school is to have new tile installed over the summer. Here is a floor plan of the areas to be tiled and the colors of tile for the pattern. We need to help the school figure out how many tiles of each color to order. What tools will we need to do this? What other information will we need?

The advantages of a topic-driven plan include the ease of finding supporting material in textbooks and other sources, the obvious alignment with curriculum frameworks, and the ability to address varying levels of skill within each unit.

Thematic planning for the middle-school class. For more experienced teachers, the thematic approach offers topic integration throughout each unit. A thematic approach to curriculum planning is the development of skills, often from more than one content area, through study of a major theme or activity. Figure 4.13 offers one example of a thematic approach during a year at the middle school level. Each 9-week period is devoted to study around a theme.

Figure 4.13
Thematic Approach to Curriculum Planning

Unit	Content Areas Addressed	Related Subject Areas
Cartography	Measurement Ratios Graphing Data	Social Studies English: Reading and Writing Travel Logs
Cooking	Measurement Fractions Linear Equations	Science
Architecture	Measurement Geometry Functions	Arts and Science
Baseball	Statistics Equations Decimals	Health and PE English: Biography and Fiction

The advantages of the thematic approach include the creativity and excitement about mathematics it can involve, the development of relationships and generalizations across mathematics and other curriculum topics, and the variety of real-world applications that can be made. But there are serious drawbacks. This approach requires knowing mathematical concepts deeply, seeking many more materials and resources, coordinating these units with other content areas (and other teachers), and making sure the levels of mathematics and the other content areas are all aligned with grade-level curriculum standards.

The final caveat is the most important. One group of teachers worked during the summer to align mathematics and science standards before developing integrated units of study at the second-grade level. The second-grade mathematics standards included "understanding the number system 1 to 100." The science standards listed "understanding the distances between planets." Presumably if second graders understood numbers to 100, then teachers could try to explain that Mars is a bunch of hundreds away from the Earth. In fact, on its closest orbit, Mars is 100 groups of 100 groups of 100 groups of 100 (100,000,000) miles away. Obviously those concepts exceeded the mathematical understanding of these second graders.

In another school, a fifth-grade teacher selected the theme of the ocean for the entire year and attempted to integrate all subject area units around the theme. The classroom was a wonderful place to be—the visitor had the sensation of being at the bottom of the ocean with the various sea life suspended from the ceiling and the shells on the floor. The teacher could have addressed the fifth-grade mathematics curriculum standards within that unit with a lot of planning. However, she settled on simplistic applications, such as adding simple fractions that represented types of seashells and comparing ocean depths of different locations. Her mathematics content was at a third-grade level, at best. Thematic approaches require extensive and joint planning but can be extremely effective for deep learning and generalization.

Weeks	Problem	Content and Processes
	Figure 4.14	
	Problem-Driven Curriculum Planning	
1–4	Student store stocking	Multiplication and division Probability and statistics Patterns and algebra Making representations
5–9	Props and costumes for the class play	Measurement Decimals and fractions Communication
10–13	A new road in the community	Measurement Geometry Patterns and algebra Connections
14–18	Weather patterns	Statistics and data analysis Decimals Measurement Connections and communication
19–22	The local habitat house building	Geometry Measurement Representations and connections
23–27	Preparations for field day	Measurement (metric distance and time) Statistics and data analysis Communication
28–31	Planning a garden	Geometry and measurement Algebra and functions Connections and reasoning
32–36	Summer project and travel planning	Small-group work using multiple Content areas and processes Student-created problems

Problem-based mathematics units.   As described for the principle "present concepts in problem-solving contexts," teachers often develop mathematics curriculum around problem situations for each unit. Figure 4.14 provides an example from an upper elementary class.

Like the thematic approach, a problem-driven approach requires extensive mathematics knowledge, resources, and planning. It also has the advantage of building in applications and developing problem-solving skills within meaningful contexts. The unit forms described above can also be combined with a problem context (problem + content, problem + thematic), or unit types can be alternated during the year.

Addressing different skill levels within the same unit.   Most general, special, or remedial mathematics teachers have students with different skill levels within the same group. For example, an elementary remedial class may include seven to nine students from third through fifth grades. Some of these students haven't mastered basic math facts or operations, some may be at early stages of understanding operations or have gaps in their learning, and some may know their facts and operations quite well but have problems with applications of these skills. Does the teacher create three instructional groups within this small class? The drawback with forming groups is that each would have guided or direct instruction only one-third of class time.

A more effective approach is to plan a whole-group warm-up, provide direct instruction at different levels simultaneously, and guide the practice through individualized monitoring. This approach can be supplemented with selective peer tutoring (see, for example, Bentz & Fuchs, 1996). To illustrate, if the topic is multiplication of multi-digit numbers, all students need a warm-up on the concept of multiplication and a quick fact review. Some students can work on two-digit by one-digit, while other students can work with larger numbers. The concepts are the same. Paired tutors could elaborate and reinforce the algorithm steps and self-questions during the process. The class period could close with students creating word problems for each other to solve.

Providing this type of multi-level instruction requires advanced preparation of all examples and materials. But the preparation time for three lessons would be as much or more.

Advanced Mathematics Study in High School

The number of mathematics credits for earning a high school diploma varies by state (and local district) from two to four credits, with a number of states specifically requiring Algebra I and Geometry. Students who are college bound should study precalculus and other advanced topics. However, states differ in how high school mathematics curriculum is designed, and therefore the related textbook adoptions and end-of-grade exams. Some states require specific topics by grade level (e.g., geometry, algebra) while others allow integrated topics within each grade level. The United States is the only industrialized country where some high schools still organize the mathematics curriculum into separate content courses. The NCTM standards recommend topic integration, even for content-specific coursework. Problem solving and making connections across content areas are critical standards for advanced mathematics study.

Figure 4.15 illustrates an integrated approach to an Algebra I course, typically taken in the ninth grade but sometimes divided into parts A and B over two years for one credit. High school teachers should plan together to assure progressive development of curriculum topics and integration of mathematics concepts across courses.

The challenge of those alternative high school schedules.   One 1990s answer to increasing content coverage at the high school level was to implement various alternative scheduling schemes (block or intensive scheduling). Although there are advantages for special education programs (see for example Santos & Rettig, 1999; Weller & McLeskey, 2000), very little research has been conducted to establish academic benefits of these

Figure 4.15
Integrated Algebra Course

Quarter	Algebra Topics	Integrated Mathematics Topics
1	Equations and Inequalities Linear Functions Matrices	Statistics: Probability concepts
2	Transformations Exponents	Geometry: Volume, Solids
3	Polynomials and Factoring Quadratic Functions	Statistical Analysis and Graphing
4	Radicals Rational Functions	Geometric Theorems and Properties

arrangements, especially for students with disabilities. These schedules have been devised primarily for management reasons—save time changing classes, reduce student opportunities for misbehavior, increase class time for labs and community-based programs, increase credits earned per year, and reduce lesson preparations for teachers.

The most common are the AB schedules, with classes alternating days, and the 4/4 semester schedules, with classes running 80 to 100 minutes long for only one semester. Many versions have been implemented, including schedules with four 80-minute periods and one 60-minute flex period, and those that meet either Monday and Wednesday or Tuesday and Thursday with alternating Fridays.

These alternative schedules can present problems for students with learning problems in both the use of instructional time and in long-term program planning. The limited research on block schedules for special education students recommends the use of an additional flex period for academic support or a full co-teaching model in mathematics classes (Bugaj, 1998; Weller & McLeskey, 2000).

The alternating day schedules for mathematics classes can be supported on alternative days for students with disabilities by resource or support time. The resource or remedial teacher can pre-teach and re-teach topics covered in the general mathematics class and provide more practice and generalization time. This support model requires close collaboration among general, special, and remedial mathematics teachers.

The long class periods may be a problem for students with disabilities unless an inclusive, co-teaching model is used. Is 100 minutes of math every day for one semester really equivalent to 50 minutes a day all year? Mathematically the time is equivalent. But how the time is used may not be. Two possible ways of dealing with this scheduling problem follow:

1. Pair a mathematics teacher with either a special education or remedial mathematics teacher and implement a full co-teaching model (see, for example, Cook & Friend,

1995). Structure a 80-minute class as if it were 5-40-10-20-5. The first 5 minutes is the warm-up time with mental math and estimation activities. During the 40-minute block a concept is introduced or continued from a previous class with a traditional model-guided practice format. The next 10-minute piece is for something different—to get up and move around, solve a puzzle, or read something math-related from the newspaper. The next 20-minute block would address a different math area than the first, but relationships would be developed. For example if equations were the first topic and geometry the second, then students could use equations to predict geometrical patterns. Or problem-solving applications could enhance the concept developed during the first part. The last 5 minutes provides time for a quick review, closure, and beginning homework assignments.

2. Team a mathematics teacher with a special education or remedial support teacher, divide the class into two periods (one for mathematics and one for support and study skills), and work all year. Teachers would swap groups of students in this model. Or plan to offer mathematics and English in 50-minute periods all year within the larger block time in a co-teaching model for both classes. One advantage of this approach is that students will not have an eight- to twelve-month gap in their mathematics learning.

Other recommendations and issues about block scheduling were discussed by Santos and Rettig (1999); Weller and McLeskey (2000); Bugaj (1998); and Bottge, Gugerty, Serlin, and Moon (2003). Issues and barriers included: special educators must work proactively to ensure schedules that meet individual student needs, no differences in achievement were found based on schedule alone, there was a need for more support teachers and collaboration among teachers, students were often confused by alternating schedules, and absences were magnified. Benefits for students: inclusion in mainstream classes with access to the regular mathematics curriculum, longer classes allow for more hands-on and in-depth learning, and additional support from either co-teaching or resource class models.

TEACHER COLLABORATION FOR INSTRUCTION

Most students with mathematics learning challenges are served in the general education classroom with some level of support from remedial or special education teachers. How can these professionals collaborate to provide the most effective instruction? What program models hold the most promise for this collaboration?

General education mathematics teachers may have no training in methods for teaching students with learning problems. They typically teach in single, large groups, using lessons that incorporate little or no differentiated instruction (Baker & Zigmond, 1990). General educators don't typically introduce specialized adaptations when confronted by student confusion or difficulty (Kagan & Tippins, 1991; Fuchs, Fuchs, & Bishop, 1992), even when co-teaching arrangements are used.

Many special education and remedial mathematics teachers have had no training in mathematics instruction or the training was limited to an elementary education mathematics course. These teachers' understanding of mathematics concepts in depth or across the curriculum may be likewise limited or just developing.

The most promising models for serving students with learning problems are the limited pull-out or support class model and the full co-teaching model. These models offer students the expertise of two professionals and the benefits of their collaboration. However, it should be emphasized that program model or setting alone will not result in learning. It is the quality of program implementation and resources that make the difference (Zigmond, 2003).

Students with more severe learning problems may be served for mathematics by a special educator alone. A promising model for this approach is for the special educator to specialize in mathematics and work closely with general education mathematics teachers, especially at the middle and high school levels. This model allows teachers to spend more time with quality preparation and provides students with a change in teachers during the school day. Some teachers specializing in mathematics serve two classes with a mixture of "resource" and "separate class" (pull-out) students, and work in valid co-teaching models for another couple of classes. The additional time is spent serving consultation-only students, giving mathematics assessments, and planning. These teachers are truly part of the mathematics teams of their schools. Current federal requirements for highly qualified content teachers might cause restrictions on the ability of special educators to teach mathematics without additional coursework in mathematics or close work with mathematics teachers (NCLB, 2001).

Regardless of the program model, general, special, and remedial teachers providing mathematics instruction in their schools should work together. Here are some specific recommendations for teachers collaborating to deliver instruction:

■ Special education and remedial teachers should meet with general mathematics teachers to find out their long-range plans for instructional units, testing methods, homework requirements, and in-class expectations. Ask teachers which topics give students the most problems. View student work samples.

■ During the first week of school, conduct a comprehensive survey of students' mathematics achievement. Follow up with specific, curriculum-based probes to determine areas of weakness. Pay attention to how students solve problems and the strategies they use. Share and discuss the specific strengths and needs of students.

■ When working in a co-teaching model with parity, invest time in joint planning. Make an effort to use consistent mathematics language with students. Clear, elaborated explanations and carefully planned routines offer promise for successful inclusion.

■ If supporting math instruction with additional time in a resource or support model, plan preview activities before units of study to firm up concept understanding, language, and basic skills. Provide reinforcement, re-teaching, and additional practice during the units of study. Build in connections, generalization opportunities, and problem solving, especially if these are not taught explicitly in the regular class.

Figure 4.16
Accommodations for Mathematics Classes

Typical Accommodations for Mathematics Classes

Instruction
- Important words highlighted
- Partner review at lesson closure
- Peer tutoring
- Practice pages in smaller sections
- Copies of overheads or charts provided
- Word problems read aloud or on tape
- Simplified language

Materials
- Graph paper
- Supplemental texts
- Additional manipulatives
- Calculator (if calculation is not goal)
- Computer tools

Assessment
- Directions read aloud
- Word problems read aloud
- Simplified language
- Calculator (if not assessed)
- Extra time (if not timed)
- Alternative setting or grouping
- Partitioned test
- Alternative response mode
- Timing: breaks, time of day

Setting during Instruction
- Special seating
- Specified group assignments

■ Share expertise. Mathematics teachers can offer great activities, thoughtful examples, and sometimes loan materials. Special education and remedial teachers may have more experience with individual assessments, strategy instruction, and tracking student progress.

■ Discuss the instructional and assessment accommodations and modifications outlined on IEPs. The general education teacher should know that these tools are not optional but could be modified through the IEP process if they are not effective or realistic within the setting. As depicted in Figure 4.16, accommodations can be made to instruction, materials, assessment, or classroom setting, as long as the curriculum standards are upheld. Modifications, on the other hand, are more radical and typically lower the standard for an individual student (e.g., different form of test with less complex material, alternative assignment). Both accommodations and modifications (sometimes termed nonstandard accommodations) should be established based on individual assessment results, not "gut" feelings or decisions for groups of students. Fuchs, Fuchs, Eaton, Hamlett, and Karns (2000) found that teachers tended to over-award accommodations (to students who would not profit from their use) and that curriculum-based measures should supplement teacher judgment in determining appropriate accommodations for individual students.

Occasionally a regular mathematics classroom offers little or no appropriate mathematics instruction. Mathematics has been reduced to a note-taking exercise, busywork, and punishment. Inexperienced teachers may rely on a page-by-page rush through the textbook, never pausing to check student understanding. ("If it weren't for the students I could finish this textbook.") Because of the teacher shortage, many mathematics teachers are only provisionally certified and have no pedagogical training. If collaboration is not successful, the special educator or remedial mathematics teacher must usually address this situation with the school administration. Either another classroom should be found or the student should be served in the pull-out setting. A year of no mathematics achievement is more than a lost year for students with learning problems.

Fortunately, the situation described above is not typical. In most schools, mathematics teachers are keenly interested in mathematics and have deep understandings of concepts and relationships. Special education and remedial teachers have a repertoire of skills for adapting, enhancing, and augmenting instruction. Together these teachers provide well-planned mathematics instruction that meets the needs of learners with special needs.

CHAPTER SUMMARY

- Key principles for planning and delivering mathematics instruction are:
  - Ponder underlying concepts and connections,
  - Link prior knowledge to new learning,
  - Activate positive attitudes,
  - Present concepts in problem-solving contexts,
  - Establish an effective sequence of instruction,
  - Consider the appropriate degree of explicit instruction for the content,
  - Plan for variety within structure,
  - Remember the importance of language,
  - Recognize the power of strategies, and
  - Ensure transfer-of-learning.
- When planning for mathematics instruction, teachers should consider the NCTM standards, the instructional principles, and typical problem areas for students with learning problems.

- Student-centered mathematics curricula should focus on fewer topics more deeply.
- Teachers can plan units by content topic, themes, or problem situations.
- High school schedules present more challenges for students with disabilities and their teachers.
- Special educators may want to specialize in mathematics instruction within their schools and work more closely with other mathematics teachers.
- Because students with mathematics learning problems are served primarily in the general mathematics class, collaboration among general, special, and remedial teachers is essential.

RESORCES

For more resources on teaching the concepts and skills addressed in this chapter, go to the NCTM's Illuminations web site: http://illuminations.nctm.org

Akers, J., Tierney, C., Evans, C., & Murray, M. (1998). Fraction Track Game. *Investigations in number, data, and space.* Parsippany, NJ: Dale Seymour Publications.

Iwamoto, J. R. (1994). *Coming together: Integrating math and language.* Englewood Cliffs, NJ: Prentice-Hall.

Office of English Language Acquisition, Language Enhancement & Academic Achievement for Limited English Proficient Students (OELA), www.ncela.gwu.edu.

Whitin, D. J., & Whitin, P. (2000). *Math is language too: Talking and writing in the mathematics classroom.* Reston, VA: NCTM with the National Council of Teachers of English.

Chapter 5

Chapter Questions

1. Why are problem-solving skills emphasized in mathematics standards and assessments?
2. What traits do good problem solvers share?
3. How do students with mathematics disabilities perform on problem-solving tasks?
4. How should problem solving be taught to students with learning problems?
5. What sequences and strategies are most effective for solving routine and nonroutine problems?
6. How can problem solving be effectively integrated in the mathematics curriculum?

Problem-Solving Instruction for Students with Learning Problems

A GREAT discovery solves a great problem but there is a grain of discovery in the solution of any problem.
—*How to Solve It,* Pólya, 1945, page v.

One train departs from Miami at the same time another train departs New York. Many adults get sweaty palms just hearing the first line of this memorable word problem. Of course "word" or "story" problems aren't representative of most problem-solving demands in real life but they are the way problem situations are presented to students in mathematics textbooks and on standardized tests. This chapter will explore strategies for teaching students how to interpret and solve word problems. But first, read the following problem and think about how it could be solved:

You have been contracted to paint the town's water tower—a huge metal-covered cylinder with a height of 15.5 meters and the radius of the circular base of 7.1 meters. What is the surface area of the tower? If it takes 1 gallon to paint 20 square meters, how many gallons of paint should you order?

Think: What are the reading demands for understanding this problem?
Is personal experience useful?
In how many different ways can this problem be solved?

This problem was of the pragmatic type—it is taken from an actual problem situation a painter may encounter. Another problem type is the abstract problem—one that challenges thinking for the sake of the mental exercise.

For solutions to the problems presented in this book, visit the Companion Website at www.ablongman.com/gurganus1e.

Try this example:

> The letter "E" represents any even digit (2, 4, 6, 8) and the letter "D" represents any odd digit (1, 3, 5, 7, 9). If E + D = 15 and 2E + D = 21, what are the values of E and D?

> Think: What makes this problem different than the previous one?
> What are the reading and experiential demands?
> In how many ways can this problem be solved?

Problem solving is one of the most complex, ubiquitous, and critical skills developed in mathematics curricula. The next section elaborates on this importance. ■ ● ▲

THE IMPORTANCE OF PROBLEM-SOLVING SKILLS

"Problem solving means engaging in a task for which the solution method is not known in advance . . . . it is not only a goal of learning mathematics but also a major means of doing so" (NCTM, 2000, p. 52). The national mathematics standards (1989, 2000) emphasized problem-solving skills throughout the K–12 curriculum and across all topics of mathematics. One compelling argument is found in the section titled "The Need for Mathematics in a Changing World." The authors emphasized that we live in a time of accelerating change and that the applications of mathematics have never been greater in everyday life, the workplace, and in the scientific and technological community (NCTM, 2000, p. 4). Problem solving is one of the five process standards, the ways students acquire and use their content knowledge. It is important to note that all the other process standards include problem-solving aspects: reasoning and proof, communication, connections, and representation.*

Problem solving should be the basis for mathematics understanding, not an afterthought or later application of skills learned in isolation. Consider the format of mathematics textbooks more than ten years ago. A new skill was introduced, such as adding and subtracting decimals, with a title across the top of the page followed by a rule and a couple of examples of the steps for working through these calculations. Then students were presented with an "A" section of calculations to work for guided practice and then a "B" section for seatwork or homework. At the very bottom of the page were two or three word problems that used the previous calculation skills. The teacher was encouraged by the instructor's manual to explain these problems to students, but more often they were ignored or assigned without instruction. Students didn't have to think about the solution method—it was obviously an application of the computation presented in the lesson. Somewhere later in the chapter was a section called "problem solving" or "applications" and teachers often treated these sections as new concepts.

Consider a scenario that begins with problem solving—or, more specifically, a problem situation that needs solving.

> The weather station workers need to prepare a monthly report on the weather data they have been collecting. The precipitation amounts over the month were: 1.2 cm, 0.8 cm,

*Reprinted with permission from *Principles and Standards for School Mathematics*, copyright 2000, by the National Council of Teachers of Mathematics. All rights reserved. Standards are listed with permission of the Council of Teachers of Mathematics (NCTM). NCTM does not endorse the content or validity of these alignments.

1.075 cm, and 0.25 cm in four precipitation events. How can we find the month's total precipitation?

A skillful teacher would turn it over to the students, with guidance, for the whole group or even small working groups to discuss *how* to go about finding the total amount. The teacher would prompt students to discuss what they know about the problem, drawing from experiences. The questions could be, "What do we know? What are we looking for? What do you already know about how precipitation is measured and reported?" Then she would ask for some ideas, without judgment, on possible strategies for solving this problem. As students listen to others, they tend to re-form ideas or variations on ideas. The teacher can also "hear" her students' thought processes.

As each group of students settles on a way to solve the problem, the teacher encourages each to apply its strategy. One group may draw the rain collector on graph paper and draw in each precipitation event. Another group may use one centimeter as a reference point and use a sort of number line to see how close to one centimeter each week's measurement falls. Another group finds a calculator and simply plugs in the numbers and quickly arrives at a solution, then spends time examining why the solution makes sense by working backwards through algorithms. The fourth group attempts to line up the numbers and simply add them up—arriving at 11.20 centimeters. Then they exclaim, "That can't be right!" and begin discussing where to put the decimal point.

Eventually groups begin to settle on the same solution from a variety of directions. As they share their processes with each other, the meanings of the concepts involved deepen. At this point the teacher could demonstrate the most common algorithm and remind students of the place value concepts involved. Guided practice with two or three similar problems will help students feel confident with the algorithm and problem pattern. At this point in the lesson, particularly for students with disabilities, it is important for the teacher to explicitly describe the problem type or pattern and strategies used for solving the problem (but not necessarily only one strategy). It is also critical that the teacher not allow a faulty strategy, such as using the keyword "total," that might work in this problem but not another. And, of course, a master teacher would intentionally build on this problem pattern (several like quantities to *combine* into one amount) later in the curriculum.

Problem solving is a critical part of today's high-stakes testing. High-stakes testing is a term that refers to those district- or state-wide tests with significant implications for students, teachers, or schools. The outcomes of these tests may determine a student's promotion, a teacher's paycheck or contract, and a school's leadership and funding. Most states' end-of-course, end-of-grade, and exit exams are heavily weighted with mathematics problem solving. In some cases students must show their work and explain their answers in writing. This emphasis on problem solving over calculation is a direct result of the NCTM standards and their influence on states' curriculum standards. See Figure 5.1 for examples of specific state test items that involve problem solving.

> **TRY THIS**
> Select one mathematics concept or algorithm and develop a problem-solving context in which it could be introduced. Use one from a student's IEP or select one from the following list:
> - addition of simple fractions
> - graphing a set of binary coordinates
> - computing the area of a rectangle

All students, including students with disabilities, are required to participate in state and district-mandated testing programs. As discussed in Chapters 1 and 3, districts are struggling to interpret IDEA and NCLB regulations: Should students be tested on grade level if they haven't been exposed to grade-level curriculum? What accommodations are possible without changing the standards of the test? How many grade levels below a student's assigned grade level would be feasible for testing with useful results? How should life skills mathematics that are not from curriculum standards but on individual student IEPs be assessed? Which students qualify for alternative assessments and what forms should those take? There are more questions than answers—a frustrating situation for teachers, students, and parents.

TRY THIS

Find examples of specific state or district mathematics test items for a given grade level. (Many states post sample items on the web.) Analyze the sample for problem-solving requirements. What type of problem solving is required? What is the student asked to do (processes) and know (content) when solving the problems?

Problem solving is an integral part of life, not just within the study of mathematics. Many of the strategies developed for mathematics problem solving and the ways of thinking that are promoted can be applied across other situations—science, social skills, reading comprehension, social studies, school-wide conflict resolution, the world of work, and community living. Problem-solving abilities are some of the most important outcomes of education. For example, in a comprehensive study of job requirements in the United States, Murnane and Levy (1996) found that the "new basic skills" for entry-level positions include the ability to solve semi-structured problems in which hypotheses must be formed and tested, in addition to collaboration and communication skills and basic reading, mathematics, and computer literacy. In a more recent study (2004), the researchers found that two types of skills are most important in the job market: expert thinking (solving new and more complex problems) and complex communication (accurate interpretations). However, the 2003 Organization for Economic Cooperation and Development's Program for International Student Assessment (PISA), an international test of the application mathematics skills to real-world problems, found that 15-year-olds in the United States were outperformed by their peers in 25 countries, and only 40 percent were prepared to be successful in college-level mathematics courses or in the workplace.

If the outcomes of our educational programs are adults who are productive and successful in their careers, members of functional families, and contributing and lawful citizens within communities, then problem-solving abilities must be developed through-out the curriculum in schools and reinforced at home. Regardless of the subject area or social context, active problem solving requires the solver to move through a sequence of thinking and decision-making steps. Generally speaking, these are:

1. Identify what the problem is and really attempt to understand it.
2. Generate a list of possible methods or strategies for solving the problem, drawing on previous experiences and available resources including input from other people.
3. Follow through with the most feasible method.
4. Examine what resulted for its effectiveness or validity.
5. Reflect back on the whole process. If the process wasn't successful, what went wrong? If it was successful, why did it work and will it be useful in the future?

Sometimes the steps are simplified: understand, plan, carry-out, and look back. Problem-solving sequences are examined in more depth in a later section in this chapter.

TRY THIS
Apply the first two steps of the generic problem-solving steps to at least one of the following problems. Or if a real problem is available, try all five steps.
1. Two students in your class constantly bicker and call each other names. The situation is disruptive to instruction and distracts the other students.
2. A social studies class has been challenged to find the most cost-effective and viable way to provide humanitarian aid to a draught-stricken African country.
3. In science class, groups of students must identify as many characteristics as possible of several unknown liquids. The only information they have is that none of the chemicals is hazardous for touch, smell, heating, or cooling situations.

CHARACTERISTICS OF PROBLEM SOLVERS

Interesting research has been conducted on the characteristics of excellent and poor problem solvers. Most of this research does not specifically address individuals with disabilities but helps illuminate the many facets of problem-solving ability. Figure 5.2 summarizes the characteristics of excellent problem solvers (see for example Scheid, 1993; Schoenfeld, 1992).

Others have studied poor and novice problem solvers and found virtually the reverse characteristics (Havertape & Kass, 1978; Montague & Bos, 1986; Montague & Applegate, 1993; Parmar, Cawley, & Frazita, 1996; Lucangeli, Coi, & Bosco, 1997). These students:

- don't spend time analyzing and understanding problems
- decide on a strategy to try too quickly
- rely on a trial-and-error approach
- switch strategies too impulsively
- have gaps in knowledge base and make more computational and procedural errors
- lack metacognitive awareness and strategies
- have difficulty representing problems (linguistically or graphically)
- don't see patterns or familiar aspects of problems
- have difficulty generalizing
- have problems sorting the information provided

These traits of poor problem solvers can be linked directly to the learner characteristics discussed in Chapter 2. Students with disabilities and other learning problems may have gaps in prior knowledge, often have comprehension problems, tend to have immature habits such as guessing or switching strategies without thinking, lack solid cognitive

---

Figure 5.2
Characteristics of Excellent Problem Solvers

Characteristics of Excellent Problem Solvers

- Have a sound knowledge base (math concepts)
- Understand the general nature of the problem
- Can generate mental pictures
- Have a set of strategies
- Spend more time analyzing problems than other students
- Can self-monitor during problem solving
- Have good estimation (prediction) skills
- Can perceive likenesses, differences, and patterns
- Can switch methods easily, but not impulsively
- Able to generalize with only a few examples
- Possess strong self-esteem, low test anxiety

strategies, and don't generalize from experiences automatically. These students will need more explicit problem-solving instruction in the strategies good problem solvers use. Each phase of the problem-solving sequence will need repeated instruction using many types of problems. This problem-solving instruction should be closely aligned with mathematics content instruction and build deeper concepts and skills across grade levels.

Research on Students with Disabilities

Students with disabilities in mathematics share many of the characteristics of poor and novice problem solvers. When first presented with a problem, these students have trouble identifying the important information within the problem, understanding what the problem is all about, and organizing an efficient strategy for solving the problem (Havertape & Kass, 1978). They often lack critical self-regulation, attention, and memory skills necessary to carry out the process (Miles & Forcht, 1995). Students with mathematics disabilities perform lower than their peers on problems that include indirect questions, extraneous information, and multiple steps (Parmar, Cawley, & Frazita, 1996). And they often use the wrong algorithms, leave out steps, or attempt ineffective strategies such as using "key words" (Montague & Bos, 1990).

Researchers are beginning to acknowledge the critical role language skills play in problem-solving ability. Reading the problem, finding the question, and locating the important information while discounting the unimportant are essentially reading comprehension tasks. When working through possible problem solutions, language becomes a tool for our thought processes. When good problem solvers believe they have a solution, they ask, "Does this answer make sense in the original context?" Students with disabilities typically have significant reading comprehension problems, are unable to separate the important from unimportant, have trouble "holding" necessary information in working memory, and rarely ask themselves if they have seen similar problems or if the answer makes sense.

To explore how significant reading problems are related to deficiencies in problem solving, Fuchs and Fuchs studied the problem-solving performance of students with mathematics disabilities with and without co-morbid reading disabilities (2002). Eighteen students with mathematics disabilities and twenty-two students with both mathematics and reading disabilities were tested on arithmetic story problems, complex story problems, and real-world problems. As the problem complexity increased (sentence and word length, number of steps, irrelevant information), students' accuracy decreased. The math disability group scored 75 percent on arithmetic problems, 14 percent on complex problems, and 12 percent on real-world problems. Students with both reading and mathematics disabilities performed much lower on all levels of problem-solving tasks, 55, 8, and 5 percent respectively.

Van Garderen and Montague (2003) studied the specific use of visual imagery while solving word problems by sixth-grade students with learning disabilities in mathematics, average students, and students identified as gifted. The researchers studied the types of visual-spatial representations used during problem solving and their effects on performance. On an assessment of thirteen nonroutine, multistep word problems, students with

A *pictoral representa-
tion,* in this case, is a
drawing of the surface
story, whereas a
*schematic representa-
tion* is a way of repre-
senting the underlying
structure, elements, and
relationships of a
problem, as with a
chart, diagram, or
symbol recording.

learning disabilities used more pictoral and fewer schematic representations than the other two groups. Pictoral representations were less successful strategies because they tended to depict the cover stories of problems, while schematic representations depicted spatial relationships and transformations among problem parts.

A research program in understanding mathematics disabilities with regard to problem solving has only recently been initiated and has many unanswered questions to address. How can we identify students with specific mathematics disabilities and what forms do those disabilities take with regard to problem solving? How can teachers most effectively assess problem-solving abilities for instructional planning? How are language disabilities related to those in mathematics? How can problem-solving deficits be identified earlier? Researchers, those in the fields of mathematics, psychology, and special education, need to more carefully describe study participants' individual characteristics (cognitive, metacognitive, language, and attitudes) and relate those to intervention effects.

PROBLEM-SOLVING SEQUENCES

Problem-solving sequences have been virtually the same, give or take a few intermediate steps, since the work of Pólya in the 1940s. The 1980 NCTM yearbook included the Pólya problem-solving sequence on the flyleaf (Krulik, 1980). Problem-solving literature in such diverse fields as political science, psychology, chemistry, computer science, and educational leadership from the 1970s cited his model. However, criticisms at the time noted that Pólya's strategies were descriptive rather than prescriptive; they had only face validity and lacked rules for implementation (Schoenfeld, 1987). Only since the 1980s has research supported the use of specific problem-solving strategies first described by Pólya (Schoenfeld, 1992).

Pólya (1945) outlined a four-step process and described in detail heuristics, or strategies, that were useful for devising and carrying out a problem-solving plan. Heuristics proposed by Pólya—such as analogy, decomposing and recombining, and working backward—are those that are invoked when dealing with new and unfamiliar problems, not standard algorithms that can be memorized (Schoenfeld, 1992). The Pólya problem-solving sequence was:

1. **Understand the problem.** The problem solver should ask: What is the unknown? What are the data? What is the condition?
2. **Devise a plan.** The problem solver should ask and do: Have I seen it before? Do I know a related problem? Look at the unknown and find a connection. Can I solve a related problem part of the problem?
3. **Carry out the plan.** The problem solver should ask: Is the plan working with each step? Have I checked each step? Do I need to retrace steps?
4. **Look back.** The problem solver should ask: Can I check the result? Does the result make sense in the problem's context? Can I use the result, or the method, for some other problem?

Most mathematics basal textbooks introduce a problem-solving sequence in an early chapter and teach specific heuristics throughout the book and series (Houghton Mifflin,

2002; McGraw-Hill, 2002; Everyday Learning Corporation, 2002). The problem-solving steps are essentially Pólya's sequence: understand (read for understanding), plan, solve, and look back (check). Basal texts also recommend strategies for solving problems: making lists or tables, preparing diagrams, writing number sentences, reasoning, solving a simpler problem, working backward, guess and check, and find a pattern.

Research with students with disabilities has investigated the use of problem-solving sequences. Montague and Bos (1986) developed a more detailed sequence for problem solving with four steps for "understand the problem," two steps for "devise a plan," one computation step for "carry out the plan," and "look back" reduced to a check-your-work step:

- Read the problem
- Paraphrase the information
- Visualize the information
- Identify the problem
- Develop a hypothesis
- Estimate the answer
- Compute the problem
- Check your work

Montague, Warger, and Morgan (2000) created an instructional program for the middle grades called *Solve It!* that incorporates most of these steps ("identify the problem" was omitted) with prompts for self-questioning during the process. The program was developed through three studies involving eighty-four students with learning disabilities (Montague & Bos, 1986; Montague, 1992; Montague, Applegate, & Marquard, 1993). The 1986 study, with six high-school students with learning disabilities, was an initial study of the original eight-step strategy using the acquisition steps of the Deschler, Alley, Warner, and Schumaker *Strategy Intervention Model* (1981). Five of the six students made substantial progress on post-intervention measures, increasing by five to six correct responses on a set of ten routine, two-step word problems. The 1992 study focused on six middle-school students with learning disabilities and underscored the need for both cognitive and metacognitive strategy training, attention to individual student characteristics, and explicit distributed practice. The 1993 study, with seventy-two students in grades 7 and 8, demonstrated that students with learning disabilities could be taught a problem-solving routine with explicit cognitive and metacognitive strategies and achieve similar criterion results (at least 7 of 10 problems) as the average-achieving group.

Enright and Beattie (1989) proposed a problem-solving sequence that was closely aligned with Pólya's approach and applicable to routine and nonroutine word problems. The sequence offered a mnemonic device for learners. The SOLVE sequence included the following steps:

- Study the problem
- Organize the facts
- Line up a plan

The term *routine* refers to those word problems that are solved by standard algorithms; *nonroutine* are those that require alternative methods.

- Verify the plan with computation
- Examine your answer.

Marsh and Cooke (1996) applied the SOLVE sequence in a study on the use of manipulatives (Cuisenaire® Rods) to facilitate problem understanding but did not study the sequence effectiveness.

Case, Harris, and Graham (1992) developed the following sequence for teaching students with learning disabilities to solve simple word problems:

- Read the problem out loud
- Look for important words and circle them
- Draw pictures to help tell what is happening
- Write down the math sentence
- Write down the answer

Four students were instructed in each step of the process and encouraged to self-instruct during problem solving. After students demonstrated mastery and understanding of the steps, they were guided through problem-solving examples with prompts and corrective feedback. After students could solve six of seven problem sets with guidance, they moved on to independent practice, also in seven problem sets. Students' problem solving increased from 56 percent (equation and answer) to 95 percent of simple addition and subtraction word problems. Maintenance checks indicated 88 percent success over eight to thirteen weeks after the intervention. This study was limited by the narrow definition of word problems, its focus on key words that were conveniently included within problems, and the number of students involved. This sequence is also deficient in that it doesn't prompt reflection or asking whether the answer makes sense.

Mercer and Miller embedded a problem-solving sequence within their *Strategic Math Series* for teaching basic arithmetic operations (1991–94). The sequence begins with the concrete stage where students label the operational problem with the objects used, such as blocks or chips. Next, students label problems with representations used, such as tallies or boxes. Then students begin labeling problems with short real-life one-word and phrase appendages; for example, 4 blue socks in 3 brown bags results in 12 blue socks. Next, sentences appear with numbers aligned and extraneous information is added. Finally, regular word problems involving the operation under study are presented and students are encouraged to create their own word problems of the same type. Research with this graduated sequence of problem solving instruction with students with disabilities indicated significant gains in multiplication and subtraction problem solving (Miller & Mercer, 1993). But this program is limited in that it doesn't vary problem types or provide mixed practice.

Other researchers have taken a problem-conceptualization approach and developed strategies for determining problem type, analyzing underlying schemas, and applying related solution strategies.

Jitendra, building on the schema work of Marshall (1995), developed a schema-based word problem solving approach for students with mathematics disabilities (Jitendra &

Hoff, 1996). Her work began with single-subject studies of instruction in routine addition and subtraction word problems. Students were taught to represent each problem with a graphic representation and then apply the solution strategy indicated by the graphic. After instruction, students were able to discuss the specific problem types, represent problems graphically, find problem solutions, and maintain these skills over at least 10 weeks (Jitendra, DiPipi, & Perron-Jones, 2002).

Fuchs and Fuchs (2003) emphasized the nature of problem solving as a transfer issue and applied the work of Cooper and Sweller (1987) on problem-solving transfer and that of Salomon and Perkins (1989) on broadening schemas to explicit problem-solving instruction. Cooper and Sweller asserted that problem solving transfer required mastery of problem solution rules, development of problem categories, and matching new problems to familiar types. Salomon and Perkins described problem solving as a "high-road transfer" task in which the solver is searching for abstract connections between new and familiar tasks. They described both forward-reaching and backward-reaching situations where transfer can be achieved.

The Fuchs developed a tutoring strategy for explicitly teaching four problem structures and transfer strategies. In a study with fourth-grade students, forty students with mathematics disabilities were assigned to four groups—tutoring, computer, tutoring and computer, and control. All students were taught a background unit of six lessons on approaching word problems. After twenty-four sessions within treatment groups, the tutoring group's effect sizes compared with the results of the control group were 2.10 on story problems and 1.67 on transfer story problems, but transfer to real-world story problems was not significantly different. Computer-assisted practice did not enhance problem-solving ability, perhaps due to its limitations in providing individualized elaborated examples as needed by the student. Transfer to real-world problems was not achieved because the problem types taught were routine structures: multiply and then add a list of items purchased (shopping list); fractional part of a whole set (half problem); total items in bags; and interpreting a pictograph problem. Transfer to similar problem structures was achieved because the problems changed only superficially—different format, different key words, larger context, and additional questions—and these superficial changes also were taught explicitly.

Research on effective problem solving strategies is difficult to design because of the wide variability of problem types. If the researcher limits the instruction and corresponding measurement instruments to only one or two problem types, then the research results are limited to those types. For example, some studies taught students key words to connect with problem operations (not a recommended method), then measured the results with carefully controlled problems using the same keywords (see for example, Bottge & Hasselbring, 1993; Shiah, Mastropieri, Scruggs, & Fulk, 1994–5). Another study encouraged students to consider the size of numbers given (the big number rule) to determine the correct operation (Wilson & Sindelar, 1991). These studies resulted in student learning but had serious generalization issues. Math problems in textbooks, on statewide tests, and in the real world are not so carefully controlled. Problem-solving research is also made difficult by the complexity of the problem-solving task: reading comprehension, abstract connections, multi-step situations, and numerous solution strategies. It is difficult for researchers to control some aspects of the problem-solving process while intervening with the variable(s) under study. Researchers have noted other issues as they grapple with the difficulties of this area of study: promoting and assessing maintenance and generalization of new skills, accounting for individual learner characteristics, and examining the efficient use of limited time for instruction and practice (Xin & Jitendra, 1999; Rivera, Smith, Goodwin, & Bryant, 1998).

TEACHING PROBLEM-SOLVING STRATEGIES

Most problem-solving sequences supported by research employ the four-step process proposed by Pólya, elaborated with strategic prompts and additional steps for understanding the problem. The following sections provide specific methods for each phase of this problem-solving process. These are followed by a review of problem-solving programs.

Strategies for "Understand the Problem"

For solving real-world problems, the most challenging step for most people is defining the problem and understanding its components. The homeowner who notices water collecting around the foundation of her house must seek out the problem. The scientist who identifies a decline in one fish species in a river must first clarify the problem. The automobile mechanic whose client is complaining of a strange engine noise must diagnose the problem. A teacher who is working with a student with significant learning problems in mathematics must first identify the student's prior knowledge and concept gaps. A clear understanding of the problem is essential before solutions can be considered.

Mathematics students are faced with "word" or "story" problems in textbooks and on state and district tests. Problems are presented in sentences that describe key elements and ask for solutions. The first step in the problem-solving process is to understand the problem. Successful students will need a number of strategies for this step.

The first questions students should ask involve **problem typology.** "What type of problem is this?" and "Have I seen a problem like this in the past?" Mathematics problems can be categorized as *routine*, those for which basic mathematics operations can be directly applied, and *nonroutine*, those problems that require alternative strategies. Problems also can be classified as one-step, two-step, or multi-step. Consider the characteristics of the problems depicted in Figure 5.1. Which problems are routine and nonroutine? Which ones require more than one step?

Routine problems typically require one or two steps of the application of basic operations. Riley, Greeno, and Heller (1983) studied addition and subtraction word problems and identified three basic types: change, combine, and compare. *Change* problems involve some quantity being increased or decreased. The unknown is the starting amount, the change amount, or the ending amount. For example, *Erica had a dozen blocks before giving half to Amy. How many did Erica have left? If Mr. Brown filled up his tank with 10 gallons and it holds a total of 25 gallons, how many gallons of gas were in the tank originally?*

Combine (group) problems involve at least two quantities that are combined. The unknown is either the total or the amount in one of subsets. For example: *When Leslie and Sarah put their baseball cards together there were 24 cards. If 10 belonged to Leslie, how many were Sarah's?* Notice that the word "together" does not mean to add. Keywords can be deceptive and are not reliable problem-solving tools. Students should be encouraged to consider the structure or what is happening over the course of the problem (Gurganus & Del Mastro, 1998).

Compare problems involve a comparison between two quantities using the relations more or less. The unknown is the referent, the compared quantity, or the difference between the two quantities. For example, *Whitney had four more books to carry than her sister. If her sister had 3 books, how many did Whitney have?*

In her seminal work *Schemas in Problem Solving* (1995), Marshall referenced her 1985 study of sixth-grade, eighth-grade, and remedial college textbooks that identified only five strategies for the majority of word problems (71% of sixth grade, 65% of eighth grade, and 58% of remedial college textbooks). The types were change, group, compare (as described above), restate, and vary. Other word problems identified required geometric formulas, estimation, probability, range, map interpretation, or distance-rate-time formulas.

The *restate* problem type involves a relationship that can be expressed between two distinct but similar things, such as two children, two bicycles, or two buildings. Each thing has some common property that can be counted (age, cost, length, weight, height). One is described in two different ways (restated). For example, *A new bicycle costs 3 times as much as a used one. If a new bike costs $150, how much is the used one?*

The *vary* problem type includes the expression of a per unit value. The relationship can be centered on one property of an object: *You want to purchase 9 yards of cloth that costs $4 per yard.* Or the relationship can be between two different things: *For every 5 students we have 2 balls. How many balls do we have for 25 students?*

Jitendra furthered this work on problem types or schemas by applying the graphic representations for each type to specially-designed instruction for students with disabilities (Jitendra & Hoff, 1996). Research using these word problem schemas found that students with disabilities could be taught this conceptual-representation strategy and could generalize its use to novel problems (Jitnedra & Hoff, 1996; Jitendra, Hoff, & Beck, 1999; Jitendra, DiPipi, & Perron-Jones, 2002). The Jitendra schema-based strategy is discussed in more detail later in this chapter.

As seen with the restate and vary problem types above, multiplication and division problems are more difficult because they involve more than one kind of object or unit (Reed, 1999). For example: *Our class is in charge of packaging cookies for the parent open house. If there are 15 dozen cookies and we need three in each package, how many packages will we have?* Another example: *If each truck in the Ajax Trucking Company has 16 tires and the trucking company runs 20 trucks each day, how many tires are in service at one time?* Multiplication and division problems involve a transformation of referents and are based on the concept of intensive quantity (Schwartz, 1988). An intensive quantity is not measurable alone, rather is the ratio of two measurable quantities. For example, 50 miles per hour is actually the ratio of a measurable distance (in miles) divided by a measurable amount of time (in hours). As discussed in content strand B, multiplication and division can be depicted in a number of models: grouping and partitioning, scalar (no dimensions), rate (value per unit), Cartesian product (set pairings), and area (length by width of a rectangle).

In studying multiplication and division problem types, Greer (1992) described four main classes of situations: common equivalent sets or equal groups (vary), multiplicative comparison (restate), Cartesian product, and rectangular area (or array). An example for equivalent sets (vary), where two clearly different factors are identified: *The book sale committee has collected 10 boxes of books with 20 books in each box.* "Boxes" is the multiplier that operates on the multiplicand or "books in each." If the product were known first, this example would generate two types of division problems—partitive division (if the number in each set were unknown) and quotitive division (if the number of sets were unknown).

Another multiplication-division type is the multiplicative comparison (restate) situation. For example, *Crystal has four times as many quarters as her sister. If her sister has 5 quarters, how many does Crystal have?* This is the division version—if the problem were worded the other way around, it would require multiplication. English (1997) terms this problem type "asymmetrical" because one entity has x times as many things as the other entity.

A third multiplication-division type is the symmetrical Cartesian product, where two factors are matched into pairs. *If you are buying a new bicycle and have the choices of ten colors and three models, how many options do you have in all?* Each color is matched with each model, resulting in thirty options. The division version would provide the total options and one set of choices would be unknown.

Finally, the area model of length by width can require multiplication or division, depending on which dimension is unknown. Consider these examples: *The area of a rectangular floor is 60 square feet. If one side measures 12 feet, what is the length of the connecting side? If a poster is 40 inches by 20 inches, how many square inches of glass is needed for framing?*

With complex word problems, such as in algebra, strong students detect the mathematical structure and relationships within the problem, while less able students tend to focus on the surface structure or "cover story" of the problem (Krutetskii, 1976; Mayer, 1981; Hutchinson, 1993; Bassok, Wu, & Olseth, 1995). Hutchinson recommended that students with learning disabilities in mathematics be taught explicit methods for developing schemata for algebra word problems including how to translate propositions and integrate them into a structure.

Hutchinson (1993) identified three algebra word problem types: relational, proportional, and two variable-two equation problems. An example of a relational problem is: *One swimmer swims 100 meters farther than another swimmer. If the total distance swum by both swimmers is 1,500 meters, how far did each swimmer swim?* An example of a more complex problem based on the same type: *One swimmer swam 50 meters less than 1.5 times his opponent. The total distance swum by both swimmers was 1,500 meters. How far did each swimmer swim?*

Proportion problems provide one set of data by which to compare one or more other sets of data. For example, *Amy drew a picture of a building on a scale of 1 cm to 2 meters.*

If a window is 1.5 cm tall in Amy's drawing, how tall is the actual window? A more complex proportion problem: *We are planning a party for 20 people and will need 5 gallons of punch and 3 dozen cookies. How much food would we need for 30 people?*

Two variable two-equation problems involve two unknowns where one equation becomes an elaboration of the other. For example, *one brand of cereal (rice) weighs 383 grams per box. Another brand (corn) weighs 510 grams per box. There are 15 boxes of cereal in all at a total weight of 6,634 grams (6.634 kg). How many boxes are there of each brand?*

As can be seen by the previous word problem examples, another strategy students should use to understand the problem is to ask themselves **informational questions** about the problem. *What is known and what is unknown? What is important information and what is not necessary (extraneous)? What are the relationships among the data in the problem?* Identifying the unknown or unknowns may lead to later use of variables, equations, and effective reflection strategies.

When reading mathematics word problems, students should draw on effective **reading comprehension strategies.** Specific techniques such as paraphrasing, visual imagery, underlining or crossing through parts that are important or not important, and asking what is the main idea or question are all effective comprehension strategies that can be applied to reading and understanding math word problems. Consider the following problem:

> The parent-teacher organization of the school has decided to replace the front sidewalk that has been in place 20 years, but is now cracking, with concrete blocks. The sidewalk is 36 feet long and 9 feet wide. Each concrete block is 15 inches square and there will be a one-half inch gap between blocks. About how many blocks should the school order?

Is this a routine or nonroutine problem? What is its structural type? Can you visualize the project described? Can you paraphrase the question? What information is important for solving the problem and what is not needed? Students need practice with understanding the problem, without actually solving the problem, using effective reading strategies. Discussing problems within small groups will assist students in the cognitive processes involved. Students find it interesting to discuss a problem's features without having to actually solve the problem. Further, students who begin grasping a specific problem type can solidify that understanding by creating their own problems for others to identify.

Strategies for "Develop a Plan"

The next stage in problem solving is to develop a plan for finding a solution or solutions. By the time students are in high school, they should have a repertoire of strategies. Some strategies (using objects) can be introduced as early as first grade, while others (developing a formula) are more abstract and are introduced in later grades. Additionally some strategies introduced early can become more sophisticated with higher-level applications.

Many of these strategies, such as draw a figure, working backward, setting up equations, and using a related problem, were proposed by Pólya (1945) in his "Short

Dictionary of Heuristic," a chapter in *How to Solve It*. Curiously arranged in alphabetical order, this dictionary offers an almost conversational discussion of various strategies with examples, both mathematical and nonmathematical.

Students should first consider the problem type, as developed in "understand the problem." If the problem is routine and a previous problem structure can be recalled, then that solution strategy can be implemented—typically applying one or more of the four operations to the selected information provided in the problem. If the problem type is clearly specialized content—such as interpreting or creating a graph, determining probability, measuring a figure, determining perimeter or volume, constructing lines or angles, or solving an equation—then the problem directions and format should prompt the strategy. Finally, if the problem is nonroutine or a previous structure cannot be recalled, students should apply one of the following heuristics.

1. *Relate a new problem to a familiar one.* As discussed in the previous section, students who are weak problem solvers tend to relate the "cover story" or superficial aspects of problems rather than the mathematical structure of problems. We need to teach students to examine and recognize the underlying structure. Which of the following three problems has a similar structure?

    a. A couple set out to hike the Hadrian's Wall Path of 84 miles. They walked an average of 12 miles a day with sightseeing about 2 hours each day. How many days did the hike take to complete?

    b. Two people hiked the coastal pathway of 90 miles, walking about 3 miles per hour. If they walked for 6 hours the first day, 7 hours the second day, and 6.5 hours the third day, how many miles do they have left to hike?

    c. If a factory worker can package 45 boxes in one hour, how many boxes can he package in a 40-hour week?

Problems (a) and (c) are both equivalent sets (vary) types: 84 miles at 12 miles a day equals 7 days; 45 boxes an hour for 40 hours equals 1800 boxes. Problem (b) has the same "cover story" as problem (a) but is structurally different. It requires equivalent sets, then two change steps (addition and subtraction): $(6 \times 3) + (7 \times 3) + (6.5 \times 3) = 18 + 21 + 19.5 = 58.5$ miles from 90 miles yields 31.5 miles.

Saloman and Perkins (1989) identified two types of problem transfer. Forward-reaching involves teaching structures and abstractions when the problem type is initially learned. Backward-reaching transfer requires students to think back to previous problem types for common structures. Students with disabilities need explicit instruction in making both types of transfers.

2. *Estimate a reasonable answer (guess and check).* Estimation is a critical skill for step four (look back) but also can be part of an effective problem-solving strategy. This strategy is particularly helpful for state-required mathematics tests with multiple-choice options. Consider the following problem from grade 4 (no calculators were allowed):

a. Miguel wants to buy 3 bags of potato chips. Each bag of potato chips costs $2.69. If he uses a coupon for $1.00 off the price of one bag, how much will Miguel owe for the 3 bags of potato chips?*

A. $1.69
B. $3.72
C. $7.07
D. $8.07

We can estimate by using $3 a bag for 3 bags would be $9 and a dollar off would leave $8. This estimate would quickly eliminate A and B. Closer examination would reveal that D is too close to $8 because our estimate would be about 90 cents too high. The best answer is C. The student with time for an exact calculation could check this estimate by multiplying 3 by $2.69 and subtracting $1 or by starting with $7.07, adding $1 for $8.07, then dividing by 3 for $2.69.

Some problems ask for estimation rather than an exact answer. For example:

b. According to the 2000 United States Census, Florida had an average of 296 people per square mile. The state of Florida is listed as 53,927 square miles. Which of the following is the best *estimate* of the total population?

A. 12,000,000 people
B. 14,000,000 people
C. 16,000,000 people
D. 18,000,000 people

The previous problem forced students to select from four estimates. When problems do not provide a choice for answers and require an estimate, students with learning problems often try to find the exact answer, regardless of the directions. The concept and process of estimating can be more difficult than conducting a routine computation for these students. Consider the following problem: *Mr. Sterner is shopping for a few items in the grocery store. If the items cost $4.95, $1.75, $2.20, $8.10, and $6.89, provide an **estimate** to the nearest dollar of the total cost.*

3. *Solve a simpler problem.* This strategy is effective when large numbers or complex situations are presented and simplification can be combined with other strategies. Once the student can set out a solution for and solve a simpler version of the problem, the same solution strategy can be applied to the actual problem. Consider the following problems and how they can be simplified.

a. A rectangular park measures 587 feet wide and 1398 feet long. How long would a diagonal pathway be in feet?
b. The surface area of the United States (50 states and District of Columbia) is 9,631,418 square kilometers. Of this area, 9,161,923 sq km is land and 469,495 sq km is water. What percentage of the total area is water? (Data source CIA: The World Factbook, 2004)

*From *Release of Spring 2003 Test Items*, Massachusetts Department of Education. Reprinted by permission.

4. *Use objects.* Some problems lend themselves to the use of objects because they are about objects (see example a). Abstract objects, such as cubes or straws, can be used to represent real-life objects in some problems (example b).

    a. If Ramon had 10 crayons after giving 6 to his brother, how many crayons did he start with?

    b. Gail, Hannah, Isabelle, Joyce, and Kay are standing in line for baseball tickets. Gail and Isabelle are next to each other. Joyce is last. Kay is not next to either Gail or Hannah, nor is she first. List these baseball fans in the order they are in line.

5. *Draw a picture.* Like using objects, some problems are explicit in calling for a diagram (examples a and b) and others can be solved in many ways including a drawing (see example c). Teachers should note that pictures and other diagrams are at the representational level and may be difficult for concrete-level learners to use. Instruction in this strategy should include modeling that explicitly links the picture to the components of the problem.

    a. Study the pattern of the figures shown below. Draw the next 3 figures in the pattern.

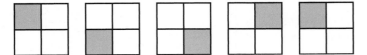

    b. Draw a ray that bisects the angle below:

    c. A lumberyard charges 45 cents per foot of 2″ by 2″ lumber and 10 cents a cut to reduce the 8-foot lengths to custom measures. How much would it cost to order four lengths that are 1 1/2 feet long apiece?

    d. The following are coordinates of points in a coordinate plane: $(-1, 2)$, $(3, 2)$, and $(3, -2)$. What would the coordinates of a fourth point have to be so that a square will be formed by connecting the points with line segments? (South Carolina PACT, 2001, Copyright S.C. Department of Education, reprinted by permission.)

6. *Act it out.* Word problems that involve action or change can be acted out with students to model what happened in the problem. Younger students may need to act out problems involving simple addition and subtraction to see the difference (example a). Even older students need convincing sometimes with problems such as example (b). Acting these out can assist students with keeping up with the steps of multi-step problems.

a. Angela had 10 books on her desk. She loaned 3 to her sister. How many books did she have left? Her sister returned one book. How many does she have now?

b. Ms. Shaw saw a porcelain vase at a flea market and bought it for $30. Her friend, Ms. Leggett, begged her to sell it so she sold it for $40. Ms. Shaw changed her mind but had to pay $50 to get the vase back. A dealer spotted the vase on the way out of the market and offered Ms. Shaw $60. If Ms. Shaw takes this offer, will she come out ahead, even, or behind? By how much?

7. *Create a list, table, or chart.* Problems that present a lot of data or ask about combinations, a number of possible answers, or a sequence of events lend themselves to making lists, tables, or charts. Even if another strategy is eventually needed for solving the problem, this graphic representation of data can assist the problem solver in understanding critical aspects of the problem.

a. At a local restaurant, diners can select one meat and two vegetables from the blue-plate menu. If 4 meats and 8 vegetables are available today, how many possible combinations could the restaurant serve?

b. A local shopping mall is being renovated so that each store's owner will have a choice for colors for the front, door, and awning. The possible choices are: front (gray, cream, or teal), awnings (maroon or yellow), and doors (black or green). Show all possible outcomes of the color choices.

Developing a chart is a useful strategy for mapping out known and unknown information in algebra problems such as example (c) as follows:

c. For a given rectangle, the length is 1.6 times the width. Find the perimeter and area of rectangles with the width of 8, 16, and 24 inches.

8. *Solve part of the problem (decompose and recombine).* Problems that are multi-step or have complex structures lend themselves to decomposition of parts. However, Pólya cautions about "a very foolish and bad habit with some students to start working at details before having understood the problem as a whole" (p. 72). Once students consider the complete problem by asking, "What is not known? What is the information?" they should ask, "Would it be helpful to separate parts for better understanding or partial solutions?" Consider the following example:

Construct an equilateral triangle within a circle with a diameter of 6 inches. The student must consider each broad concept—diameter of circle, characteristics of equilateral triangles—and then the two concepts recombined. The examples that follow are other problems that can be decomposed and recombined.

a. On Monday Kim's mother gave her school money for the week. She spent $2.80 for lunch every day for five school days. She paid a $ .75 book fine at the library and bought school supplies for $3.50. If Kim had $1.75 left at the end of the week, how much did her mother give her on Monday? (Texas Assessment of Knowledge and Skills, Released Grade Eight, Pearson Educational Measurement, Copyright © 2004, Content used here under license. All Rights Reserved.)

b. Two groups of tourists each have 60 people. If $\frac{3}{4}$ of the first group and $\frac{2}{3}$ of the second group board buses to travel to a museum, how many more people in the first group board buses than in the second group? (From *TIMSS Released Sample Middle School Mathematics Test* (Grades 7 and 8), copyright 1995, permission to reprint by the International Association for the Evaluation of Educational Achievement.)

9. *Use a formula.* The most common problems requiring the application of formulas are those in geometry and measurement. Formulas describe the relationships among points, lines, and surfaces for two- and three-dimensional objects. They describe other relationships such as conversions between measurement systems, trigonometric functions, and even compounded interest, calorie intake calculations, and batting averages. Many students with disabilities have trouble remembering specific formulas because concepts underlying formulas are not understood or they view each formula as a separate, abstract memorization task. Consider the two examples below, both addressing surface area:

a. What is the area of a room 12 feet long by 8 feet wide?
b. What is the area of a parallelogram whose two long sides measure 12 inches and the height measures 8 inches?

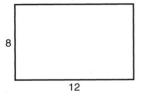

If students understand the concept that area is a square unit measure of length by width in very rough terms, they will readily determine that the floor is 96 square feet. If they also understand that this rough length by width can be applied to the parallelogram by visually chopping off one side with a perpendicular line (shown dotted above) and placing it on the other side, the parallelogram is 96 square inches. Hands-on tools such as geoboards or graph paper can assist this spatial understanding.

Other formulas are called for when a "standard" reference is provided in the problem. What is the temperature, interest payment, batting average, length in meters, volume, or sum of squares, given specific data that can be plugged into a formula?

c. At 3 p.m., the temperature outside was 75° Fahrenheit. What was the temperature in degrees Celsius? (Apply the formula $C = (F - 32)/1.8$)
d. Nolan Ryan pitched 149 innings in the 1981 regular season and gave up 28 earned runs. What was his earned run average (ERA) that season? (Apply the formula: (number of earned runs $\times$ 9) divided by (number of innings pitched).

Some statewide tests provide formulas for students to apply (example e); others expect students to recall formulas, then apply them (example f). A few states provide a page at the front of the test booklet listing common formulas and conversions (e.g., Texas, Virginia, and Florida).

e. The variables x and y are related by the following formula:
$(x + 10)/6 = y$
If $x = 8$, what is the value of y?

f. The slope of a ramp is 30° as pictured below. If the ramp is 40 feet long, how high is the ramp at the tallest point?

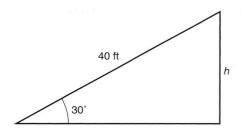

10. *Write an equation.* Similar to applying a formula, an equation uses symbols to represent the unknown information in a problem. Some problems require two or more simultaneous equations because there is more than one unknown or more than one "data statement" (see example b). For students with disabilities, it is often helpful to use special letters to represent unknown variables (e. g., s for student, t for teacher).

a. At this school there are 20 times as many students as teachers. If there are 25 teachers, how many students are in this school?

b. The third-grade class is planning a party for their parents. If 30 sodas and four dozen cookies are ordered, the cost would be $40. If 40 sodas and five dozen cookies are ordered, the cost would be $51.25. How much do sodas and cookies cost?

Many state-level tests include items that require students to create equations (example c) or select from a list of equations (example d).

c. Rosie bought 12 yards of fabric for a total of $59.40. Write an equation that could be used to compute the cost per yard.

d. Mora downloaded 15 songs to her personal player. Sara downloaded 3 times as many as Mora. Allison has 4 songs more than Sara. Which equation shows how many songs Allison has (z)?

A. $15 + 3 + 4 = z$
B. $4 - (3 \times 15) = z$
C. $4 \times (15 - 3) = z$
D. $(15 \times 3) - 4 = z$
E. $(15 \times 3) + 4 = z$

As is discussed in content strand E, Functions, many students hold a restricted view of variables and tend to consider them concrete objects or labels rather than numbers in equivalence statements that demonstrate functional relationships (Küchemann, 1978).

11. *Work backward.* This strategy has been used for years by students who discovered the answers to some problems at the end of their math textbooks. It is also an excellent

strategy for solving problems when a reasonable answer can be estimated or may even be known but a solution strategy is not apparent. Some problems begin with the "final" information and ask for the pieces along the way that led to the answer (examples a and b).

   a. The book sale yielded $925 for the school. If 637 hardback books were sold at $1 and paperbacks cost 50 cents, how many paperbacks were sold?

   b. The diver needs a total of 287 points to beat the other divers at a competition. The first two dives yielded a total of 190 points from the scores of ten judges on a 10-point scale. What should the average score by judges be for the final dive to win the competition?

   c. How can you bring the amount of liquid in a container up to six quarts when you have only two containers, one four quarts and one nine quarts (from Pólya, 1945, pp. 198–201).

   12. *Look for patterns.* Patterns are systematic repetitions. They may be in numerical, visual, or event (action) forms. Patterns are used in problems that call for predictions and generalizations. The following examples demonstrate problems calling for numerical (example a), visual (example b), and event (example c) forms.

   a. The first five terms in a sequence are 1, 2, 4, 7, and 11. What will be the eighth term in this sequence?

   b. Draw the design that will be fifth in this pattern.

   (Adapted from the *NC End of Grade Mathematics Grade 3 Sample Items*, copyright 2003, reprinted by permission, North Carolina Department of Public Instruction/State Board of Education, Accountability Services, North Carolina Testing Program.)

   c. Mr. Smith has decided to sell his XYZ stock when it reaches $100 per share. The chart below shows the growth of his stock by weeks. When should he sell his stock if it continues to grow at the same rate?

Week	Price Per Share
1	$ 5
2	$10
3	$20
4	$40

Students with learning problems should be taught these alternative strategies explicitly, with many examples connecting the solution strategy to problem types. Some teachers use code words to prompt strategy use, for example, Patterns, Simpler Case, Guess, Table, or Model. Students also should be taught critical vocabulary in word problem directions, such as solve, compute, simplify, estimate, graph, construct, measure, select, find, which expression, or which statement.

Strategies for "Carry Out the Plan"

Selecting a solution strategy will not result automatically in the correct solution. Students who are poor problem solvers generally apply a strategy without monitoring its effectiveness. They should be taught the essential metacognitive processes that accompany problem solving. Montague defines metacognitive processes for mathematics as awareness and regulation of cognitive processes (1992). Metacognition is the executive control part of the information-processing system and includes selecting appropriate strategies, monitoring progress during work, evaluating whether a solution strategy was successful, and reflecting back on what was learned in the process.

First, teachers should model "think-aloud" strategies for students and encourage them to use this mental talk during the problem-solving process. Students with disabilities may need question starters to prompt this self-talk: Am I applying the strategy in a logical manner? Do I have all the necessary information? Have I calculated accurately? Am I keeping track of each step of my work in case I have to back track? Do I need to change my approach or try a different strategy?

Keeping track of work is especially important in multi-step problems. Students should begin recognizing problems that have several steps. Some may actually be short in terms of wording but it is evident that information has not been presented in a direct form without a first or second step of information manipulation. For example, *Joe bought 5 gallons of gas for his lawnmower for $9.75. If he burns 1 gallon in 1.5 hours, how much should he compute for the cost of gas in a 3-hour job?*

Even when a solution strategy isn't successful, students should understand they can sometimes use part of the process or at least learn from the process. Again, prompting questions help guide this type of thinking. Did any part of the solution make sense? Can I use some of the information? At what point did the solution strategy break down?

Strategies for rescuing a partially successful strategy include going back to ask if all relevant information was used, estimating the solution to gauge the work ahead, considering whether there may be more than one solution, and applying a new strategy (such as charting or drawing a picture) at the mid-point. Strategies for starting over after a failed process are starting with a different perspective on the problem, simplifying the problem, and using a different heuristic.

Strategies for "Look Back"

Students with mathematics disabilities are often satisfied with any answer. They write it down and are finished. Good problem solvers, however, engage in a final step that not only increases the probability of a correct solution but also informs them more deeply on the problem type for future reference.

Once a solution (or solutions) is determined, the problem solver should compare it with expectations. Does it make sense in the context of the problem? Is it close to the original estimate? Has the problem question or implied question been answered? Can I check the solution by inserting it back into the problem or working backward? Generally the more pragmatic and real world the problem, the more sense making can be made. However, students can fail to complete this step in even the most obvious problems. A physics teacher was teaching about electric current (newton, joule, watt, volt, ohm). She used an example of a 100 W light bulb (100 Watt-hours). She asked the class to compute the cost of burning a light bulb all night (6 hours) if a kWh costs $ .0577. The results should have been energy times rate or .6 kWh $\times$ 0.577 = $ .03462 (just over 3 cents). Some students returned with results such as $34.62 and even $346,200!

Students should be encouraged to study the problem type for future reference (forward-reaching transfer). Was this a compare or combine problem? Why did a chart strategy work with this information? Could I have used a simpler strategy and still achieved the solution?

Some statewide tests require students to explain their answers in writing. For example, *what can be the greatest number of days in two months? Explain your answer.* This task is especially challenging for students with a combination of mathematics and language disabilities. Practice throughout the year in providing oral explanations of problem solutions, listening to other students provide reasoning, and occasionally writing out these explanations with corrective feedback is critical for success. Students with disabilities often provide faulty or superficial reasoning such as "it was the best answer" or "because that's what it came out to be" or "because one number was bigger than the other."

▲■●▲■●▲■●▲■●▲■●▲■●▲■●▲■

TRY THIS

Solve and write out an explanation for the following problem.

Mr. Riley grows four different crops on his 300-acre farm. Each acre has the same number of plants. Of the total acres, 25% is wheat, 35% is corn, 20% is cotton, and the rest are beans. Mr. Riley thinks that if he plants wheat in all of the acres that are now beans, more than half of his farm would be wheat. Is he correct? Explain your answer.

Adapted from *Release of Spring 2003 Test Items,* Massachusetts Department of Education, by permission.

▼■▼●▼■▼●▼■▼●▼■▼●▼■▼●▼■▼

CURRICULUM CONCERNS

One of the most challenging aspects of problem solving is integrating assessment, content standards, instruction, and practice across mathematics topics and grade levels. Some content areas lend themselves to specific solution strategies such as formulas in geometry and equations in algebra. Younger students need

Figure 5.3
Problem-Solving Strategies by Grade-Level Band

Grade-Level Span	Initial Strategy Instruction
K–2	Use manipulatives Act it out Draw pictures Make simple lists Discuss with others Use whole number models
3–5	Paraphrase Represent data in a variety of forms (tables, charts, models) Identify patterns Use trial and error Distinguish important from irrelevant Use basic logic (and, or, not) Make valid and invalid arguments
6–8	Break problems down Work backward Understand different approaches to same problem Generalize from pattern Use a variety of reasoning and logic abilities
9–12	Apply a wide variety of strategies Construct multi-step algorithms Conduct proofs Use math notation as representations Implement a variety of modeling strategies

more concrete strategies, while older students should have developed a large repertoire of skills. Recommended solution strategies by grade level bands are depicted in Figure 5.3 (see, for example, Cook & Rasmussen, 1994; Stiff & Curcio, 1999).

Teachers should decide how problem-solving instruction will be related to the total mathematics curriculum for students. One powerful approach is to use realistic problems as the context for teaching mathematics content and for assessing content understanding. For example, when beginning a unit on statistics, students are presented with a class problem—to find data on students' music preferences and analyze results by gender and age. This approach is motivating for students, connects content with problem types, and develops the other mathematics processes at the same time. However, teachers should plan a range of problems, providing students extended practice, not just a few "super" problems.

Another approach is to teach problem solving simultaneously with content instruction. Most mathematics basals incorporate problem solving within each unit of specific content development. A new lesson typically begins with a problem and most lessons close with a small set of related problems. The Miller and Mercer *Strategic Math Series*, described in the next section, pairs a graduated problem-solving sequence with instruction in arithmetic concepts. This approach has an advantage in enriching content understanding through problem solving and providing multiple examples of problems related to specific content. However, unless mixed practice is planned, students may have difficulty with transfer and generalization.

Finally, teachers can use specialized problem-solving curricula as supplements to a regular basal or unit approach to content instruction. Montague's *Solve It!* and Jitendra's *Teaching Word Problem Solving to Students with Learning Disabilities* are research-based instructional programs developed for special needs learners and are described in more detail in the next section. Another option is adapting a general education problem-solving program, such as *Problem-solving Experiences: Making Sense of Mathematics* (Charles & Lester, 2005), that has a sound research base and effective instructional elements.

Other supplements, such as Cohen's *Figure it Out* (2003) and The Math Forum's problems of the week, are not full research-based curricula but can offer additional practice if matched carefully to curriculum goals. Teachers should select or create word problems that are aligned with content standards and promote understanding of problem types, use of specific problem-solving strategies, and instructional-level mathematics language. When examining a word problem, teachers should consider: What content and problem type is reflected? Is the problem stated in a question or implied? How many steps are involved? Does the problem contain extraneous material or omit necessary information? Are students prompted to use a specific strategy? Have students been exposed to the mathematics terms and concepts in the problem? Figure 5.4 illustrates a checklist for evaluating problem characteristics. Teachers should work through each problem, considering possible strategies and anticipating difficulties, before posing problems for students.

Problem-Solving Curricula

Miller and Mercer developed the *Strategic Math Series* (1991–1994) as an instructional program for teaching arithmetic facts to students with disabilities. Based on a concrete-semiconcrete-representational model of instruction, these instructional modules incorporate a graduated sequence of problem solving instruction within each lesson. During the concrete-level lessons, students label number problems with concrete descriptors such as "cubes" or "red disks." In the semiconcrete lessons, the labels change to "tallies" and "circles." Beginning with the abstract lessons, students encounter number problems requiring short realistic phrases (brown bags and chocolate cookies). Then sentences appear with numbers aligned, followed by the typical word problem. The program next introduces the notion of extraneous information for students to discover and cross out. Finally, students are encouraged to create their own problems using the same structure for the given operation. The multiplication and subtraction strategies' word problem effectiveness were studied with 67 elementary students and resulted in gains from solving no problems prior to intervention to post-intervention results from 84 to 92 percent, with 60 to 91 percent success on student-created problems (Miller & Mercer, 1993).

Solve It! (Montague, 2003) is a problem-solving curriculum for secondary students with learning problems in mathematics. This program includes a sequence of scripted lessons in which students are taught to apply cognitive and self-regulation strategies in the context of mathematics problem solving. The program includes an informal

Figure 5.4
Analysis of Word Problem Characteristics

Word Problems:

1. Walter brought 7 books back to the library on Monday. That was 4 more than he brought on Friday. How many books did he return on Friday?

2. Karen wants to buy five apples. The sign says six apples for $3.25 and bananas for $.99 a bunch. How much would she pay for five apples?

3. A recipe calls for three times as much flour as milk. Make a list of the amounts of flour needed for 1, $1\frac{1}{2}$, 2, and $2\frac{1}{2}$ cups of milk.

4. Jane and Bob are driving from Raleigh to Orlando. If they average 56.5 miles per hour for the trip, how long will the drive take?

	Problem 1	Problem 2	Problem 3	Problem 4
Math Content	Whole number operations	Whole number operations	Rational number operations, Measurement	Rational number operations, Measurement
Problem Type	Compare	Equivalent sets (vary)	Restate	Equivalent sets (vary)
Vocabulary	No specialized vocabulary	No specialized vocabulary	Cups	Miles per hour
Question	Direct	Direct	Indirect	Direct
Steps	One	Two	Multiple	Two
Information	All provided and needed	Extraneous	All provided and needed	Distance needed
Strategies	Subtract Diagram Act it out	Divide, multiply Proportion Diagram	Multiply Diagram/chart Equation Pattern	Divide Diagram Equation

assessment tool, the *Math Problem Solving Assessment-Short Form* (Montague, 1996). Lessons 1 and 2 provide instruction in the seven-step problem-solving routine. Lessons 3 through 5 involve practice with the routine. Beginning with Lesson 6, students practice the strategy with sets of ten math problems. Lesson 8 is the first progress check. Practice and mastery problem sets were drawn from a pool of 400 arithmetic operation problems (whole number and decimals) in one-, two-, and three-step formats. Teacher's materials emphasize research-based instructional practices including explicit strategy instruction, process modeling, visualization of problems, peer coaching, performance feedback, student charting of their own progress, mastery learning, and distributive practice.

Teaching Word Problem Solving to Students with Learning Disabilities introduces a research-based approach for teaching mathematics problem solving (Jitendra, 2002).

Building on the work of Riley, Greeno, and Heller (1983); Zawaiza and Gerber (1993); Hutchinson (1993); and Marshall (1995), Jitendra developed and validated a series of lessons in which students are taught three types of addition/subtraction problems (one and two steps) and two types of multiplication/division problems using adaptations of the Marshall schemas (diagrams) for each problem type (see Figure 5.5). The sequence of instruction includes pretesting, teaching each schema diagram for addition/subtraction using problem stories with full information (no unknowns), teaching a strategy for setting up an equation using unknowns, solving problems using the strategy, then providing mixed problem practice. Students move on to two-step problems and multiplication/division problem types in later lessons.

Extensive, rigorous research with *Teaching Word Problem Solving* has yielded significant results for learners with disabilities. The 1996 study (Jitendra & Hoff) with three students on addition and subtraction problem types was extended in 1998 (Jitendra et al.) with thirty-four students. Students with disabilities using traditional materials increased their word problem solving ability from 49 to 65 percent, while students in the schema group increased from 51 to 77 percent. The scores for a control group of third graders remained about 82 percent. Scores on generalization and delayed posttests also yielded significant differences in favor of the schema group.

An exploratory study (Jitendra, DiPipi, & Perron-Jones, 2002) of two multiplication/division strategies (vary and multiplicative comparison) with four middle school students resulted in substantial improvements for all subjects over twelve training sessions and on generalization and maintenance measures (after ten weeks). Most importantly, teachers reported that students were using the strategies independently on district tests and actually enjoyed this type of problem solving. This research was extended by a study with twenty-two middle-school students (Xin, Jitendra, & Deatline-Buchman, 2005). The schema-based instruction group significantly outperformed the general strategy instruction group on immediate posttests and delayed posttests and transfer tests of multiplicative comparison and proportion type problems. Jitendra and her colleagues have also validated curriculum-based measures to assess word problem growth and proficiency (Jitendra, Sczesniak, & Deatline-Buchman, 2005).

Problem Solving across the Curriculum

The problem-solving sequence employed in mathematics is useful for other applications, including science, social studies, writing, social skills, and real-world problems. The wide applicability of this process has the potential to mold a problem-solving approach in students that will serve them in many situations, both in school and in other settings.

In science, problems related to physical, chemical, and/or biological aspects of the world and beyond are considered opportunities to develop and test hypotheses. The scientific process of inquiry (formerly termed the scientific method) has its roots in the work of Aristotle, Bacon, Galileo, and Newton. The essential elements can be compared with the mathematics problem-solving process: characterization (define all relevant concepts related to the subject of the investigation); hypothesis (suggested explanation); prediction (logical deduction); experiment (test of the prediction); and conclusions.

Figure 5.5
Schematic Diagrams for Problem Stories

Change

Bonnie had 45 CDs of her favorite music. She now has 57 CDs after receiving 12 more for her birthday.

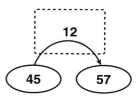

Group (Combine)

Michael wanted to organize his Reds baseball cards by decade. He had 59 cards from the 1970s, 64 cards from the 1980s, and 95 cards from the 1990s. He had 218 cards altogether.

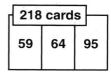

Compare

Allan did 14 of his mathematics homework problems on Friday and 23 on Saturday. On Saturday he worked 9 more problems than on Friday.

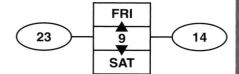

Multiplicative Comparison (Restate)

Deborah has 6 purple crayons. She has 7 times as many red crayons. She has 42 crayons.

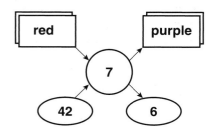

Vary

The cost of a tangerine is 30 cents. Six tangerines will cost $1.80.

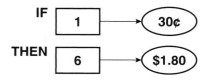

Situation diagrams from: *Schemas in Problem Solving* (p. 135) by S. P. Marshall, 1995, New York: Cambridge University Press. Reprinted by permission of Cambridge University Press. For Jitendra's adaptations, see Jitendra (2002) and Xin, Jitendra, & Deatline-Buchman (2005).

Scientists today emphasize that this process is not linear; observations lead to new questions or clarification of the hypothesis, leading to new predictions.

A reading and study skills strategy related to the problem-solving process is the KWL procedure (Ogle, 1986). Before reading, either as an individual or with a group, examine what you already **know** about the subject. Determine what you **want** to learn (and **how** you will find out). Read the material and reflect on what you **learned.**

A closely-related writing process includes six steps: determine topic or brainstorm, engage in prewriting activities such as mapping, write a rough draft, revise, edit, and share or publish (see, for example, Harris & Graham, 1996). The *process* of writing is emphasized in this self-monitoring, strategic approach and it mirrors the process that experienced writers use.

For social skills, decision-making, or interpersonal dilemmas, a common strategy involves: recognize and define the problem, list possible solutions with probable outcomes, select and implement a solution, evaluate the results. For example, a student may be faced with the social skills problem of not engaging successfully in a friendly conversation. In examining the problem, the student first thought the other students were rude and not friendly because they kept walking away. Upon closer inspection, the student revised the problem to each student's inability to find a common topic and carry on a discussion about the topic. Possible solutions he listed were finding new friends with the same interests, finding out more about the interests of these students, and getting an independent party involved to keep the conversation going. The second option seemed to be the most realistic for the situation so the student set out a plan of asking a lot of questions about the other students' interests, then reading up on the topics. When the solution strategy was actually implemented, the student found that they all had one common interest (musical instruments) but from their different experiences could learn from each other.

Some schools have implemented school-wide problem-solving procedures that employ similar problem-solving steps for behavioral issues as well as curricular applications (see, for example, Rasmussen, 2002). In those schools everyone—teachers, students, administrators, and staff—is using the same language and holding students responsible for applying these strategies in a wide range of settings.

Problem-Solving Instructional Guidelines

Research on effective strategies for solving mathematics word problems and their use by students with learning problems is beginning to converge into a few key guidelines.

- Connect problem solving with other mathematics content.
- Introduce a problem-solving sequence that can be applied to both routine and nonroutine problems and includes understanding the problem, developing a plan, carrying out the plan, and reflecting.
- Teach students to recognize problem types, using the deeper mathematical structure of the problem rather than surface-level semantics.
- Assist students in building their problem-solving strategy repertoire with more sophisticated heuristics each year.

- Select mathematics word problems that are correlated with curriculum goals and testing formats and provide for practice in explicit problem types.
- Provide explicit, carefully sequenced instruction in effective problem-solving strategies including graphic representations, transfer of problem types, problem visualization, equation creation, and estimation.
- Use effective general teaching approaches during problem-solving instruction: create a positive climate, engage learners, provide specific feedback, use elaborated examples, and plan for distributed practice and generalization opportunities.

Problem solving can be the most challenging and rewarding aspect of the mathematics curriculum. Teachers should model the critical dispositions of curiosity, persistence, interest, and enthusiasm they want their students to develop.

> *. . . the trains passed each other in Charleston, South Carolina, 12 hours after their departures. What was the average speed of each train?*

CHAPTER SUMMARY

- Problem-solving skills are important for mathematics concept understanding, success in high-stakes testing, and in real-life activities and work.
- Good problem solvers spend more time, utilize strategies, have a strong mathematics concept understanding, are good estimators, can perceive patterns, and are persistent with problem solutions, characteristics that are goals for struggling students.
- Students with mathematics disabilities often lack organizational, self-regulation, sequencing, and reading comprehension strategies.
- Most problem-solving sequences employ a version of Pólya's approach: understand the

problem, devise a plan, carry out the plan, and look back.
- Specific strategies for each phase of the problem-solving sequence can be taught explicitly. These strategies should be developed across the K–12 curriculum.
- Teachers should decide on a problem-solving approach: problem-driven curriculum, simultaneous problem-solving instruction, or supplemental problem-solving curriculum.
- Problem solving is also taught and reinforced in other content areas and for social skills instruction.

RESOURCES

Baroody, A. J. (1993). *Problem solving, reasoning, and communicating, K-8: Helping children think mathematically.* New York: Merrill.

Burns, M. (1996) *50 Problem-solving lessons.* ETA/Cuisenaire.

Krulik, S., & Rudnick, J. A. (1996). *The new source-book for teaching reasoning and problem solving in junior and senior high school.* Boston: Allyn and Bacon.

Meyer, C., & Sallee, T. (1983) *Make it simpler: A practical guide to problem solving in mathematics.* ETA/Cuisenaire.

Miller, E. D. (1998) *Read it! Draw it! Solve it!* A problem-solving program from reading readiness through third grade. Dale Seymour Publications.

O'Connell, S. (2000). *Introduction to problem solving strategies for the elementary math classroom.* Portsmouth, NH: Heinemann.

Reys, B. J. (1999). *Elementary School Mathematics: What every parent should know about estimation; What every parent should know about problem solving* (2nd ed.). Reston, VA: NCTM.

Stevenson, F. W. (1992). *Exploratory problems in Mathematics.* Reston, VA: NCTM.

Taylor, L. & Taylor, H. (1997) *You think you've got math problems!* Dale Seymour Publications.

The Math Forum (http://mathforum.org). Problems of the week by grade level and mathematics topic.

Chapter 6

Chapter Questions

1. How does the concept of universal design impact the selection of mathematics methods and materials?
2. What curriculum programs are available for use with special-needs learners?
3. What are some concerns with general education mathematics programs and how can those be adapted for special-needs learners?
4. How are manipulatives and other hands-on materials best used in mathematics instruction?
5. How can technology enhance instruction?
6. What other resources are available for planning and teaching mathematics?

Materials and Resources to Support Mathematics Instruction

Angela Smith, Joseph Lopez, and Chris Johnson are in their sixth month of new teaching assignments in special, general, and remedial education classes with the Pine Hills School District and were just informed that the district will be adopting new mathematics textbooks and supplementary materials for the next school year. They have been asked to serve on committees to review and select these materials. During a staff development meeting of new teachers, they once again compare experiences and discuss this new challenge.

Angela (the special educator): I'm interested in finding supplementary mathematics materials for both pull-out and integrated middle-school classes. I don't need to teach a complete program, but fill in some missing gaps with interesting approaches that will work.

Joseph (teaches high school Geometry and Algebra classes): I wonder if new textbooks might better meet the needs of a wide range of learning needs. I'm having to search for too many additional materials on my own.

Chris (elementary math support teacher): A lot of our classroom teachers have boxes of mathematics manipulatives but don't appear to use them much with instruction. I would like to see teachers' guides that make these connections and assist teachers. ■ ● ▲

All three teachers will be reviewing mathematics textbooks and supplementary materials influenced by the mathematics curriculum standards of 1989 and 2000. However, textbooks and other materials have varying instructional and research support for special-needs learners because the mathematics curriculum standards do not call for specific, validated methods for diverse learners. The Individuals with Disabilities Education Act (1997, 2004) requires that all students be given access to the general education curriculum, including related instruction, technology, textbooks, and other materials and that scientifically-based methods be employed. The 2004 reauthorization also emphasized universal design concepts for curriculum and materials.

UNIVERSAL DESIGN

The concept of **universal design,** first developed for architectural applications, is now applied to concepts of curriculum interface where diverse learners seek access, or appropriate instructional methods and materials, to the same curriculum standards. Universal design for learning "means the design of instructional materials and activities that allow the learning goals to be achievable by individuals with wide differences in their abilities to see, hear, move, read, write, understand English, attend, organize, engage, and remember" (Orkwis & McLane, 1998). For curriculum materials, universal design is the built-in flexibility of use. However, no materials will ever be universally applicable. The goal of promoting universal design features is to increase the adaptability of materials for the most efficient use by teachers for the most effective use by most students. As with the concepts of architectural design, universal curriculum design is not about lowering standards or applied only to students with disabilities, it is to make the current learning environment more flexible for a wider group of learners. The best design features allow flexible use by the most students.

The joint Council for Exceptional Children/Office of Special Education Programs stakeholder's meeting on universal design in fall 1997 developed a framework of universal design for curriculum development that has spurred further research and development (Orkwis & McLane, 1998). Each aspect of this framework is illustrated here with examples from mathematics curriculum materials. These examples focus on alternatives that reduce cognitive barriers rather than the more apparent physical disabilities—vision, hearing, speech, or motor barriers.

1. *Provide flexible means of representation.* Making representations is a key NCTM process standard important for both teacher and student representations of concepts. This component, however, addresses the nature of new information represented to students for learning. Students learn about mathematics concepts and strategies by observing teacher models, reading textbooks, viewing models and charts, collecting data, working with concrete materials, and viewing the work of others. Among the recommended strategies to enhance representations is emphasizing the big ideas of content, rather than a multitude of details. For example, a big idea in computation is base-ten regrouping for addition. A student does not have to learn all possible algorithms for performing these computations. A

student with working memory issues might work best with a partial-sums addition method (see content strand B). Another recommended strategy is determining and building background knowledge. For the previous example, the student who learned partial sums for addition may learn left-to-right subtraction algorithms more effectively. In addition to considering the big idea, teachers should examine any printed materials for readability level, vocabulary demands, language clarity, and overall organization of printed materials. If alternatives are not provided with the materials, teachers can adapt printed materials to reduce vocabulary load, items per page, or readability level using assistive technology.

2. *Provide flexible means of expression.* This component addresses the expression of learning by students, including demonstration, writing, drawing, and speaking. Flexibility in format for expressions, for example oral rather than written descriptions, are encouraged when some formats will not allow full expression of what has been learned. Or when students are learning new formats (initial writing or English as a second language), they can be assisted with the use of translators until the new format is a stronger tool. For example, a student has been asked to write out in words how she solved a math problem. The student's written language ability is below her math ability so she explains her reasoning aloud and a scribe writes the verbatim description. Another student struggles with keeping numbers and other math symbols organized on paper. The teacher provides graph paper for working specific textbook problems. In mathematics classes where so much work is cooperative and students view and discuss the work of others, it is especially important that curriculum design be universal—applied, if appropriate, to all students so that it is natural, not stigmatizing, and promotes better learning by everyone.

3. *Provide flexible means of engagement.* Student engagement in learning can be affected by other factors, such as motivation and cultural background. Concrete materials are excellent tools for motivating reluctant learners in mathematics, if used effectively within the curriculum. As will be discussed later in this chapter, concrete materials should be selected carefully and used to promote learning of important concepts. Teachers who are assigned new students from other cultures should attempt to understand the previous mathematics approaches used with the student, through talking with family members, viewing student records, or meeting with community support groups. Those alternative approaches to powerful mathematics concepts taught in classrooms around the world should be incorporated, valued, and shared. Mathematics is particularly rich in multicultural applications, as will be illustrated in the content strands later in this text. If a student's mathematics abilities are higher than his English learning ability, teachers should allow work with translations or in both languages until the English-based understanding of mathematics catches up. Engagement with mathematics also means student practice opportunities and cooperative grouping. These instructional arrangements have a wide range of options to meet individual student needs.

The components of universal design addressed above apply to all aspects of teaching and learning, not just materials design. But curriculum materials have an enormous influence over classroom teacher decisions about "what" and "how" curriculum is taught,

Assistive technology includes devices that assist individuals with disabilities to increase, maintain, or improve functional capabilities; also services that assist them in acquiring or using such devices (Technology Act, 1988).

especially those who view the textbook as the primary resource for the class (Duffy, 1987; Kon, 1994). Adopted textbook series, especially developmental basals, tend to set the scope and sequence of mathematics topics for the school year, outline the way lessons are introduced, and schedule practice, application, and review opportunities. Other materials, supplemental books or manipulative kits, are also common in general, remedial, and special education classrooms to offer support to the regular basal. This chapter will examine books, materials, and other resources available for teachers like Angela, Joseph, and Chris and discuss their best use with learners with mathematics disabilities.

Textbook series and other curricula are typically developed and validated through expert opinion, alignment with standards, and limited field review. Teachers or school committees selecting materials should consider the following elements when making decisions about mathematics curriculum adoption:

■ Materials are aligned with the NCTM content standards (or parts of the standards), and therefore provide access to the general curriculum and high-stakes testing programs. The content concepts are interconnected throughout.

■ Instructional design is universal, providing teacher and student flexibility for representation, expression, and engagement. Instructor's materials are based on effective instructional methods and provide appropriate instructional supports (scaffolds) for students with learning differences.

■ Materials have been validated through field-testing with clearly defined control groups, student characteristics (including students with disabilities, English language learners, minority groups, and low-income students), and outcome measures.

Many textbook series have been aligned with NCTM curriculum standards but have limited research on actual effectiveness with students (Carnine & Gersten, 2000). Very few quantitative experimental studies exist to support the use of commercial mathematics materials. Even fewer control instructional elements or break out research results for specific student populations.

TRY THIS
Review an adopted textbook series for universal design elements and research support.

Some commercial mathematics materials can be considered **comprehensive and developmental** because they address the full mathematics curriculum in a sequenced, grade-level approach. Other materials are clearly **remedial**, addressing earlier mathematics concepts for older students who have gaps in learning. Still other materials are **supplemental,** focusing on one domain, such as computation or problem solving, or a very focused application, such as telling time or solving proportions. Supplemental materials can support developmental, remedial, or even teacher-constructed programs.

CURRICULA FOR SPECIAL-NEEDS STUDENTS

Several programs have been developed specifically for students with learning problems or those at risk of low performance. Prominent examples include the *Strategic Mathematics Series* (Mercer & Miller, 1991–94), *Direct Instruction Mathematics* (Stein, Kinder,

Silbert, & Carnine, 2006), *Adaptations for Special Populations* (Saxon Publishers), and *TouchMath* (Innovative Learning Concepts, 2000/05). The features and research bases for these programs are addressed briefly in the next sections.

Strategic Math Series

The *Strategic Math Series* (Mercer & Miller, 1991–1994) is a series of well-researched procedures for teaching basic computational skills with simultaneous problem solving, a supplemental program. The series is based on the best of behavioral and cognitive research involving students with learning problems (LD, ED, MD, and at-risk). Behavioral aspects include carefully structured direct instruction lessons involving modeling, guided practice with feedback, independent practice, and progress charting. Cognitive aspects are goal setting, self-monitoring, mnemonic devices, and a concrete–representational–abstract (CRA) sequence of instruction. The seven phases for instruction within each computation area are:

1. Pretest
2. Teach concrete application (three lessons)
3. Teach representational application (three lessons)
4. Introduce the "DRAW" strategy (seventh lesson)—(Discover the sign; Read the problem; Answer, or draw and check; Write the answer)
5. Teach abstract application (three lessons)
6. Posttest
7. Provide practice to fluency (eleven or twelve more lessons)

Titles in the series to date include addition facts 0 to 9, subtraction facts 0 to 9, place value, addition facts 10 to 18, subtraction facts 10 to 18, multiplication facts 0 to 81, and division facts 0 to 81. Materials included with the teacher's manual are reproducible "learning sheets," detailed teaching notes, progress charts, and ideas for fluency practice with the program's unique "pig dice." The sheets (see Figure 6.1) are called learning sheets because they are used during instruction with clear model, prompt (guided practice), and check (independent practice) sections. Items are presented randomly using both vertical and horizontal formats and the items for early skills are presented with letters rather than numbers to prevent confusion with the actual computation. Each lesson incorporates part of a graduated word problem sequence (Miller & Mercer, 1997).

The authors conducted field tests to validate the concrete–representational–abstract (CRA) instructional sequence and specific lesson procedures with teachers in a variety of settings for students with disabilities. Experimental research further validated the instructional procedures and resulted in significant student achievement (see, for example, Peterson, Mercer, & O'Shea, 1988; Harris, Miller, & Mercer, 1995).

Although the series was developed for initial learning of number and operation concepts, these materials have been used with middle-school students who had never mastered basic facts. The materials are not age specific, and students are able to quickly master (and understand) basic facts and operations in only a few lessons. Teachers should be aware that these materials are for basic fact mastery and related word problems, not

Figure 6.1
Learning Sheet

Learning Sheet 9

Describe and Model

1) $\begin{array}{r} 8 \\ \underline{\times 5} \end{array}$

Guided Practice

2) $\begin{array}{r} 8 \\ \underline{\times 6} \end{array}$ 3) $1 \times 7 =$ ______ 4) $\begin{array}{r} 5 \\ \underline{\times 0} \end{array}$

Independent Practice

5) $\begin{array}{r} 1 \\ \underline{\times 9} \end{array}$ 6) $5 \times 4 =$ ______ 7) $\begin{array}{r} 6 \\ \underline{\times 1} \end{array}$

8) $\begin{array}{r} 4 \\ \underline{\times 4} \end{array}$ 9) $3 \times 2 =$ ______ 10) $\begin{array}{r} 9 \\ \underline{\times 4} \end{array}$

Problem Solving

11) 3 plates
of 7 oatmeal cookies
oatmeal cookies

12) 9 metal cages
of 5 red birds
red birds

13) 7 brown bags
of 2 big books
big books

Source: From *Strategic Math Series: Multiplication Facts 0 to 81* (p. 114), by C. D. Mercer and S. P. Miller, 1992, Lawrence, KS: Edge Enterprises. Copyright 1992 by Cecil D. Mercer and Susan P. Miller. Reprinted by permission.

other mathematics concepts or applications. Multiple operation review and concept connections are not included in the current materials. Further, multiplication and division concepts are limited to those of equal groups, so the teacher should provide additional practice with other multiplicative models (see content strand B).

Direct Instruction Mathematics

Direct Instruction Mathematics, developed for low-income and other at-risk students (Stein, Kinder, Silbert, & Carnine, 2006), has been translated into three series of math programs published by SRA/McGraw-Hill: *Connecting Math Concepts, Corrective Mathematics,* and *DISTAR Arithmetic.* The Direct Instruction approach involves specifying instructional objectives; sequencing skills; selecting a teaching procedure that matches the learning task; designing a format or specifically what the teacher will say or do;

selecting examples; and planning practice, review, and progress-monitoring procedures (Stein, Kinder, Silbert, & Carnine, 2006). These elements of Direct Instruction were incorporated into the published series. The materials are known for their teacher scripts, frequent student responding including choral responding, focus on representational and symbolic levels of understanding, explicit and standardized mathematics procedures, and built-in assessment and recordkeeping systems. Of particular note is the lack of emphasis on concrete materials; lessons typically involve pictures and symbolic forms. The authors asserted several issues with using manipulatives for mathematics learning: inefficient use of instructional time, lack of transfer from concrete to symbolic forms, and the difficulty of monitoring student performance with concrete objects. If concrete materials are used, they should be used only after students have been taught a specific algorithm, according to the authors. They promoted using structured worksheets with algorithms and rules or pictures during instruction and practice. Student drawings and written work are preferred over manipulatives for assessment activities.

DISTAR Arithmetic I and II (2nd ed.) (Engelmann & Carnine, 1975) is a two-level program of beginning math skills (grades K–3) taught through small sequential steps in a mastery learning, direct instruction model. Materials for each level include the teacher's scripted presentation book, teacher guide, student take-home workbooks, and progress charting materials. The promotional materials state that lessons "emphasize thinking and understanding before memorization."

Connecting Math Concepts (Engelmann, Carnine, Kelly, & Engelmann, 1992) is a basal math program for grades 1 through 6 and a bridge module between fifth and sixth grades. Rather than addressing mathematics topics by unit, this program introduces ideas gradually and emphasizes the connections between concepts. Each lesson is organized into paths (strands) of 5- to 10-minute segments that address several different topics. For example, one lesson might have a segment on mental addition, then subtraction, a geometry piece, and also a fraction component. Over time these small steps lead to mastery of difficult concepts. Teachers adopting this program should be aware of this structure—it is not a program to use in parts or pick up midyear. Materials for this program include the teacher presentation book, teacher guide, answer keys, student workbooks, and student hardcover textbooks (grades 3 through 6).

Corrective Mathematics (Engelmann & Carnine, 1982) is a series of topical modules for remedial mathematics grades three through adult. The modules include addition; subtraction; multiplication; division; basic fractions; fractions, decimals, and percents; and ratios and equations. As with the other Direct Instruction programs, *Corrective Mathematics* modules include a teacher presentation book, student workbooks, answer keys, and placement tests. This remedial program emphasizes teaching students strategies to master basic math skills efficiently and effectively.

In a 1996 review of thirty-four intervention studies contrasting DI with typical basal programs, 87 percent favored DI programs and 64 percent found significant differences (Adams & Engelmann, 1996). A substantial effect size of 1.11 in favor of DI math programs was found in thirty-three of the thirty-seven comparisons that included a math component. Other studies since this review have indicated mixed results. A study with nineteen secondary students using peer-delivered *Corrective Mathematics* found average effect sizes of 2.11 in calculation and .86 in applications as measured by the *Woodcock-Johnson Revised Test of Achievement* (Parsons, Marchand-Martella, Waldron-Soler, Martella, & Lignugaris/Kraft, 2004). A study with forty-six fourth-graders comparing *Connecting Math Concepts* with a typical mathematics basal found no statistically significant differences as measured by the *National Achievement Test* (Snider & Crawford, 1996).

Adaptations for Special Populations

Saxon Mathematics offers a four-book series (Math 5/4, Math 6/5, Math 7/6, and Math 8/7) to support the middle grades (grades 4 to 8) mathematics instruction of special-needs students, including those with problems in visual-motor integration, spatial organization, receptive language, fine motor, anxiety, verbal expression, or distractibility. The adaptation binders provide additional teacher guidance, student worksheets, tests, student reference guides, and supplemental activities. The adaptation notebooks are not currently available for the K–4 series or the high school texts. The scope and sequence guide for the four middle-grades textbooks claims full content coverage and alignment with the NCTM standards. However, most lessons are clearly focused on numbers and operations, and some middle-grades topics are not addressed at all (e.g., computing with negative integers or solving polynomials). Problem-solving strategies are limited to estimation and translating word problems into equations.

The regular Saxon mathematics series is known for its systematic approach to the mathematics curriculum, with distributed practice and continuous assessment rather than unit or chapter-based organization. Each lesson begins with a warm-up activity (8–10 minutes), followed by introduction of a new concept through rules and examples (10–15 minutes), with immediate practice with the new concept (5–10 minutes), followed by mixed practice including previous concepts (20–30 minutes). Lessons are not organized by unit of study; rather, a mixture of lesson topics are simply labeled lesson 1 through lesson 140. The extensive mixed practice that accompanies each lesson has the flavor of the random calculation and application word problems one would find on a statewide test.

The company's supporting materials for the regular program cite the research base for effective instructional practices and several studies that compare student groups using other curricula with groups using Saxon materials. The studies cited break out student results by ethnicity and students qualifying for free lunch, but not by disabilities. Outcome measures were typical end-of-grade tests such as the *Stanford Achievement Test 9* or the *Ohio State Proficiency Test*. Several quasi-experimental studies reported student gains, from a low range of thirteenth to thirtieth percentile, to between the sixty-first and seventy-eighth percentile, but these gains were not by the same group of students; rather, they were grade-level scores over a three-year period.

TouchMath

TouchMath is a multi-sensory system, with origins in the Orton-Gillingham approach, for introducing mathematics skills and concepts. It has evolved since 1975 to serve a

● ● ● ● ● ● ● ●
Distributed practice refers to spaced rather than massed practice: review of important skills and concepts spaced out over two or more years within a curriculum (see, for example, Dempster & Farris, 1990).
● ● ● ● ● ● ● ●

wider audience of students. The distinguishing feature of this system is the use of visible "TouchPoints" superimposed on the symbols for numbers. Students learn the Touch-Points as they learn the digits through nine and use the TouchPoints with beginning addition, subtraction, multiplication, and division. For example, as a student adds 3 + 5, he touches and counts the three TouchPoints on the 3 and continues to count the additional five TouchPoints on the 5 to reach the answer of 8 (see Figure 6.2). Later he would be taught to say "5" and add on with the TouchPoints of the 3. The visible points are gradually phased out and students only use the TouchPoint process if they cannot recall a basic fact. Actually, the visible TouchPoints provide a representational level as an overlay to the symbolic number. In any event, using TouchPoints is more efficient than putting the pencil down and remaining dependent on concrete counters.

The *TouchMath* system (4th edition) includes kits for number concepts, addition, subtraction, sequence counting, multiplication/division, story problems, time, money, and fractions. Each kit includes activity masters, progress tests, fact mastery materials, teaching aids, a kit guide, and an instructional manual (Bullock, 2000). The company will also provide a video for teacher training. These materials are intended to supplement a math program and are appropriate for general and special education settings. The research base for TouchMath programs includes materials on the theoretical base, connection with NCTM standards, and several independent studies with children. Scott (1993) studied the implementation of the addition and subtraction elements with three students with mild disabilities. In a multiple-probe design, all three students made significant improvement (from pretest scores of 0 to 20 percent, to posttest scores of 94 to 100 percent) in addition and subtraction skills and demonstrated maintenance of skills over six weeks. Simon and Hanrahan (2004) studied multi-digit addition with three students with learning disabilities, also a multiple-probe design, and found all three students mastered this level of addition and retained learning between one and one-half to four and one-half months after the end of instruction.

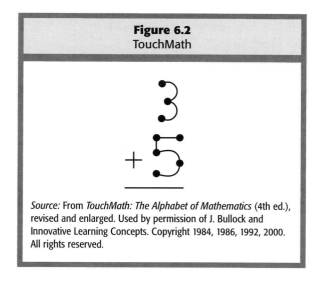

Figure 6.2
TouchMath

GENERAL EDUCATION MATERIALS: CONCERNS AND ADAPTATIONS

Basal mathematics series are typically adopted by mathematics educators, under the purview of local and state boards of education, for use in general education classrooms and have varying components for students with special learning needs. This section will discuss the criteria and review process for general education textbooks and supplemental materials, typical components of these series, and primary concerns and additional modifications that may be needed for use with students with learning problems.

Mathematics Textbooks: Criteria and Review

Criteria for mathematics textbook and materials adoptions have been influenced primarily by the NCTM standards and NCLB requirements for scientifically based materials. Selection of textbooks and other instructional materials varies widely; sometimes a list is adopted by a state-level board, other times districts or even schools may conduct their own adoption procedures. Adoptions are typically by expert committee, often with public input, and are guided by specific criteria.

State and district criteria typically include the following:

- Scientifically based evidence of effectiveness: Instructional methods and practices that have been verified through rigorous, systematic research, evidence of student achievement as a result of the program, and achievement sustained over time
- Demonstrated effectiveness with diverse students (low-achieving and gifted), especially elements of universal design
- Correlation with the NCTM and/or state mathematics standards
- Capacity for technical assistance and details about what resources are necessary for program implementation, including assistance from publisher
- Big ideas emphasized, with clear connections among concepts
- Background information required for new learning
- Links to future concepts
- Suggestions provided for implementing best practices in the classroom
- Ongoing, integrated, multiple forms of assessment
- Assessment addresses whether students understand concepts, can apply them, and communicate their learning
- Problem-solving, investigation, writing, reasoning found throughout the program
- Tasks required of students are worthwhile, promote higher-order thinking, provide practice opportunities, and allow students to use a variety of tools, such as manipulatives and technology, for learning

There is no evidence that any single mathematics program meets all these criteria. In 2002 the U.S. Department of Education established the "What Works Clearinghouse," administered by the Institute of Education Sciences. This is a consolidation of the previous ERIC clearinghouses and an attempt to provide a central source of scientific evidence of what works in education. One portion of the Clearinghouse is concerned with conducting systematic reviews of K–12 interventions for increasing mathematics achievement (curricula, textbooks, and software programs), beginning with middle-grade interventions, with elementary and high school interventions to follow. The What Works Clearinghouse conducted an "exhaustive literature search" covering a twenty-year period and identified forty-four curriculum-based interventions for middle-school students (2005). The research on each intervention was reviewed for scientifically based effectiveness (randomized controlled trials and quasi-experimental studies) with enough information on students, intervention, and outcome measures to be deemed valid. Only five interventions met these criteria:

- *Connected Mathematics Project.* Three quasi-experimental studies were conducted with sixth-, seventh-, and eighth-grade students. The results included no information on student demographics. Two studies found effect sizes of .32 and .43, but the third found a statistically insignificant negative effect.
- *Saxon Math.* Two studies—one randomized, one quasi-experimental—were conducted with only thirty-six eighth-graders; one was with talented students but the other did not describe the students. Statistical significance was not established (.11).
- *Cognitive Tutor.* One randomized study of this software-based intervention was conducted with regular education ninth-graders. Findings included significance for an effect size of .23.
- *The Expert Mathematician.* One randomized study was conducted of this computer-based intervention with 70 regular education students. There were no significant effects.
- *I CAN Learn Mathematics Curriculum.* This computer-based curriculum was researched in three studies—one randomized, two quasi-experimental—two with regular education students, one with gifted and remedial students. Only the randomized study (regular education students) found statistical significance (.41).

None of the middle-school curricula identified by the U.S. Department of Education was demonstrated to be effective with students with learning problems. The Clearinghouse researchers called for more and better studies of published interventions, since only four well-designed randomized controlled trials could be identified over twenty years, but did not call for studies to deliberately include special groups of students in their criteria. Critics have charged the Clearinghouse with valuing only one type of intervention research.

A special issue of the journal *Exceptional Children* (Graham, 2005) was devoted to the issues involving research in special education and evidence of effective practices, in an effort to establish criteria for quality indicators and guidelines for evidence-based practices published by the journal, and potentially the field. The authors of one article (Odom et al., 2005) termed the What Works Clearinghouse's criteria a "gold standard" but for only one type of quality research. Four types of quality intervention research were described—experimental group, correlational, single subject, and qualitative—that should be used to identify and understand effective practices. The other articles in this issue provided guidelines for each type. Programs of research into the effectiveness of interventions involve stages: preliminary observations and piloting; classroom experiments, qualitative studies, single-subject studies, or quasi-experimental studies; controlled randomized trails or single-subject studies in natural settings; and, finally, research on implementation factors involving correlational, qualitative, or mixed methodologies. Each article in the issue emphasized sufficient description of participants in studies to allow other educators to use the interventions with students with similar characteristics.

Until studies of mathematics curricula are subjected to broader quality criteria and include more diverse student populations, educators have two strategies for selecting interventions:

1. Evaluate curricula based on other criteria, such as alignment with standards, and well-established effective instructional methods
2. Carefully monitor the implementation of any curriculum for effectiveness with all students using frequent curriculum-based measures

Even "scientifically based" curricula can be ineffective with some students or not used in ways that maintain fidelity with program design. It is the quality of instruction, not the textbook or program alone, that makes a difference in students' mathematics learning.

General Education Materials: Research Base

Typically commercial materials are developed by committees of experts—mathematics professors and K–12 teachers at all grade levels—and are sometimes piloted in classrooms but rarely undergo independent research. Some national-scope validation studies have evaluated mathematics textbooks in recent years, especially since the passage of the NCLB Act, and are encouraged by the What Works Clearinghouse as described in the previous section. The National Science Foundation, through the K–12 Mathematics Curriculum Center, supports three projects that promote specific standards-based textbooks:

- Alternatives for Rebuilding Curricula (ARC) supports three elementary projects:
  - Investigations in Number, Data, and Space (TERC)
  - Math Trailblazers (University of Illinois at Chicago)
  - Everyday Mathematics (University of Chicago)
- Show-Me Center (National Center for Standards-Based Middle Grades Mathematics Curricula) at the University of Missouri-Columbia is assisting middle schools with mathematics curricula:
  - Connected Mathematics Project (Michigan State University)
  - Mathematics in Context
  - MathScape: Seeing and Thinking Mathematically
  - MATH *Thematics* (University of Montana)
- Curricular Options in Mathematics Programs for All Secondary Students (COMPASS) promotes integrated curricula at the high school level:
  - Contemporary Mathematics in Context: A Unified Approach
  - Interactive Mathematics Program (IMP)
  - MATH *Connections*: A Secondary Mathematics Core Curriculum

- Mathematics: Modeling Our World (ARISE)
- SIMMS Integrated Mathematics: A Modeling Approach Using Technology

With the nationwide promotion of these projects and their companion professional development, these curricula are being implemented widely across the country. However, none of the projects provide impact data for students with disabilities.

A large-scale study of the three elementary curricula in Massachusetts, Illinois, and Washington state with 100,875 students in third and fourth grades *excluded* all special education students (10 percent of the original number) (ARC Center, 2003). The study concluded that use of the "reform" curricula resulted in significantly higher achievement in both grade levels and across student groups (socio-economic status, English proficiency, and ethnicity)—an effect size of .10 or about 4 percentile points overall. Effect sizes for computation (.10) and measurement (.14) were the largest, and geometry (.08), algebra (.09), and statistics (.025) were smaller, as measured using state-mandated standardized achievement tests. Effect sizes for Asians, Whites, and Blacks were similar (.106, .100, and .092 respectively), but those for Hispanics were only .021, or just above 1 percentile point. Effect sizes of .10 and .14 may be statistically significant, especially given the sample size, but may not be practically different than the control curricula.

Woodward and Baxter (1997) compared five third-grade classrooms using *Everyday Mathematics* with four classrooms using a traditional basal series. Of the 104 students in the intervention classrooms, 16 were learning disabled or low-achieving in mathematics; of 101 comparison students, 22 were learning disabled or low-achieving. After a year-long instructional cycle, formal and informal measures were again administered to all students—yielding computation, concept learning, and problem-solving ability measures. The innovative program (*Everyday Mathematics*) group benefited the majority of students in those classrooms. Low-achieving students made marginal improvements on the whole but not nearly as much as average and above-average students. The authors noted that the limited effects for low-achieving students might be due to the relatively limited exposure to an alternative curriculum (one year), limited resources for meeting the needs of low-achieving students, or the structure and content of the curriculum.

The middle-grades textbooks were identified by Project 2061, sponsored by the American Association for the Advancement of Science. In 2000, Project 2061 evaluated thirteen textbook series developed specifically for middle grades mathematics (grades 6 to 8), excluding K–8 curricula. Evaluative criteria included building on prior knowledge, coherence of curriculum, complexity and connection of concepts, accuracy, promoting student reasoning, alignment of assessment, and supporting all students. The median ratings of only four of the series fell primarily within the satisfactory range: *Connected Mathematics* (Dale Seymour), *Mathematics in Context* (Encyclopedia Britannica Educational Corporation), *MathScape* (Creative Publications), and *Middle Grades Math Thematics* (McDougal Littell). This study did not review student achievement data.

Clearly, more research is needed on the effects of "reform" curricula on disabled and low-achieving students, as programs based on NCTM standards are adopted across the country. Collaborative research, with special education and mathematics researchers jointly designing and evaluating quality interventions in general education and support settings, is especially needed. Even the RAND Mathematics Study Panel, in its guidelines for mathematics education research *Mathematics Proficiency for All Students*, failed to include students with disabilities in the list of at-risk student groups, including only children of poverty, children of color, English language learners, and girls (2003). This report did call for a wider range of research than the federal initiatives—descriptive studies that would examine the effects of instruction on different groups of students, experimental studies to test models of instruction, and design and development studies to create and determine the effects of professional development and various curriculum materials in different settings. Research methods "should be appropriate for investigation of the chosen question" (RAND, 2003, p. 63).

Adapting Mathematics Textbooks

Many researchers have noted the problems with using basal mathematics textbooks with students with learning problems. The primary concern is that few materials provide research support for diverse groups of students, as discussed in the previous sections. Other concerns involve curriculum design and instructional methodology. Stein, Kinder, Silbert, and Carnine (2006) found that most teacher's guides for these texts provide only general instructional procedures, and student lessons lack adequate practice and review (see also Carnine, Jitendra, & Silbert, 1997). Cawley and colleagues (2001) found that mathematics textbooks are laden with new vocabulary while the comprehension of text by students with disabilities, including that of word problems, is often below the level required—while their computation skills may be higher.

In the teacher's guides for mathematics basals, brief suggestions are typically offered with each lesson for students with individual learning needs: students who are accelerated, English language learners, and students with disabilities or learning problems, frequently called *inclusion* students. The suggestions for students with learning problems include creating an atmosphere of high expectations but support and acceptance, creating consistent routines, making assessment criteria clear, considering multiple approaches to problem solving, providing additional practice sets, and occasionally offering specific suggestions for alternative instruction and re-teaching if some students are not succeeding with the strategies presented in the teacher's manual. Many teachers' manuals, curiously, emphasize addressing different learning styles, where teachers are encouraged to allow students to learn math in the most comfortable style for each student—visual, auditory, kinesthetic, linguistic, logical, social, or individual—a seemingly confused mix of multiple intelligences and learning styles theory—neither of which has research support for effective mathematics intervention.

With the emphasis on access to the general education curriculum and state-mandated testing programs, most students with mild to moderate disabilities and other learning problems are working in general education classrooms with district-adopted mathematics textbooks. Although the first adaptation considered by the IEP committee might be using the text of a lower grade level, that choice may not be most appropriate decision for the general education teacher or student. It is likely the teacher's class includes students with a wide range of abilities and levels of mathematics achievement, so a more universal curriculum design with adaptations to the current text and supplements would be more manageable than using several different grade-level texts. Further, many students with learning differences have gaps in learning, not comprehensive delays, and their goals include reaching grade-level performance.

Consider the following description of a fifth-grade series of lessons on addition and subtraction of integers (composite lessons from several typical sources). The total estimated time for this series of lessons is six days of 45-minute lessons.

Integers include negative and positive whole numbers and zero.

Lesson 1: Using Models to Add Integers—Two color counters (red and yellow) are used to represent positive and negative integers; students are asked to find the sums using counters.

Lesson 2: Using Number Lines to Add Integers—A number line is shown and students are reminded to always start at the zero and move right for positive and left for negative integers. Algebraic equations (those with an unknown in the expression) are also presented for solving.

Lesson 3: Using Models to Subtract Integers—The two-color counters re-appear with new rules for subtracting positive and negative integers.

Lesson 4: Using Numbers Lines to Subtract Integers—The number lines are used again with the equation $-6 - -3 = n$ requiring students to start at the zero, move left for the negative 6, then right for the negative 3 because subtracting a negative is the opposite procedure.

Lesson 5: Using Rules to Add and Subtract Integers—Students are taught three new rules involving sums of negative and positive integers and the concept of absolute value.

Lesson 6: Problem Solving with Integers—Word problems involving football yardage and temperature are presented. Students are prompted to use previous problem-solving strategies.

To plan for the adaptation of the lessons on this integer topic or other lessons and units of study, teachers should plan together considering some key questions. (A checklist of these questions can be found in the appendix. These questions are congruent with the instructional principles in Chapter 4, the related principle is in italics.) Teachers should consider first these broad questions:

1. Is this topic important, a key idea for future mathematics learning? If not, focus on another concept. *Linked to instructional principle 1, big ideas.*
2. What is the primary instructional objective? For example, students will add and subtract negative and positive integers.
3. What prior knowledge (informal or formal) do students have about this topic? Conduct an informal assessment, because students' prior knowledge will vary.

For example:

Through the fourth grade, students have had extensive experience with whole number operations and properties. Fourth-grade texts only briefly mention negative numbers in a unit on measurement with the thermometer application. Coordinate graphing in fourth-grade texts is in the first quadrant only—positive, positive.

Linked to instructional principle 2, prior knowledge.

4. What prior knowledge is essential for success with this objective? For example:

For students to add and subtract negative and positive integers, they need to know the whole number concepts of "properties" (inverse, commutative, zero) and the operations of addition and subtraction.

Also linked to principle 2, prior knowledge.

5. What future skills will be developed based on this learning? Look ahead in the text and the series to answer this question. For example:

Later in the same text students will work with the coordinate plane, functions that provide ordered pairs of negative and positive integers, and graphing equations onto a plane. The sixth-grade text also has lessons on adding and subtracting integers with the extension of the commutative and associative properties using parentheses. The seventh-grade text includes graphing and ordering integers, adding and subtracting whole and decimal integers, and multiplying and dividing integers, with extensions into solving algebraic equations and graphing linear equations. These concepts are actually developed over a three-year period.

Linked to instructional principle 9, transfer-of-learning.

Teachers should next anticipate learning difficulties with this topic:

6. What vocabulary will be challenging? Obvious examples might include absolute value, negative integer, positive integer, and inverse operation. Yet some students will still confuse terms like *greater* and *less*. *Linked to instructional principle 7, language.*

7. What concepts will be confusing? Anticipate the difficulties. For example:
   - Negative and positive signs are the same as plus and minus signs
   - Directionality on the number line
   - The sum of two negatives is a positive but the sum of a negative and positive integer depends on the greater absolute value
   - Some practice examples are written as equations but others don't have equals signs: $-4 - -9$.
   - The whole number rule that we cannot take a smaller number from a larger number will no longer apply.

Linked to instructional principle 8, strategies.

8. Are the examples appropriate for these students? For example, some students may understand football yardage and temperatures below zero; others may not. Consider expanding the examples to include altitude, golf, playing other games with points, or profits and losses. *Linked to instructional principle 8, strategies.*

9. Is the sequence of instruction appropriate? Think of modifications that might work better for your students. For example:

Consider teaching the addition and subtraction concepts simultaneously and using consistent equation formats. The overall CRA sequence (concrete: counters, representational: number lines, and abstract: equations) should be effective with these concepts if each is connected with the next form; however, an initial lesson might be added, to begin with prior knowledge of negative numbers as a concept. Further, the two-color counters don't represent zero, so a zero piece or empty circle might be added.

Linked to instructional principle 5, sequence.

10. Is practice with new concepts sufficient? Put on a critic's hat as you consider the number and types of practice opportunities. For example:

Each lesson has six to eight guided practice examples and twelve to fifteen independent practice examples. Those are followed by algebra equations and word problems to solve, without additional instruction or practice. The textbook pages are extremely busy, full of different types of practice. Consider varying practice activities to include number cards, partner work, individual white boards, and small-group games. The unit pieces from algebra tiles would also make good models, because those will be used in later lessons with variables.

Linked to instructional principles 6, variety, 8, strategies, and 4, problem solving.

11. Has judicious review been planned in future lessons? Again, critique the review opportunities provided in future lessons in this text and in the series. For example:

An extra practice set is located at the end of the unit. Brief review of one previous concept is found at the end of all lessons, but with little direction. The next units—on data analysis and graphing, computation with fraction and decimal numbers, geometry and measurement—do not refer to integers at all.

Linked to instructional principle 9, transfer-of-learning.

12. Do extensions and applications in future lessons have concept fidelity? For example:

Only one future unit—that of coordinate-plane graphing and linear equations—makes use of these concepts. Most of the text remains focused on positive numbers.

Linked to instructional principle 9, transfer-of-learning.

Teachers should now decide if extant lessons are sufficient or whether adaptations are required. If adaptations are designed, which teachers will be involved and how much time will be necessary for the revised instruction? The special education or remedial teacher could provide preview or remedial instruction prior to the lessons, reinforce concepts during the lessons through additional examples and practice, and design followup instruction and review for later lessons.

A developmental mathematics basal may provide the sufficient "bones" for a flexible program for diverse students if teachers work together to analyze and adapt instruction and learning experiences and monitor effectiveness. Supplemental programs will always be needed for some students, to provide extra practice, alternative methods, remediation, or extensions for learning. It is how materials are used that makes the difference in learning.

TRY THIS
Select another series of lessons from a basal text—elementary, middle, or high—and use the previous questions to adapt the lessons for students with learning problems.

SELECTING, CREATING, AND USING MANIPULATIVES

There has been disagreement in the research literature about the merits of mathematics manipulatives for students' learning. Sowell (1989) concluded in a meta-analysis of sixty equivalent-comparison group studies (between 1954 and 1987), that regular use of manipulatives by knowledgeable teachers over a school year or longer, but not shorter durations, was correlated with significant group differences in mathematics achievement across the curriculum. Evans (1990) found that beginning instruction with manipulatives was less efficient than beginning with an algorithm followed by manipulatives' use. Carnine (1997) cautioned that manipulatives should be used only in a time-efficient manner and reminded educators that it is not the manipulative but the explicit construction of connections between object use and symbols that results in learning.

A few studies have indicated positive results for manipulative use with students with learning problems. Peterson, Mercer, and O'Shea (1988) found that introducing place value concepts with brief manipulative use (cubes and place value strips) resulted in successful place value identification that was maintained over time. This CRA teaching sequence was also successful for addition, subtraction, multiplication, and division fact mastery (Mercer & Miller, 1992); for algebra word problems, using algebra tiles worked (Maccini & Hughes, 2000); and for teaching fraction concepts, using construction paper models was effective (Jordan, Miller, & Mercer, 1999). Funkhouser (1995) successfully used a five-frame with jellybeans to teach basic number concepts involving the digits 0 to 5 to five- and six-year-olds. Marsh and Cooke (1996) demonstrated the effectiveness of using Cuisenaire Rods to support problem-solving instruction with students with LD. Cass, Cates, Smith, and Jackson (2003) used manipulatives (geoboards) to teach perimeter and area concepts to students with LD, and demonstrated the effectiveness of manipulative use for initial instruction, transfer to abstract models, and long-term maintenance of skills.

Special educators have noted the dearth of research on manipulatives' use with students with learning problems, while acknowledging the potential benefits (Marzola, 1987; Cass, Cates, Smith, & Jackson, 2003). Manipulatives provide opportunities for students to explore new concepts and relationships. They can be motivating for reluctant learners, support real-world applications of mathematics concepts, and promote transfer of mathematics concepts and language to more abstract representations. Since mathematics is essentially a science of number and space and their interrelationships, concrete materials and semi-concrete representations support student understanding of these relationships.

However, the effective use of instructional materials takes time, reflection, and practice. Manipulatives do not make math easy or cause automatic concept understanding or transfer. Teachers must invest planning time understanding concepts at deeper levels and selecting materials that enhance the understanding of that content where it is most appropriate in the learning cycle—for concept introduction, guided learning experiences, individual practice and application, transfer of learning, or assessment.

The next two sections address concrete manipulatives, those that are teacher-made or purchased for hands-on manipulation. Virtual manipulatives are computer-based simulations of the concrete versions and are discussed in a later section.

Creating Materials

The most effective concrete and representational materials for mathematics are those that are:

- valid representations of important concepts
- inexpensive enough for each student to have adequate materials
- durable enough for repeated student use (unless consumable)
- age-appropriate

Teacher or student-created materials and inexpensive everyday items can meet all of these criteria. Additional requirements may include the ease of creating larger or over-head versions for demonstration, safety with specific students, the ability to send materials home with assignments, and storage capability. This section will provide useful examples of simple materials and should spark the reader's imagination for additional adaptations or creations. A list of free and inexpensive items for a mathematics classroom is featured in Figure 6.3.

Number concepts and place value.   Simple counting objects such as toy blocks, buttons, bottle caps, crayons, game board objects, and other everyday objects with similar characteristics can be used to develop whole number concepts for numbers up to 20. Smaller or edible objects (e.g., beans, macaroni, candy) should be used with care, as will be discussed in a later section. Younger children developing number concepts to 10 may find using five- or ten-frames easier to visualize than scattered objects. These simple frames may be created from boxes or line drawings and encourage children to name the total without counting each item by judging parts of five. The transition from concrete to representational versions of a ten-frame is depicted in Figure 6.4.

Concepts of larger numbers, requiring place value representations, can be developed using bundled straws, wooden sticks or coffee stirrers, or, in more representational forms, coins (penny, dime, dollar) or sections of graph paper (units, strips of 10, blocks of 100, cube with 100 on each face). Place value mats (see appendix) are useful devices for organizing objects by place, engaging in trading (regrouping) activities, and transfer into symbol (number) form. Library card pockets or small envelopes can be labeled with places and attached to a bulletin board for creating larger or smaller numbers using number cards.

Teachers and students can represent decimal forms of number using the objects identified above if the one's place is the larger grouping (i.e., the bundle, cube, or dollar is one unit) that can be divided into 10 parts to represent tenths and 100 parts to represent hundredths. The place value mat, in this case, would include a decimal point.

To demonstrate the properties of sets and groupings, objects can be placed on paper plates or sheets of construction paper, in clear plastic cups or sections of cup-cake pans, or in other containers that are easy to view and manipulate. Number lines are flexible representations of the sequence of whole numbers and can be adapted for negative integers and other rational numbers. Number lines can be drawn in small

---

Figure 6.3
Free and Inexpensive Materials for the Mathematics Classroom

Paper Products
  butcher paper
  envelopes
  construction paper
  library card pockets
  menus
  cardboard cake or pizza circles
  paper cups and plates
  paper bags
  cardboard inserts
Plastics
  clean food trays
  coffee stirrers
  straws
  buttons
  clear plastic cups
  beads
Cloth
  ribbon
  string
  yarn
  felt
  cloth scraps
Wood
  popsicle sticks
  toothpicks
  paint sticks
  yard and meter sticks
  wooden dowels

Kitchen Items
  scales
  thermometer
  measuring cups and spoons
  empty food containers (cubes,
    cylinders)
  egg cartons
  dry beans
  cupcake pans
Other Household Items
  shoeboxes
  paper clips
  paper brads
  small mirrors
  newspapers and magazines
  calendars
  file folders
  sponges
  shower curtain
  maps
  tape measures
  poker chips
  playing cards
  dice
  tiles
  children's blocks
  clocks
  coins
  game boards and pieces

---

versions for students' individual use or in large formats across the classroom floor or wall.

Hundreds charts have powerful applications for a range of number concepts including sequencing, count-bys, multiples, and factors. Hundreds charts can be depicted in 0 to 99 format or 1 to 100 format, in either right-to-left or left-to-right sequences. They can be teacher made or downloaded from a number of websites (see appendix). Larger pocket versions allow for removal and manipulation of numbers and number patterns. Hundreds charts can be used with plastic or paper markers or drawn on directly.

Rational numbers.   Many free and inexpensive materials can be adapted to represent fractions, percents, decimals, ratios, and probability. Although teachers often reach first for the paper pizza example, strips of construction paper (e.g., 3" by 11") are better representations, with one intact strip representing one whole, and folded or cut sections

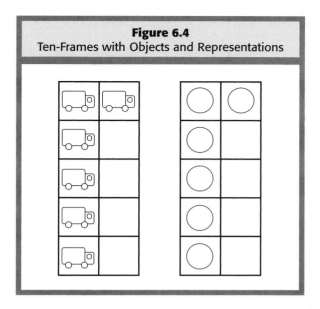

Figure 6.4
Ten-Frames with Objects and Representations

representing parts. These strips are easily folded, torn, labeled, and glued. Fraction concepts can be extended with representations for mixed numbers and with more than one strip representing the "whole." Students can explore the answers to questions such as, "What are other names for $\frac{1}{2}$?" and, "How do we divide a fraction by a fraction?" using paper strips. Then rational number concepts can be extended with more than one piece of paper representing the unit.

Because percents are units per hundred, materials representing percents should clearly depict that base. Examples include pennies and dollars, 100s grids or graph paper squares, or meter sticks with centimeters labeled. Metric graph paper with darker lines for blocks of 100 is available from scientific or drafting supply stores or online through downloadable PDF files.

Ratio comparisons can be made within sets of similar items or between different items, so materials representing ratios should include those with similar (cubes, crayons, coins) or different (collections of objects, pictures) characteristics. Standard ratios (rates) (e.g., miles per hour, price per yard) should be represented with realistic materials (*realia*) such as maps or advertisements.

Probability of events can be represented with many concrete objects: dice, spinners, coins, cards, cubes, and semi-concrete grids and patterns. It is important that students have experience with a variety of objects for the generalization of concepts. Even data sets (surveys, weather data, baseball statistics), magazine clippings (ads, photographs), and game boards (checkers) can be adapted for probability experiments.

Spatial concepts of geometry and measurement.　Two- and three-dimensional figures and their features come to life when constructed by students. Construction paper, graph paper, straws and string, paper brads, clay, and food packaging are inexpensive and flexible construction materials.

Paper folding activities have been used to develop many geometric concepts such as angles, shapes, symmetry, lines, rotations, and other transformations. Cubes and pyramids can be constructed with thick paper using simple directions that actually demonstrate the concepts of face, vertex, and volume. Straws strung together with string can create open three-dimensional shapes with the straws representing edges. These activities can also be used to check concept and math language understanding, develop general spatial sense, and promote overlapping fraction concepts (see, for example, Wheatley & Reynolds, 1999).

Measurement tools can be standard devices or alternatives. For measuring distance, paper tape measures and free or inexpensive rulers and yardsticks are used for standard units, while any object with a constant length can make alternative measures (e.g., shoe, block, wooden dowel, vinyl floor tile, unsharpened pencil, paper clip). Dollar store measuring sets for liquid volume sometimes include both metric and customary units. Other everyday containers are marked with units (pint of milk, liter of soda, 32 oz. of juice). Teachers often use water with a drop of food coloring for easier reading, or, when liquids are not feasible, inexpensive dry goods such as rice. Measures of nonliquid volume and capacity (cubic units) can be made with the same materials using three-dimensional geometric objects.

Problem solving.   Concrete objects can assist problem solving, as described in Chapter 5. Objects can represent portions of the problem (crayons represent people) or be the actual object from the problem, as below:

> Mary Jo had 5 CDs and Jared had 4. If they each bought two new CDs, how many does each now have?

Using concrete objects with problem solving connects mathematics concepts to the real-world aspects involved. And a problem like the one above can be elaborated to connect other areas of mathematics:

> If the CDs play 45 minutes of music each, how much music can be heard without repeating songs? If the new CDs were originally priced $12 and discounted by 15 percent, how much did Mary Jo and Jared spend on the new CDs?

Safety and individual-use issues with manipulatives.   There are a number of publications on using edible manipulatives (such as M & M's, pretzels, jelly beans, etc.) for mathematics instruction. Edible manipulatives can be extremely motivating and a change in routine, but teachers should be aware of their disadvantages. Many students have severe allergies to food items, especially peanuts, tree nuts, and products containing milk, eggs, or wheat. The use of food for working with math concepts is usually unsanitary, unless carefully controlled. Rice or corn used for measurement activities should be composted, not cooked. "We're going to put the ones we've used in the compost and cook a fresh batch to eat afterward." Some food items, such as beans and corn kernels, are too small for safe use with younger children.

Other math tools pose safety hazards, especially for students with behavioral and self-control issues. Students should be taught how to safely use the rubber bands with

For solutions to the problems presented in this book, visit the Companion Website at www.ablongman.com/ gurganus1e.

geoboards or, if not practical, substitutes such as interactive web, string, or dot paper should be used. Compasses with metal points are especially dangerous; safety compasses, offering the same construction capabilities, should be used instead. Scissors are available in safer versions with blunt tips. Other construction supplies, such as glue, crayons, markers, toothpicks, building clay, and straight edges, should be checked for toxicity or sharpness and monitored for safe use.

Although not safety issues, some manipulatives are not appropriate for use with some students because of individual needs or some objects may need adaptations. Students who do not discern between specific colors will not be successful with color-coded manipulatives unless the colors are selected with care or also have patterns. Students with fine motor problems may need larger versions of manipulatives or even web-based simulations. Children who cannot use vision for learning or have low vision will need adaptations to manipulatives and diagrams such as number lines, graphs, and hundreds charts. If these students are served under an IEP, those adaptations should be specified on the IEP and provided. Other students with disabilities can access adaptations under 504 plans.

Commercial Manipulatives

Catalogs and websites for teachers offer dozens of concrete materials to support mathematics instruction. This section will describe select commercial materials that have the power to demonstrate big ideas and connect critical concepts. These materials are only a sampling of what is available and were selected because they frequently appear in classroom kits that accompany textbooks.

Cuisenaire Rods, invented by Emile-Georges Cuisenaire in 1930 in Belgium to convey critical mathematics concepts to his students, were described in the collaborative book *Mathematics with Numbers in Colour* in partnership with Caleb Gattegno (1953). The rods, now available in wood or plastic, were designed in various lengths (one unit to 10 units) and colors to be visual representations of numbers.

Cuisenaire Rods are continuous representations (not scored or separable) of number and therefore have arithmetic and algebraic properties (see Figure 6.5). For example, the white rod is one unit, the red two units, the green three units, and the purple four units. Four whites equal one purple. Two reds equal one purple. The purple is twice as long as the red. The white is $\frac{1}{4}$ the length of the purple. If the white represents 8 fish, then the red would represent 16 fish. For a full-color view, please visit the ETA/Cuisenaire website at www.etacuisenaire.com.

Cuisenaire Rods have powerful applications in developing number and spatial sense, geometry, measurement, probability, and statistics. Students with learning problems need explicit orientation to the value of the rods with each activity. Rods are typically called by their color names, but their values are intentionally variable. Students who cannot discriminate colors may need their rods coded with letters, as in Figure 6.5.

Geoboards also have a direct connection to Caleb Gattegno, who referred to the *Gattegno Geoboard* in a 1954 article (as cited by Tahta, 2004). Geoboards, available in wood and plastic in many sizes, have pins or nails arranged in rectangular arrays or

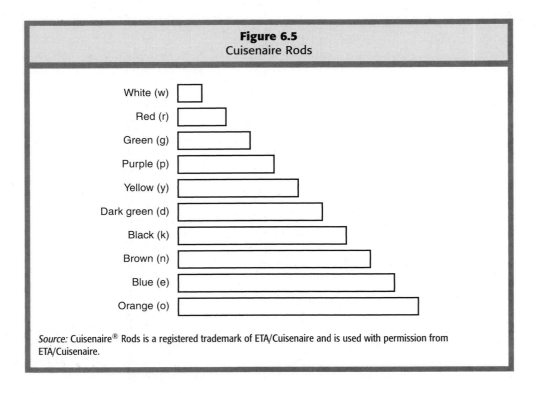

Figure 6.5
Cuisenaire Rods

White (w)
Red (r)
Green (g)
Purple (p)
Yellow (y)
Dark green (d)
Black (k)
Brown (n)
Blue (e)
Orange (o)

Source: Cuisenaire® Rods is a registered trademark of ETA/Cuisenaire and is used with permission from ETA/Cuisenaire.

circular patterns (see Figure 6.6). Geometric figures are created on geoboards using rubber bands. Painted-surface geoboards can be marked with chalk. Clear plastic geoboards are useful for overhead demonstrations and comparing patterns by overlay. Geoboards were developed to demonstrate geometric concepts such as perimeter, area, circumference, line, angle, symmetry, and transformations. Additional mathematics concepts, such as those of rational numbers, multiplication, and graphing, also can be modeled with geoboards. Students who cannot safely use rubber bands may need adaptations using elastic thread or yarn with actual geoboards, or simulations using dot paper or web versions.

Unit cubes are available in many sizes, colors, and materials. The smallest commercial cubes are 1 cm^3 and weigh 1 g, too small for younger children, but perfect for developing base-ten and decimal system concepts. The most commonly used cubes for younger children measure 2 cm^3, $\frac{3}{4}$ in^3, and 1 in^3, appropriate for exploring a range of number and spatial concepts. Many commercial-brand cubes (e.g., Unifix, Multilink, Snap, and PopCubes) have connection devices on two or more sides, for creating cube towers and other shapes. Some cubes are plain, while others feature dots, numbers, and other symbols on the sides (like dice). Cubes are useful for developing number and spatial sense through activities such as counting, sorting, comparing, measuring, and constructing.

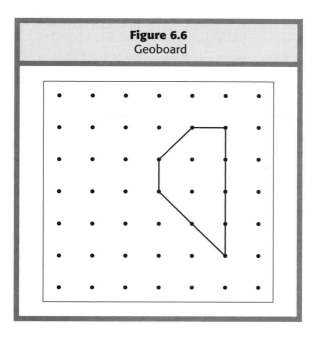

Figure 6.6
Geoboard

Base-ten blocks were most likely developed by the Hungarian Mathematician Zoltan Paul Dienes (Picciotto, n.d.), and are sometimes called Dienes Blocks. Base-ten sets are available in wood, and plastic versions in many colors. However, since color is not the attribute of concern in most base-ten applications, single-color sets are recommended, especially for students with learning problems. Each set should include unit blocks, rods (a connected bar of 10 units), flats (a connected square of 10 rods or 100 units), and cubes (representing 1,000 units, sometimes called decimeter cubes). Sets are also available in clear and soft versions. Useful supplements are the overhead sets, stamps, and place value mats (see Figure B.4 on page 279).

Attribute blocks are common in early childhood classrooms but also have applications for more advanced mathematics topics. Attribute blocks are proportionally sized blocks with five shapes (circle, square, rectangle, triangle, hexagon) in two sizes (small and large), three colors (yellow, red, and blue), and two thicknesses. They can be purchased in wood, plastic, or foam or made by the teacher using patterns, templates, or stamps. Attributes are characteristics of objects that can be compared, sorted, identified, and used for object description. The concept of attributes is important for the concepts of geometric properties, logical reasoning, problem solving, probability, and set theory. Students with learning problems sometimes have trouble distinguishing more than one attribute at a time or identifying the important attributes for creating shapes or finding members of sets.

Pattern blocks are often confused with attribute blocks but are distinct—they come in six specific polygons (square, triangle, trapezoid, hexagon, rhombus, and parallelogram) that can form fractional parts of each other. Pattern blocks can be obtained in a single-color set or mixed colors in many sizes and materials. Also available are pattern block overhead sets, templates, stamps, paper repeating patterns, and die cutters. Pattern blocks can be used throughout the mathematics curriculum for concepts such as patterns, geometry, fractions, tessellations, problem solving, estimation, and probability.

Commercially available representations of rational numbers include **fraction pieces** such as squares and circles; fraction, decimal, and Percent Tower cubes; and various versions of fraction tiles and number lines. When using these concrete representations, the teacher should make explicit references to the specific rational number types, not just parts-of-whole concepts (see content strand D).

Tangrams and **pentominoes** can extend students' concepts of spatial relationships such as area, flips, turns, perimeter, ratio, and properties of triangles and rectangles. Tangrams, most likely an ancient Chinese game, are actually squares that have been divided into seven pieces: five triangles, one square, and one parallelogram (see Figure C.4 in strand C). By turning and flipping pieces, students can create different shapes with just the seven pieces. Pentominoes are five connected square blocks, and, although they may be older, the name is attributed to Solomon Golomb from a lecture in 1953 to the Harvard Mathematics Club (Bhat & Fletcher, 1995). A set of twelve different shapes are identified by the letters, which assist with identification: T, U, V, W, X, Y, Z, F, I, L, P, and N. Challenges for pentominoes include creating 6×10, 5×12, 4×15, and 3×20 rectangles using all twelve. Students may also enjoy creating full sets of triominoes (three squares) or tetrominoes (four squares).

Algebraic concepts were first modeled using base-ten blocks by Dienes and later, using multi-base blocks, by Laycock (Picciotto, n.d.). Rasmussen developed a tile form for convenience and added a frame with a corner and color on each side for positive and negative. When selecting the appropriate model for students, teachers should consider the range of concepts to be addressed, students' cognitive flexibility, and the limitations of some visual models. These geometric-based models of algebraic concepts have the additional advantage of connecting math concepts and prior student knowledge.

Algebra Tiles and other xy tiles are inexpensive and widely available. Algebra Tiles include three pieces—the small square (x), the larger square (y), and a rectangle (xy). The small and larger squares are not proportionally related. Negative values are represented by red; the other colors indicate positive values. Algebra Tiles are limited to representing two dimensions and the tiles can represent units (whole numbers) or variables, but cannot represent whole numbers and more than one variable at a time. The representation of negatives and positives with color also limits their use and may cause misconceptions if extended too far. Algebra Tiles can assist initial algebra concepts such as modeling polynomials, performing the four operations with polynomials (including the distributive property and factoring), and modeling quadratic equations. Figure 6.7 illustrates multiplication of the polynomials $(x + 2)(3x + 1)$.

Algeblocks provide a three-dimensional view of algebraic equations that include units and two variables. Algeblocks offer a quadrant map to assist with more accurate representations of minus. They are also limited in representing minus in operations

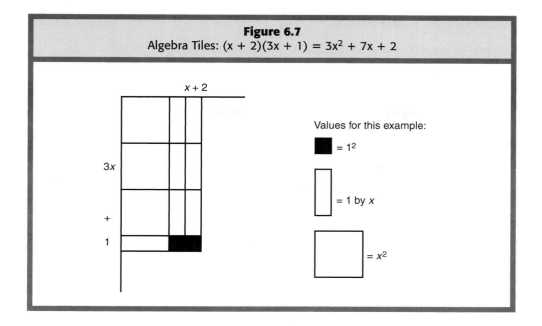

Figure 6.7
Algebra Tiles: $(x + 2)(3x + 1) = 3x^2 + 7x + 2$

x + 2

3*x*

+

1

Values for this example:

■ = 1^2

▯ = 1 by *x*

□ = x^2

but can expand polynomial concepts to two variables with units and extend the distributive property to include examples such as $(x^2)(x + 5y)$.

The Lab Gear (Creative Publications) model involves two different representations at once, positions related to the mat and blocks on top of each other, which allows for a geometrically sound representation of minus but may be initially more difficult to understand. The Lab Gear model was developed for high school algebraic applications and includes models for 5 and 25 per the original Rasmussen and Laycock models, and can be extended with base-ten blocks. The Lab Gear model includes a unit piece with scored flats for 5, 25, 5*x*, and 5*y*; a rod representing *x*; a longer rod representing *y*; flats representing x^2, y^2, and *xy*; and cubes representing x^3, y^3, x^2y, and xy^2.

Teachers should spend some time exploring the use of these algebraic models before introducing them to students. Consider what might be confusing or supportive during student instruction. If introduced gradually, with clear and explicit references to numbers and variables depicted and deliberate transfer activities to other representations such as graphs, these models have the potential to unlock critical high-school algebraic and related geometric concepts for students. No representative model will be a perfect match for the more abstract forms of mathematics, but they offer sound conceptual visualizations that can scaffold, or support, fragile and superficial understanding.

TRY THIS

Select one of the following big ideas of mathematics and explain how concrete manipulatives can introduce the concept.

Place value (ones, tens, hundreds)
Equivalence
Proportional reasoning
Factoring
Perimeter and area

TECHNOLOGY SUPPORT

Technology is a tool for mathematics learning with ever-evolving applications. This section will provide a brief overview of current applications with demonstrated support for learning. As with manipulatives and textbooks, technology itself will not enhance learning, it is how technology is used that will make the difference. *Note:* Check the resources mentioned in this section for updates that may have occurred since this manuscript went to press.

Calculators

Calculators are devices that assist with simple or lengthy computations. The earliest calculator, the abacus, is still in use in many cultures. Between 1600 and 1960, various mechanical calculators were used—including the logarithmic rule (1620) and slide rule (1622), the Odhner pin-wheel calculator (1874), and the Dalton 10-key add-listing machine (1902) (Tout, 2005). In 1961, the first electronic desktop calculators were sold in England. The first all-transistor calculators appeared in 1964 for about the price of a car at the time. Sharp produced the first battery-powered hand-held calculators in 1969, and the microprocessor-based calculator appeared in 1971. Hewlet-Packard introduced the first scientific pocket calculator in 1972 and by 1975, prices for all handheld calculators had dropped significantly, allowing use by classroom teachers and students. Solar-powered calculators were introduced in 1978. The *Little Professor*, a dedicated calculator for mathematics practice, appeared in the same year (Texas Instruments) and assumed the opposite function of a calculator—it gave the question and asked for the answer (2 + 7 = ?).

Today, calculators are available in many sizes (even on cell phones and in notebooks) with varying functions and applications. The basic types used in school are four-function, scientific, and a range of graphing calculators. Other dedicated calculators (hand held or web-based) are used for specific applications such a loan amortizations, measurement conversions, and currency conversions.

The calculator is considered an "assistive technology device" under IDEA. Calculators can be purchased through special education funding if designated on an IEP and used "to increase, maintain, or improve the functional capabilities of [individuals] with disabilities" (§300.5). However, the IEP team must specify how such an assistive device is to be used to enhance access to the general education curriculum. If calculator use is determined necessary and required per the IEP, it must be allowed to the extent specified.

Requirements for calculator use on district or state-level tests vary considerably, with some tests requiring calculators, some permitting calculator use, and some prohibiting their use. The SAT allows calculator use and recent studies indicated that students using graphing calculators performed better that those using less sophisticated versions, but these results may be due to those students taking more advanced mathematics classes that require graphing calculators (see, for example, Wendler, Zeller, & Allspach, 2003). Other studies of student achievement also indicate that calculator use is more prevalent among white, middle-class students and this difference in technology use contributes to the achievement gaps associated with race and SES (Lubienski & Shelley, 2003).

Teachers cannot simply hand out calculators and expect students to use them effectively and efficiently. The type of calculator needed for the mathematics application should be considered. Elementary students typically are introduced to the four-function calculator in first grade, but many students will have already had calculator experiences at home. This type of calculator is limited to numbers expressed in decimal form and the four arithmetic operations. By middle school, calculators with more advanced functions are needed (e.g., square roots, percent, fractions, and statistics). High school students should learn to use graphing calculators for algebraic, trigonometric, statistical, and other pre-calculus applications.

Calculators are more difficult to learn than computers due to the limits of on-screen icons and prompts, so explicit and guided instruction on a common model is recommended, especially for students with learning problems. Teachers should demonstrate calculator use through modeling (overhead projector versions) and think alouds. Students' initial use should be guided with corrective feedback. Instruction may need to begin with locating each key and learning the effects of each function (e.g., pressing the + key followed by a number and the = will add to my previous amount).

Teachers should also emphasize questions to prompt accurate use. For example, "the problem states that we should find the average height of five students with heights of 4′9″, 4′0″, 4′7″, 5′3″, and 5′4″. How can we use the calculator to assist us with this problem? My first question is about the form of the data—can my calculator add feet and inches? My next question is procedural—how do we compute averages on a calculator?" Students with learning problems may need other accommodations, such as larger keys and display screens, paper printouts for monitoring inputs and outputs, or prompting sheets with step-by-step directions for entering specific types of equations or creating graphs (see Figure 6.8). Calculators may actually make advanced mathematics concepts accessible for more students, minimizing the number crunching and tedium of long or multi-step computations.

Figure 6.8
Example Cue Sheet for Calculator Use

To average a set of numbers:
1. Enter each number with ⊞ between each number.
2. Press the ⊟ button.
3. Record the answer (sum) unless using paper tape.
4. Press the ⊞ and enter the total number of items in the data set.
5. Press the ⊡ button for the average (mean) of the data set.
6. Record the average.

Software

Since the microcomputer became common in classrooms and homes in the mid 1980s, software for educational purposes has developed into a range of options for teachers and parents. In the area of mathematics education, the following types are most common: tutorial, drill and practice, simulation (discussed in a later section), problem solving, and reference.

Tutorial software provides a complete teaching and learning experience (Foshay & Ahmed, 2003). This complex software includes content presentation, practice with feedback, review loops, and other organizational devices that the learner can control. Simple tutorials tend to be linear, while more sophisticated programs have complex branching capabilities that are keyed to student responses and questions. This type of software can include drill and practice, simulation, and assessment modules. An example of tutorial mathematics software is *A + LS Algebra* (American Education Corporation), a program that provides individual activities to develop concepts in beginning algebra such as solving quadratic equations.

Drill and practice software provides repetition and reinforcement of knowledge and skills already learned. Content is typically factual in nature—algorithms, vocabulary, math "facts," and simple problems. Programs range in sophistication from flash card simulations to those that branch depending on student responses (Bitter & Pierson, 2005). Examples for mathematics include the *Mighty Math Carnival Countdown* for place value (Riverdeep) and *Math Blaster* (Knowledge Adventure).

Much problem-solving software could be classified under simulation or tutorial. In mathematics, however, problem solving is so integral for learning that it deserves special attention. Problem-solving software requires the application of higher-order thinking and concept synthesis to solve problems. Some programs may allow guessing, while others provide learner control to move through and track various solution strategies. An example of problem-solving software is *Fizz & Martina's Math Adventures* (Tom Snyder Productions) that includes video clips of problem situations and is appropriate for cooperative learning groups.

Reference software provides factual information in the form of text, pictures, or other multimedia. This type of software differs from tutorial in that there is limited interactivity and practice. Most commonly used with science and social studies content areas, reference software does have some mathematics applications, such as locating data for analysis, tracing the history of a math problem, or exploring algorithms used by different cultures.

Desirable features of instructional software packages for mathematics include:

- Accurate and current content that addresses the full range of the domain. Mathematics software materials should address alignment with the NCTM content standards.
- Features that also tap one or more NCTM process standards: communication, making representations, reasoning, problem solving, and making connections.*

*Reprinted with permission from Principles and Standards for School Mathematics, copyright 2000, by the National Council of Teachers of Mathematics. All rights reserved. Standards are listed with permission of the Council of Teachers of Mathematics (NCTM). NCTM does not endorse the content or validity of these alignments.

- Language that is consistent with the instructional language of the classroom and appropriate for target students, including reading level, mathematics terminology, and mathematics symbols.
- Appealing and age-appropriate graphics and multimedia, yet not superfluous with animation and sounds. Flashing lights may be a concern for students with seizure disorders.
- Appropriate responses to the learner with corrective feedback, automatic level adjustments based on responses, and scaffolding to the next level.
- Higher-order thinking is promoted.
- Accessible for students with vision, hearing, language, or motor impairments.
- Content is free of bias or stereotypes.
- A management system that allows learner control, teacher access, recordkeeping, and back-up capabilities. Some software allows for teacher modification of content level, practice items, and feedback schedule and methods.

Some software is designed for independent use, others for pair or small-group work or for entire class demonstration. Teachers should review software from their own and students' points of view before using it with students, even if the software accompanies the text or has been reviewed in journals. Students with learning problems may have difficulty accessing and using software without explicit instruction and guidance, so teachers should plan for its use as with any other instructional activity.

Teachers can also use productivity software for instruction and instructional support. Spreadsheets have many applications for mathematics concepts, including data analysis and statistics, functions and graphing, and formula development. For example, students can enter data into cells and create formulas to analyze the data. They can ask "what if" questions and immediately test their hypotheses. They can also create different types of graphs and charts, even trigonometric applications.

Equation editors supplement word processing programs to enable teachers to create mathematically accurate worksheets and other written materials. Symbols from algebra ($\sqrt{}$), trigonometry (θ), statistics ($\overline{X}$), set theory ($\subseteq$), calculus (∂x), and geometry ($\sphericalangle$) can be embedded in equations and other expressions in correct format.

Graphing calculators are common with most PC software packages. Type in an equation and it is automatically graphed to the parameters selected. These calculators are also found on the web in many locations, some educational but others clearly commercial. Graphing calculators are available in a wide range of sophistication. Other software for computers, termed dynamic geometry software, includes *Cabri Geometry II* (Cabrilog) and the *Geometer's Sketchpad* (Key Curriculum Press).

Statistical analysis packages are useful for high-school level data analysis or integrated research. Even the simplest packages yield descriptive statistics such as means and standard deviations, while more sophisticated programs can conduct t-tests and analysis of variance. Examples include *Graphers* (Sunburst Technology), *The Graph Club* (Tom Snyder Productions), and *SPSS* (SPSS, Inc.).

Assessment tools are often built into the other instructional software types or may be single-application forms of software. Gerber, Semmel, and Semmel (1994) described the development and use of *DynaMath*, a computer-based dynamic assessment system, for assessing student performance on multiple-digit multiplication problems. The system was field tested with secondary students with mild disabilities over three years, demonstrating its potential to assess many aspects of mathematics computation beyond the "correct answer" including procedures selected, level of assistance required, and tempo of work. Teachers can also use test-creation software to develop individualized assessments. *Discourse*, by ETS, is a software package that allows teachers to develop instructional and assessment modules for any subject area.

TRY THIS

Review a software package that accompanies an adopted mathematics textbook, using the criteria described in this section.

Interactive Web

The World Wide Web (known as "WWW", "Web" or "W3") began as a networked information project at CERN (the European Organization for Nuclear Research) and is the universe of network-accessible information (W3C, 2005). The directors of CERN declared in April 1993 that the web would be free and by September of that year the Mosaic browser (National Center for Supercomputing Applications) was released for all common computer platforms. The web has grown from 10 hosts in 1991 to over 57,000 by 2005. It is essentially a body of software in hypertext and a set of common protocols so that anyone can browse and contribute.

Software available on the web is similar in type to stand-alone software. There are simulations, drill and practice, tutorials, reference materials, calculators, and other applications for mathematics. However, software on the web can offer immediate links to other locations, frequent updates, and viewing from virtually anywhere in the world. Disadvantages of web-based software include its potentially ephemeral nature, commercialization of many sites, threats of viruses and privacy invasion, and, often, questionable sources of information. Using web applications for mathematics instruction requires even more teacher preparation and monitoring than stand-alone software. But free access to thousands of excellent instructional sources makes using the web worth the extra effort.

Computer Environments

Computer software, whether stand-alone or web-based, can support powerful mathematical thinking and processes. Often termed "computer environments," these technology applications support the processes and broad content areas of mathematics at all levels. Although overlapping in features, these special environments are loosely classified for mathematics applications as virtual manipulatives, learning objects, and microworlds. Other environments, such as computer and web language development, are beyond the scope of this text.

Students and teachers can access **virtual manipulatives** on many websites, including the NCTM Illuminations and National Library of Virtual Manipulatives sites. Virtual manipulatives are simulations of actual concrete manipulatives or representations such as graphs, created using JAVA, a robust, but neutral, dynamic computer language (Heath, 2002). JAVA "applets" are immediately accessible to the student; these tools don't require special keystrokes or syntax like other software. They have applications from kindergarten through graduate-level mathematics. Applets can also be created by using the directions found on many websites, such as the English/Japanese site "Manipula Math with JAVA."

Another powerful learning tool for mathematics are **learning objects,** modular digital resources that include various forms of software such as simulations, calculators, animations, tutorials, video clips, graphs, and assessments (Wiley, 2001). Learning objects (sometimes called "widgets") have the potential to provide individualized learning experiences with teacher-selected instructional objectives and can be used with any content area or level. The Wisconsin Online Resource Center includes the following criteria for quality learning objects: small (2 to 15 minutes), independent, stored in a searchable data base, based on a clear instructional strategy, interactive, reusable, and groupable. An example of a learning object on the Washington State University website is the Dollars and Cents Widget for practicing making change up to $5.00, estimating cash back, and identifying exact amounts for purchases (Miller, Brown, & Robinson, 2002).

Simulation software creates **microworlds** that can be manipulated by the user, who is able to view the consequences of manipulations immediately. Simulations can range from real-world applications (e.g., flight simulator, electric motor, whitewater rafting) to gamelike fantasy worlds. The earliest mathematics simulation tool was LOGO, built into microcomputers in the mid 1980s (Papert, 1980). LOGO is a programming language for moving objects (in early versions, an abstract "turtle"; later, "robots") around space and analyzing spatial relationships and properties. Available today through commercial sources or online freeware in many versions, LOGO activities offer countless mathematics applications (Logo Foundation, 1991). Another microworld for mathematics is *Blocks Microworld* (Thompson, 1992), based on Dienes' blocks. Children can create and explore their own algorithms or follow formal routines for addition and subtraction. Other microworlds include *Conservation of Area and its Measurement* (Kordaki & Potari, 2002) and *Mathwright 32 Author* (Bluejay Lispware).

A final note is warranted about the use of technology to support mathematics instruction. There is no doubt technology is powerful and can assist student learning. However, teachers must make decisions about how it is used. Goldenberg offered six principles "for thinking about technology use in math classrooms" (2000, p. 2):

- choose technologies that further existing learning goals (rather than create artificial goals so technology can be used)
- allow calculator use when computation gets in the way of instruction's purpose
- consider when the analysis (process) of the problem is as important as the answer
- be cautious when technology might be replacing the student's development of important thought processes
- be aware of the effects of removing content from the curriculum just because the technology can substitute (e.g., square roots, trigonometric functions)
- encourage students to learn a few tools well rather than attempting to expose students only superficially to many tools

Applets are programs written in the Java programming language that can be included in HTML web pages. These programs are animated and can be interactive.

Like their students, teachers must have time to learn new technologies and their applications for mathematics. Calculator and computer technologies require significant resources and support services from the school and district level.

OTHER RESOURCES

Mathematics is literally all around us—the environment is rich with materials and applications for mathematics connections. This brief section will remind the reader of other options for mathematics resources.

Newspapers and Print Media

Many schools and homes receive daily newspapers and magazines that offer a plethora of mathematics tools and applications. Newspapers include weather charts, advertisements, stock prices, sports statistics, various maps and graphs, and references to other statistics within articles. Newspapers and magazines frequently publish special features on topics in science, health, ecology, elections, history, bridges and other architecture, the community, and government.

Other printed materials that may be useful for mathematics and are readily available include phone books, restaurant menus, tax worksheets, sales charts, sizing charts, bus schedules, road maps, house plans, and travel brochures. Materials that have personal or confidential information, such as check stubs, electric bills, or medical reports, should not be used, but simulated with teacher-developed materials.

Organizations and Projects

In recent years, several mathematics organizations and projects have earned the reputation for providing quality information to teachers and their students about mathematics. The following list is not exhaustive, but the sources included have been reviewed as those that are nonprofit, broad based, and accessible. Many of these projects include links on their websites to additional resources.

■ CAST: Center for Applied Special Technology. Research, development, professional training, and products in universal design for learning: www.cast.org.

■ The National Council of Teachers of Mathematics offers professional development and support through conferences, journals and newsletters, web-based resources (Illuminations), and publications: www.nctm.org.

■ The Eisenhower Science and Mathematics Consortium, funded by the U.S. Department of Education until September 2005 and now by subscription, is a clearinghouse of curriculum and professional development resources for mathematics and science: www.goenc.com.

■ National Library of Virtual Manipulatives, a NSF-supported project, began in 1999 to develop a library of uniquely interactive, web-based virtual manipulatives or concept tutorials, mostly in the form of Java applets, for mathematics instruction (K–12 emphasis). Utah State University: http://matti.usu.edu/nlvm/nav/vlibrary.html.

■ The Math Forum@ Drexel is an internet-based center for mathematics and mathematics education. Provides resources, materials, activities, products, and services such as discussion boards, Ask Dr. Math, Problems of the Week, Teacher2Teacher, Problems Library, and Teacher Exchange: http://mathforum.org.

■ Project Interactivate is sponsored by the Shodor Education Foundation, Inc. Its goals include the creation, collection, evaluation, and dissemination of interactive Java-based courseware for exploration in middle-school science and mathematics: www.shodor.org/interactive.

■ The Gateway to Educational Materials (GEM) is a consortium effort to provide educators with easy access to thousands of educational resources on the web: www.thegateway.org.

■ The K–12 Mathematics Curriculum Center, funded by the National Science Foundation through the Education Development Center, is charged with assisting schools and districts with the implementation of standards-based mathematics curricula: www2.edc.org/mcc.

■ AIMS Education Foundations (Activities Integrating Mathematics & Science) is a nonprofit research and development organization dedicated to the improvement of teaching and learning through a meaningful, integrated approach. AIMS creates hands-on, standards-based activities and curricula and offers professional development and resources: www.aimsedu.org.

■ International Education Software (IES) Math Education and Technology website based in Japan offers instructions for creating JAVA applets, a collection of several hundred math applets, and other software for mathematics education: www.ies.co.jp/math/indexeng.html.

■ Wisconsin Online Resource Center offers several dozen learning objects for mathematics instruction as well as guidance in creating learning objects: www.wisc-online.com/index.htm.

■ The LOGO Foundation was established in 1991 as a nonprofit educational organization to facilitate communication, professional development, research, and product dissemination about LOGO: http://el.media.mit.edu/logo-foundation.

■ PBS TeacherLine offers professional development, interactive applets, online videos, live chats, and resources that support all subject areas: http://teacherline.pbs.org/teacherline/welcome.cfm.

■ Federal Resources for Educational Excellence is a clearinghouse of free educational resources offered by federal organizations and agencies: www.ed.gov/free/index.html.

■ The University of Virginia's Center for Technology and Teacher Education has compiled a list of websites for collecting data, maps, and charts: http://teacherlink.org/content/math/relatedlinks/datacollection.html.

Angela, Joseph, and Chris met again during their March inservice and exchanged notes on their curriculum review committee work. Angela explained to Joseph and Chris how valued she felt after the process. "The group understood my concern for the gaps in the adopted series and decided to adopt supplementary materials that I recommended. My cooperating teachers and I can use these supplements for reteaching concepts or providing extra practice with new skills. These are not those mindless workbooks that my students hate, but additional activities for concept development and varied practice opportunities."

Joseph explained that the high school curriculum committee had decided to integrate geometry and algebra. "I was so excited to be part of this decision from the beginning. I believe all the students in my courses will understand the concepts more deeply because I can demonstrate the connections. We also are recommending the district provide basic graphing calculators for each class so students can use the same calculators at home."

Chris described her experience reviewing elementary mathematics curricula. "The three series we reviewed each included classroom manipulative sets at each grade level. But the series we recommended for adoption actually provided instructional materials for using the manipulatives with adaptations for students with special needs."

The three teachers agreed that the time between textbook adoption and the beginning of the school year would allow them to become familiar with the new textbooks and study the best methods for integrating technology, materials, and adaptations. ■ ● ▲

CHAPTER SUMMARY

- Universal design applied to curriculum allows a wide range of students accessibility to the curriculum. Curriculum design should be flexible in terms of means of representation, expression, and engagement.
- A few mathematics curriculum programs have been developed for students with learning problems. These include components for strategic instruction, explicit modeling, providing immediate feedback, charting progress, and supplementary activities for additional practice.
- A number of national clearinghouses support specific general mathematics programs that are based on NCTM standards. These programs do not provide impact data for students with disabilities or low-achievers. Research is needed in this area.
- Teachers should work collaboratively to adapt general curriculum programs for special-needs students. A principle-based planning strategy can be useful for making these adaptations.
- Mathematics manipulatives should represent concepts well and be inexpensive, durable, and age-appropriate.

- Teachers and students can create their own powerful manipulatives to support mathematic learning.
- Both concrete and virtual manipulatives can support K–12 mathematics learning by students with learning problems if careful study and planning take place.
- Calculators have evolved to be powerful mathematics tools at all grade levels. Students with learning problems need explicit guidance in calculator use.
- Educational software for mathematics should be evaluated by recognized criteria. Software types include tutorial, simulation, drill and practice, problem solving, and reference.
- Productivity software that is useful for mathematics learning includes spreadsheets, equation editors, graphing software, statistical packages, and assessment tools.
- The World Wide Web offers the same software types and other interactive applications such as virtual manipulatives, learning objects, and microworlds.
- Other resources for mathematics instruction include newspapers, print media, and national-level nonprofit mathematics projects, research centers, and clearinghouses.

RESULTS

American Education Corporation (A + LS Algebra software): www.amered.com.

Bluejay Lispware (Mathwright 32 Author software): www.mathwright.com.

Cabrilog (Cabri Geometry software), Grenoble, France: www.cabri.com.

Carnegie Learning, Inc (Cognitive Tutor): www.carnegielearning.com.

Creative Publications (Algebra Lab Gear): www.creativepublications.com.

Curriculum Associates, Inc.: www.curriculumassociates.com.

Edge Enterprises (Strategic Math Series): 785-749-1473.

ETA Cuisenaire (Cuisenaire Rods and other materials): www.etacuisenaire.com.

ETS (*Discourse* software): www.ets.org/discourse/index.html.

Everyday Learning Corporation: www.sra4kids.com/everydaylearning.

Glencoe/McGraw-Hill MathScape: Seeing and Thinking Mathematically, Contemporary Mathematics in Context: www.glencoe.com.

Holt, Rinehart and Winston (Mathematics in Context):www.hrw.com.

Innovative Learning Concepts, Inc. (TouchMath) 6760 Corporate Drive, Colorado Springs, CO 80919-1999 (1-800-888-9191): www.touchmath.com.

It's About Time, Inc. (MATH Connections): www.its-about-time.com.

James Joseph Baker: www.expertmath.org.

JRL Enterprises, Inc. (I CAN Learn Mathematics Curriculum): www.icanlearn.com.

Kendall Hunt Publishing Company (SIMMS Integrated Mathematics): www.kendallhunt.com; (Math Trailblazers): www.mathtrailblazers.com.

Key Curriculum Press: Interactive Mathematics Program, Geometer's Sketchpad: www.keypress.com.

Knowledge Adventure (math software): www.adventure.com.

McDougal Littell (MATH Thematics): www.classzone.com/start/math_thematics.cfm.

Prentice Hall (Connected Mathematics Project): www.phschool.com/math/cmp.

Riverdeep (math software): www.riverdeep.com.

Saxon Mathematics (Adaptations for Special Populations): www.saxonpublishers.com.

Scott Foresman (Investigations in Number, Data, and Space): www.investigations.scottforesman.com

SPSS, Inc. (SPSS software): www.spss.com.

SRA/McGraw-Hill (Direct Instruction Mathematics: Connecting Math Concepts, DISTAR Arithmetic, Corrective Math): www.sra4kids.com.

Sunburst Technology (math software): www.sunburst.com.

Tom Snyder Productions (math software): www.tomsnyder.com.

W. H. Freeman and Company (Mathematics: Modeling Our World): www.whfreeman.com.

Wright Group/McGraw-Hill (Everyday Mathematics): www.wrightgroup.com.

Chapter 7

Integrating Mathematics with Content Areas and Life Skills

Chapter Questions

1. What are the benefits and concerns about integrating mathematics instruction with other content areas?
2. What are the big idea concepts and processes that are common for mathematics and science, social studies, reading, writing, and the visual arts?
3. What mathematics skills are critical for adult career (life) domains: personal, interpersonal, leisure, home life, employment/education, and community living?
4. How should life-skills mathematics instruction be designed for students with learning problems?
5. How can teachers identify the mathematics concepts and skills necessary for specific occupations?
6. What mathematics preparation should be considered by a transition planning team?

The entire staff of Pine Grove Elementary School, including Chris Johnson, the remedial mathematics support teacher, is attending an August training session on integration of content areas across the elementary curriculum. Segments of the in-service training address the integration of mathematics and science standards, the use of children's literature across subject areas, writing across the curriculum, and using the arts with other content areas. Chris discusses her concerns with the other teachers at her table before the first session begins. "I feel so pressured to cover the math standards in time for spring testing, I can't imagine how we can fit in more content."

David Schmitt, a kindergarten teacher, replies, "The early childhood curriculum is already integrated. We don't separate subject areas like in the other grades. But I would like to understand the curriculum at other grade levels so I can better prepare my students."

"I've had concerns for several years about curriculum connections," offers Mei Wang. "My fifth-grade students just aren't able to use their math skills in social studies or science. They act like they've never heard of fractions or measurement with those applications, even though we completed units in both areas. It seems to me there are many commonalities among the content areas that we don't stress enough. My concern is having enough planning time." ■ ● ▲

INTEGRATING MATHEMATICS WITH OTHER CONTENT AREAS

The teachers of Pine Grove Elementary voiced some of the most common concerns with curriculum integration—planning and instructional time, content coverage, consistency of curriculum goals across grade levels, and preparation for annual testing. Other concerns include diluted content-area standards, inadequate resources (including textbooks), narrow teacher training and experience, shallow exposure due to fragmented integration, inadequate assessment, and rigid school schedules. But many educators point to the benefits of curriculum integration, such as promoting the generalization of new concepts and skills, connections with real-world problems and applications, bonus instructional time, relevance and motivational aspects for students, and better preparation for college and work requirements. The NCTM Task Force on Integrated Mathematics concluded that integration within mathematics and across other contexts "has the potential for enhancing the scope and power of mathematics teaching and learning" (Dickey et al., 1997, p. 12). But, the group warned, it also has the potential for undermining the coherence and focus of the mathematics curriculum. Integrated activities that are trivial or disconnected don't substitute for worthwhile mathematics tasks. Like all other content standards committees (e.g., science, social studies, the arts), this mathematics task force emphasized that the standards of its discipline must drive and serve as the core of any curriculum integration.

Major learning obstacles for many students with low mathematics achievement include poor attitudes about mathematics and difficulty generalizing skills from mathematics class to other settings. Integrated learning activities, whether in remedial settings, general education mathematics classes, other classes in school, or in community situations, can promote more positive attitudes and generalization. Integration can also provide a broader prior knowledge base for future learning, offer more powerful applications for technology, emphasize a common problem-solving approach, encourage more reinforcement and review of concepts and skills, and reduce gaps in learning. Unfortunately, the primary rationale for benefiting students with learning differences provided by many articles on mathematics curriculum integration is the ease of addressing different learning styles, a shallow and simplistic argument (see Chapter 2 for discussion).

Content integration involves careful planning for the inclusion of grade-level content standards, dynamic assessment strategies, robust applications, and the consideration of cross-curricular instructional strategies, student processes, and the big idea concepts. Common instructional strategies that should be considered for integrating mathematics with other subjects include student grouping, individualization techniques, investigations, demonstrations, concept mapping, vocabulary building activities, and problem-driven learning, among others. The NCTM processes—problem solving, communication, making representations, reasoning, and making connections—are important for other content areas. Many major concepts for mathematics are interdisciplinary: functions, change patterns, spatial relationships, number sense, and properties of different types of relationships. Content integration has the potential to offer more time for in-depth study with meaningful applications rather than surface-level and isolated content coverage.

Figure 7.1
Continuum of Cross-Curricular Integration

Minimal	Moderate	Full
One teacher	Two or more teachers	All teachers
Primary subject with select examples from other subjects (Within subject)	More than one subject area (Across subjects)	All subjects (Themed)

Content area integration can be considered along a continuum from minimal to full integration, as depicted in Figure 7.1. Minimal integration takes place in one setting with one subject area such as mathematics. The mathematics teacher plans examples from other subject areas to introduce lessons, write word problems, or develop applications. A social studies teacher demonstrates a minimal level of integration by reviewing and applying specific mathematics skills for map making. All teachers in a school should be implementing minimal-level content integration by being aware of the concepts and skills students are learning in other subject areas and planning some integrated applications. It is particularly important that students with learning problems in mathematics have planned and explicit application and generalization activities for new mathematics concepts and skills.

A more involved integration model is where two or more teachers plan lessons or units together so that concepts and skills can be taught and reinforced by all the teachers. For example, a mathematics and an English teacher teaching the same group of students wanted to reinforce the concept of descriptive language. The English teacher asked students to write descriptions of objects, settings, and events using rich language. The mathematics teacher asked students to verbally describe three-dimensional shapes and then write descriptions using accurate mathematics vocabulary. A high school vocational education teacher worked with the school's special education mathematics support teacher on students' fraction concepts for measurement. After the special educator determined the understanding gaps of each student, both teachers retaught concepts with real-world measurement applications. The integration of two content areas may be the most effective and time-efficient model, because the standards of each area are more likely to be upheld and connections reflect the most important concepts for each subject.

Full content integration, at the most intensive end of the continuum, is implemented by a team of teachers at a given grade level or by an entire grade level or school. Full content integration involves every unit of study planned around a theme by which every content area's standards are addressed. As discussed in the section on unit planning in Chapter 4, the most critical concerns for full integration are maintaining the integrity of each set of content area standards and making time for team planning. An example unit for fifth graders could be planned around the theme of the book, *Pedro's Journal* (Conrad, 1991), a fictional account of Christopher Columbus's voyage told by a young cabin boy on the *Santa Maria*. The English teacher would take the lead for language arts standards including reading comprehension, vocabulary development, and written language skills, all related to the book. The social studies teacher would guide study into the rich history and geographic aspects of Christopher Columbus' journey, expanding on the concepts in the book, including those of the exploitation of indigenous people and distinguishing historical fact from fiction by expanding study to other sources. The science teacher would integrate biological, physical, and earth science concepts related to the sea, human nutrition, and tropical climates. And the mathematics teacher would plan charting, graphing, spatial concept, and problem-solving lessons related to navigation, planning trips, and volume of provisions.

Some students served by this team of teachers might also be served by a support teacher for learning strategies, pre-teaching, or re-teaching, depending on each student's needs. The support teacher should be a part of the planning team for this unit of study. All the teachers on this team began using similar problem-solving procedures and concept mapping with their students, an unexpected benefit of collaborative teaching. Similar units can be planned at any grade level as long as the appropriate standards for each subject area are addressed. A planning map for teachers integrating the Pedro Unit is shown in Figure 7.2.

Fogarty (1991) proposed ten specific curriculum integration models organized by interdisciplinary, intradisciplinary, and student-based orientations. Within a given subject integration can be fragmented, connected, or nested. Across subjects it can be sequenced, shared, webbed, threaded, or integrated (rearranged and overlapping). At the student level, the learner can be individually immersed or work with a network of other students. Usiskin (2003) described five kinds of mathematics integration: unifying concepts, merging areas of mathematics, removing distinctions between areas, teaching strands each year, and interdisciplinary integration. He recommended that curriculum developers focus on the "size of curriculum" when planning integration—from the single problem to the lesson, unit, and course to the school's mathematics curriculum and overall curriculum.

The following sections discuss specific means for integrating mathematics concepts and skills with those of science, social studies, writing, literature, and art. Integrations can also be made with health, physical education, music, foreign language study, computer science, vocational education, and other subject areas. Many sources are available to assist teachers in planning high-quality integration activities and units of study. Some of these are listed at the end of the chapter. Additionally, recent mathematics textbooks and curriculum projects have offered integrated approaches (e.g., Connected Mathematics Project at Michigan State University, Contemporary Mathematics in Context of the Core-Plus Mathematics Project at Western Michigan University).

The Math–Science Connection

Curriculum standards for science and mathematics are closely related, as they both deal with understanding the physical world. Both content areas rely on a similar problem-solving approach and tools such as observation, comparison, measurement, and communication.

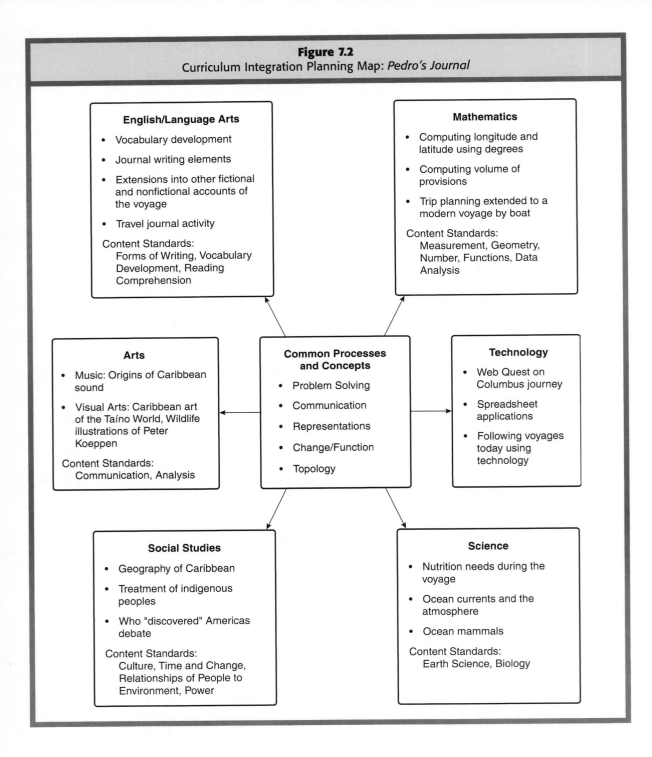

Figure 7.2
Curriculum Integration Planning Map: *Pedro's Journal*

English/Language Arts

- Vocabulary development
- Journal writing elements
- Extensions into other fictional and nonfictional accounts of the voyage
- Travel journal activity

Content Standards:
Forms of Writing, Vocabulary Development, Reading Comprehension

Mathematics

- Computing longitude and latitude using degrees
- Computing volume of provisions
- Trip planning extended to a modern voyage by boat

Content Standards:
Measurement, Geometry, Number, Functions, Data Analysis

Arts

- Music: Origins of Caribbean sound
- Visual Arts: Caribbean art of the Taíno World, Wildlife illustrations of Peter Koeppen

Content Standards:
Communication, Analysis

Common Processes and Concepts

- Problem Solving
- Communication
- Representations
- Change/Function
- Topology

Technology

- Web Quest on Columbus journey
- Spreadsheet applications
- Following voyages today using technology

Social Studies

- Geography of Caribbean
- Treatment of indigenous peoples
- Who "discovered" Americas debate

Content Standards:
Culture, Time and Change, Relationships of People to Environment, Power

Science

- Nutrition needs during the voyage
- Ocean currents and the atmosphere
- Ocean mammals

Content Standards:
Earth Science, Biology

Even some big ideas are the same: change (function), systems, and classification (Gurganus, Janas, & Schmitt, 1995).

In young children's activities, it is difficult to separate mathlike and sciencelike enterprises because children are exploring and trying to make sense of their world. Children engaged in sorting, describing, building, and experimenting with objects are preparing for more formal mathematics and science activities in school. Teachers of young children should guide these activities so that language skills and concept development grow and expand beyond incidental learning.

Several curriculum projects for elementary and secondary students encourage the integration of mathematics and science lessons. One example is the *AIMS Education Foundation*, a nonprofit organization dedicated to improving the teaching and learning of math and science through an integrated approach. The AIMS (Activities Integrating Mathematics & Science) Foundation creates hands-on, standards-based activities and curricula and supports those with professional development and other resources. Another is the professional organization *American Association for the Advancement of Science*, dedicated to advancing science and technology throughout the world. Among its twenty-four sections are specific organizations on mathematics, engineering, education, linguistics, statistics, and social sciences. In addition to *Science*, the largest peer-reviewed journal in the world, AAAS supports research such as the middle-school mathematics textbook project, a science-news website, and many other publications and initiatives.

An example of the integration of mathematics and science standards is provided in Figure 7.3, depicting the big idea questions for a unit of study for ninth- and tenth-graders on the use and recovery of fossil fuels and impact on the environment, with the mathematics standards relating to data analysis and functions. In this unit, both mathematics and science standards appropriate for ninth grade were addressed, processes and methods maintained fidelity to both fields, and the topic for study was relevant for a real-world investigation.

TRY THIS

Review the mathematics and science curriculum standards for a specific grade span. Select one science goal and articulate the relationship with mathematics concepts and skills. For example, a science goal for grades 9–12 is to relate the transfer of heat energy to the patterns of wind belts (Earth Science, Energy Systems). What mathematics concepts and skills at the same grade levels would be incorporated with this study?

Mathematics as a Tool for Social Studies

Social studies are essentially studies of humankind, where people live, how they are organized, how they change, and how individuals fit within society (South Carolina Social Studies Curriculum Standards, 2005). Within the social studies domain are many disciplines, including anthropology, archaeology, history, philosophy, economics, geography, political science, psychology, religion, and sociology—although K–12 studies focus primarily on history, political science, geography, and economics. Likewise there are many sets of national standards including specific standards for civic education,

Figure 7.3

Integrating Mathematics and Science: Ninth–Tenth Grade Unit on Fossil Fuels, Data Analysis, and Functions

Unit Problem: How are fossil fuels used today, what is the impact on the environment, and what are the alternatives?

Questions	Science Concepts	Mathematics Concepts
What percentage of the world's energy use is from fossil fuels?	Fossil fuels are organic chemicals created by living organisms millions of years ago and transformed by high pressures and temperatures into coal, petroleum, and natural gas.	Data collection and analysis of the fuel reserves and rates of consumption around the world. Exploration of functional relationships.
What is the environmental impact of the use of fossil fuels?	Burning of these fuels produces oxides of carbon, sulfur, nitrogen, soot, and fine-particulate ash. Carbon dioxide contributes to global warming.	Data analysis and functional relationships between rate of fossil fuel use, atmospheric concentrations of gasses, and climate change. Longitude, latitude, and Earth rotation concepts are factors.
What alternatives to fossil fuels are viable environmentally and economically?	Exploration of methanol, ethanol, wind, and solar energy.	Data collection and functional analysis of alternative resources and their impact on the environment. (Functional relationships can be depicted with tabular, equation, graphical, or geometric models.)

Source: Science portions adapted by permission from a unit developed by Susan S. Van Biersel (2004), *Fossil fuel sources, usage and alternatives: What are the options?* prepared in a seminar sponsored by the Yale-New Haven Teachers Institute (www.yale.edu/ynhti), part of the national League of Teachers Institutes (teachers.yale.edu).

economics, geography, and history. The National Council for Social Studies developed general social studies standards (1994). A perusal of these standards across the grade levels brings to mind many mathematics applications. Many of the same methods from mathematics are used in social studies. Making connections in social studies includes those across time and cultures, viewing patterns in history, or the effects of events on people. Problem solving skills can be applied to simple or complex problems such as developing systems for food and water in third-world countries or studying the impact of political change. Communication skills are critical for studying and understanding interpersonal and intercultural relationships, the effects of media, and researching topics of interest. Reasoning is essential for solving problems, making connections, applying theory, and making predictions. Representations are used in social sciences to convey ideas through charts, graphs, maps, and tables.

Study of history involves a mental number line that represents time and patterns of events. Study of geography requires spatial sense, measurement, and proportions. Anthropology, economics, sociology, and political science all depend on data analysis, probability, and statistical representations. And archaeology combines most other disciplines. The content strands in this book include cultural connection sections that relate specific mathematics concepts to applications in other cultures.

Some examples of social studies and mathematics activities include:

- Developing surveying skills using maps and compasses
- Comparing wages, taxes, and prices among several countries after converting currencies according to official listings. Comparisons can also be made for one country across time.
- Collecting population data for analysis and prediction using spreadsheets
- Researching how mathematics differs in other cultures
- Interpreting and creating charts and graphs to depict economic, political, geographic, cultural, and sociological phenomena
- Engaging in service-learning projects that meet community-level needs while addressing social studies, mathematics, and other content standards and cross-curricular processes. Examples include environmental surveys, community transportation studies, children's education projects, and parks and recreation projects for diverse citizens.

TRY THIS
Select one of the following social studies topics and describe a companion mathematics unit for the same grade level: fourth grade—(U.S. History) resources of various regions and their impact on occupations of citizens; seventh grade—(World Regions) economic relationships of trading partners such as the U.S., European Union, and China; ninth grade—(World Geography) the effects of water sources on people.

Writing in Mathematics

Writing across the curriculum became a national trend in college curricula in the mid 1970s with the realization that traditional curriculum areas, such as mathematics, could benefit from more creative and active methods of learning than traditional lecture and rote learning. At about the same time, researchers began to recognize that disciplines have their own communication styles that students need for college and careers in specific fields. By the 1980s the initiative moved to elementary and secondary classrooms to better prepare students for post-secondary communication demands. The NCTM standards (1989, 2000) emphasized communication skills as one of five process standards for engaging in mathematics. As a result, state and district

Figure 7.4
Example Test Items Requiring Written Responses in Mathematics

Example 1
Is the number 35 even or odd? Explain in words how you know.

Example 2
Examine the line for $2x + 5 = y$ in the graph below. Explain in words the effect on the slope of the line if the $+5$ were changed to -5 in the equation.

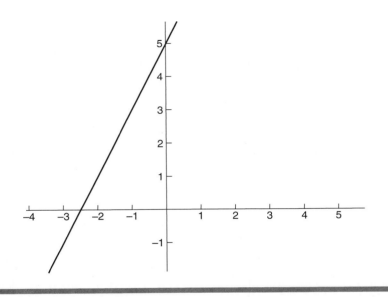

mathematics tests often require students to write out procedures or explain their responses in writing (see Figure 7.4).

Mathematics teachers find themselves planning more writing activities as a result of these initiatives. Typical activities include keeping a mathematics journal or daily log of new concepts and experiences, recording definitions for new mathematics terms, writing word problems for other students to solve, producing summaries of investigations, developing story or problem books for younger students, and creating reports on careers or historical figures in mathematics. Some teachers even explore mathematics poetry and cartoons as a means for connecting mathematics to student interests through language.

Having students explain their responses in writing benefits mathematics learning by offering teachers a view of student thinking and requiring students to consider whether the "answer makes sense." However, some students with language disabilities or limited English may not be able to adequately express their mathematics reasoning in writing. Consider the following students' written explanations of the same mathematics problem. Al has a mathematics disability but average language skills, Tami has mathematics and language disabilities, and Ciara has been learning English for only six months but was on grade level in mathematics in her native China.

The problem: Convert this expression into its simplest form: $5(4x + 2y^2) + 2x + y$.

Al: I followed the steps in "Please Excuse My Dear Aunt Sally" and did the parentheses first, getting $20x + 10y^2 + 2x + y$, and then I couldn't do anything with the exponent and there was no multiplication or division so I then I added the like terms, getting $22x + 10y^2 + y$. I rearranged that in the correct order for $22x + y + 10y^2$.

Tami: The (and) things first and so the answer is $20x + 10y^2 + 2x + y$ because that's the answer.

Ciara: The 5 many the $4x$ and the $2y^2$ and the $20x$ and the $2x$ so $= 22x + 10y^2 + y$.

Please Excuse My Dear Aunt Sally or variations of this mnemonic device remind students of the order of operations—parentheses, exponents, multiply, divide, add, subtract.

All three students were observed beginning their work the same way and both Al and Ciara simplified the expression completely. Only Al was able to provide an understandable written explanation with the protocol for his final result, but his reasoning was purely procedural rather than conceptual. Both Tami and Ciara struggled with accurate vocabulary. A more conceptual written description would have been:

> The distributive property should be applied first, distributing the 5 to the terms $4x$ and $2y^2$ by multiplication. No other division or multiplication can be performed, so then look for common terms to add. We can combine the $20x$ and $2x$ into $22x$. No other terms can be combined, so put the terms in order of degree to get $22x + y + 10y^2$.

For students with limited vocabulary or written language skills, mathematics teachers should allow alternative means of expression, such as oral explanations or diagrams, while building writing skills. Mathematics vocabulary can be developed through activities similar to those in language arts: charts of new terms, morphological analysis, mnemonic devices, repeated use of new words by students in both oral and written forms, and personal mathematics dictionaries or word banks. Producing quality written descriptions of mathematics reasoning also requires instruction, practice, and reinforcement. Students should share their descriptions with others for clarification, view and discuss model descriptions, develop descriptions in cooperative groups, and practice critiquing descriptions for elements of logical reasoning. Like language arts writing activities, mathematics writing can take many forms, such as reflections, descriptions, captions, word problems, and technical reporting. Students should have grade-appropriate practice with many forms and specific and corrective feedback on their efforts.

There is research support for the effects of writing activities on learning mathematics. Jurdak and Zein (1998) used journal writing with teacher-created prompts with middle-grade students and found that the students engaged in this writing outscored their peers in concept understanding, procedural knowledge, and mathematical communication, but there were no differences for problem solving, attitudes, or math achievement in the twelve-week study. Thayer and Giebelhaus (2001) conducted a four-week study with high school geometry students and found significant differences in achievement for the group that received instruction in summary, process, and analytical writing. In only four weeks, with no additional class time, the group engaged in writing about mathematics understanding outperformed their peers.

Teachers encouraging writing for mathematics should also be aware of special writing conventions. Mathematics writing is not simply using correct vocabulary, there is a discipline-specific writing style. These conventions also are expected for college-level writing in mathematics (Crannell, 1994; Countryman, 1992; Morgan, 1998).

■ For problem solving, most sources recommend explaining the problem first, then stating the answer in a complete sentence, and then describing the solution strategy. Sometimes writers will describe the features of a problem that are interesting or challenging. Sometimes they will provide more than one solution method.

■ Mathematics writing should be simple, clear, uncluttered, and well organized. It should not be flowery or full of forced synonyms. Use complete sentences to enhance clarity. Many times the same phrases will be repeated as with, "To solve for . . . ," and, "we see that," and, "we can show . . . by . . . ," and "given the value . . . ." It is not considered redundant to repeat these phrases. Attempting alternative wording in mathematics typically results in less clear language.

■ Clearly label all charts, tables, graphs, and other representations using words. Define all variables and formulas. Don't assume that the reader will understand that $P = 4s$ means the perimeter of the object in the drawing is equal to four times the length of a side.

■ Avoid using words that can cause confusion such as "time," "center," and "first." If necessary, use these multiple-meaning words very precisely with modifiers. For example, t stands for the time in seconds and the first term of the four terms in this polynomial. Sometimes students create their own words or phrases, which can be creative, but should be accompanied by an explanation. For example, "I'm going to call the group of cubes left over after sorting, the 'outsiders.'" But students may inadvertently use a mathematics term incorrectly (e.g., remainders).

■ Use symbols within sentences for clarity. The following sentence is accurate for mathematics writing: *If A = area, L = length, and W = width, then we can find the area of a rectangle given the formula A = LW if we know the values of L and W.* But avoid other abbreviations and symbols that are not clearly mathematical or accurate for the situation (e.g., etc., re, OK, #, ea, and &).

■ Often mathematics problems involve multiple steps and students tend to use multiple equals signs to show change. This practice may lead to confusion for the reader, as can be seen by this example: $3x + 5x + 3(2y + x) = 8x + 6y + 3x = 11x + 6y$. Inserting phrases such as "In step one we combine the terms . . ." will be clearer.

■ Tables, graphs, or diagrams should be clearly labeled and referenced within the text of the student's narrative. They should not stand alone, but be explained in terms of how they were created and what they mean.

■ Teach students to use the equation editors that accompany word processors to make the actual mathematics symbols. This expression does not mean the square root of

5: √5. while this expression does: $\sqrt{5}$. Use the option key and special character keys to find the clearest method for creating symbols: 34 - 5 = 19 uses the hyphen key. But 34 − 5 = 19 uses the option-dash (en-dash).

■ Have students write for a specific audience, such as their peers, rather than writing for the teacher. Collect "quick-write" prompts for journal writing and use a rubric for evaluation. For example, *Which is easier to visualize, ratio or percentage? Explain.* or *Describe the differences in these problems: $\frac{1}{4} \times \frac{3}{12}$ and $\frac{1}{4} = \frac{3}{12}$",* (Cleland, Rillero, & Zambo, 2003)

■ Older students should read mathematics articles on their concept level for exposure to mathematics writing. Good sources include *Pi (π) in the Sky*, *Plus Magazine*, and the American Mathematical Society (www.ams.org).

Writing is a critical communication skill across curriculum areas but has specific applications for mathematics that merit development. Good writing instruction for mathematics is not simply telling students to "write in your math journal" but involves planning, appropriate instruction, and ongoing, standards-based assessment as with any other curriculum goal.

> **TRY THIS**
> Write out an explanation for the following solution using math-style writing conventions. *The eight students' grades were 91, 76, 84, 95, 89, 89, 86, and 90. The mean grade for the group was 87.5.*

Literature and Mathematics

One of the most popular curriculum integrations has been that of children's literature with mathematics concepts. But popularity doesn't necessarily mean research-based, effective instruction. In fact, very little research has been conducted to connect the use of literature with mathematics learning. Most resources on using literature cite increased student motivation as the primary rationale for this integration. Literature can also be a vehicle, like a problem situation, for introducing a concept or applying a math skill.

Literature for children and adolescents that is appropriate for making mathematics connections can be divided into three categories: literature developed specifically for mathematics connections, literary works that have the potential for strong mathematics connections, and literature that has only incidental or minor connections to mathematics. Books and stories in each of these categories range from high quality to downright terrible and include both fiction and nonfiction. Examples of high-quality fiction are *Grandfather Tang's Story* (Tompert, 1990), developed to demonstrate the origin and use of tangrams; *Alice's Adventures in Wonderland* (Carroll, 1865/1981) that includes many complex mathematics concepts such as shape changes and proportion, logical argument, time, space, and puzzles; and *A Year Down Yonder* (Peck, 2000) with its incidental references to train travel in 1937, seasonal changes on a farm, and depression-era wages. Special mathematics series include *Stories to Solve: Folktales from Around the World* by Shannon, and the *Sir Cumference* series by Neuschwander. Nonfiction examples include *Fermat's Enigma* (Singh, 1977) for high school students, *Crafts around the Ancient World* (Jovinelly, 2002) for middle schoolers, and *Food Chains in a Meadow Habitat* (Nadeau, 2002) for elementary students.

Teachers who want to integrate literature with their mathematics activities should consider these guidelines:

1. Consider the mathematics concepts that the selection supports. They should be aligned with grade-level mathematics standards and offer the opportunity for deeper exploration and understanding rather than just a bit of humor or simplistic treatment. Are the mathematics connections so motivating and powerful that the use of literature is the best method and worth the additional preparation time for a given unit of study?

2. Use reference books, journals, and websites to locate and read reviews of appropriate literature.

3. Read and reread the book or story carefully before using it with students. A book with a great title and wonderful illustrations still can be poorly written, inappropriate, or inaccurate regarding mathematics concepts.

4. Decide whether the selection is appropriate for the age, interests, and reading levels of students. A work written for younger children actually can be used by older students for deeper analysis and extensions as long as students do not view the work as too babyish. The length of the work, vocabulary needs, and relationship to other subject areas also should be considered.

5. Plan whether to use a good literary work to introduce a mathematics concept, to develop the concept, or to reinforce the concept after instruction. For example, the book *How Big Is a Foot?* (Myller, 1962) serves as a good introduction to the concept of units of measure. *The Doorbell Rang* (Hutchins, 1986) helps to develop the concept of partitive division. After much practice with two-digit numbers and their meaning, the book *17 Kings and 42 Elephants* (Mahy, 1987) brings together many mathematics concepts and skills such as place value, number sense, combining, grouping, and comparing.

6. Select works or portions of works that increase in value with repetition. Literature selections are typically reread and explored rather than given a "once-through."

7. Plan mathematics extensions for the literary selection, such as creating similar problems or researching related data.

Many reading comprehension skills overlap with mathematics skills such as making predictions, focusing on the main idea, understanding a problem, and visualizing content. Making predictions about the events in a narrative story or for a mathematics application requires background knowledge or data upon which to base reasonable predictions. The main idea of a story or that of a word problem is identified by students who can comprehend the meaning of the selection and eliminate extraneous information. Many stories include problems or dilemmas that the characters must understand and attempt to solve as with mathematics problems. And reading and mathematics both require visualization of events, relationships, space, and/or time. These comprehension skills common to reading and mathematics are the big ideas of reasoning and problem solving.

TRY THIS

Select one book (fiction or nonfiction) for children or adolescents and analyze its possible use for teaching or reinforcing mathematics concepts.

The Art of Mathematics

The entire mathematics curriculum could be taught through an artist's point of view. From early childhood concepts of two-dimensional symmetry and visual patterns to the dynamical systems and chaos theory of advanced mathematics, art can be a vehicle for making sense of the numerical, functional, and spatial properties of mathematics. Mathematics is also a tool for creating art.

The ancient Egyptians used mathematics in architecture but did not demonstrate perspective in their drawings because those were not intended to represent reality, but rather to project a symbolic re-representation of the world based on proportions (University College London, 2002). Construction of the pyramids (the Great Pyramid dates to 2575 B.C.E.) depended on geometric concepts such as surface area and volume of the pyramid, slope, degree of angles, and cross-section analysis of solids. There is actually a lot of disagreement about the mathematical theories of the pyramids—were the measurements' relationship to the golden number a coincidence or a deliberate application of mathematical formulae? The golden number is $\frac{1 + \sqrt{5}}{2}$ or 1.6180 . . . and an angle based on this number will have the measure 51°50′ (O'Connor & Robertson, 2000). The sides of the Great Pyramid have angles of 51.5° degrees, the Khafre pyramid 53°7′48″, and the Menkaure pyramid 51.3° (PBS-Nova, 1997). Mathematicians have made more precise analyses of the dimensions and angles using spreadsheets in order to better understand the mathematics behind the construction and still disagree about the level of mathematics that was actually used in construction (Tompkins, 1978). Since lengths were measured in cubits based on palm length (of the hand) and distance in rods is the distance one can travel the river in one day, the precision with which the lengths of each edge of the Great Pyramid were made is remarkable. For example, the four original lengths around the base are hypothesized to be 230.253 m, 230.391 m, 230.454 m, and 230.357 m plus or minus 6 to 30 mm, according to metrum.com, resulting in only $\frac{1}{1500}$ to $\frac{1}{2000}$ error.

The early Greeks contributed the golden section and proportion concepts that have permeated art, architecture, photography, design, music, and even poetry. The golden section, with a proportion of 1 : 1.618 (or .618 : 1), appears in the proportions of the Parthenon in Athens, and a construction for the golden section point was found in Euclid's *Elements* from 300 B.C.E. (Knott, 2005). But nature most likely provided the inspiration: the patterns in seashells (the nautilus shell), the spiral growth patterns of plant stems (phyllotaxis) and pinecones, and even human proportions. The golden section is also related to the numerical sequence known as the Fibonacci sequence: 0, 1, 1, 2, 3, 5, 8, 13, 21, 34, . . . as depicted in Figure 1.2 (page 4) that is created by adding the two previous terms in the sequence. Students of all ages enjoy explorations and applications with these universal concepts.

Another major application of mathematics for art was the development of the concept of perspective during the Renaissance. Brunelleschi is credited for making the first correct formulation of linear perspective in 1413 with the concepts of vanishing point (and the convergence of parallel lines toward that point) and that of scale as the relation between the measurement of an actual object and the object in the picture (O'Connor &

Robertson, 2003). Teachers can demonstrate these mathematics principles by having students study works of art (e.g., Alberti's *Vanishing Point*) or produce their own scale-perspective drawings.

Perspective is actually an optical illusion that uses mathematical principles to "fool the eye" into viewing what has been drawn on a two-dimensional surface as three-dimensional space. Leonardo da Vinci (around 1490) furthered the work on perspective, writing about related mathematical formulas and two types of perspective: artificial (with foreshortening) and natural (with consistent relative sizes) (O'Connor & Robertson, 2003). Dürer (around 1525) extended theories of perspective to shadows cast by objects. Hogarth (1697–1764) and Escher (1898–1972) are both known for deliberately misusing perspective in their art. Escher's work has been the topic of many mathematics classes, especially those in hyperbolic geometry.

> ● ● ● ● ● ● ● ● ●
> *Hyperbolic geometry* is a non-Euclidean geometry having constant sectional curvature. There are infinitely many parallels to a line that pass through the same point.
> ● ● ● ● ● ● ● ● ●

Another application of mathematics for art is the use of patterns, tilings, and tessellations by all cultures for fabric (rugs, quilts, wall hangings, etc.), architecture (windows, floors, roofs, fences, etc.), and decorations for baskets, pottery, wallpaper, and many other applications. These patterns have been made popular by the work of Escher, who was inspired by the art of thirteenth to fifteenth-century Alhambra, Spain (of Islamic influence). Besides the mathematics concepts of plane symmetry, groups, and properties of various two-dimensional shapes, these patterning applications explore flips, rotations, and construction methods.

Students enjoy creating mathematical patterns and exploring other applications in the visual arts, as is demonstrated everyday in hands-on museums for mathematics, science, technology, and the arts. The Goudreau Museum of Mathematics in Art and Science in New Hyde Park, New York allows children and youth to build a variety of mathematical models (www.mathmuseum.org). The Minnesota Children's Museum offers activities for children exploring shapes and patterns that connect mathematics concepts to the arts and sciences (www.mcm.org). Other interactive and integrative museums can be found through the Exploratorium website (www.exploratorium.edu) and the Association of Science-Technology Centers (www.astc.org).

Other activities that incorporate mathematics concepts with art include:

■ Create polyhedra using repeated two-dimensional patterns of regular polygons: triangles for tetrahedrons (four faces), octahedrons (eight faces), and icosahedrons (twenty faces); squares to create cubes; and pentagons for dodecahedrons (twelve faces). These are the five platonic solids. There are thirteen Archimedean solids that use two or more types of regular polygons. Remember to use tabs along the edges of each polygon so that the shapes can be connected.

■ Explore the properties of Möbius (Moebius) strips, discovered simultaneously by Möbius and Listing in 1858 (Derbyshire, 2004). To create a Möbius strip, take a long strip of paper and give it a half twist. Tape the two ends together. Some activities with the strip include determining how many sides there are by drawing a line down the middle of the strip, cutting the strip along the line to see what happens, and predicting what will happen with a second cut along the midline (mathforum.org). The mathematics related to the Möbius strip depend on trigonometric functions. The Möbius strip and its extensions (double Möbius, surfaces achieved by attaching disks, etc.) have been applied to architecture, physics, and even symbolism (infinity, religion).

■ Create mathematical mobiles after studying the work of Alexander Calder. The concepts of balance, fulcrum, and distribution are critical for creating a mobile that is balanced, yet interesting in motion. There are also virtual mobile sites on the web. The National Gallery of Art's website for teachers features lesson plans connecting mobile making and mathematics with connections to an online gallery of Calder's work (www.nga.gov/education/classroom).

■ Study the architectural features of buildings in the community. Look for examples of the golden proportion, other proportions, the Pythagorean triangle (ratio 3 : 4 : 5), and arches. Students can also draft floor plans of classrooms or public spaces to apply measurement and geometric concepts.

■ Use origami to explore mathematics concepts. In Japanese, the word *origami* refers to any type of paper folding. The traditional methods typically involved a single square of paper. But origami applications have expanded to modular forms with several sheets and differing dimensions of paper. Huzita (1992) formulated a set of six basic axioms for origami, including the most basic: "given two points P_1 and P_2, we can fold a line connecting them." The rest develop systematically through two points and two lines with mapping points onto lines. Other mathematicians have proposed origami theorems. For example, Kawasaki's Theorem (1989) states that if the angles surrounding a single vertex in a flat origami crease pattern are $a_1, a_2, a_3, \ldots a_{2n}$, then:

$$a_1 + a_3 + a_5 + \cdots + a_{2n-1} = 180 \text{ and}$$
$$a_2 + a_4 + a_6 + \cdots + a_{2n} = 180$$

(If you add up the angle measures of every other angle around a point, the sum will be 180.) Origami applications can be as simple as paper folding to gain experience with basic shapes and lines of symmetry, or as advanced as topology and combinatorics.

The visual arts offer many applications for in-depth connections with mathematics concepts while providing motivating activities and the groundwork for future studies. Technological applications, such as virtual websites and Geometer's Sketchpad, are additional tools for integrating these disciplines. Teachers without arts training should take advantage of the expertise of other colleagues, community volunteers, and area museums. Like other content areas, the arts have national curriculum standards (Consortium of National Arts Education Associates, 1994). The arts standards address communication skills, making connections, studying cultural forms, intellectual methods of inquiry, and *connecting the arts with other disciplines*.

TRY THIS

Explore the mathematics concepts embedded in the following paper folding activity. To make a basic swan, take a square of paper (different colors on each side if possible) and make a diagonal fold, then unfold (Figure 7.5, A). Turn the square so the folded crease is up and down (make each crease sharp and match edges exactly). Fold the left and right corners and the edges of the square below those in to meet the center crease. Your shape now looks like a kite (B). Turn that shape over and repeat the last step—fold the left and right corners and edges below them to meet the center crease (C). Fold the bottom point (the long, thin angle) close to but not reaching the top point, creasing a horizontal line at about the middle (D). Fold that tip down again not quite half way (forming the head E). Fold the entire shape in half along the original crease, with the "head" on the outside (it should look identical on each side—symmetrical). Pull on the swan's head and neck until it looks right, then crease the neck into position (F). It should stand like it's floating across a lake!

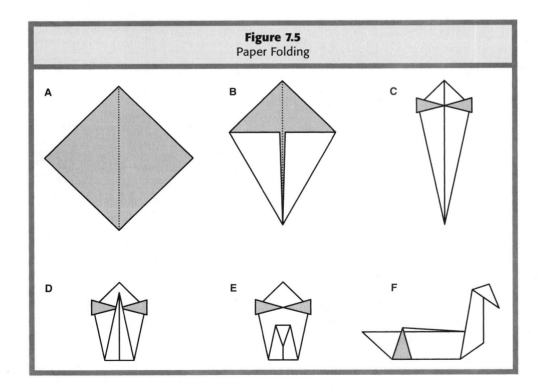

Figure 7.5
Paper Folding

Other Considerations for Content Area Integration

Integration of mathematics concept development with other content areas has the potential to boost student interest in mathematics, create deeper understanding, scaffold generalization of new mathematics skills, and prepare students for the next levels of learning. Integration with integrity requires fidelity with all content area standards, careful research and planning, and the continued application of effective instructional methods, including the ongoing assessment of student learning.

Many teachers place content integration in the "extras" category of activities to fill time once the content required for the next test has been "covered" and the weeks of testing have been completed for the year. However, isolating these activities will reduce their effectiveness and make actual concept connections less viable. Successful integration should be planned to introduce new concepts, provide real problem situations, assist with concept development, or serve as culminating experiences to units of study that will connect and extend new learning. Content integration is only as powerful as the planning invested and integrity with which it has been designed.

High school teachers are the most resistant to content integration because of the amount of pure mathematics content in coursework and the isolating effects of traditional high school curriculum design (Ballheim, 2001). An excellent source for higher-level mathematics integration is the *Mathematics Awareness Month* website, supported by the Joint Policy Board for Mathematics, a committee of representatives of four mathematics organizations (www.mathaware.org), and the NCTM. The purpose of the awareness month initiative (April is the target month) is to increase the visibility of mathematics as a field of study and to communicate the power of mathematics to a wider audience. The website offers an archive of themes back to 1986, including features on art, the ocean, biology, the environment, and medicine.

CAREER EDUCATION AND LIFE-SKILLS MATHEMATICS

Angela Smith and other middle and high school special educators have signed up for an August workshop on teaching life-skills mathematics. As she finds a seat in the training center, Angela is thinking about the assigned readings. When she signed up for the training, she thought "life-skills mathematics" meant how to keep a checkbook and make change. The readings, however, covered mathematics applied to many more aspects of life than using money and "career education," which she discovered did not mean vocational training. "This workshop is going to expand my ideas about mathematics applications," thought Angela. "I hope to learn how to teach mathematics skills so students can generalize them to these other settings. But I wonder how these mathematics skills relate to the NCTM standards and the state's required assessments." ■ ● ▲

Previous sections in this chapter addressed the integration and application of mathematics concepts with other content areas. The following sections will extend these applications to career education and the role of the mathematics curriculum for real-world applications and transition planning for post-school settings. *Career education* is the umbrella term for students' preparation for all their future roles in adult life. Included within career education are vocational education, applied mathematics, consumer mathematics, life-skills training, and college or continuing education preparation. For students with learning problems, these are particularly critical areas for making school meaningful (preventing drop-outs), generalizing knowledge and skills, and achieving personal goals.

Educators in general seem to be susceptible to the latest trends without considering historical perspective or research-based evidence of curricular effectiveness. In the case of mathematics for real-world applications, the most recognized philosophical movement in education was pragmatism (Peirce, James, & Dewey) that emphasized the practical application of ideas in real-world problems in the early 1920s (Gutek, 2004). This very American outlook on the purpose of education also emphasized cross-curricular problems but focused on the individual's interaction with the environment and society rather than external standards. An outgrowth of pragmatics was the progressive movement that was formalized from 1919 to 1955 with the Progressive Education Association but has continued with other names and forms with recurring curriculum reform cycles. Progressive education is described as child-centered and practical, a rejection of the traditional, academic focus of the disciplines. Educational "reforms" in the U.S. have not been scientifically based or measurable improvements, but cyclical (and predictable) swings between the extremes of "pure academics or back to the basics" and "applied, integrated, wholistic curriculum" studies. Our schools desperately need educators willing to take a balanced curriculum approach who are not afraid to be exacting in terminology (even if it is outdated), deliberate with implementation that is measurably effective, and careful to allow for student differences that are not trivialized.

Students with lower academic abilities have been, in phases, separated from general education and its opportunities, or expected to meet (or fail) a common set of curriculum standards, again, educational practice via extremes. The language of curriculum, career education, vocational training, and transition planning has been different for different sets of students, leading to lower expectations, restricted program options, and crisis-level school drop-out rates. The next section discusses the broader view of career education adopted by special educators. That is followed by discussions of life skills and applied mathematics and an examination of transition planning needs of all students.

Career Education

Career education includes those instructional activities throughout school that prepare students for a variety of roles in adult life, including those at work, home, leisure, with family and friends, in continuing educational settings, in one's own physical and emotional being, and in the community. The word *career* means course or progress through life and originates from the Latin *carraria*, meaning carriageway (*The American Heritage Book of English Usage*, 1996). In special education, the terms *functional skills* or *life-skills education* are also used to describe those skills needed to accomplish everyday tasks. General educators tend to partition career education related to mathematics into specific vocational training, consumer mathematics, and applied mathematics.

The seminal work on career education for students with disabilities was Brolin's *Life Centered Career Education* (LCCE) (1978). This functional curriculum is organized into daily living skills, personal–social skills, and occupational guidance and preparation with 22 competencies and 94 sub-competencies (see Figure 7.6). LCCE is a competency-based curriculum with a history of research and teacher training. A more recent version of the LCCE curriculum is geared toward students with moderate disabilities (Loyd & Brolin, 1997).

Cronin and Patton (1993) proposed a life-skills curriculum with six domains: employment and education, home and family, leisure pursuits, community involvement, physical and emotional health, and personal responsibility and relationships. This framework includes twenty-three subdomains and 146 major life demands. Described as a top-down approach to curriculum development, the curriculum evolved from study of the major demands of adult life. But the authors cautioned that community-specific demands may vary considerably (e.g., using a bus). They also described how life skills could be infused into the content of existing courses, augment coursework through special units, taught in distinct generic or special topic life-skills courses, or taught as a cluster of courses.

Dunn and Rabren analyzed both curriculum frameworks for their mathematics skills and were able to identify specific skills in all domains (1996). For example, home management clearly involves budgeting and paying bills. Taking care of one's health requires using a thermometer. Preparing food involves planning nutritious meals, which requires measurement and budgeting.

Mathematics educators have developed curriculum models for real-world mathematics according to the domains of mathematics or by real-world topics. For example, Cawley (1985) outlined adult skills and competencies by numbers, operations, sentences, geometry and measurement, relations and functions, probability and statistics, reasoning, and general skills (those not in the standards such as banking or computing taxes). Huff (1999) organized skills by topics such as investing, measuring things, building things, your car, travel, and business decisions.

A framework for career education that will support infusion of mathematics concepts and skills or the creation of life skills units or courses is proposed in Figure 7.7. The domains of life are depicted as overlapping, much like the Cronin and Patton model, but are arranged environmentally, from personal outward to community-based. Figure 7.8 depicts a curriculum-planning chart with cells including sample concepts and skills keyed to mathematics content standards. A blank planning chart can be found in the appendix. Other examples from each domain will be developed in the next sections on instruction for life-skills mathematics and applied mathematics.

TRY THIS
Develop at least two additional mathematics concepts or skills to add to each cell in the third column (examples) of Figure 7.8.

Figure 7.6
Life-Centered Career Education Curriculum

Curriculum Area	Competencies	Sample Subcompetencies
Daily Living Skills	1. Managing personal finances	4. Calculate and pay taxes
	2. Selecting and managing a household	8. Use basic appliances and tools
	3. Caring for personal needs	16. Practice personal safety
	4. Raising children and meeting marriage responsibilities	17. Demonstrate physical care for raising children
	5. Buying, preparing, and consuming food	23. Prepare meals
	6. Buying and caring for clothing	27. Purchase clothing
	7. Exhibiting responsible citizenship	32. Demonstrate knowledge of citizen rights and responsibilities
	8. Utilizing recreational facilities and engaging in leisure	37. Plan vacation time
	9. Getting around the community	40. Find way around the community
Personal–Social Skills	10. Achieving self-awareness	43. Identify interests and abilities
	11. Acquiring self-confidence	50. Develop confidence in oneself
	12. Achieving socially responsible behavior	52. Recognize authority and follow instructions
	13. Maintaining good interpersonal skills	58. Make and maintain friendships
	14. Achieving independence	60. Demonstrate self organization
	15. Making adequate decisions	65. Recognize nature of a problem
	16. Communicating with others	67. Recognize and respond to emergency situations
Occupational Guidance and Preparation	17. Knowing and exploring occupational possibilities	71. Locate sources of occupational and training information
	18. Selecting and planning occupational choices	77. Identify requirements of appropriate and available jobs
	19. Exhibiting appropriate work habits and behavior	81. Follow directions and observe regulations
	20. Seeking, securing, and maintaining employment	93. Know how to adjust to change in employment
	21. Exhibiting sufficient physical/manual skills	96. Demonstrate manual dexterity
	22. Obtaining a specific occupational skill	Varies

Source: From *Life Centered Career Education: A Competency-Based Approach* (5th ed.) by D. E. Brolin, 1997, pages 12–13. Copyright 1997 by The Council for Exceptional Children. Reprinted by permission.

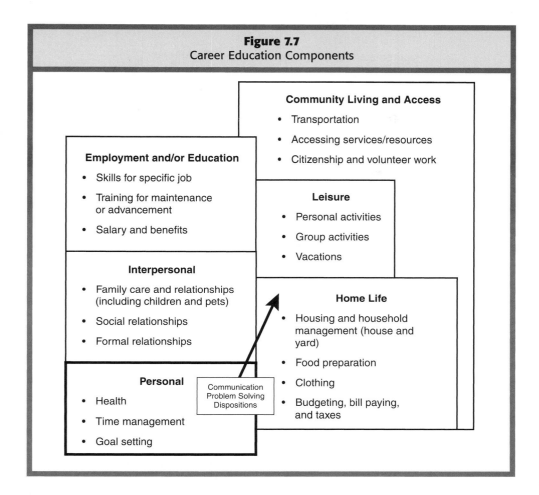

Figure 7.7
Career Education Components

Community Living and Access

- Transportation
- Accessing services/resources
- Citizenship and volunteer work

Employment and/or Education

- Skills for specific job
- Training for maintenance or advancement
- Salary and benefits

Leisure

- Personal activities
- Group activities
- Vacations

Interpersonal

- Family care and relationships (including children and pets)
- Social relationships
- Formal relationships

Home Life

- Housing and household management (house and yard)
- Food preparation
- Clothing
- Budgeting, bill paying, and taxes

Personal

Communication
Problem Solving
Dispositions

- Health
- Time management
- Goal setting

Life-Skills Mathematics

Life skills should be developed throughout school, from the concepts of responsibility and value of money in the early grades to advanced study for specialized applications such as budget trend analysis and investments. Many of the mathematics-related life skills are not addressed in the NCTM content standards but rely on similar concepts and processes for development. For example, working with money is not listed within the NCTM competencies explicitly but relates to those in both number and measurement. Using money also involves concepts of equivalence, function, and decimal forms of number. In special education, life-skills topics are often called functional mathematics and appear on students' IEPs because they may not be addressed adequately in the general curriculum or students may need more explicit instruction and generalization strategies in these areas. For students with other special needs, such as those from disadvantaged homes or those who are English language learners, these life skills may also need special attention.

Figure 7.8
Mathematics-Oriented Career Education Planning Chart

Life Domain	Subdomains	Mathematics Concepts and Skills—Examples
Personal	Health	Reading % of daily allowance on food containers (N)
	Time Management	Projecting the time needed for a task (M)
	Goal Setting	Earning a bonus (N)
Interpersonal	Family Care and Relationships (including children/pets)	Determining the body temperature of a sick child (M)
	Social Relationships	Planning the costs for a movie night (N)
	Formal Relationships	Meeting with an insurance agent about payments on a policy (N)
Home Life	Housing	Determining how much paint to order (N, G, M)
	Food	Preparing cookies (N, M)
	Clothing	Sewing a simple skirt (N, M, G)
	Financial	Computing taxes (N, F, D)
Leisure	Personal Activities	Pursuing the hobby of carpentry (N, F, M, G)
	Group Activities	Watching a baseball game (N, F, M, G, D)
	Vacations	Planning the route to drive to the mountains (N, F, M, G, D)
Employment/Education (specific to the position)	Job Skills	e.g., Lab technician—reading various measuring devices (M)
	Training	e.g., Bank clerk training to be associate—computing mortgage rates (N, F)
	Salary and Benefits	Determining co-pay for health costs (N)
Community Living (specific to the community)	Transportation	Computing miles per gallon (N, M)
	Accessing Services/Resources	Grocery shopping (N, F, M, D)
	Citizenship and Volunteering	Studying a proposal for a vote on road improvements (N, F, M, G, D)

Mathematics Content Codes:

N = Numbers

F = Functions

M = Measurement

G = Geometry

D = Data Analysis

This section will provide an overview of example topics for life-skills mathematics with recommendations for instruction—telling time, using currency, writing checks, taking out a loan, and reading sports statistics. Each of these areas involves many mathematics competencies, so this discussion will focus on selective competencies and their assessment and instructional strategies.

Telling time is a critical skill that relates to all of the career education domains but especially personal and interpersonal areas of life. Units of time for everyday life include years, months, weeks, days, parts of days, hours, minutes, and seconds, measured with tools such as clocks and calendars. Sometimes time telling should be precise and other times it can be estimated. With the popularity of digital clocks, many students find it difficult to read, interpret, and set analog clocks. Students with learning problems often have problems with the general concept of time—estimating time needed or time elapsed.

Informal assessment of students' abilities to set clocks, read clocks, and interpret time can be conducted through daily activities. The teacher should attend carefully to each student's level of understanding (e.g., a student understands days, portions of days, and hours but cannot set or tell time to the nearest minute). Students who are English language learners may find it difficult to change from time-telling conventions such as saying "half six" to mean 5:30 or 6:30, depending on the culture, or the use of the 24-hour method for telling time. Other native speakers of English with language deficits may struggle with relational vocabulary such as before, after, quarter to, quarter 'till, o'clock, and half-past. Sometimes several phrases can mean the same time: three forty-five; quarter' till four; fifteen minutes to four.

Instruction in telling time should include both clock setting and clock reading, beginning with the larger units of time and moving to shorter segments—hour, half hour, quarter hours, five-minute increments, minutes—with real clocks. Tactics that help students discriminate between the large and small hands and the portions of the clock face include color-coding, clock overlays for specific portions, and prompting phrases such as "begin with the small hand and say the hour it is on or just passed." Teachers should not assume that any student, regardless of other abilities, has mastered time-telling skills, because they are easily disguised within the classroom.

Using currency is related to the domains of home life, leisure, work, and community living. This area involves using coins, bills, making change, computing costs, converting currencies, and many other applications with actual currency. One of the most difficult skills, after students have learned the values of coins and combining amounts, is to compute change. Again, the teacher should conduct an informal assessment on student understanding of coin and bill values, combining amounts, and making change from a given amount before beginning instruction.

For students with lower cognitive abilities, Schloss and Kobza demonstrated the effectiveness of peer tutoring for teaching money skills (1997). They employed the next-dollar strategy (developed by Test, Howell, Burkhart, & Beroth, 1993), in which six individuals with cognitive disabilities were taught to make purchases using one more dollar than asked for by the salesperson. For example, if the clerk asks for three dollars and fifty-seven cents, the student would provide four dollars. Instruction took place in peer tutoring teams and involved counting dollars to ten, reading and saying dollar and cents amounts displayed on index cards, and finally stating the next dollar amount, gradually increasing the dollar amounts. Students also practiced their skills in community settings for generalization. Five of the six students were able to provide the correct number of dollars with only natural cues in the environment.

Making change is much more difficult, even for average students, but there are several possible approaches. The most difficult, but used most often in consumer settings, is counting up from the price to the amount given. The most tedious method is computing with paper and pencil using subtraction with decimals. Another method is checking change given using a calculator, but that is too visible and slow for those waiting in line for the cashier. The counting up method requires the student to count by 1's to the next number divisible by 5 or 10. Then a decision has to be made about using quarters, dimes, or nickels to reach the next even amount. Finally, counting by dollars, five dollars, and ten dollars if needed. For example, if an item cost 32 cents and a dollar was provided, then the student should count as follows: thirty-three, thirty-four, thirty-five (three pennies); forty (one nickel); fifty (one dime); seventy-five, one dollar (two quarters). An alternative for transitional learning could be to count up using pennies, then count by 5's the rest of the way using nickels, then trading out most of the nickels for quarters and dimes. However, that method may lead to confusion or providing too much change in a retail setting.

For finding out if you received the correct change that was not counted out for you, start with the cost of the item, and add on using the coins in the order from least value to most value. Subskills that are essential for making change in this manner are quickly recognizing coins and their values and doing count-bys using fives, tens, and twenty-fives. A common practice in real settings is for the consumer to hand the clerk $5.03 for an item costing $3.38. The three cents reduces the price to $3.35, therefore divisible by 5 and avoiding pennies in return.

Understanding other forms of money, such as banking accounts and **check writing,** is related to the domains of home life, employment, and community living. Many students will set up their own bank accounts while they are still in school because their parents want to teach financial skills and responsibility. Check writing and balancing accounts is also taught as a part of a life-skills or consumer mathematics curriculum. Many banks will provide kits for teachers who want to teach a unit on check writing, with realistic checks and balance booklets (see, for example, the Federal Reserve Bank of New York at www.ny.frb.org/education). Online and commercial materials are available with example expenses and pay checks provided. A more realistic activity would be to have students select jobs (entry-level, no college degree), research salaries in their community, and research the costs of monthly expenses such as automobile expenses, housing, food, electricity, telephone, and extras. This type of unit not only addresses check writing and balancing a checking account, but a sense of the expenses adults face when living on their own as well as legal and ethical aspects of financial transactions.

Check writing can be challenging for students because it requires them to record payments in numerical and word form, legibly and accurately. During instruction, each part of the check face should be explained and students should practice with differing amounts (e.g., forty-six and 00/100, two hundred three and 23/100). Balancing accounts by hand requires a running list of balances to which expenses are subtracted and deposits are added. Reconciling a statement takes the unit a step further.

Jitendra and Nolet (1995) demonstrated that the functional skill of using a check register could be taught to students with disabilities using direct instruction. They recommended a six-step process for teaching this and similar life skills: specify instructional objectives, sequence the skills to be taught, identify the task content and select an appropriate teaching procedure to match, provide systematic practice and review, and evaluate student progress. An example objective for using a check register was "given a check register, students will correctly enter information such as date, check number, description of transaction, payment or deposit, and new balance in 100% of the opportunities" (p. 31). A sequence of necessary skills was following directions, writing checks, adding and subtracting money, understanding critical vocabulary, entering information into a check register, determining whether to add or subtract to find the new balance, and determining whether or not a new check may be written given the balance.

The concept of taking out a **loan** is related to using credit cards, purchasing more expensive items (car, television), and a means for attending college. Taking out a loan involves many mathematics concepts, including goal setting, time management, percentages, and functions such as amortizations and interest concepts.

The basic functional concepts related to loans are amount of principle (amount borrowed), rate of interest (including frequency computed), payment schedule, and duration of loan period. An example of a simple loan would be a principle of $5,000 at an interest rate of 8% (computed monthly), with monthly payments over 3 years. Amortization tables are found on many web sites and can provide quick computation so instructional emphasis can be on concept understanding and data analysis. Figure 7.9 shows a table using the example above. The formula for computing a monthly payment is:

$$M = P\left(\frac{J}{1 - (1 + J)^{-N}}\right)$$

where P is the principal, J is the monthly interest in decimal form (equal to the interest divided by (12×100), and N is the number of months (length in years $\times$ 12) (Chou, 2003). For the example in Figure 7.9, $P = 5,000$, $J = .0066667$, and $N = 36$. Giving $(1 + J)^{-N}$ to be .78725369 from one is .21274631; therefore, the denominator is .21274631 $(1 - .78725369)$. The resulting payment is 5,000 $\times$ (.0066667/.21274631), or $156.68. Fortunately, most spreadsheets include a PMT function so that students can explore, predict, and develop concepts rather than bog down with computations. Concepts related to loans can be much more complex, such as with credit card methods of computing interest on average daily balances, early loan payoffs, variable interest loans, and penalties.

The **leisure** domain is as essential to quality of life issues as work or home life. Leisure time contributes to personal health and interpersonal relationships. Leisure activities include hobbies, travel, and watching or participating in sports. In order to fully enjoy sporting activities and discuss them with others, students need an understanding of the rules, scoring, and participant roles within various games. Sports can be individual or

Figure 7.9
Amortization Schedule

Pymt #	Date	Principal	Interest	Balance
1	8/1	123.34	33.33	4,876.65
2	9/1	124.17	32.51	4,752.48
3	10/1	124.99	31.68	4,627.48
4	11/1	125.83	30.84	4,627.48
5	12/1	126.67	30.01	4,374.97
6	1/1	127.51	29.16	4,247.46
7	2/1	128.36	28.31	4,119.09
8	3/1	129.22	27.46	3,989.87
9	4/1	130.08	26.59	3,859.79
10	5/1	130.94	25.73	3,728.84
11	6/1	131.82	24.85	3,597.02
12	7/1	132.70	23.98	3,464.32
13	8/1	133.58	23.09	3,330.73
14	9/1	134.47	22.20	3,196.25
15	10/1	135.37	21.30	3,060.88
16	11/1	136.27	20.40	2,924.60
17	12/1	137.18	19.49	2,787.42
18	1/1	138.09	18.58	2,649.32
19	2/1	139.01	17.66	2,510.30
20	3/1	139.94	16.73	2,370.35
21	4/1	140.87	15.80	2,220.47
22	5/1	141.81	14.86	2,087.66
23	6/1	142.76	13.91	1,944.89
24	7/1	143.71	12.96	1,801.18
25	8/1	144.67	12.00	1,656.50
26	9/1	145.63	11.04	1,510.86
27	10/1	146.60	10.07	1,364.25
28	11/1	147.58	9.09	1,216.67
29	12/1	148.57	8.11	1,068.10
30	1/1	149.56	7.12	918.53
31	2/1	150.55	6.12	767.98
32	3/1	151.56	5.11	616.41
33	4/1	152.57	4.10	463.84
34	5/1	153.58	3.09	310.25
35	6/1	154.61	2.06	155.64
36	7/1	155.64	1.03	0.00
Totals		**5,000.00**	**640.54**	

Principal: $5,000.00
# of Payments: 36 (3 years)
Interest Rate: 8.00% (compounded monthly)
Monthly Payment: $156.68

group oriented and range considerably, depending on community resources. This example will review some of the major concepts needed to watch or participate in a baseball game.

Baseball is a game of statistics and spatial relationships. The goal of the game is to earn more runs than the opposing team, each run achieved by a player running a circuit of four bases that form a diamond shape. A player can only begin running the bases when one of the following occurs: he makes a safe hit of a baseball thrown by the pitcher from the center of the diamond, he is "walked" (by four pitches out of the strike zone), he is hit by a pitched ball, he is able to run after a wild pitch or the catcher misses the ball on strike three. (As this example shows, sports aren't easily described in words; they are best diagramed, experienced, viewed, and discussed.) The functional and spatial relationships of baseball come into play with the speed of the ball thrown toward a base compared with the speed of a runner, the angle of the run of an outfielder attempting to catch a fly ball on a certain trajectory, and the path and speed of the pitched ball, to name a few examples. Statistics are maintained for every aspect of the game—pitches, hits, runs, batters hit, outs, fly-outs, and so forth. These statistics are compiled for every play and player in the game and used to compare players, detect trends, and even predict pitches.

An interesting statistical application for mathematics class is computation of a player's slugging percentage, a statistic for determining a player's average number of bases per at-bat, that helps predict the players most likely to hit for extra bases. This statistic is calculated using the following formula:

$$\frac{1B + 2(2B) + 3(3B) + 4(HR)}{AB}$$

where $1B$ is the number of times the player hits safely and reaches first base for a single, $2B$ is the number of doubles, $3B$ is the number of triples, HR the number of home runs, and AB the number of times the player is at-bat. See NCTM's Illuminations lessons for examples of using spreadsheets to compute and analyze baseball statistics (http://illuminations.nctm.org) and many other baseball statistics websites for teachers and students. Similar mathematics concepts can be developed for basketball, football, soccer, golf, pool, and other sports.

Instruction in most life-skills mathematics applications requires a careful task analysis, informal assessment, direct instruction, and planned generalization in real settings with natural cues. Two examples of task analyses are provided in Figure 7.10, one for using a vending machine and one for inflating a tire to the correct pressure. A functional assessment involves observation of student performance of as much of the task as possible, with the task analysis serving as a checklist. Instruction would then be started where the student made mistakes or expressed concept confusion through verbal or nonverbal language. Students with higher cognitive abilities typically learn quickly through demonstration and minimal practice. Students with more involved learning problems may need forward or backward chaining of the skills for their learning and practice. An example of forward chaining for teaching ATM use is to have the student begin the task (with entering the card in the correct position and typing in the code) and the teacher complete the steps the student cannot complete, repeating this pattern

Using Vending Machine

1. View selections and decide on one choice.
2. Read the price and determine if you have at least that much money.
3. If the price is a dollar or less, insert a dollar bill with the picture matching the dollar in the same direction. If more than a dollar, insert more than one dollar bill (next highest dollar strategy).
4. If you have only coins, begin with quarters and add coins until the price (or over) is displayed. Do not deposit pennies.
5. Press the letters and numbers matching your item.
6. Retrieve the item and your change (if any).

Inflating a Tire Using a Coin-Operated Machine

1. Position the car in relation to the air pump.
2. Determine the cost (e.g., 25¢, 50¢) and time, coins or bills accepted.
3. Consult the manual for the tires and determine correct pressure (e.g., 35 pounds per square inch).
4. Place the correct amount of money into the machine.
5. Take off the cap from the tire and store safely.
6. Press the hose end onto the tire stem until air flow begins.
7. Check the pressure with hand-held or attached device with quick motion and read the scale.
8. Visually inspect tire for nail heads and worn spots.
9. Recap the tire stem.
10. Continue to monitor the tire after driving.

until the student can perform all steps (through putting the ATM card, money, and receipt in a safe place). Backward chaining would have the teacher complete the first steps, and then the student would perform the last step. Gradually the student would perform the next-to-last step and so forth until she could perform the entire task. These students may also need varied settings for full generalization (e.g., an ATM machine in the grocery that asks for a fee and the bank's ATM machine, one with a touch screen in addition to keypad).

TRY THIS

Develop a task analysis of a real-life task such as mixing pancake batter, looking up the time for a bus, or making a purchase in a grocery store.

Several commercial curricula, besides LCCE, are available for life-skills mathematics. *Real-Life Math: Living on a Paycheck* (Glisan, PRO-ED), includes simulations for using a check register, budgeting, job searching, procuring an apartment, and making payments for cars, groceries, clothes, and other needs. *Family Math II: Achieving Success in Mathematics* (Coates & Thompson, EQUALS) is for students in grades K–6 and their families and includes real-world activities such as the Zoo Game and Grandpa's Coins for reinforcing mathematics concepts. *You're on Your Own* (Cavazos & Glisan, PCI Education) is a consumer education curriculum for simulating living in the real world for secondary students. Educators should be aware that most "consumer mathematics" curricula and materials are simply booklets of worksheets and not connected with powerful mathematics concepts and skills.

Life skills involving mathematics are critical for all students. These skills are not necessarily watered down or less conceptually demanding than standards-based mathematics, but may be underemphasized on state curriculum standards and assessments. For students with learning challenges, these are skills that cannot be substituted or compensated—they must be applied in everyday life for an individual to be successful as a family member, friend, worker, citizen, or consumer.

Applied Math

The area of applied mathematics is more focused on job-related skills than life-skills mathematics, but there are certainly overlapping concepts and applications. In some secondary schools teachers in mathematics, vocational, technology, and even special education plan applied coursework together so they can pool their expertise and plan powerful and realistic tasks (see, for example, Bottge, 2001). In other schools, application tasks are integrated into existing coursework that addresses algebra, geometry, trigonometry, and calculus. For example, The Mathematical Sciences Education Board's *High School Mathematics at Work* (1998) provided integration tasks such as analyzing the data from 911 emergency calls for recommending the regions for each response station, scheduling elevators in a multi-story building, computing the anti-inflammatory drug in a student's system after 24 hours, comparing the quality of two hospitals, and comparing internet service providers. Other schools are implementing rigorous interdisciplinary senior projects or service learning projects to make the connection between school learning and real-world applications (Steinberg, Cushman, & Riordan, 1999). But to be successful, these projects require community support and reorientation of the school's structure and focus.

Other researchers have compared the demands of real jobs with the mathematics taught in school. Nunes, Schliemann, and Carraher studied the emergence of mathematics competencies in Brazil's working class, those without formal schooling in mathematics (1993). They concluded that "street mathematics" involves understanding mathematical relationships embedded in specific activities, technologies, and situations. In order to function well, individuals must understand both the mathematical invariants and the context. Their problem-solving strategies may be so situational as to be limited in application. School mathematics is directed beyond the particulars of situations to systems of knowledge, thus more flexible for a wider range of applications.

Jurdak and Shahin compared the spatial reasoning abilities of plumbers with those of high school geometry students in Beirut, specifically the transformation of two-dimensional surfaces into three-dimensional solids and vice versa (2001). Tenth-grade students and traditional (Arabic) plumbers were asked to construct a cylindrical container with a bottom, of one-liter capacity and height of 20 cm. The students had previous problem-solving experience with volumes of cylinders but no construction experience; the plumbers had constructed other cylinders of standard dimensions but different than this task. The plumbers employed a process that moved from perception-cognitive (a three-dimensional task to two-dimensional descriptions), to cognitive-mnemonic (using formulas and estimation), to perceptual (testing and adjusting). The students used symbols first in a cognitive-mnemonic phase, then moved to a cognitive phase (recalling alternative solutions), and finally the perceptual phase preparing for construction. The students had a broader understanding of concepts and could compute the correct answer but not complete the construction. The plumbers eventually completed the construction but could not generalize their approach. Again, the conclusion is that mathematics in the workplace is more meaningful but school mathematics is more powerful (flexible and generalizable). An integrated approach is supported.

Secondary schools should have coursework and programs that more directly connect mathematics concepts to real-world applications. Britton, Huntley, Jacobs, and Weinberg (1999) identified six types of connections between curriculum and workplace contexts: providing students with workplace experiences, simulating workplace activities in the classroom, adding mathematics topics found in the workplace to the curriculum, using workplace examples to explain subject matter, illustrating how mathematics is used in different occupations, and obtaining information from workplaces. However, real-world applications are not neatly packaged by discrete academic areas such as physics, biology, algebra, geometry, or even consumer mathematics (Britton et al., 1999). Increased specialization in these mathematics courses through the grades and into college makes it more difficult for students to understand patterns and applications. Explicit and deliberate applications, such as community-based projects and internships, can balance the effects of specialization by providing a setting for the application of interconnected concepts. More importantly, collaborative curriculum development with creative scheduling can assure a balance of content rigor and meaningful application.

Transition Planning

Assisting students with planning for the transition from school to work and adult life has been the purview of high school guidance counselors, with the primary focus on the application process for college. But many constituents, including business and industry and colleges, assert that more explicit planning for mathematical and technological occupations is required at the secondary level if students are to move successfully into post-school educational and employment settings. Colleges are most concerned that students are not prepared for the demands of their coursework. Businesses are seeking closer partnerships with schools to ensure rigorous training for the jobs of the future. A report by the National Academy of Sciences titled *Preparing for the 21st Century: The*

Education Imperative (1997) emphasized, "an understanding of science, mathematics, and technology is very important in the workplace. . . . Our nation is unlikely to remain a world leader without a better-educated workforce" (p. 1).

Federal initiatives resulting from these forces included the passage of the School-to-Work Opportunities Act of 1994, that required career exploration and counseling beginning by seventh grade, election of a career major by eleventh grade, integrated academic and vocational learning, work experiences, regular evaluations, and procedures to facilitate students' transition to additional training or postsecondary education. The legislation required community support for schools in these efforts. Although federal funding for this Act ended in 2000, many states have continued with school-to-work initiatives (Brown, 2002).

The 2006 reauthorization of the Carl D. Perkins Career and Technical Education Act included requirements for stronger integration of academic and technical skills and better linkages between secondary and postsecondary educational settings. This act subsumed the previous Tech-Prep initiatives and emphasized rigorous academic content, local (not federal) determination of curriculum content and funding appropriations, and accountability for effective programs that meet the needs of the business community.

The National Research Council's Mathematical Sciences Education Board has published several reports about the mathematical preparation of the technical work force (*Everybody Counts*, 1989; *Reshaping School Mathematics*, 1990; *Mathematical Preparation of the Work Force*, 1995; *High School Mathematics at Work*, 1998). These reports addressed a range of topics, including integrating vocational and academic education, transition programs, preparing for the SAT, and preparing students for postsecondary education. They are replete with real-world problem tasks that illustrate the integration of standards-based mathematics with the demands of work, college, and other life settings.

Transition initiatives for students with disabilities actually predated these general education requirements. In the mid 1980s, when students with disabilities had been through school entirely under the protections of the Education for All Handicapped Children Act (P.L. 94-142, 1975) and with more potential than ever, projects were funded by the U.S. Department of Education to explore the best programming and support services for successful transition to an adult lifestyle that would be productive and meaningful. These projects led to the passage of requirements for transition services for students with disabilities with the reauthorization of EHA (into IDEA) in 1990. The 2004 requirements defined transition services as:

> a coordinated set of activities . . . designed to be within a results-oriented process, that is, focused on improving academic and functional achievement of the child with a disability to facilitate the child's movement from school to post-school activities, including postsecondary education, vocational education, integrated employment, continuing and adult education, adult services, independent living, or community participation. . . . Based on the individual child's needs, taking into account the child's strengths, preferences, and interests. . . . includes instruction, related services, community experiences, the development of employment and other post-school adult living objectives, and when appropriate, acquisition of daily living skills and functional vocational evaluation. (§300.43)

IDEA (§300.320.b) requires that transition services "beginning not later than the first IEP be in effect when the child is 16, and updated annually thereafter (1) appropriate measurable postsecondary goals based upon age-appropriate transition assessments related to training, education, employment, and where appropriate, independent living skills; (2) the transition services (including courses of study) needed to assist the child in reaching these goals." Some states and school districts have elected to keep the age 14 requirement of the 1997 reauthorization so that transition planning can begin before students enter ninth grade or drop out of school. It is interesting to note the use of the term "child" and specific ages in IDEA while vocational education and NCLB legislation tend to use "adolescents" or "youth" and refer to grade levels.

Transition services for students with disabilities, like school-to-work planning for all students, include projecting post-school goals, planning for coursework that will prepare the student for those goals, and providing other support services such as job training, career counseling, or tutoring for the SAT or licensing exams. Each student's transition portion of the IEP is individually designed. Transition planning teams should ensure the following:

- Exploration activities by middle school as a means for determining student interests and abilities
- Academic planning prior to ninth-grade to design an appropriate, realistic curriculum
- Student involvement (self-determination) in every aspect of transition planning
- Goals for the full scope of adult life beyond high school, including home life, personal and interpersonal skills, leisure, community life, and work or postsecondary education
- Work or internship experiences during high school that further assessment activities and instructional goals (in compliance with fair labor laws)
- Support services that are necessary for success (e.g., transportation, counseling, adaptive devices, etc.)
- Participation by representatives from adult services, business, or local colleges on schoolwide transition planning groups
- Frequent program evaluation to ensure the needs of students, families, and the community are addressed and kept current

The U.S. Department of Labor's Bureau of Labor Statistics (and state-level equivalents) offers many resources for students, teachers, counselors, and employers on occupational trends and training requirements (www.bls.gov). The *Occupational Outlook Handbook* (2004–2005) predicted that the jobs projected to grow the fastest over the next ten years are medical assistants, network systems analysts, and human services assistants. Declines were predicted to be in farming, sewing, and secretarial work. The *Handbook* also includes detailed descriptions of specific occupations, organized by professional categories. For example, tool and die makers typically train for four to five years (10,400 hours) in apprenticeships and are very highly skilled workers, with the middle 50 percent earning between $16.33 and $25.64 per hour in 2002. They must use blueprints and various tools and computer technologies to fashion tools and dies. Classroom training includes mechanical drawing, tool designing, tool programming, blueprint reading, and mathematics courses including algebra, geometry, trigonometry, and statistics. Computer skills are increasingly important for these workers.

TRY THIS

Locate another occupation in the Department of Labor database and evaluate its mathematics requirements.

A number of sources have identified requisite mathematics skills needed by high school graduation in order to be successful in general college mathematics coursework or in technical positions in the workplace. Ballheim (2000) and the editorial panel of *Dialogues* (a newsletter of NCTM) polled members for their views on mathematics needed beyond high school. College-bound students should have the equivalent of two years of high school algebra with problem solving, graphing calculators, and matrices; geometry; pre-calculus and calculus; iterative and statistical reasoning; trigonometry; decimals; and life skills. Students not attending college need basic arithmetic skills including number sense, estimation, consumer mathematics, applied mathematics; proportional reasoning; algebra including matrices; geometry and logical reasoning; programming; statistical reasoning; discrete mathematics; probability; and trigonometry.

The Learning First Alliance (1998) called for higher expectations for mathematics learning by all students, including algebra and geometry year-long courses by the end of ninth grade and the foundations for algebraic thinking, mathematical reasoning, and geometric concepts begun in grades K–4. The organization noted that many eighth graders are still working on mastering arithmetic concepts while their peers in other countries are studying advanced mathematics at the same age. Students in high school should study advanced mathematics topics in preparation for post-secondary education, and general mathematics coursework at the secondary level should be eliminated.

There have been widespread misperceptions that school-to-work programs are a lesser education for non-college-bound students; however, research indicates increased advanced course taking and college applications in schools with school-to-work programs (Britton et al., 1999). In the United States especially, college is viewed as the only acceptable option for students; anything else is often viewed as substandard. College attendance by graduates and SAT scores are common means of rating the effectiveness of high schools. Other countries with high living standards support more alternatives for post-secondary education and training.

Other misperceptions are the views that students with disabilities or other learning problems cannot engage in rigorous mathematics applications in work-directed or college-preparatory programs, or that they are the only students who need life-skills curricula. Recent trends in education are toward more specialized, narrow, standards-based curricula with college preparation as the primary goal. A better balance, to meet the needs of individuals and their communities, would be to offer a range of programs that teach powerful mathematics concepts and challenge students but prepare them for varying post-school goals. The one-size-fits-all model of many secondary schools does not serve students, their families, or society very well in the long term. Students who have powerful and meaningful mathematics experiences in school will have more options in careers and other life choices and be able to introduce their own children to mathematics concepts through positive example. Imagine a family at the dinner table discussing a mathematics problem the parent encountered at work or the application of the children's mathematics concepts to a household event. That infusion of math curiosity and sense making into everyday life activities is a primary goal of mathematics programs for all students.

After the week's workshop, Angela Smith was enthused about the new applications for mathematics she learned. "My middle school students were so unmotivated about doing mathematics. They viewed it as steps to learn and answers to produce without much thinking. Now I have some great real-world examples to use when teaching about fractions, decimals, geometric solids, linear equations, and statistics. And, more importantly, these applications will build the concept connections among those topics as well as require students to use the other processes of mathematics—communication, problem solving, reasoning, and making representations. Rather than having students complete skills worksheets on isolated topics, I know how to pose a problem situation that will keep students engaged for several days with good mathematics learning. I realize that these applications will actually prepare students better for our state's problem-based tests. As a teacher, I've had very little experience in other types of work. Now I have many resources for understanding the mathematics of other jobs." ■ ● ▲

CHAPTER SUMMARY

- Integration of mathematics instruction with other content areas has potential benefits of motivating students, providing realistic problems for application and generalization of mathematics skills, reducing learning gaps, and reinforcing the common concepts and processes across the curriculum.
- Concerns about curriculum integration include undermining the focus and standards of the mathematics curriculum, teacher preparation time, alignment with annual testing, and inadequate resources.
- Curriculum integration can range from minimal, within one primary subject area, to full integration across all subjects.
- The mathematics process standards are also common processes for other subject areas such as science, social studies, language arts, and visual arts.

- Other subject areas have similar big idea concepts as mathematics, such as change (function), classification, systems, patterns, and predictions based on data.
- Writing for mathematics should include instruction in content-specific conventions.
- Literature has the potential for enhancing mathematics for reluctant students or providing problem situations, but should be selected carefully for mathematics concepts, student level, and purpose for instruction.
- Mathematics skills are critical for all adult career domains: personal, interpersonal, leisure, home life, employment/education, and community living.
- Some students may need life skills instruction that is not typically part of the mathematics curriculum or testing programs, such as using currency or writing checks.

- Life-skills instruction requires a functional task analysis, individualized assessment, direct instruction of new skills, and planned generalization strategies.
- Mathematics specific to job skills are often called applied mathematics and offered within secondary coursework or in separate courses. The study of mathematics applications in the real world is as rigorous as "pure" mathematics and provides students more flexibility in their use of mathematics concepts and skills.

- In planning for the transition from school to adult life, teachers and counselors should consider the mathematics demands of continuing education, employment, and home settings to assure appropriate coursework and support services during school. Students with disabilities must have a written transition plan as part of their IEP planning from age 16.
- Secondary programming should offer a range of applied coursework and community-based experiences so that mathematics concepts can be deepened and generalized for post-school preparation.

RESOURCES

Integrating Mathematics

American Mathematical Society (www.ams.org) *Pi (π) in the Sky* and *Plus Magazine*.

Connected Mathematics Project at Michigan State University, www.mth.msu/cmp.

Contemporary Mathematics in Context of the Core-Plus Mathematics Project at Western Michigan University, www.wmich.edu/cpmp.

House, P. A. (Ed.) (1995). *1995 yearbook: Connecting mathematics across the curriculum*. Reston, VA: NCTM.

McGraw, S. A. (Ed.) (2003). *Integrated mathematics: Choices and challenges*. Reston, VA: NCTM.

Resources for the Math-Science Connection

AIMS Education Foundation: Activities Integrating Mathematics & Sciences resources (www.aimsedu.org).

American Association for the Advancement of Science, www.aaas.org.

Hynes, M. C., & Dixon, J. K. (Eds.) (2005). *Mission Mathematics II* (PK–2; 3–5; 6–8). Reston, VA: NCTM. This series of books are investigations that integrate mathematics and science developed by NASA and NCTM. The book for grades 9–12 was edited by P. A. House and R. P. Day.

The Eisenhower Science and Mathematics Consortium, funded by the U.S. Department of Education until September 2005 and now by subscription, is a clearinghouse of curriculum and professional development resources for mathematics and science, www.goenc.com.

Resources for Social Studies

Hallerberg, A. E., Baumgart, J. K., Deal, D. E., & Vogeli, B. R. (1989). *Historical topics for the mathematics classroom*. Reston, VA: NCTM.

Smith, D. E. (1995). *Number stories of long ago*. Reston, VA: NCTM.

Resources for Writing in the Mathematics Curriculum

McIntosh, M. E. (1997). 500+ writing formats. *Mathematics Teaching in the Middle School*, 2(5), 354–358.

Whitin, D. J., & Whitin, P. (2000). *Math is language too: Talking and writing in the mathematics classroom*. Reston, VA: NCTM with the National Council of Teachers of English.

Resources for Integrating Literature

Burns, M. (1993). *Math and literature* (K–3). ETA/Cuisenaire.

Thiessen, D. (Ed.) (2003). *Exploring mathematics through literature: Articles and lessons for prekindergarten through grade 8*. Reston, VA: NCTM.

Thiessen, D., Matthias, M., & Smith, J. (1998). *The wonderful world of mathematics: A critically annotated list of children's books in mathematics* (2nd ed.). Reston, VA: NCTM.

Society of School Librarians, http://falcon.jmu.edu/~ramseyil/sslihome.html

Welchman-Tischler, R. (1992). *How to use children's literature to teach mathematics*. Reston, VA: NCTM.

Whitin, D. J., & Whitin, P. (2004). *New visions for linking literature and mathematics.* Reston, VA: NCTM with the National Council of Teachers of English.

Resources for the Art of Mathematics

Bruter, E. P. (Ed.) (2002). *Mathematics and art: Mathematical visualization in art and education.* Springer.

Olson, A. T. (1975). *Mathematics through paper folding.* Reston, VA: NCTM.

Ivars Peterson column in www.sciencenewsforkids.org

Runion, G. (1990). *The golden section.* Palo Alto, CA: Dale Seymour Publications.

Resources for Life-Skills Mathematics and Transition Planning

Ethnomathematics Digital Library: www.ethnomath.org.

Harrington, T. F. (Ed.). (2003). *Handbook of career planning for students with special needs* (3rd ed.). Austin, TX: PRO-ED.

Glisan, E. M. (2001). *Real-life math: Living on a paycheck.* Austin, TX: PRO-ED.

Dadila-Coates, G, (2003) *Family math II: Achieving success in mathematics.* Berkeley, CA: Lawrence Hall of Science.

Cavazos & Glisan (2004). *You're on your own.* PCI Education.

Introduction to the Content Strands

The following sections offer a more in-depth study of the "big ideas" of K–12 mathematics content. These key concepts are not only foundational to mathematics understanding, they provide the framework for most other concepts and skills throughout the curriculum. If teachers develop good understandings of these concepts at their core, they will be able to develop curriculum connections, plan applications and problem situations, prepare students for the next levels of mathematics learning, and have confidence in their ability to adapt and modify the mathematics curriculum to meet students' needs. Another reason for offering these content strands is to provide specific instructional suggestions for students with mathematics learning challenges.

While there are dozens of key mathematics concepts, the following were selected because of their power for overall mathematics understanding. The strands are not organized by NCTM content standards, rather the big ideas featured in each strand are important for more than one standard. The strands also are not organized like mathematics texts so teachers can more readily view the big ideas that connect topics across mathematics.

A. Number Sense and Place Value
B. Whole Number Relationships
C. Spatial Sense
D. Rational Numbers
E. Functions

Each content strand provides an overview of key concepts, makes connections to other mathematics concepts, outlines problems for students with mathematics disabilities, and describes specific instructional techniques. The sections close with resources for additional study and discovery.

Comparison of "big idea" content strands with NCTM content standards

NCTM ⇓	Number Sense and Place Value	Whole Number Relationships	Spatial Sense	Rational Numbers	Functions
Number and Operations	✓	✓		✓	✓
Patterns Functions, and Algebra	✓	✓	✓	✓	✓
Geometry and Spatial Sense			✓		✓
Measurement	✓		✓	✓	
Data Analysis, Probability, and Statistics	✓	✓	✓	✓	✓

Strand A   Number Sense and Place Value

After studying this strand, the reader should be able to:

1. Discuss number sense and its importance for the range of mathematics topics
2. Implement several strategies with K–12 students that promote stronger number sense
3. Use teacher language to boost students' concept understanding
4. Determine student place value understanding and plan activities to build those concepts
5. Discuss a range of applications for data analysis across the K–12 curriculum

Emily, a student in Pine Grove Elementary's 5th-grade remedial mathematics class, was asked by Ms. Johnson to estimate and then quickly count a group of 217 unit cubes. She estimates 100 cubes but cannot explain how she selected that estimate. Then she counts each cube, stumbling over the numbers after 30, 80, and 110.

Ms Johnson: Let me ask you a question. When you are counting, let's say you counted to 90, tell me the number before that and the number after that.

Emily: 89

Ms Johnson: And the number that comes after 90?

Emily: 100

Ms Johnson: OK, now I'd like to hear you count by 2s, starting with zero up to 20.

Emily: 2, 4, 6, 8, 9, 10, 12, 14, 15, 18, 20.

Ms Johnson: Can you count by 5s beginning with zero?

Emily: 0, (slowly counting in head) 9, 14, 19.

Ms Johnson: Thank you. Now I'd like to see you write a number. Can you write the number three hundred two?

Emily: (writes 31002)

Ms Johnson: Can you read that number?

Emily: Three hundred and two. ■ ● ▲

Emily demonstrates significant problems with numbers, including patterns of numbers, place value knowledge, and estimation. As a fifth-grader, she still is struggling with memorizing basic facts, applying operations to numbers, and solving problems involving whole numbers. Ms. Johnson noted that Emily works well with spatial concepts such as describing features of geometric figures and interpreting graphs.

Virtually all mathematics in the elementary and secondary curriculum is strongly grounded in number, even extensions of geometry and measurement. This strand explores the importance of understanding number, ways of representing number, number sense, number relationships, number values, and how teachers can promote the development of these understandings throughout the mathematics curriculum.

NUMBER SENSE

Number sense is "an intuition about numbers that is drawn from all varied meanings of number" (NCTM, 1989, p. 39). Children with number sense understand that numbers are representative of objects, magnitudes, relationships, and other attributes; that numbers can be operated on, compared, and used for communication. Number sense is a cognitive ability that has roots in fundamental mental processes but is heavily influenced by experience and other abilities such as language and spatial sense. It is the fundamental knowledge that mathematics, grounded in number and with all its rules and operations, has an inherent "sense" that can be used by the student in flexible ways to solve problems.

Sowder (1988) described number sense as a well-organized conceptual network that enables students to relate number and operation properties and to solve number-based problems in creative ways. Abilities in students that indicate good number sense include: inventing their own procedures for conducting operations, representing a number in several ways, recognizing number patterns, recognizing errors of magnitude, and discussing general properties of a numerical expression without depending on precise computation.

Gersten and Chard (1999) proposed that number sense in mathematics may be analogous to phonemic awareness in reading development, especially for early mathematical experiences (Gurganus, 2004). They built a strong case for the importance of number sense development in early, pre-formal schooling experiences. Number sense was identified as the missing component of early math facts learning, the reason rote drill and practice doesn't lead to significant improvement in mathematics ability. Gersten and Chard further posited the need for students with mathematics disabilities to build deeper understandings of number concepts that form the foundation for problem solving, strategy development, and generalization abilities.

While parts of the Gersten-Chard framework for conceptualizing the role of number sense in mathematics learning are certainly useful, the premise that the two constructs are largely analogous is questionable. Phonemic awareness is a much more narrow ability and is most critical in early reading skill development. It is an auditory processing ability that, when later linked with alphabetic (symbolic) understanding, leads to development of reading skill in languages whose alphabets are phonetic. It has been established to be one of the strongest predictors of later reading success.

Number sense, on the other hand, continues to be developed throughout a student's mathematics education and life experiences and applies to a wide range of number-related concepts. There may be other fundamental mathematics abilities—such as temporal and spatial senses—that contribute to critical concept development. Mathematics, unlike reading, is a content area with a wide range of symbols for representing concepts.

Gersten and Chard's observation that the study of mathematics disabilities and effective interventions has been neglected is accurate. They are correct in asserting the need for a framework to guide research into mathematics interventions that is as well constructed as those in reading, leading to more coordinated and effective intervention strategies. Many special educators have been guilty of oversimplifying mathematics content into fragments of fact and algorithm mastery without attending to underlying concepts, strategies, problem-solving skills, or higher-order processes. But this neglect has been due, in part, to the lack of guiding research.

Perhaps a more specific concept of "early number sense structures" would more clearly describe one construct that seems to be related to later success in formal (school) mathematics. Early number sense structures could include the demonstration of skills in counting, stating the total number for a group of objects, recognizing amounts larger or smaller, and performing simple combining and taking away procedures. These skills would precede the "numerical understanding" that comes with recognizing numerals and using numerals as symbols.

Brain researchers have concluded that most of us are born with a sort of mental number line (Kunzig, 1997). Located in the inferior parietal lobe, this function enables us to identify one number as larger or smaller than another, to specify a number between two others, and do simple addition and subtraction tasks such as adding on to a given number by one, two, or three. Interestingly, the brain finds it easier to compare distant numbers, such as 1 and 9, than close ones, 6 and 7. Even six-month-old infants discriminate between large sets of objects if the number of objects being compared is a wide ratio, such as 8 to 16 (Xu & Spelke, 2000).

IMPORTANCE OF NUMBER SENSE FOR MATHEMATICAL ACHIEVEMENT

The National Council of Teachers of Mathematics emphasized the role of number sense in the 1989 and 2000 national standards.

> understanding number and operations, developing number sense, and gaining fluency in arithmetic computation form the core of mathematics education for the elementary grades. As they progress from prekindergarten through grade 12, students should attain a rich understanding of numbers—what they are; how they are represented with objects, numerals, or on number lines; how they are related to one another; how numbers are embedded in systems that have structures and properties; and how to use numbers and operations to solve problems (NCTM, 2000, p. 32).

In each of the grade-level bands of the NCTM standards, the development of number sense is fundamental. In the early grades children develop a sense of whole number by counting objects and comparing whole numbers (greater than, less than, first, third). They strengthen their concept of whole numbers by adding and subtracting and developing an understanding of properties such as identity and commutative. Children in grades 3 through 5 extend their concept of number beyond counting numbers: fractions, negative numbers, and decimal forms. The operations of multiplication and division are compared with addition and subtraction and extended through the additional properties of these operations. Children develop the concepts of factor and equivalence and continue developing estimation skills. Middle-school students develop a deeper understanding of rational numbers and use a wider range of number representations, such as scientific notation and exponents. High school students are expected to compare the properties of various number systems, explore new systems such as vectors and matrices, and understand less common types of number such as complex and random. They use algebraic symbolism to study the properties of number and operations. A concept map of the real number system is depicted in Figure A.1.

The 1996 National Assessment of Educational Progress found that fourth- and eighth-grade students showed weaknesses in number sense. "While U.S. students seem to be fairly strong in basic whole number computation, they seem to lack the flexibility to apply those skills to new or unusual situations. The emphasis in the curriculum should move beyond basic paper and pencil computations with numbers to include such topics as computational estimation and mental computation. . . . In a world where problem solving and reasoning are highly valued, mental strategies and the ability to judge the reasonableness of an answer are more important than ever" (Wilson & Blank, 1999, p. 12).

Special educators typically have emphasized computational practice without acknowledging the importance of understanding number and number relationships. An example is requiring students to master basic facts without teaching supportive strategies based on number sense. The student knows $2 + 2$, $3 + 3$, $4 + 4$, and $5 + 5$ but is stumbling with $3 + 4$ and $4 + 5$. Students who appear to have mastered their facts sometimes fall back on number sense to figure out that $3 + 4$ is just one more than $3 + 3$ or that $4 + 5$ is one less than $5 + 5$. Students with learning problems may need explicit practice with number patterns and instruction in these strategies.

PROMOTING NUMBER SENSE DEVELOPMENT

Given the importance of number sense for developing deep mathematical understanding and promoting continuous achievement through the grade levels, what can teachers do to develop this ability in students with learning problems? This section will focus on four areas critical for developing number sense within any mathematics curriculum—mental math, estimation, number meaning, and language.

Mental Mathematics

All engagement with mathematics is, of course, mental. But mental mathematics denotes "doing math" in your head without paper and pencil or other assistive devices. It forces students to visualize numbers and their relationships. Many teachers view **counting**

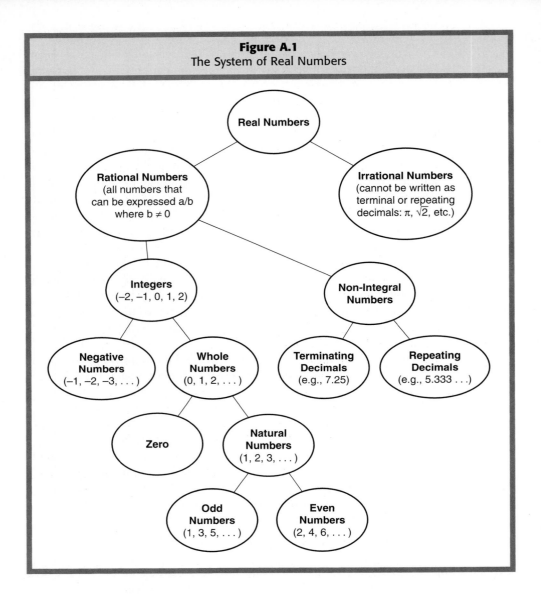

Figure A.1
The System of Real Numbers

exercises before a math lesson as coaches view stretches before a workout. These quick drills can strengthen students' sense of numbers and their patterns.

Begin with counting up to 30 or 40 by 1s, 2s, 5s, and 10s, then have students count back down again. On other days challenge students to count by 3s, 4s, 6s, 7s, 8s, and even 9s. With practice, students can continue patterns such as 1, 2, skip 2, 5, 6, skip 2 , 9, 10, skip 2 . . . or 1000, 1050, 1100, 1150 . . . or create their own patterns.

If students with specific learning problems have trouble with counting exercises, try some of the following modifications:

- Start with a few numbers and practice until firm:
  0, 5, 10, 15, 20—20, 15, 10, 5, 0.
- Allow students to count using a number line or chart at first, then fade its use.
- Use familiar objects associated with the number (coins for 5s, 10s, 25s; shoes for 2s; clover for 3s; dogs feet for 4s; etc.), then fade their use.
- Have students respond chorally until comfortable before calling on individual students to count alone.
- Individualize the counting challenge for each student; scaffold students to the next hardest level without causing frustration.
- Encourage students to make up poems and songs to accompany counts.
- Have students toss bean bags or bounce balls while counting.

Visualizing numbers, objects represented by numbers, and number patterns can also strengthen number sense. Ask students to name their personal associations with specific numbers. For example, 12 is typically associated with a carton of eggs or a child's age. The number 9 may remind students of a baseball team or the number of their classroom. Younger students tend to view numbers as labels, like names, rather than the total number of items in a set. While the nominal form is common for addresses and other means of identification, mathematics uses primarily cardinal and ordinal forms in problem solving.

Students can also be asked oral questions about the relationships between numbers: Which number is larger, 47 or 52? How many numbers fall between 39 and 44? How many even numbers are between 40 and 50? What two digits added would equal 10? What is 46 minus 2? What is 41 minus 2? Just don't overburden students' capacities for mental math by presenting problems better computed by pencil or calculator. Many students with learning disabilities have working memory problems, as discussed in Chapter 2.

Students who have difficulties can be assisted with number relationship problems through the initial use of number lines (Figure A.2) and charts or having examples modeled using explicit strategies. Create large number lines across the floor using tape and large numbers. Have students stand on reference points and compare actual distances.

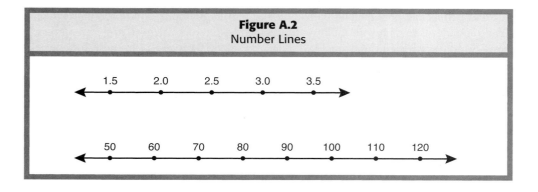

Figure A.2
Number Lines

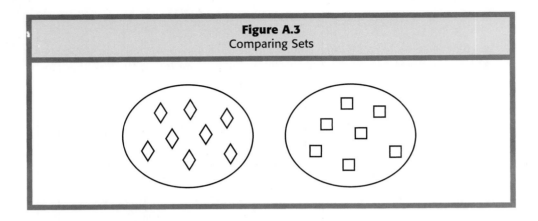

Figure A.3
Comparing Sets

This is a great way to teach rounding numbers to the nearest 10. Or tape large versions of 100s charts on the floor or painted onto concrete common areas.

Teachers should not just hand a number line to students with learning problems and expect understanding. The teacher should model its use with lots of examples and clear, consistent language. "I'm putting my red markers on the 10, 20, and 30. My blue marker is on the 23. Is my blue marker closer to the 20 or 30? Is 23 closer to 20 or 30? If I want to round 23 to the nearest 10, I record 20." Older students should be challenged with segments of number lines depicting decimals, fractions, very small, and very large numbers.

A final type of visualization involves the presentation of objects (concrete) or diagrams representing objects (representational) and asking students to enumerate or compare sets (see Figure A.3). Research on instant enumeration of objects in a set demonstrated that humans could quickly identify three objects, but started making errors with four (Mandler & Shebo, 1982). The first three objects do not have to be counted one-by-one. With larger numbers human brains have a hard time instantaneously identifying five objects from four $(n - 1)$ or six $(n + 1)$, especially when spacing and configuration are varied. It takes practice and some cognitive scaffolding to increase one's speed and accuracy with rapid enumeration and comparison.

A third method for using mental mathematics to promote number sense is to present **number games** that challenge visualization and mental manipulation. Variations on dominoes and dice assist with rapid enumeration of whole number sets and set comparisons. Simple games with playing cards or teacher-made flash cards can build number concepts and associations. And "magic squares" promote mental problem solving with number patterns. Magic squares (also magic triangles and sudoku—the 3 by 3 blocks of 3 by 3 magic squares) have some numbers missing from the grid and all number relationships are based on a rule. For example, the rule for the rows, columns, diagonals, and the four central squares in Figure A.4 is the sum of four numbers is 34. The rule can be found by placing letters in unknown boxes and solving simultaneous equations or through guess and check methods. For younger students, provide the rule for the square or use a three-by-three square instead.

• • • • • • • • •
For solutions to the problem presented in this book, visit the Companion Website at www.ablongman.com/gurganus1e.
• • • • • • • • •

	15		12
8	10		13
		16	
14		9	7

Estimation

Until the 1990s, mathematics texts rarely emphasized estimation skills. Occasionally there would be a special box with one or two estimation practices. More frequently students were encouraged to round and then compute. Some teachers attempted to explain the importance of estimation by warning students that if they couldn't estimate they would be terribly embarrassed in the grocery store check-out line one day when they didn't have enough money for their purchases. Not only did these teachers not fully grasp the importance of estimation, they didn't teach it as a mathematical strategy or help students generalize it in useful ways.

A more realistic explanation of the value of estimation comes from a closer examination of its use. Some things cannot be exacted—the measurement of a coastline, the number of cells in your body. Some offer no practicality for exactness—there are about 150 oysters in a bushel, it will take a little more than two gallons of paint to paint this porch, we expect about forty people at our party. The importance lies in good estimation based on a sense of number, space, and time.

Estimation is a critical part of problem solving. Using estimation assists students in selecting operations and judging the relative sense of their answers. Good problem solvers begin a problem with a sense of the range of reasonable answers and complete the problem-solving sequence by asking themselves, "Does my answer make sense given what I've established as the important parts of the problem?" These students tend to notice number patterns and make connections between past experiences and the current problem.

Estimation is developed over time through practice with lots of different problems. Students with difficulties in this area may be anxious about not having an exact answer, may not have estimation strategies such as rounding, or may not have a sense of the approximate "size" of an expected number, as with the mental number line.

Students should first have experience estimating relatively small amounts or sizes. About how many students are seated at each table in the cafeteria rather than about how many students are in the cafeteria. About how long is this bulletin board? Students often mistake estimation with guessing and should be taught to consider a reasonable range and begin relating their experiences with familiar distances, numbers, or areas with more challenging ones. Examples of problems without possible precise answers but requiring reasonable ranges:

■ It is 20 miles between our school and the mall. If you could run about 6 or 7 miles per hour, about how long would it take to run to the mall?

■ We know it is 100 miles from Charleston to Columbia because we took a field trip there last week. If this distance on your map is 100 miles, about how far is Washington?

Teachers should model strategies such as using referents and chunking so that students have estimation tools (Lang, 2001). **Using referents** involves finding number or amount benchmarks with which the student is already familiar and using those to estimate unknowns. For example, the student may be familiar with the length of a baseball bat and be able to use that in estimating someone's height. **Chunking** is like *sampling* in statistics—breaking a total into parts, estimating a part and then applying that back to the whole. This section of the auditorium has about 25 students, so there must be about 200 students in all.

Estimation with larger numbers can develop a stronger sense of number and place value. This square inch of turf has fifteen blades of grass. We can estimate that a square foot would have 2,000 blades. How many blades would be in a football field? A city subway carries an average of 250,000 riders per hour during peak periods and 50,000 riders per hour at other times. About how many riders does the subway carry between 6 a.m. and midnight?

Number Meaning

Students who have more and varied experiences with numbers develop a deeper understanding of numbers and number structures. They develop a sense that numbers represent other things and can themselves be represented in various ways. In addition to the number line and number game activities described in the previous sections, teachers can promote deeper understanding of number meaning by:

■ Guiding students through 100s charts explorations. Using both 1 to 100 and 0 to 99 charts (see appendix), students cover up various number patterns and actually see relationships such as factors, doubles, and primes. Figure A.5 shows part of a 100s chart with every fourth square covered.

■ Demonstrating the use of objects or pictures to represent numbers. Interlocking cubes can represent various number patterns or groupings. Graph paper is a wonderful, inexpensive tool for showing the relationship between number and space.

■ Incorporating number experiences into other content areas. Teachers should make a point to use number and estimation skills in social studies, reading, science, and other areas to promote generalization and reinforce number concepts. Often number skills are essential for the development of concepts in these areas—map skills, graphing, making comparisons, and grouping. There are also many sources for the use of children's literature in developing number concepts (see Chapter 7).

1	2	3		5	6	7		9	10
11		13	14	15		17	18	19	
21	22	23		25	26	27		29	30
31		33	34	35		37	38	39	

■ Teaching the concept of zero. Many children think zero means nothing. But in the system of real numbers, zero holds a position on the number line. In computation, zeros have place value. Many children have trouble positioning a ruler because of their lack of understanding of zero as a starting position (Figure A.6). To promote better understanding, use games with negative and positive numbers, incorporate zero into the number line, and include zero in counting exercises.

■ Representing numbers in other forms. When familiar numbers take on unfamiliar positions such as in the denominator of a fraction or to the right of the decimal point, many students with learning problems are confused or attempt to maintain a whole number concept. Begin these new concepts at the concrete level with familiar examples. Use language and modeling to make each number's role explicit. One fourth of our floor is covered with carpet. Our floor has four parts and one part is carpeted. Only one of the four parts has carpet. Three-fourths is covered in tile.

■ Connecting number meaning with number functions. From the number line, hundreds charts, graph paper, and other number experiences, students are better able to conceptualize the actions, relationships, and properties represented by addition, subtraction, multiplication, and division.

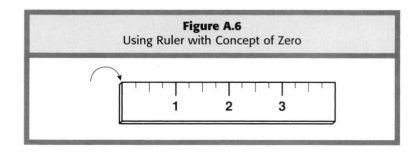

Figure A.6
Using Ruler with Concept of Zero

The Language of Mathematics

Teachers sometimes forget that mathematics learning depends on language. The teacher uses language to explain new concepts. Students use language (aloud or in their heads) to clarify relationships and express understanding. Math number systems and concepts have their own challenging vocabulary. And many state-mandated mathematics tests require students to explain their answers in writing.

Students with language disabilities or differences may have compounded problems in mathematics achievement. Of particular concern are those students with problems in word naming, manipulating morphemes, making sound–symbol connections, expanding vocabularies, asking questions, and applying syntax in creating sentences. No current standardized tests adequately measure language skills in a mathematics context. Teachers must attend to students' language use during teacher-developed diagnostic procedures.

Some ideas for promoting language development in addressing number sense:

■ Mindful teacher talk: the teacher should use mathematics terms carefully and consistently. For example, when teaching about subtraction, teachers may use the terms subtract, minus, take away, and less. Teachers should begin with one consistent term until that is firmly understood and then gradually add the others to the repertoire. While these terms are introduced by the teacher, it is essential that students use the terms with the teacher and each other (expressive form of language). Teachers should model verbal expressions for students using "thinking aloud" or "self-talk" strategies. Teachers' language should connect objects and pictures with numbers and symbols. Teachers should pose questions carefully to promote the use of math language by students.

■ Scaffolding concept understanding via language: teacher questions and prompts can ratchet a student's understanding up to the next level. For example, the student who believes that the only pattern for covering a 24-square-foot area is 4 by 6 could be asked to show 4 by 6 on graph paper and then be asked to shade in another rectangular area of 24 blocks that do not have four on one side. And asked again for another example. Then the teacher could ask the student to examine the pairs of numbers for a pattern. The student's thinking is scaffolded, through the teacher's language, to make the connection between area and factors.

■ Promoting language as a problem-solving tool: The first step in problem solving is understanding the problem. Reading or hearing the problem, restating the problem, and discussing the problem with others are language tasks that clarify the problem. "About how many newspapers does the class need to sell? We don't need the exact answer, why not? *About* means approximate or estimate within a reasonable range."

■ Encouraging student use of self-talk: many students may not know that good problem solvers talk to themselves. They ask themselves questions, restate problems, prompt themselves to the next step or to a different tactic, question the reasonableness of answers, and reinforce themselves when they've been successful. Teachers should explicitly explain and model this process and encourage out loud self-talk (thinking aloud) along the way. Listening to student explanations is one of the most effective diagnostic tools. Students should be encouraged to use mathematical terms and more precise language. Rather than, "That number just seemed to cover the same amount as part of that side of this block and that block," a student should say, "One face of the rectangular prism is the same area as one face of the cube because the edges are the same length."

■ Providing practice with speaking and writing justifications: have students explain their conclusions and reasoning. It is particularly important that students write out justifications if those are required on state tests. But teachers must provide immediate, corrective feedback. Without practice and feedback, students with learning problems tend to offer irrational or simplistic justifications such as, "it was the best number" or "it was the biggest number because it was the biggest of all."

All students need to develop a strong sense of number and number relationships throughout school, but students with learning problems may need more explicit strategies to develop these fundamental understandings. Number sense may be key to most other mathematics learning. The next section extends number sense development to the big idea concept of place value.

PLACE VALUE

As children enter formal mathematics instruction, place value is an essential concept that evolves in complexity throughout the curriculum. The concept of place value—the quantity that a digit represents varies depending on the place it occupies in a number—is one of the most fundamental for modern mathematics. Many teachers, regardless of grade level, begin the school year with place value review and extension activities. Students are also fascinated to learn that our system of number is not the only system (Figure A.7, discussed in the following section).

Before Place Value

The earliest number systems were developed as people needed to express larger numbers and make computations, such as those for astronomy. If each real number had its own name and symbol, one couldn't get much past 33 distinct digits, as in the New Guinea system in the mid-twentieth century, before losing track of the amount (see Dehaene, 1997, p. 94). Consider the challenge of memorizing each digit (that they assigned to body parts) and performing addition and subtraction by moving forward and backward. Go beyond the body positions and one's ability to understand larger number concepts is restricted.

Early systems for numbers included grouping—the Egyptians (1600 B.C.E.) used groups of ten in an exponential fashion. The Babylonians (2000–3000 B.C.E.) used groups of 60, which seems awkward today but allowed for the expression of the factors of 2, 3, 5, and 6, and simplified the most common fractions. The primary problem of these early systems was the lack of a zero as a placeholder. Zero represented nothing or null.

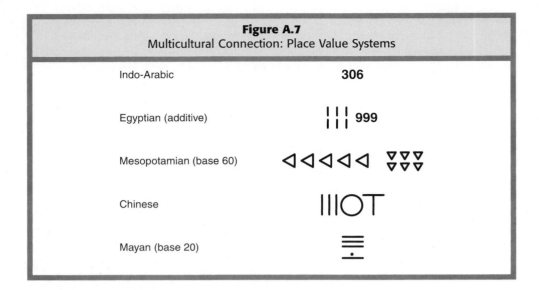

Figure A.7
Multicultural Connection: Place Value Systems

Indo-Arabic	**306**
Egyptian (additive)	||| **999**
Mesopotamian (base 60)	◁◁◁◁◁ ▽▽▽▽▽▽
Chinese	IIIOT
Mayan (base 20)	≡•

The Mayans (at least two thousand years ago) used a base-20 system with a zero using a bar (stick), dot (stone), and shell (zero). They were able to perform astronomical calculations but the procedures have been lost (Zaslavsky, 1996).

The Hindus used an extensive positional number system with a zero placeholder sometime between 650 and 800 C.E. They used a dot or small circle to indicate the zero position. This system was translated into Arabic about 800 C.E. and into Latin about 1200 C.E. (thus the Western world calls this system Arabic). Hindu mathematicians also developed the first system of arbitrary symbols to represent the ten digits rather than countable tallies for some digits (Dehaene, 1997, p. 100).

The Value of Place Value

It doesn't matter whether our place value system uses 2, 5, 10, or even 20 digits, any system using zero can become operational. Twenty might be too many to recall, especially for math "facts." Computer systems use binary systems (only two digits), represented in code with "0" and "1" for the circuit off and on positions. However, a binary system results in very long number representations. A checkbook would have to be a foot long. Some historians have posited that a ten-digit system is natural for humans because we have ten fingers, harking back to body-based counting some call "digital computation."

Having a decimal (base 10) number system with a manageable number of digits, meaningful relative positions, and zero serving as a placeholder allows us to express very large and small numbers, make complex computations, and express rational numbers in different forms. We can read and understand the size of a number such as 50,002,600. We can use exponential notation such as 2.15×10^9 to represent 2,150,000,000 (hint:

there are 9 digits to the right of the 2 so the exponent is 9) or .00043 can be expressed as 4.3×10^{-4}. With a place value system we can compute using the operations (and the properties of the operations) for addition, subtraction, multiplication, and division for the entire set of rational numbers. We can express fractions in decimal form so comparisons are more easily made, measurements are more precise, and technological tools (calculators and computers) more useful. For example, consider which fraction is larger, $\frac{4}{15}$ or $\frac{6}{16}$. A difficult comparison! But it is easy to compare .2667 with .375 ($\frac{6}{16}$ is the larger fraction). If students have a deeper understanding of place value, they can devise (or at least understand) nonroutine algorithms (see content strand B).

TEACHING PLACE VALUE CONCEPTS

As discussed in Chapter 2, young children tend to view numbers as labels. As they learn to count, the numbers are names. *I'm three years old. There are five cookies.* It's much harder to add to or take away from the amount labeled with a number name. Even when children count up to 12, numbers have discrete names (in English and most European languages). For young children counting by rote, the numbers up to 20 remain discrete. It's only when they attempt twenty-one, twenty-two, and so forth that the place value pattern is apparent. The numbers from thirteen to nineteen are particularly tricky. *Thir* in *thirteen* and *fif* in *fifteen* may not sound like *third* or *fifth* to a child. The *teen* suffix represents "plus ten" and is reversed when we reach the 20s and 30s and so forth. It is interesting to investigate how other languages deal with the decimal system in verbal form (e.g., *ten*—English, *diez*—Spanish, *dix*—French, *ti*—Norwegian, *zehn*—German, *dieci*—Italian, *kumi*—Swahili, *Wikcemma*—Sioux) (Helton & Micklo, 1997).

Consider the following examples of two students whose teachers did not understand the importance of place value. One student was working with subtraction of whole numbers and had been taught to subtract single digits using a number line. His teacher continued to use the number line when she taught him to perform two-digit minus one-digit computations (e.g., 17 − 5 =). Perhaps she could not imagine that he would ever subtract larger numbers such as 398 − 127. Another student had been taught two-digit addition with small digits, not requiring regrouping. Her teacher was careless and never noticed that she was computing left to right. After all, she was getting correct answers. However, when larger digits were required and the teacher tried to explain regrouping and starting in the one's position, this student was extremely resistant to a different procedure. It took three times as long to re-teach addition from a place-value perspective.

There is some evidence that children are not cognitively ready to understand place value until seven or eight years of age (Kamii, 1985). The earliest experiences with place value, besides counting and reading large numbers, involve two-digit and three-digit addition and subtraction. To understand and effectively use the place value of numbers for these operations, children must have a conservation of number (making one ten into ten ones doesn't change what I have) and practice with the multiples of ten and hundred (the difference between a 2 in the ten's place and a 2 in the hundred's place). They must also have skills in combining and partitioning values, naming the places for digits within a number, and recognizing the difference between the face value of a number and its complete value within a place. Some children lack place value understanding until fifth or sixth grade or even later (Resnick & Omanson, 1987).

For developing place value concepts with two-digit numbers, Varelas and Becker (1997) recommended adding a notation step between the concrete manipulatives (place value blocks) and written number. They taught students using two-color disks with face value on one side and complete value on the other (e.g., 8 on one side and 80 on the other) by placing the disks in a two-box frame. After this strategic instruction, students were able to distinguish between face and complete values of digits within two-digit numbers and add up the total values.

Fuson (1990) argued that mathematics textbooks were flawed in their sequence and focus of place value instruction related to addition and subtraction. Reading, writing, and computation with two-digit numerals up to 20 or 30 should precede larger numerals that require different cognitive conceptual structures. Addition and subtraction with all single digits should precede multi-digit addition and subtraction. Place value instruction should accompany multi-digit addition and subtraction. Multi-digit addition and subtraction with three and four digits should be attempted earlier (second grade) so that the operations without trading (regrouping) are not prolonged and over-generalized. Textbooks provide inadequate support for developing multi-unit conceptual structures. Students should use place value blocks and spoken number words to support place value and regrouping understanding with multi-digit addition and subtraction. A study using these curriculum modifications with second graders (all achievement levels) produced much more understanding of place value and addition/subtraction with multi-digits than that of older students (Fuson & Briars, 1990). Fuson also warned that English-speaking students may have the most difficulty with two-digit numbers because of the lack of "tens" names in English (other than the confusing "teen" or "ty") as compared with hundreds and thousands.

Baroody (1990) offered modifications to Fuson's place-value curriculum sequence. He recommended exposing children to multi-unit numbers concretely, in reading and writing activities such as newspaper reading, before instruction on multi-unit addition and subtraction procedures. This sequence would build deeper number concepts. He suggested additional concrete and pictorial place-value models: interlocking blocks, Dienes blocks (pregrouped), colored chips, trading frames, tallies, and Egyptian hieroglyphics. Baroody agreed with Fuson that textbooks are inadequate in their treatment of place value and that procedures with larger numbers can be introduced earlier.

Additional strategies for teaching place value concepts:

■ Use a single ten-frame (Figure A.8) to assist students' automatic recognition of zero to ten objects (attributed to Wirtz, 1974). Adding 4 + 5 will leave one spot open on the frame. Adding 7 + 4 will fill the frame, with one left-over object.

■ Provide place value mats and number cards for practice reading numbers and constructing numbers read aloud (Figure A.9). Longer mats can include a decimal point. These mats can be extended to form grids for addition and subtraction.

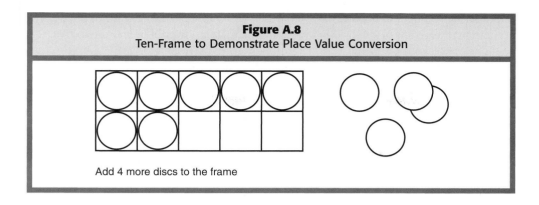

Figure A.8
Ten-Frame to Demonstrate Place Value Conversion

Add 4 more discs to the frame

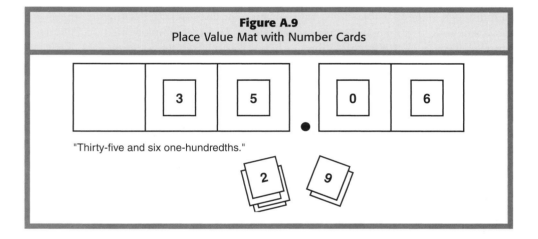

Figure A.9
Place Value Mat with Number Cards

| | 3 | 5 | • | 0 | 6 |

"Thirty-five and six one-hundredths."

2   9

■ Stress the patterns in reading larger numbers. One strategy is the concept of three houses in each block on a street, always ones, tens, hundreds, and a comma separating each block indicating where students should say the name of the block. For example: two hundred thirty-five *million*, three hundred fifteen *thousand*, six hundred forty-seven. Place value exercises are also excellent for mental math activities. Reading large numbers, adding on in different places, rounding numbers to a given place, and writing dictated numbers are some of the activities that promote facility with place value. These activities can continue throughout the elementary and middle school years with the inclusion of decimal numbers and expanded notation.

■ Money is sometimes a good tool for reinforcing place value. It is motivational! Using dollars for hundreds, dimes for tens, and pennies for ones, demonstrate the trading procedures. Then set up simple dice games where students roll the dice, earn pennies and can trade in 10 pennies for a dime and 10 dimes for a dollar. Money can also be used to demonstrate decimal positions (dollar is one's place, dime is tenths, and penny is hundredths). Younger children may be confused with money because it is not physically proportional; base-ten blocks or other proportional materials would be more effective.

■ Students who are having difficulty with place value concepts may not have a solid conservation of number. Back up and work on simpler trading activities: one nickel for five pennies, one solid color Cuisenaire rod for the same number of discrete cubes, items with marked prices (two 5¢ pencils for one 10¢ pen), number cards with numbers on one side and circles or tallies on the other, and invented values such as "one red button is worth 3 green ones."

■ Practice adding on by 10s, 100s or even greater multiples using calculators. Call out a number (2,315), and have students enter it. Then say, "Add 100 and try to predict." Then have students push the equals button and read the result.

■ Older students having trouble with place value conversions are typically involved in multi-digit addition, subtraction, multiplication, or division with decimals. Using lined paper sideways or graph paper can assist students in keeping columns lined up. Alternative algorithms such as those described in strand B can lessen the memory load. If students are taught procedures by rote rather than through understanding, they will experience difficulty when faced with difficult situations such as zeros, decimals, or numbers that don't need regrouping. Other strategies for older students include decomposing numbers (3,127 = 3000 + 100 + 20 + 7) and estimating answers before computing:

- ■ 389 + 214 will be about 600
- ■ 427 × 59 will be close to 400 × 60, or 24,000
- ■ 4.036 × 29.1 will be close to 4 × 30, or 120
- ■ 58.12 divided by 2.3 will be close to $\frac{60}{2}$, or 30

Place value is what gives our number system its power. This big idea of mathematics is developed throughout the curriculum, with some concepts rather simple, others quite complex.

DATA ANALYSIS

Data are "sets of quantities or information gathered from a sample of a population when surveys or experiments are done" (Sidebotham, 2002, p. 145). Data can be qualitative (e.g., describe attitudes, appearance, gender) or quantitative (e.g., number of employees, temperature). Qualitative data can be nominal (e.g., hair color) or ordinal (e.g., attitude scales), while quantitative data can be discrete (countable) or continuous (measurable). *Statistics* is "a branch of mathematics concerned with the collection, display, and analysis of numerical data in order to draw conclusions or make predictions" (Sidebotham, 2002, p. 428).

Skill with data analysis is developed throughout the K–12 mathematics curriculum. The 2000 standards document recommends that study in this area be generated by student questions. A question such as, "Which foods are most popular in our cafeteria?"

can lead to the methods needed to gather, organize, analyze, and display or report results. Younger children are naturally curious and can design simple data-collection strategies, such as tallies or objects, and represent data on bar graphs. They should understand that data representations provide information about their world. By middle school, the emphasis should be on planning the most appropriate data collection and analysis methods and comparing methods. Their tools and skills expand to include different graphing forms, statistical symbols, the meaning of aggregated data and various measures of data, and technology applications for collection, analysis, and representation. By high school the range of applications increases, as do the methods and tools. Students compare data sets (univariate and bivariate), study trends, use simulations, and apply more advanced concepts such as correlation and regression. They also explore related issues: bias, randomization, error concepts, types of studies, and probability (statistical predictions).

Data analysis also is important in life and job settings. For example, an individual reading the newspaper in the morning may study data related to weather, the stock market, and a favorite basketball team. This analysis will assist her in deciding what to wear, when to sell some stock, and whether to reserve seats for the next game. At work managing a large wholesale club, she will use sales data to predict the number of cashiers to schedule each day the following week and to plan special sales. She will prepare charts depicting annual sales trends for the next regional meeting. Even things that don't seem numerical in nature can be analyzed using data, such as opinions of consumers or the quality of a musical performance.

Students with learning problems in mathematics may have gaps in this curriculum domain because emphasis for many of these students was primarily on computation. Other students may have specific problems with generalization, number size and visualization, new terminology and formulas, and developing an intuition about the reasoning required to understand statistics. Older students with weaknesses in rational numbers, number sense, spatial sense, and proportional reasoning will also have difficulty with data analysis and probability.

Students with trouble generalizing basic mathematics concepts to data analysis applications tend to over-apply arithmetic concepts and problem-solving procedures. For example, the mean of a data set is the simple average or the sum of each item divided by the number of items. The mean differs in concept from median and mode but all three are ways to describe central tendencies of data sets and each has its purpose. A student may better understand the effects of simple addition and division operations on a data set if these processes are explicitly tracked and described and the size of the data set limited during initial learning.

New terminology and formulas may not have meaning, especially if procedures are taught by rote, situations are unfamiliar, or quantities very large and abstract. Students may be able to memorize formulas and carry them out, but have no sense of the concepts or be able to apply formulas in new situations.

A strong grounding in number sense and further development of number concepts, especially those of rational numbers, prepares students to deal not only with the properties of numbers and operations but their application within real-world problems. Some researchers have proposed the term "statistical reasoning" to differentiate the type of mathematics thinking required, that students should be prompted to "think statistically" (Rossman & Chance, 1999; Garfield & Ahlgren, 1988). By using a problem-solving approach with real data sets and exploring new statistical concepts as they are needed, students develop the concepts and intuitions required to solve new problems. In statistics, data are not just numbers; they are numbers in a context. The context provides the meaning (Cobb & Moore, 1997). For example, reading that the mean of a data set is 40 and the standard deviation is 12 has no meaning without a context such as class grades on a test with 60 possible points.

Here are some recommendations for developing data analysis skills:

■ Use real data sets, student questions, and real-life problems as the basis for introducing new concepts in data analysis. These explorations can be extremely motivating if connected with student interests.

■ Provide hands-on (physical) objects for simulations with initial learning, not just computer-generated simulations. For example, real students for a study of arm length, real candy for a survey on preferences.

■ Use technology for its exploratory and efficiency properties. Students who have the fundamental concepts can ask "what if" questions of a data set and see immediate results without having to work through lengthy calculations.

■ Remember the importance of language for new mathematics concepts and vocabulary. Ask students to explain and discuss their results, not simply record answers.

■ Provide examples of how statistics can be misused, to demonstrate potential sources of bias. Younger students, especially, tend to believe numbers are correct, absolute, and unquestionable. But the premise of statistics is the variability of the world.

■ High school students should have a solid understanding of data analysis and statistics concepts before the more theoretical and abstract concepts of probability are introduced.

Data analysis should begin with the youngest students and be expanded and developed throughout the grade levels. It should be a tool for problem solving throughout the curriculum, not just for mathematics class.

RESORCES

Bosse, N. R. (1995). *Mathematical pathways through literature.* Mountain View, CA: Creative Publications.

Burrill, G., Burrill, J. C., Coffield, P., Davis, G., Resnick, D., & Siegel, M. (1992). *Data analysis and statistics across the curriculum series, grades 9–12.* Reston, VA: National Council of Teachers of Mathematics.

Burton, G. M. (1993). *Number sense and operations: Addenda series, grades K-6.* Reston, VA: National Council of Teachers of Mathematics.

Fosnot, C. T., & Dolk, M. (2001). *Young mathematicians at work: Construction number sense, addition, and subtraction.* Portsmouth, NH: Heinemann.

Illuminations: Understanding a Child's Development of Number Sense. NCTM's website for teaching assistance with the standards. Provides lessons, video clips, and additional references. Available at: http://illuminations.nctm.org.

Muschla, J. A., & Muschla, G. R. (1995). *The math teacher's book of lists.* Englewood Cliffs, NJ: Prentice Hall.

Reys, B. J. (1991). *Developing number sense: Addenda series, grades 5–8.* Reston, VA: National Council of Teachers of Mathematics.

Strand B   Whole-Number Relationships

After studying this strand, the reader should be able to:

1. Compare the properties and operations of addition, subtraction, multiplication, and division with whole numbers
2. Describe difficulties of students with learning problems in computing with whole numbers
3. Create example addition and subtraction problems using change, compare, and combine situations
4. Identify applications for which the concept of equivalence is critical
5. Create example multiplication and division problems using equal groups, multiplicative comparison, Cartesian product, and area or array situations
6. Demonstrate at least one alternative algorithm for each of the four operations using whole numbers

Keera is working on whole number problems with Ms Smith in the special education classroom at Maple Street Middle School. The current problem states, "There were 176 students in the 6th grade at the beginning of the year but 19 students moved. How many are still in the 6th grade at our school?"

Ms Smith: How do you think we should solve that problem?

Keera: Plus it? Plus that number and that number (pointing to the 176 and the 19)?

Ms Smith: If students have moved away, then we will have fewer students. What should we do?

Keera: Take away.

Ms Smith: Good, can you write the problem and solve it?

Keera: Writes: 176
             −19
            ——
            163

Ms Smith: Please tell me how you worked that problem.

Keera: First I just wrote down the one, then I said 7 take away 1 is 6. Then I did take away 6 from 9 and got 3. The answer is 163.

Ms Smith: Think about this: if we started with about 175 students and almost 20 students moved, would we have about 165 still here?

Keera: I wrote 163.

Ms Smith: Let's add 19 to 163 and see if we get the beginning number back. ■ ● ▲

One of the most widespread myths of mathematics reform is that computation and fluency are not emphasized. Actually, these skills should be strengthened by the reorientation of the new standards. The NCTM 2000 document posits that, ". . . understanding number and operations, developing number sense, and gaining fluency in arithmetic computation form the core of mathematics education for the elementary grades" (p. 32).

What has changed is an emphasis on developing a deep understanding of number, number systems, and the meaning and interrelationships of the operations. Rote learning is out. Teaching for understanding is in. Research on mathematics learning by students with and without learning problems is compelling—students learn more and are able to maintain and generalize learning that is taught through context, developing concepts and strategies, rather than rote learning through drill and practice of isolated computations (see, for example, Carpenter, Franke, Jacobs, & Fennema, 1998). Developing fluency is still important and is emphasized in all four grade-level strands. But fluency means more than rapid recall of facts. Computational fluency is the "connection between conceptual understanding and computational proficiency" (NCTM 2000, 35). Fluency includes the deeper understanding of concepts and flexible, ready use of computation skills across a variety of applications.

In general education classrooms, whole-number addition and subtraction are developed to fluency in grades PreK through 2, and multiplication and division concepts are introduced. In grades 3 through 5, fluency in all four whole number operations is expected and students begin extending these operations to a deeper understanding of their interrelationships and applications with fractions and decimals. By sixth grade, whole and rational number computations should be fluent and used in a variety of applications. For many students with mathematics disabilities, these skills won't be mastered in the same time frame required in general education.

Many teachers assume the basic whole-number operations are simple and students can virtually teach themselves. However, the underlying number system structures can be challenging, well worth the time to study before planning instruction. This strand explores whole number concepts including properties of the four operations, single-digit combinations, multi-digit computation, and alternative algorithms. Recommendations for developing concepts and skills with students with learning problems are provided in each section.

UNDERSTANDING SINGLE-DIGIT OPERATIONS

For years, teachers and parents urged children to learn their math facts—referring to the 400 addition, subtraction, multiplication, and division combinations of single-digit numbers. The term *fact* erroneously implies an isolated bit of information that must be memorized, so the mathematics community now uses more accurate terms such as *single-digit combinations* or *basic number combinations* instead (Kilpatrick, Swafford, & Findell, 2001), although mathematics textbooks still refer to fact learning. Extensive research into how children learn single-digit operations demonstrates that children move through individually determined sequences of progressively more abstract and more efficient methods of working out the answers. Immediate recall and rapid procedures eventually become students' primary means of computing, but students who sometimes forget a quick solution and understand the basic concepts can figure out sums, differences, products, and quotients in a number of ways.

Counting, Addition, and Subtraction Concepts

The concept of addition is the earliest of the four operations developed by children and can be observed in activities such as counting discrete objects and assigning a number to a whole group of things. Children between the ages of two and five develop the underlying concepts of number sequence, enumeration (one-to-one correspondence), cardinality, and relative magnitude (Baroody, 1987). A child counts his buttons: one, two, three, four, five . . . and announces, "I have five buttons. You have only three so I have more than you."

Addition is adding items to an existing set. Addition is putting two or more amounts (sets) together to result in a larger, combined amount (with positive whole numbers). Subtraction is the inverse operation—counting back or removing items from a set. Subtraction is a more difficult concept because it is restrictive; it does not have identity, commutative, or associative properties (see Figure B.1). We cannot subtract from zero, reverse the order of numbers to be subtracted, or regroup numbers to be subtracted. Young children (18 to 24 months) develop early, initial concepts of addition and subtraction by manipulating objects. About age two children begin learning and using number words to count and name small groups of objects (Fuson, 1992).

Identifying the total of a set (cardinality) and comparing sets (relative magnitude) lead to other critical concepts for addition and subtraction development: equality or inequality, subitizing (automatically recognizing number of objects without counting), and conservation of number (what action effects a change in number and what does not). Preschool children should recognize that explicitly adding or taking away items from a set will change the total number of the set, but children may still be fooled when the items in a set are changed in their spacing but not number. Four-year-olds typically can identify a number plus 1 but it might take another year before they readily identify 1 plus a number because of their dependence on counting skills and lack of understanding of the commutative property (Starkey & Gelman, 1982). By age seven children should readily identify plus or minus 1 up to 10 in any order and apply a variety of operational strategies (Fuson, Richards, & Briars, 1982).

When children begin counting they start with the number 1. (They are actually using the positive integers but most teachers call them counting numbers.) The concepts of empty set and adding zero to an existing set, resulting in the original number (identity property), are very problematic for children (Anthony & Walshaw, 2004). If teachers use the term "nothing" for zero, confusion increases because nothing implies no importance. There is some debate whether zero should be introduced with the other digits (1 to 9) or if its introduction should be delayed until multi-digit numbers, requiring zero as a placeholder, are addressed. Concepts involving zero form a critical foundation for algebra and should be modeled through hands-on activities and discussions as the other digits and arithmetic properties are explored. Zero concepts are also critical for number theory, measurement, geometric, and statistical concepts such

Figure B.1
Whole-Number Properties

Addition	Identity	The identity element is zero: $n + 0 = n$
	Commutative	The order of the addends does not affect the sum: $a + b = b + a$
	Associative	The grouping of addends does not affect the sum: $(a + b) + c = a + (b + c)$
	Closure	The sum of two integers equals an integer.
Multiplication	Identity	The identity element is one: $n \times 1 = n$
	Commutative	The order of the factors does not affect the product: $a \times b = b \times a$
	Associative	The grouping of factors does not affect the product: $(a \times b) \times c = a \times (b \times c)$
	Property of Zero	Any number times zero equals zero. $n \times 0 = 0$
	Closure	The product of two integers equals an integer.
Multiplication over Addition	Distributive	The product of a number and a sum is the same as the sum of two products: $a(b + c) = (a \times b) + (a \times c)$

as computing with negative integers, measuring length, the concepts of line and plane, and graphing data.

One major problem with how beginning arithmetic is taught and depicted in text-books is the use of symbols for addition (+), subtraction (−), and equals (=) before those concepts are fully developed. Addition and subtraction problems each involve three quantities—two addends and a sum—with one element unknown.

$4 + 5 = 9$	Addend plus addend	$9 - 4 = 5$	Sum minus addend
$5 + 4 = 9$	equals sum.	$9 - 5 = 4$	equals addend.

The situations for which these operations can be used vary conceptually by three basic types—compare, combine, and change—in two forms—active and static (Fuson, 1992). The equals sign is usually introduced as a horizontal line below two numbers to be added or subtracted, so most children assume it means "and the answer is," an *operator* meaning, rather than "equal to the amount" below, a *relational* meaning; this leads to more confusion when higher-level concepts are introduced.

A more mathematically powerful approach to addition and subtraction concepts is to present problem situations orally and with the use of objects until children can describe and manipulate the concepts flexibly and with their own strategies. Mathematics is not always a paper-and-pencil task. For example, consider the types of addition and subtraction prompted in the following discussion.

> **Teacher to Amy and Billy:** I am going to give each of you five crayons. Help me count them out.
> **Children:** One, two, three, four, five, one, two, three, four, five.
> **Teacher:** Good, do you both have the same number?
> **Children:** Yes, five.
> **Teacher:** Amy, would you please loan Billy one crayon? Amy hands a crayon to Billy. Amy, do you now have fewer or more than five?
> **Amy:** I have four.
> **Teacher:** OK, do you have more or does Billy have more?
> **Amy:** He gots more cause he gots mine, too.
> **Teacher:** That's right, Billy has more crayons now. And you have fewer crayons because you loaned him one of yours. Let's say what happened. Amy had five crayons and gave one to Billy so now she has four. Can you say that?
> **Children:** Amy had five crayons and gave one to Billy and now Amy has four.
> **Teacher:** Can you tell me what happened with Billy's crayons?
> **Amy:** Billy got six.
> **Teacher:** OK, but what did he start with and how does he now have six?
> **Children:** Billy had five crayons and got one from Amy so he has six now.

This discussion illustrates the **change** situation in addition and subtraction. In the crayon exchange, the original number of five changed with the addition or subtraction of a crayon. There is a beginning amount, change amount, and ending amount. If the teacher were to ask the children next to compare the number of crayons Billy and Amy have, they would be in a **compare** situation, Billy has two more than Amy, Amy has two less (fewer*) than Billy. If the teacher asked the children to put all their crayons together into one group, a **combine** situation arises and the children would count ten crayons. In all three situations, the element not known determines the operation. Further, the concept of equal has been enhanced by explicitly comparing groups of crayons. But equivalence is more difficult to establish with change and combine situations because the original sets no longer exist. The use of descriptive language, diagrams, and symbols helps keep track of the original and new sets.

With more experience describing and manipulating situations involving zero to five objects, young children form stronger concepts of addition and subtraction concepts. By

---

*Mathematics terms for inequality are greater than and less than. English grammar for comparison of lower amounts is "less than," for smaller numbers, "fewer than."

the time larger digits and symbols are introduced, the concepts are understood. Seven-year-old children should be able to manipulate addition and subtraction concepts quite flexibly, adding or subtracting by one or two ($1 + 8, 7 + 2$), doubling ($4 + 4$), applying the commutative property ($4 + 5 = 5 + 4$) and even using known 10s combinations to determine those with addends of 9 ($9 + 3 = 10 + 3 − 1$). The addition and subtraction table in Figure B.2 illustrates with shading those combinations that are readily learned through strategies. If the additional strategy of adding or subtracting one from a known fact were applied, then $3 + 4$ would be one more than $3 + 3$, $4 + 5$ would be one more than $4 + 4$, and $8 + 7$ would be one less than $8 + 8$.

Computation tables, such as the one in Figure B.2, should not be used to introduce or teach arithmetic concepts. They are interesting to examine for patterns after children understand the concepts of addition and subtraction and have developed some computing strategies. Children who are dependent on these tables to find answers are not thinking or strategizing, merely copying. Children learn more about numbers by counting fingers or referring to a number line than using tables.

Figure B.2
Addition and Subtraction Combinations Learned through Strategies

	0	1	2	3	4	5	6	7	8	9	10
0	0	1	2	3	4	5	6	7	8	9	10
1	1	2	3	4	5	6	7	8	9	10	11
2	2	3	4	5	6	7	8	9	10	11	12
3	3	4	5	6	7	8	9	10	11	12	13
4	4	5	6	7	8	9	10	11	12	13	14
5	5	6	7	8	9	10	11	12	13	14	15
6	6	7	8	9	10	11	12	13	14	15	16
7	7	8	9	10	11	12	13	14	15	16	17
8	8	9	10	11	12	13	14	15	16	17	18
9	9	10	11	12	13	14	15	16	17	18	19
10	10	11	12	13	14	15	16	17	18	19	20

Fuson (1988) admonished U.S. mathematics textbook publishers for not presenting a full range of addition and subtraction problem types, overlooking effective strategies that can assist slower learners, and not introducing larger numbers early enough. She added that forcing young children to use equations to solve addition and subtraction situation problems may be unnecessary unless the equation is a model of the problem situation (rather than a solution procedure).

Teachers can promote deeper understanding of addition and subtraction concepts through the following activities:

■ Children between the ages of three and five should be engaged with a variety of objects for counting, comparing, and manipulating. Adults should ask prompting questions that will assist children with making connections, building vocabulary, and developing new concepts.

■ Although parents and school boards seem to expect it, asking four- and five-year-old children to write equations may be too developmentally challenging. If children have fine motor problems but can identify numbers in print, they can work with number and symbol cards (see appendix) to form equations.

■ For five- and six-year-olds, scaffold student understanding of number combinations by drawing diagrams for sets and changes, combinations, and comparisons. Here are three blocks and over here we have five blocks. If we put them all together, how many do we have? Yes, we have eight blocks. What if we moved two away? Yes, there would be six left. Let's draw what happened:

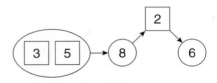

■ To strengthen students' concepts of zero, use paper plates, place mats, or simple containers for grouping objects as sets to be added together or subtracted from. Randomly use an empty plate to represent zero. Three blocks in this plate and zero blocks in this plate equals how many blocks all together?

■ An activity for strengthening fluency and number concepts is *seeking sums*. Present the sum "8" and ask students for all the ways they can create addition equations that give the sum of 8 (1 + 7, 2 + 6, 3 + 5, 4 + 4, 5 + 3, 6 + 2, 7 + 1; and don't forget 0 + 8 and 8 + 0). Present equations in noncanonical (nonstandard) forms such as 8 = 5 + 3 and 2 + 3 + 3 = 8. Then do the reverse for subtraction equations with 8 as the beginning number (8 − 5 = 3; 8 − 3 = 5) or a missing term (5 = ? − 3). Repeat with other sums.

■ Another strategy used with early subtraction practice is "counting back." This strategy can be used with minus one and minus two to promote fluency of those combinations. For example in the problem 9 − 2 = ? the student would begin with the nine, then count back twice, 8, 7, to achieve the difference. Counting backwards is difficult for many children, so they tend to use counting up instead: $9 - 2 = ?$ starting with 2, count up to 9 and keep track of the counts with fingers or tallies.

■ To emphasize the relationship between addition and subtraction, use the terms addend and sum for describing the elements of both equations. Many textbooks define sum as the answer to an addition problem and difference as the answer to a subtraction problem. This view promotes the operator meaning of addition and subtraction rather than a more global relational view needed for solving algebraic-type equations.

■ For students in first and second grade who are required to solve written combinations, consider the format (horizontal, vertical, noncanonical), spacing, and numbering of items on a page. Some students try to figure in the item number to an equation such as the following item three on a worksheet:

$3.4 - 5 =$

There is research support for moving through a concrete–representational–abstract sequence of instruction with arithmetic operations if instructional time devoted to manipulatives and diagrams is carefully controlled. Mercer and Miller's research-based *Strategic Math Series* (1991–1994) matches a range of objects with number problems in the first three lessons, then moves on to diagrams in the next three, before requiring children to compute without those devices. A strategy is introduced in lesson seven, DRAW, that offers a fall-back procedure if students have not memorized all the combinations.

D-iscover the sign
R-ead the problem
A-nswer, or DRAW
W-rite the answer

Lessons 8 through 21 provide practice in the strategy, related problem solving, and fluency practice. In multiple baseline studies of the basic combination interventions with students with disabilities, students were able to reach criterion for understanding (80%) in a limited number of formal lessons (within six 30-minute lessons) and retained the skills in follow-up tests (Mercer & Miller, 1992). All CRA lessons follow an explicit, direct-instruction format with modeling, guided practice, and independent practice portions with self-charting of progress after each lesson.

Funckhouser (1995) implemented a learning sequence that first used jelly beans glued to five-cell frames to represent numbers. During the first two weeks, kindergartners built frames for the numbers 0 to 5. In the third week, combinations of number frames were explored. In the fourth week the + symbol was introduced and after the four-week intervention, all students could recognize and match numbers 0 to 5 and add sums up to 5.

Concept of Equivalence

As mentioned in the previous section, children often view the equals sign as an operator rather than relational equivalence when it is first introduced, usually with children's first experiences with addition equations in kindergarten or first grade. Textbooks actually promote the operator view of the equals sign by using "function machines" and standard equations.

In a study with second-grade students, Seo and Ginsburg (2003) found that most students (14 of 16) held a context-based view of the equals sign rather than a generalized and integrated conception of equals as relational. The teacher in the classroom under study used more situations for equals signs than the textbooks offered, including number comparisons with greater than, less than, and equals signs; addition and subtraction within varied contexts; multiple names for the same number $(1 + 4 = 5; 2 + 3 = 5)$; measurement comparisons using Cuisenaire rods (1 red = 2 whites); equivalent coins (5 pennies = 1 nickel); and everyday-life contexts (equal number of letters in names). Children in this classroom tended to explain that the equals sign's meaning changes based on the situation. In an addition equation it meant how much is the total. With the Cuisenaire Rods it meant the two groupings of rods were the same length. Some children's interpretations depended on the language or order of symbols used. Thirteen of the sixteen children were confused by a noncanonical context, for example $5 = 2 + 3$, and insisted that the equation was backward. Eleven children viewed $3 = 3$ as an incorrect expression.

Faulkner, Levi, and Carpenter (1999) encouraged teachers to hold discussions with children that will illuminate their understandings and misconceptions about equals signs and equivalence concepts. Teachers should emphasize the relationship concept of equivalence so that children can better express a range of mathematical ideas and to build a foundation for algebraic understanding.

Recommendations for promoting an integrated and generalized view of equivalence:

■ Expose children to the different meanings of the equals sign, including nonarithmetic contexts, emphasizing the relational model (Seo & Ginsburg, 2003).

■ Be more explicit in teaching for transfer of equivalence concepts to various forms of equations.

■ Consider using another symbol, such as an arrow, for the operator meaning of simple addition and subtraction (Seo & Ginsburg, 2003).

■ Use diagnostic interviews and group discussions to assess individual student understanding and changes in understanding with experience.

■ When children begin using written equations, build the concept of equivalence by writing equations horizontally and using equivalence analogies such as balanced scales. If 10 cubes and 5 cubes are on this side of the equation, how many cubes need to be on the other side to make it balanced? $10 + 5 = 15$. If we take three cubes off this side, how many do we take off the other side? Let's write our new equation. $(10 + 5) - 3 = 15 - 3$

■ Avoid teaching students to match cue words to operations. The words *altogether*, *total*, and *sum* may not always mean to add the numbers given. For example, the museum had 817 paintings altogether. 625 were from the year 1900 to present. How many were older? Many students would see the word "altogether" and add: $817 + 625 + 1900$.

Multiplication and Division Concepts

For positive integers, multiplication is repeated addition. It is counting groups of the same number. Instead of adding $4 + 4 + 4 + 4 + 4$, we say we have five groups of four, or five times four equals twenty. Multiplication's identity element is the number 1. Any number times one equals the same number. Like addition, the order or grouping of factors doesn't affect the product (commutative and associative properties).

Division is the inverse operation of multiplication and, like subtraction, has no identity, associative, or commutative properties. Division begins with a total amount that is then shared or partitioned. Division is repeated subtraction for positive integers. Further, division can result in leftovers (remainders or fractional parts). For example, a family held a yard sale and made $200 on things they no longer needed. If there are 6 people in this family and they plan to split the money evenly, how many dollars will each person receive? Each person gets $33.33, with 2 cents left over.

Multiplication and division can be seen in four types of situations: equal groups (also called equivalent sets or vary), multiplicative comparison (also called restate), Cartesian product, and rectangular area (or array) (Greer, 1992). Consider the following situations and the multiplication or division that would be required if one of the three elements (two factors and one product) were unknown.

Equal groups (vary): *Five children have four books each to check out from the school library. They are checking out 20 books in all.* Another common example is rate: *The ribbon costs $2 per foot and Libby wants to buy 5 feet of ribbon for $10.*

Multiplicative comparison (restate): *Carmen has three times as many baseball cards as Dan. Dan has 10 cards and Carmen has 30.* The "times as many" signals the comparison, a many-to-one correspondence. This situation is sometimes called restate because Carmen's amount has been expressed in two different ways.

Cartesian product: *Emily has five blouses and three skirts. She can make 15 different outfits from these pieces.* This situation is called Cartesian product because items from each set can be matched like ordered pairs. But is it possible to have more than two sets for which members are matched. Division problems are rarely designed in this format.

Rectangular area or array: *A floor measures 8 feet by 10 feet. The area of the floor is 80 square feet.* An array version can refer to rows and columns of objects, similar in type to equal groups: *Our classroom has 24 desks, 4 desks in each row of 6 rows.*

There are other situations that call for multiplication or division operations in later mathematics. For example, linear and nonlinear functions, proportions, fractions, ratios, rate, and products of measures all depend on simple concepts of multiplication and division. Understanding the whole "conceptual field of multiplicative structures" takes at least eleven years beyond first grade for typical learners (Vergnaud, 1988). These concepts also rely on the development of rational number understanding, as will be discussed in content strand D.

The following activities promote multiplication and division concept understanding:

■ Expand the range of problem situations for multiplication and division beyond objects in groups. Include different types of groups (connected, such as egg cartons and soda packs; discrete, such as people, unit cubes, or pencils), rate (something per unit), multiplicative comparison (times as many as), Cartesian product, and area models.

■ Link multiplication and division concepts by using the terms *factor* and *product* to describe the elements in both operations. Also, integrate multiplication and division instruction by using problems that can be reversed to show the inverse operation. For example, the children have baked 64 cookies for the parent open house. If 16 parents attend, how many cookies would each receive? (division) Revised: the class expects 16 parents to attend the open house and wants to provide 4 cookies per parent. How many should they bake? (multiplication)

■ Encourage students to develop their own word problems to represent multiplication and division equations, beyond the simple equal grouping situations.

■ Use harder numbers, ones that aren't so tidy, in problem situations to expand multiplication and division concepts. If multi-digit computation has not been taught, students can use calculators, estimate, or just determine the problem type and operation. For example, *the school is replacing the panes in its windows with energy-efficient panes. Each window has 8 panes and the school has a total of 215 windows. About how many panes should be ordered, with a few extra in case of breakage?* A good estimate would be 1,600 plus 160, or 1,760 panes. This is a vary (equal groups) type of multiplication situation.

■ Like developing fluency with addition and subtraction combinations, students should be encouraged to develop strategies rather than viewing "fact" learning as a rote memory task. The most common strategies include:
   ■ The rule of zero—any number times zero equals zero.
   ■ The rule of one (the identity property)—any number times one equals the original number.
   ■ Using students' prior knowledge of counting by 5s and 10s with nickels and dimes.
   ■ Applying the inverse $2 \times 6 = 12$; $12 \div 6 = 2$ and commutative properties $(6 \times 2 = 12)$.
   ■ Multiplying by 2 doubles the number.
   ■ Nines are particularly interesting—one can use "digital computation" or the ten-finger method. Or see the pattern: any digit times nine equals a two-digit product where the first digit is one less than the multiplier and the two digits add up to nine.

   $9 \times 3 = 27$ (2 is 1 less than 3; $2 + 7 = 9$)

   $9 \times 7 = 63$ (6 is 1 less than 7; $6 + 3 = 9$)

■ For products whose factors include 6, 7, 8, or 9, another finger computation method is simple and fun (see Figure B.3). Touch two fingers to multiply, such as the pointing finger with the middle finger for 7×8. Count the touching fingers and all those below as tens—10, 20, 30, 40, 50. Next multiply the fingers above on each side—$3 \times 2 = 6$. So the answer is $50 + 6 = 56$. Figure B.3 illustrates this concept first introduced by Barney (1970).
   ■ Divisibility patterns (for even division without remainders) include:
      ■ Even numbers are divisible by 2
      ■ A number is divisible by 3 if the sum of its digits is divisible by 3

Step 1: Count off your fingers, thumbs are 6s and so forth.

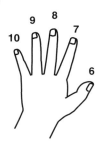
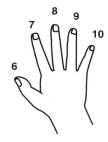

Step 3: Count touched fingers and the fingers below those as tens. (10, 20, 30, 40)

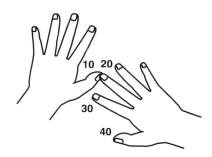

Step 2: Touch fingers to multiply. For example, 6 × 8 is being touched below.

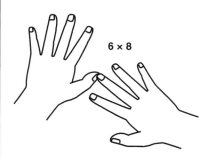

6 × 8

Step 4: Multiply the exact number of fingers above. (4 × 2 = 8)

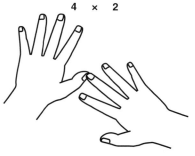

4 × 2

The answer is 40 + 8 = 48. (For 6 × 6 and 6 × 7 there is an extra step.)

- A number is divisible by 4 if the last two digits are divisible by 4
- If the last digit is a 0 or 5, the number is divisible by 5
- A number is divisible by 6 if it is also divisible by 2 and 3
- If the last three digits are divisible by 8, the number is divisible by 8
- A number is divisible by 9 if the sum of digits is divisible by 9
- If the number ends in 0, it is divisible by 10
- A number is divisible by 11 if subtracting and adding digits in an alternate format (left to right) results in 0 or 11, 22, 33 (Sidebotham, 2002). For example, 3586 is divisible by 11 because $3 - 5 + 8 - 6 = 0$.

- Provide opportunities for varied and context-based practice.

■ Avoid teaching the "facts" in isolation or one "number family" at a time. The *Strategic Math Series, Multiplication 0 to 81* (Mercer & Miller, 1991–1994) presents an assortment of facts from 1 to 4 in the first lesson. Focus is on understanding the concept of multiplication. The first ten lessons move from concrete to representational (semiconcrete) and on to abstract, encouraging students to engage in varied practice for understanding before emphasizing fluency. An example from the semi-concrete level:

This problem reads 4 times 3 equals.
That means four groups of three.
I'll draw four circles to show my groups.
Then I'll make three tallies in each group.
And counting them all up I get twelve.
Or I can count by threes—three, six, nine, twelve!

$4 \times 3 = 12$

■ Be cognizant of symbol confusion by students. The minus sign ($-$) also means negative number. Three symbols are used for equals: $=$, $\equiv$, and ___ . Various signs are used for division: $\div$, /, $\sqrt{}$ and the long horizontal line. Multiplication can be expressed by 2×3, $2*3$, and $(2)(3)$ and even $4yz$. In some countries a comma is used for the decimal.

■ Don't teach students to translate English directly into mathematical equations. For example, the statement "the zoo has 20 times as many animals as keepers" would be incorrectly translated into $20a = k$. Even college-level students stumble on these semantic problems for simple equations.

■ Anticipate that students will tend to overgeneralize their experiences with whole numbers when they begin working with rational numbers. Common misconceptions are the view that multiplication and addition will make the answer larger, and division and subtraction will result in smaller numbers.

■ Enhance multiplicative reasoning through mental math and estimation activities.

MULTI-DIGIT COMPUTATION

Working with larger numbers is challenging for students with mathematics learning problems, for a number of reasons. One is faulty conceptualization of digits within large numbers as individual numbers rather than representing a value depending on placement within the number (e.g., 78 as a 7 and an 8 rather than 70 and 8). Also, for English-speaking children, it involves translating words into numbers (e.g., 1,807 can be read one thousand eight hundred seven or eighteen hundred seven—not possible in many languages; 356 reads three hundred fifty-six—rather than three-hundreds five-tens and six). Other common problems involve following the sequence of steps in a standard algorithm, recalling one-digit combinations rapidly, holding numbers and steps in working memory while carrying out other steps, overgeneralizing addition and multiplication properties to subtraction and division, and even keeping track of numbers in written form. Also, many children ready to work with larger numbers in mental computations that can enhance place value understanding ($100 + 400$; $1500 - 100$) are forced to wait until they master their "facts."

It is easy, and common, for teachers to overemphasize practice with computations involving multidigit whole numbers. Lengthy practice keeps students busy and is simple to check. But if students have a strong grounding in place value and the operational concepts, as well as a wide range of problem types, this practice with larger numbers should not consume a large portion of instructional time. Multidigit computation, after all, is not the goal of mathematics instruction. Applying this computation when it is called for in a given problem situation is a goal.

Multi-Digit Addition and Subtraction

The first introduction of numbers with multiple digits should be accompanied by manipulatives that assist with the understanding of the values of each digit, such as base-ten blocks. The number 245 is represented by two flats, four longs, and five units—a more efficient representation than a pile of 245 units. But children need practice with trading—ten units for one long, ten longs for one flat (see Figure B.4). Later, when faced with multidigit addition and subtraction, the concepts will not be new, just strategies for working with multiple columns.

Most textbooks first introduce two-digit addition and subtraction, without regrouping, in first grade by using a tens and ones column format and encouraging students to begin with the ones column. In second grade texts, students are taught the typical algorithm for regrouping two- and three-digit problems. Some texts provide an alternative expanded notation view of these addition and subtraction processes. Beginning third graders are expected have mastered addition and subtraction, a timeline that will not be possible for many students with learning problems or developmental delays.

Transition from single-digit combinations to two-digit/one-digit computation is the first area for conceptual problems. For problems such as $17 + 4$ and $25 - 3$, it is

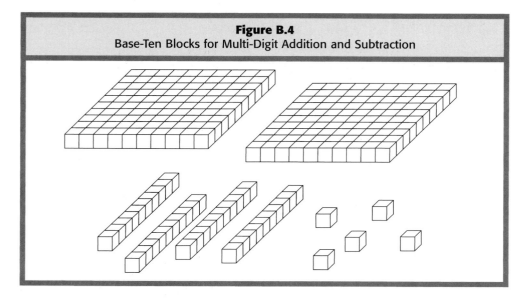

Figure B.4
Base-Ten Blocks for Multi-Digit Addition and Subtraction

tempting to continue using counting methods and number lines because the numbers aren't that large. It may be better practice to jump right into problems such as 78 + 73 or 82 − 26 so that children don't over-generalize with their comfortable counting procedures or practice too long without regrouping.

Once students move to two- and three-digit computations, the same concepts apply, with a few potential bugs. Most students are taught to perform these computations from right to left, although working left to right is not incorrect if the concepts remain intact. The most common errors are simple "fact" combination errors, using the correct operation inconsistently (in a set of mixed problems), dealing with regrouping (trading, renaming), dealing with 0s, confusing two different algorithms, and not holding amounts or steps in working memory long enough to use them.

Addition is different than the other three operations in that it can be performed with multiple addends as in column addition. A collection of addends is common for combine types of addition problems. For example, the students stocking the school store noticed that many boxes of black pens had been opened. They found 26 pens in one box, 43 in a second, 37 in a third box, 105 in a fourth, and a fifth box was unopened and had 120 pens. How many black pens are in stock? The properties of addition allow us to work this problem in a number of ways. The standard textbook approach is to list all numbers in a column, taking care to line up digits by place values, then adding each column and regrouping as needed. Alternatives are provided in the last section on alternative strategies.

Recommended strategies for providing instruction in multi-digit addition and subtraction include:

■ Make sure underlying concepts regarding place value and operations are firm.

■ Allow students to use alternative or invented algorithms as long as they are efficient and effective. Examples of the most commonly applied algorithms are described in the last section of this strand.

■ Diagnose errors carefully by watching students work computations and conducting diagnostic interviews. Have students work back through simpler problems until the basis of the error is detected.

■ Teach and encourage the use of estimation before computing. For example, the problem 578 + 213 should be about 800, not 365 or 7712. Curiously, many textbooks encourage estimation only after a strict computation algorithm has been mastered.

■ For students having trouble keeping track of columns and trading, use 1-cm graph paper and label each column with its value (see Figure B.5).

■ Use base-ten blocks for instruction, carefully connecting what is happening with numbers to the manipulation of blocks. Have students place the manipulatives on a place value mat (see Figure B.6 and appendix) and "record" each step with written symbols. My first number reads 804 so I have 8 flats, no longs, and four units and I write down 804. The second number, to be subtracted, is 78 so I write down −78 under 804 and attempt to remove 7 longs and 8 units but there aren't enough in those places. So I break apart one of the 8 flats into 10 longs and break apart one of those longs into 10 units and now I have 7 flats,

Figure B.5
Using Graph Paper with Multidigit Computation

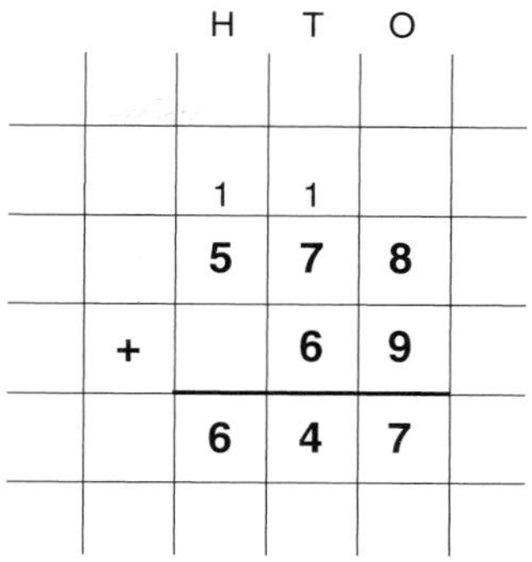

	H	T	O
		1	1
	5	7	8
+		6	9
	6	4	7

9 longs, and 14 units. Between the 804 and the 78, I'm rewriting a value for 804 as 7, 9, and 14. Removing 7 longs and 8 units leaves 7 flats, 2 longs, and 6 units. So I record that amount remaining in my problem. If I break apart too many, I can always recombine them later.

Multi-Digit Multiplication and Division

Textbooks typically introduce multiplication and division in second grade by showing pictures of groups and arrays. In third grade students are expected to move through fact fluency (usually by number families with multiplication and division in separate chapters), two-digit by one-digit numbers, using the standard renaming from right-to-left algorithm; three-digit by one-digit; two-digit by two-digit, and division by one-digit divisors in a later chapter. Some texts encourage estimation before multiplication and division, and others offer illustrative grids and expanded notation to demonstrate the effects of these standard algorithms. One text referred to multidigit multiplication as a process requiring "regrouping twice," supposedly referring to the double rows of cross-outs across the top of the problem.

Figure B.6
A Place-Value Mat for Multi-Digit Subtraction

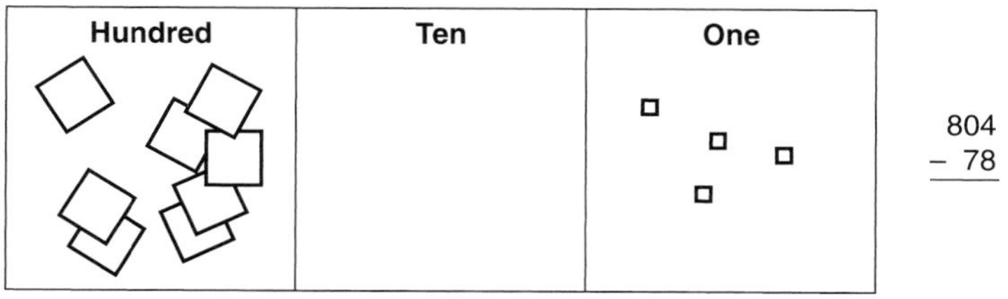

Hundred	Ten	One

804
− 78

Fourth-grade students are expected to master multi-digit multiplication and division computations with the addition of two-digit divisors.

With the above sequence of instruction, students quickly realize that using concrete objects for larger problems, even 15×8 or 36×7, is not efficient. When allowed to invent procedures to handle these larger numbers, students who understand the concepts involved tend to use variations on decomposition (Ambrose, Baek, & Carpenter, 2003). The problem 15×8 can be decomposed into $(10 \times 8) + (5 \times 8)$ if the student understands place value and properties of multiplication and addition. The problem 178×56 can be decomposed into 100×56, 70×50, 70×6, 8×50, and 8×6. Using multiples of 10 allows for simpler multiplication.

Multi-digit multiplication requires broad concept understanding: place value, multiplication and addition combinations and properties, sequencing steps to make sure all factors have been addressed, and some estimation ability. Students have the most problems with lining up numbers by place value, conducting multiplication and addition computations almost simultaneously, holding each piece of information in working memory long enough to use it in the next step, keeping track of multiple steps, and performing column addition correctly.

Clark and Kamii (1996), in studies of children's multiplicative thinking, found that it is clearly distinguishable from additive thinking and develops early (about 45 percent of second graders were at the beginning stages) but very slowly; only 28 percent of fourth graders and 49 percent of fifth graders were solid multiplicative thinkers for multi-digit situations. The authors concluded that it is critical that students be allowed to solve multiplication algorithms in their own way because of the slow developmental process and that curriculum standards may expect multiplicative reasoning too early in the grades.

Some recommended instructional strategies for multi-digit multiplication:

■ Allow students to use alternative strategies that are conceptually sound and efficient.

■ Use graphic organizers and flow charts (Ashlock, 2002).

■ Instead of manipulatives for larger numbers, use area model (array) diagrams (see Figure B.7).

■ For practice with multi-step algorithms use easy-erase surfaces such as whiteboards and chalkboards.

Students also attempt "long division" or multi-digit division by repeated subtraction. The problem $128 \div 6$ can be decomposed by subtracting 60 twice $(128 - 60 - 60)$ which leaves 8, from which 6 can be subtracted once $(8 - 6)$. So the quotient is $10 + 10 + 1$ remainder of 2, or 21 and $\frac{2}{6}$, or $\frac{1}{3}$. The problem $816 \div 13$ can be decomposed through repeated subtraction of 130: $816 - 130 - 130 - 130 - 130 - 130 - 130 = 36$, and $36 - 13 - 13 = 10$. So the quotient is 62 remainder 10 or 62 and $\frac{10}{13}$.

Long division is particularly challenging because one factor is typically placed in front of the ⌐ and the product is underneath. The standard algorithm calls for working through the product from right to left, estimating factors and then multiplying and subtracting all the way through. It truly requires a combination of all previous arithmetic

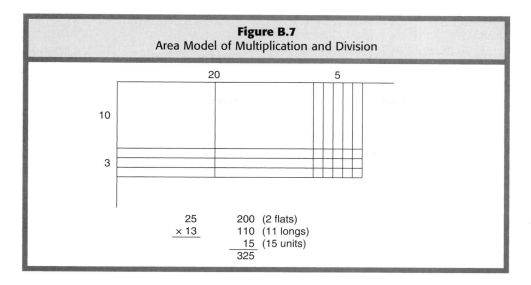

Figure B.7
Area Model of Multiplication and Division

$$
\begin{array}{r}
25 \\
\times\ 13 \\
\hline
\end{array}
\quad
\begin{array}{ll}
200 & \text{(2 flats)} \\
110 & \text{(11 longs)} \\
\underline{\ 15} & \text{(15 units)} \\
325 &
\end{array}
$$

learning to accomplish. The most common errors with multi-digit division include keeping numbers and symbols lined up, estimating products closely, holding a lot of information in working memory at one time, following an effective sequence accurately through to the final step, and dealing with those zeros and remainders.

In addition to the previous instructional strategies, recommendations for multi-digit division include:

- Focus on factor estimation practice.

- For one-digit divisors, estimate whether to expect a remainder by applying the divisibility rules before computing. For example, the problem $546 \div 5$ is not evenly divisible by 5 because it does not end with 0 or 5. Consider how a remainder should be expressed—whole number (e.g., R. 1), fraction (e.g., $\frac{1}{5}$), or decimal (e.g., .2).

- For two- and three-digit divisors, consider making a quick list of factors before beginning the division estimation process. For example, the problem $3984 \div 17$ is challenging. Making a list of the multiples of 17 will save trial-and-error time: 17, 34, 51, 68. . . . These are the most time-consuming computations and most adults simply estimate a quotient or pick up a calculator.

- Emphasize place value and use devices such as lined or graph paper to keep track of values. Even products and zeros are particularly pesky for students.

- Allow the use of alternative algorithms that are conceptually sound and efficient.

Alternative Algorithms

Alternative algorithms, sometimes termed low-stress algorithms, refer to alternative computation procedures that are usually more meaningful or efficient than the standard, textbook approaches to multi-digit computation. For more than a century, mathematicians have developed and published alternative algorithms, while others have been copied from around the world. These algorithms have several common characteristics: they are effective computational methods, they reduce the working memory demands on students, they are based on sound math concepts, and they can be a lot of fun. These approaches are not available as a cohesive curriculum program but can supplement any program. Research on alternative algorithms (Hutchings, 1976) found that they reduced the time required for mastery, increased computational power, and reduced students' stress while computing. An additional benefit is the complete record of steps available to the student while working the algorithm.

Students should be encouraged to explore these alternatives and find the approach that makes the most sense and is most efficient and effective for them. But teachers should not require students to demonstrate mastery with each type of algorithm; that is not the goal of this instruction.

The standard addition algorithm is depicted in Figure B.8a, followed by the three most common alternatives for three-addend and column addition: a partial sums method

Figure B.8
Alternative Addition Algorithms

A. Standard (Textbook) Algorithm

```
   1 1
   387
 + 936
 -----
  1323
```

B. Left-to-Right Method (Pearson, 1986)

```
   387
 + 936
 -----
  12
   11
    13
 -----
  1323
```

C. Partial Sums (right-to-left) from India (Basserear, 1997)

```
   387
 + 936
 -----
    13
   11
  12
 -----
  1323
```

D. Tens Method for Column Addition (also called *scratch method*) (Fulkerson, 1963)

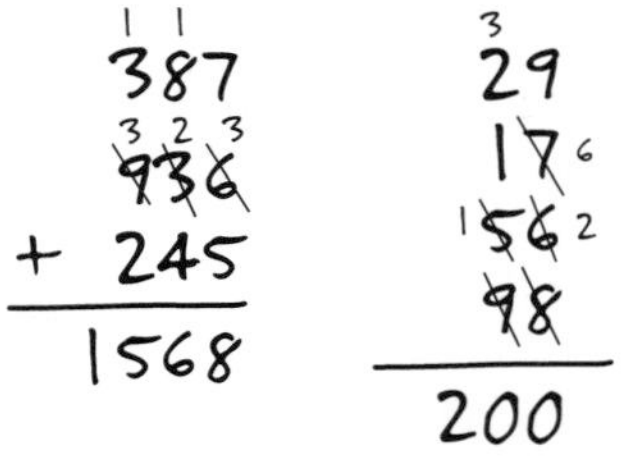

that may be 1,000 years old (Figure B.8c), Pearson's left-to-right addition (B.8b), and Fulkerson's tens method for column addition (B.8d). These addition methods place fewer demands on students' working memory because they separate rapid recall from renaming.

Figure B.9 depicts the standard and alternative subtraction algorithms. The conservation property of number is applied in the equal additions, adding constants, and adding the complement methods, because when equal numbers are added or taken away from both the minuend (top) and subtrahend (bottom) numbers, the difference remains the same.

Figure B.9
Alternative Subtraction Algorithms

A. Standard (Textbook) Algorithm

$$
\begin{array}{r}
{}^{2}{}^{16}{}^{15}\\
\cancel{3}\,\cancel{7}\,\cancel{6}\,2\\
-\,1\,9\,7\,8\\
\hline
1\,7\,8\,4
\end{array}
$$

B. Equal-Additions Method
(Randolph & Sherman, 2001)

$$
\begin{array}{r}
{}^{17}\,{}^{16}\,{}^{12}\\
3\,7\,6\,2\\
{}^{2}{}^{10}{}^{8}\\
-\,1\,9\,7\,8\\
\hline
1\,7\,8\,4
\end{array}
$$

C. Adding Constants (Mercer & Mercer)

$$
\begin{array}{rr}
46 + 2 & 48 \\
-\,28 + 2 & -\,30 \\
\hline
 & 18
\end{array}
$$

$$
\begin{array}{rr}
4000 + (-1) & 3999 \\
-3492 + (-1) & -3491 \\
\hline
 & 508
\end{array}
$$

D. Adding the Complement
(Randolph & Sherman, 2001)

$$
\begin{array}{r}
3762 \\
-\,588 \\
\hline
\end{array}
\qquad
\begin{array}{r}
3762 \\
+\,411 \\
\hline
\end{array}
$$

$$
\begin{array}{r}
999 \\
-\,588 \\
\hline
411
\end{array}
\qquad
\begin{array}{r}
{}_{3}4173 \quad {}^{-1000}\\
+1 \\
\hline
3174
\end{array}
$$

E. Low-Stress (Hutchings, 1979)

$$
\begin{array}{r}
3762 \\
\boxed{2\ \ 16\ \ 15\ \ 12}\\
-\,1978 \\
\hline
1784
\end{array}
$$

F. Left-to-right (Fitzmaurice-Hayes, 1984)

$$
\begin{array}{r}
562 \\
-\,378 \\
\hline
2
\end{array}
\qquad
\begin{array}{r}
562 \\
-\,378 \\
\hline
\cancel{2}9
\end{array}
\qquad
\begin{array}{r}
562 \\
-\,378 \\
\hline
\cancel{2}\cancel{9}\\
184
\end{array}
$$

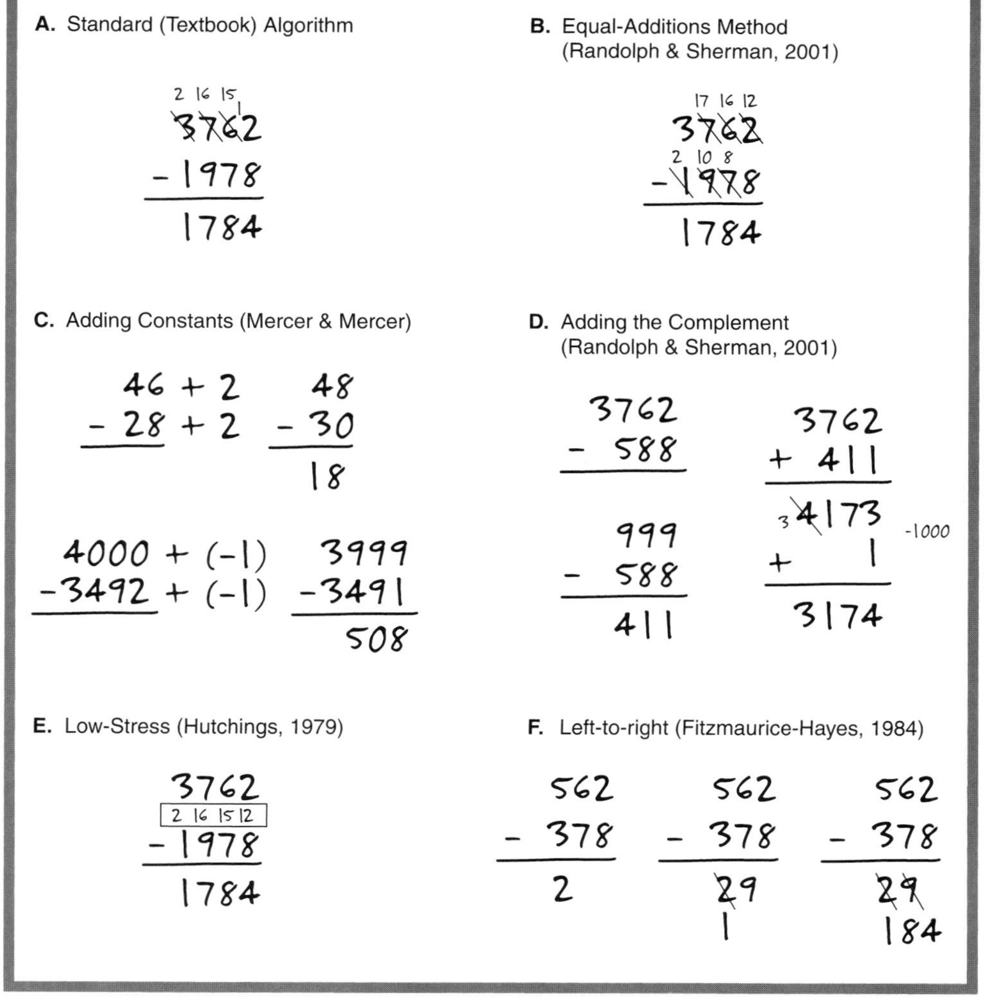

Figure B.10
Alternative Multiplication Algorithms

A. Standard (Textbook) Algorithm

$$
\begin{array}{r}
\overset{\scriptstyle 1}{\overset{\scriptstyle 3}{6}}4 \\
\times \quad 38 \\
\hline
512 \\
192 \\
\hline
2432
\end{array}
$$

B. Partial Products

$$
\begin{array}{r}
64 \\
\times \quad 38 \\
\hline
1800 \\
480 \\
120 \\
32 \\
\hline
2432
\end{array}
$$

C. Low-Stress (Hutchings, 1976)

$$
\begin{array}{r}
476 \\
\times \quad 8 \\
\hline
40 \\
8
\end{array}
\qquad
\begin{array}{r}
476 \\
\times \quad 8 \\
\hline
540 \\
68
\end{array}
\qquad
\begin{array}{r}
476 \\
\times \quad 8 \\
\hline
3540 \\
268 \\
\hline
3808
\end{array}
$$

Multiplication of multiple digit factors is complicated in the standard algorithm by keeping track of place values and overloading working memory. These issues are addressed through the partial products and low-stress methods depicted in Figure B.10. The Egyptian method is an interesting use of the concept of doubling both the first number in one factor and the other factor simultaneously, then adding terms for the first factor and the same terms for the product (see the next section, Multicultural Connection). The Lattice method of multiplication was illustrated in Chapter 4 (Figure 4.4).

As discussed in previous sections, division can be decomposed by partial quotients, factors, or multiples of 10. Some students may prefer to pyramid the quotient above the problem, as depicted in Figure B.11. These alternatives to the standard algorithm help students keep track of the steps applied and are true to multiplicative concepts.

The research-based *Everyday Mathematics* (The University of Chicago School Mathematics Project, 2001) incorporates some of these alternative algorithms into the student reference books and instructor's manuals. These include partial-sums and column methods for addition; trade-first, counting-up, left-to-right, partial differences, and same-change rule subtraction methods; partial-products and lattice multiplication; and partial-quotient division.

Figure B.11
Alternative Division Algorithms

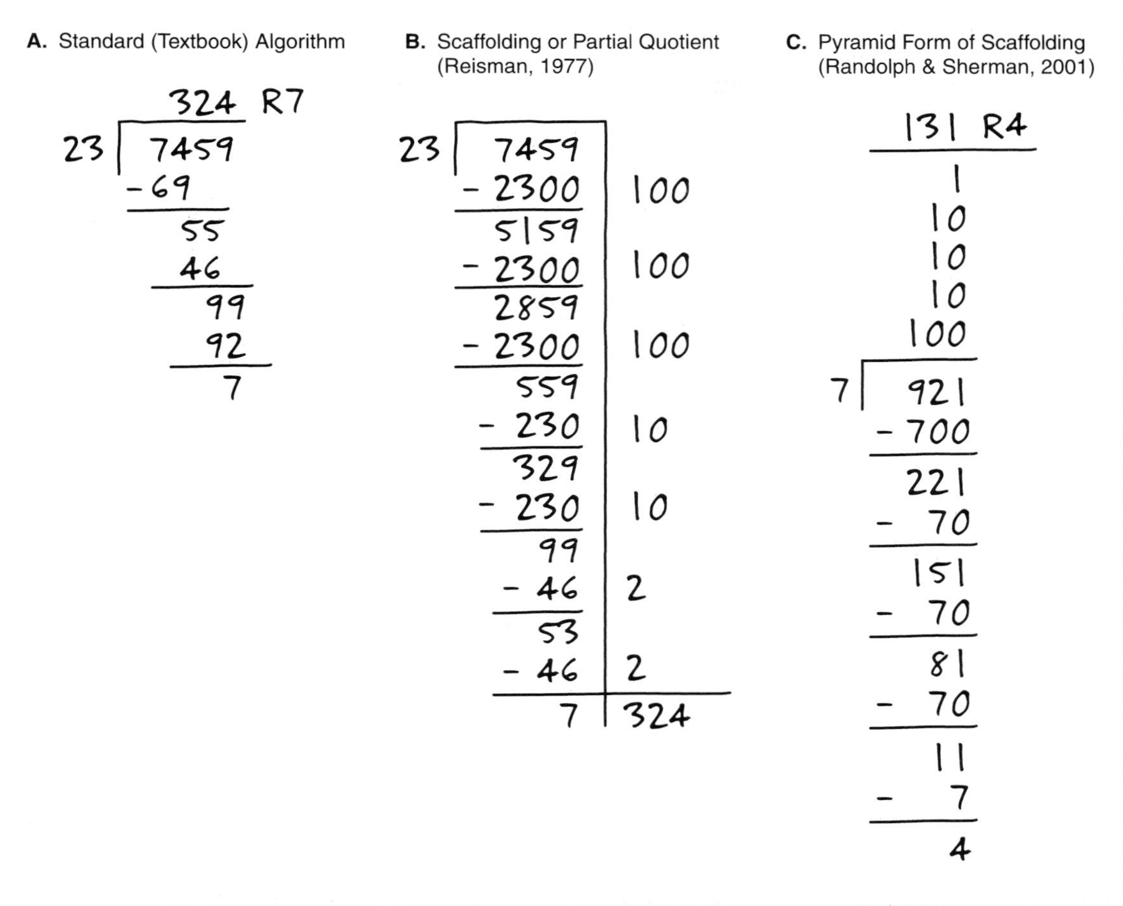

A. Standard (Textbook) Algorithm

```
        324 R7
   23 | 7459
       -69
        55
        46
        99
        92
         7
```

B. Scaffolding or Partial Quotient
(Reisman, 1977)

```
   23 | 7459
      - 2300 | 100
        5159
      - 2300 | 100
        2859
      - 2300 | 100
         559
      -  230 | 10
         329
      -  230 | 10
          99
      -   46 | 2
          53
      -   46 | 2
           7 | 324
```

C. Pyramid Form of Scaffolding
(Randolph & Sherman, 2001)

```
        131 R4
          1
         10
         10
         10
        100
    7 | 921
      - 700
        221
      -  70
        151
      -  70
         81
      -  70
         11
      -   7
          4
```

When teachers try these algorithms for the first time, they may find them confusing. Many parents and educators are skeptical about their usefulness because they are not the "standard" approach. However, for certain students they can be quite effective. These students have had trouble with traditional algorithms, especially with the notation system or memory burdens imposed by those procedures. An often-unexpected benefit is for the student to realize that he knows a math "trick" that other students want to learn.

Students can also invent their own effective algorithms if they have the requisite understanding of the underlying concepts (place value, effects of operations, properties). Student-developed algorithms should be encouraged but monitored for concept fidelity and effectiveness.

Finally, it is important to remember to embed the use of these operations with a range of number sizes into different types of problem situations, across all mathematics content areas. Applying the operation accurately and efficiently when needed is the goal of computation instruction.

MULTICULTURAL CONNECTION

The ancient Egyptian civilization spanned thirty-one dynasties and 3,000 years, until 335 B.C.E., but their contributions to mathematics and daily life are evident today in architecture, astronomy, time measurement, written language, and textiles. Through sources such as the Rhind and Moscow papyri, scholars have determined that the Egyptians could only express fractions as added unit fractions with numerators of 1. For example, 23/24 was expressed as $\frac{1}{2} + \frac{1}{4} + \frac{1}{8} + \frac{1}{12}$. They used addition to perform multiplication and division calculations (Baker & Hopwood, 1997). Multiplication involved progressive doubling and adding. In the example below, 14 times 24 begins by placing the number 1 in the first column and one of the factors, 24, in the second column (the process is quicker using the larger factor but will work with either). Double the numbers in each column until the next number in the first column would be larger than the second factor (14). In this case the last double is 8 because the next one would be 16, larger than 14. Check off the numbers in the left-hand column that add up exactly to the other factor $(2 + 4 + 8 = 14)$. Add up the corresponding numbers in the right-hand column for the final product $(48 + 96 + 192 = 336)$.

1	24
2✓	48✓
4✓	96✓
8✓	192✓
	336

RESOURCES

Morrow, L. J. (Ed.). (1998). *The teaching and learning of algorithms in school mathematics.* Reston, VA: NCTM.

National Council of Teachers of Mathematics. (February, 2003). Computational fluency (special issue). *Teaching Children Mathematics.*

Many curriculum developers now have the research base for their computational series online. For example, Curriculum Associate's Math FACTMASTER CD-ROM Program for building and assessing fact fluency: www.curriculumassociates.com.

Strand C   Spatial Sense

After studying this strand, the reader should be able to:

1. Describe the uses of spatial sense across the mathematics curriculum
2. Provide examples of student abilities at the different van Hiele levels of geometric thinking
3. Discuss issues related to the assessment of spatial abilities
4. Provide examples of methods for building spatial abilities at each grade level span
5. Discuss mathematics applications that involve both number and spatial reasoning

Steven is a tenth-grade student in Mr. Lopez' geometry class at Hilltop High School. Steven has received special education services for reading and language disabilities since the third grade and now has sufficient strategies to be enrolled in general education classes for all his core subjects. Steven has had problems interacting with peers in social situations and participates minimally in cooperative learning groups. His mathematics skills had always been average, strong computation skills and concepts, average problem-solving ability, and some difficulty with rational number representations. But high school geometry has been very difficult. Consider the following conversation between Steven and Mr. Lopez.

Mr. Lopez: Steven, what three-dimensional object is depicted on page 137 of your text? (pointing to a diagram of a cube).

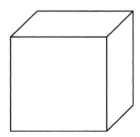

Steven: It looks like a square with sides.

Mr. Lopez: There are squares in that diagram but a square is two-dimensional. What is the three-dimensional form?

Steven: What do you mean, two-dimensional?

Mr. Lopez: It has length and width, the figure is only on a plane, it is flat.

Steven: This page is flat so that diagram is two-dimensional?

Mr. Lopez: The drawing has been done with perspective so that we can see the figure as three-dimensional. It is a cube with six squares as sides.

Steven: I see only one square and two other smaller parts. ■ ● ▲

Number sense has gained a lot of attention in the literature but other mathematical senses, such as spatial sense, have not been as visible. These senses, in some ways, are means of interpreting information from the environment, like touch or sight. But they are more cognitively involved—our abilities to make meaning of information, to understand, interpret, and organize information in ways that can be used to solve problems. Number sense, as described in content strand A, is an intuition about number, an understanding that numbers are representative of objects, magnitudes, relationships, and other attributes; that numbers can be operated on, compared, and used in flexible ways for communication and to solve problems.

Spatial sense, therefore, is an intuition about space, the relationships among objects or positions in space (including self), a sense of size, proportion, and distance, and an understanding of the properties that govern spatial relationships and the operations that create transformations, without necessarily the use of enumeration or even language. (The NCTM uses a narrower definition—the development of geometric relationships and the ability to use them in diverse settings). A quarterback throwing a football toward an imaginary point on the field where the receiver will be in a few seconds has spatial sense. A friend giving driving directions over the phone has spatial sense. A florist arranging flowers has spatial sense. A motorist pulling out to pass a slower car on a two-lane road must have spatial sense.

The terminology used in psychological and educational literature related to spatial abilities can be confusing and is not always consistent. The term *spatial orientation* has been used to describe "understanding and operating on the relationships between positions of objects in space with respect to one's own position" (Clements & Battista, 1992, p. 444). Another distinct component of spatial ability is *spatial visualization:* "comprehension and performance of imagined movements of objects in two- and three-dimensional space." A related concept is that of *imagery*—the ability to imagine or call up a mental picture of the arrangement of objects and their features from different perspectives, underlying both number and spatial senses. Wheatly (1998) used the term *imaging* as a metaphor for the mental or neural activity we cannot fully explain. Imaging is a process involving constructing an image (generation), re-representing the image (inspection), and transforming the image. Kosslyn (1980) built on those basic imaging components the process of maintaining an image while performing other cognitive functions such as problem solving.

Zimmermann and Cunningham (1991) credited technological advances for a "visualization renaissance" in mathematics (p. 1). They distinguished visualization applied in mathematics from common everyday or psychological forms that are purely mental images. "Mathematical visualization is the process of forming images (mentally, or with pencil and paper, or with the aid of technology) and using such images effectively for mathematical discovery and understanding" (p. 3).

This strand will explore the importance of spatial abilities for mathematics learning, describe the development of spatial skills, and investigate how mathematics-related spatial skills can be improved. The strand will close with a discussion of the integration of number and spatial sense.

IMPORTANCE OF SPATIAL SENSE

Persistent misconceptions about spatial skills for mathematics include the notions that these skills are only relevant for geometry and for secondary-level topics. In reality, spatial abilities are critical for most areas of mathematics and other content as well. The NCTM content strand "patterns, functions, and algebra" is highly dependent on spatial abilities—patterns can be spatial in nature, functions can be depicted graphically, and algebra is often depicted with geometric models (e.g., a cube represents x^3). The measurement strand is heavily spatial—measures of distance, volume, area, angle, and rate depend on spatial comprehension for problem solving. Data analysis, probability, and statistics often use spatial representations for depicting data and the results of analysis. Even numbers and operations rely on spatial concepts for number lines, number patterns, fractional representations, and operations such as grouping, partitioning, and factoring.

Other subjects in school draw on spatial abilities. Social studies and science make frequent use of mapping skills. Science also examines the properties of substances, objects, and living things in the Earth's environment and beyond and their relationships. Literature draws on the reader's ability to visualize for comprehension. And one of the best methods for learning new vocabulary is to use visual imagery for recalling a new word in the context of its meaning. Art, music, and physical education are inherently spatial domains. Finally, effective teaching techniques, regardless of subject area, include hands-on learning, concept mapping, diagramming, and modeling, all highly spatial methods.

Special education professionals may approach spatial sense with trepidation, given the unproductive work in the areas of modality teaching (e.g., visual learners), perceptual-motor training, and perceptual-motor assessments in the 1960s and 1970s. As a result, too many special education assessments and interventions in mathematics have focused on easy-to-measure computation and rote learning rather than more powerful mathematics concepts, such as spatial reasoning, and their connections with other concepts. Spatial abilities that are necessary for mathematics tasks are not simply visual perceptions or the integration of visual and motor senses, they are complex cognitive abilities that are difficult to assess. Perceptual-motor assessments make no connections with mathematics abilities, learning, or teaching. "We do not know what they measure because they do not measure anything consistently . . . . they are technically inadequate . . . and neither theoretically nor psychometrically sound" (Salvia & Ysseldyke, 2001, p. 511).

Mathematics curricula in the United States have received a lot of criticism for shallow treatment of geometry and spatial concepts. The typical elementary curriculum devotes very little time to "geometry," and the topics addressed are a hodgepodge of unrelated concepts, primarily recognizing and naming shapes, writing the proper symbols, and using simple formulas (Clements & Battista, 1992). In middle school, students are introduced to more symbols and formulas and are taught to use construction tools, but the time devoted to geometric concepts is minimal. The situation in many high schools may be worse, with separate courses devoted to geometry with few connections to other mathematics concepts. This separation of content is disturbing, because much of the thinking required in higher mathematics is spatial in nature (Yakimanskaya, 1991).

The dismal situation in the U.S. was reported widely by the 2003 Trends in International Mathematics and Science Study (NCES, 2004), finding that eighth graders in the U.S. did not improve in their geometry skills since the 1999 testing and answered only 45 percent of geometric items, lower than 18 other countries, equivalent to two (Romania and Cyprus), and higher than only eight. One question asked for the measure of an angle, given three other angles' measures. Only 22 percent of U.S. eighth graders could solve that problem. On the fourth-grade exam, which was not broken out by content areas within mathematics, only 39 percent of U.S. fourth graders could answer a question providing a view of one arrangement of five blocks that required them to select a turned view of the same group of blocks, lower than the responses of fourth graders (9-year-olds) in 17 other countries but higher than students in Tunisia, Armenia, Lithuania, Cyprus, Iran, the Philippines, and Morocco.

Probably the most important reason for emphasizing spatial activities and skills in the curriculum is the strong connection between spatial ability and overall mathematics achievement at all grade levels (Clements & Battista, 1992). Many mathematics concepts, even nongeometric ones, have visuospatial dimensions by which students understand and manipulate ideas. Some students need concrete representations or drawings, others can manipulate spatial concepts mentally, yet most students need spatial reasoning as a thinking tool to progress to higher levels in mathematics.

DEVELOPMENT AND ASSESSMENT OF SPATIAL ABILITIES

Everyone develops some sense of space by interacting with things in the environment. What we learn through personal experiences, without formal instruction, is called informal knowledge. As discussed in Chapter 2, young children come to school with informal mathematics knowledge but older students and adults also continue to learn informally through everyday experiences. This informal knowledge of students can be tapped to enhance formal and guided learning activities. Often, individuals are not even aware of their own tacit knowledge (Gravemeijer, 1998). For example, you may have never studied art or architecture but when you view a drawing such as the one in Figure C.1, you know that the tree is really larger than the window. You are able to interpret, without formal training, the relative sizes and distances depicted in the drawing.

Figure C.1
Perspective at Work

Teachers can determine students' informal knowledge (or misconceptions) about spatial sense through informal assessments, listening to students describe objects and their relationships. Before teaching a unit on quadrilaterals, ask students to name and describe everyday shapes. Before teaching a unit on volume, ask students to explain, in their own words, how people measure the contents of a car's gasoline tank or a large fish tank. Show students a line graph and ask them to explain what they know about it before teaching a unit on graphing using coordinate pairs. This knowledge of students' prior formal and informal understanding is invaluable for the teacher in planning meaningful instruction and assessing new learning.

Mathematical reasoning about space based on informal knowledge develops slowly and does not evolve spontaneously, however (Lehrer, Jacobson, Kemeny, & Strom, 1999). Teachers must provide high-quality, guided learning experiences. The following section discusses some of the more prominent theories of the development of spatial skills. A later section will provide recommendations for teacher-guided learning experiences to promote mathematical spatial reasoning at all grade levels.

Development of Spatial Abilities

What do we know about the development of spatial and geometry concepts in children and youth? The psychologists Piaget, Inhelder, and Szeminska studied these concepts in children in the 1940s (published in English in 1956 and 1960). Major tenets of their work included:

■ Representations of space are constructed through a developmental process involving the organization of motor and cognitive (internalized) skills; therefore, spatial reasoning is not just perceptual but an accumulation of prior experience with the environment and cognitive activity.

■ The organization of geometric ideas follows a specific order—topological relationships, projective space, and Euclidian relations. Topological discrimination is the ability to recognize features of figures such as closed or open and curved or linear (ages three to four for simple shapes; six to seven for more difficult shapes). Projective space begins when the figure is considered in relation to a point of view or perspective (about age seven). Euclidian space involves the development of a two-dimensional framework (a coordinate system) and metric relations for making spatial connections, about nine years of age.

These theories have been criticized for inaccurate uses of mathematical terms such as *topological* and *Euclidian*, and children's drawings to accurately represent their thinking. Further, there is some evidence that all three relational abilities are developing somewhat simultaneously and at some point become integrated (Clements & Battista, 1992). Yakimanskaya, a Soviet psychologist whose work from the 1960s and 1970s was translated into English in the 1990s, pointed out that the order of concept development in mathematics curricula was actually reversed, beginning with measuring and the metric (Euclidian) relations of space, followed by projective relations, and then topological relations. She posited that the difficulties noted in children's concept development, especially with transformations between two- and three-dimensional objects, is related to inappropriate curriculum and instruction.

A more current view of the development of spatial abilities is based on a modification of the van Hiele levels of geometric thinking (van Hiele, 1959/1985; Fuys, Geddes, & Thischler, 1988; Clements & Battista, 1992; Clements, Swaminathan, Hannibal, & Sarama, 1999):

■ Level 0: **Pre-recognition** (proposed by Clements & Battista, 1992). Children perceive geometric shapes but attend to only part of the shapes' characteristics. For example, a four-year-old is asked to sort attribute blocks and sorts them by color. When asked to sort them another way, she is unable to view attributes other than color.

■ Level 1: **Visual.** Students identify and operate on shapes according to their appearance and can mentally represent figures as visual images. Clements, Swaminathan, Hannibal, & Sarama (1999) termed this the syncretic level because of their findings that the synthesis of verbal declarative and imagistic knowledge are at work, not just visual matching. For example, young students worked with cut-out rectangles and triangles one day. The next day the teacher asked them to draw a rectangle and a triangle from memory. They could visualize one shape with three sides and one with four sides.

■ Level 2: **Descriptive/Analytic.** Students can characterize shapes by their properties but do not see the relationships between classes of figures. For example, a student can sort two-dimensional objects by shape, size, and texture but do not see the similarities between quadrilaterals, rectangles, and squares.

■ Level 3: **Abstract/Relational.** Students can classify figures and give informal arguments. One student justified his argument that a square is a quadrilateral by showing that a square has four sides, with opposite sides parallel and angles of 45°.

■ Level 4: **Formal deduction.** Students can use an axiomatic system to establish theorems and construct original proofs. A middle school student can use Euclid's axioms about lines, circles, and angles to construct a proof of the length of a line segment in relation to a circle's radius.

■ Level 5: **Rigor/Meta-mathematical.** Students can reason formally about mathematical systems, thinking about figures and relationships without reference models. A high school student views the formula $AB = \frac{1}{2}(AC)\sqrt{2}$, where AC is the hypotenuse of a 45–45–90 right triangle and AB is the length of either leg. The student is able to relate this formula to that of a 30–60–90 triangle without using a visual model.

Many studies have confirmed these levels as useful in describing students' geometric concept development. However, it is important to note that moving up in levels is a process of achieving a higher level of abstraction and generalization, and that all students will work at "lower" levels when they choose. There is some evidence that students do not enter level 2 until sixth or seventh grade and some students, especially low achievers, will still be performing at level 0 or 1 (Fuys, Geddes, & Tischler 1988). Movement to level two requires guided instruction. Ninth graders may be at very different levels, with 12 percent at level 1, 44 percent at level 2 with some level-1 lapses, and another 44 percent performing at level 2 with some movement to level 3. Some researchers have estimated that 40 percent of students finish high school at or below level 2, clearly not prepared for college mathematics (Burger & Shaughnessy, 1986).

The van Hieles (Pierre and Dina) asserted that progress through these levels is not due to biological maturation but facilitated by teachers and the curriculum through active and constructive but **guided** learning opportunities. Clements & Battista (1992) proposed setting earlier geometric goals for children, achieving levels 2 or 3 in the presecondary curriculum; employing more precise language in geometry instruction; and using manipulatives and real world objects to support concept understanding.

A more recent synthesis of the van Hiele model and the SOLO taxonomy (discussed in Chapter 3; see Figure 3.15) was made by Pegg and Davey (1998) to provide a means for investigating individual differences in cognitive growth in geometry. The two models were merged through applying each of the SOLO modes within each van Hiele level: unistructural (one aspect is the focus of attention), multistructural (two or more unrelated aspects), and relational (full control of the imaging process with consistent classification).

Researchers continue to explore the development of spatial abilities but need to address student differences beyond the many studies related to gender and cultural differences. Do students with visuospatial deficits demonstrate different or delayed development of spatial abilities? How are those deficits related to other abilities such as verbal and metacognitive skills? Can early interventions have an impact on spatial ability development? How can spatial abilities, that are essentially cognitive functions, be assessed with a clear relationship to mathematics learning?

Assessment of Spatial Abilities

Research on the development of spatial abilities relies on valid and reliable assessment of cognitive abilities, elusive and uneven abilities measured indirectly using overt tasks. Assessment, in turn, often depends on language or drawing skills that can skew results in favor of some children and to the detriment of others. It is critical that educators consider appropriate assessment strategies when evaluating research on spatial abilities and screening students for potential spatial deficits.

Yakimanskaya (1991) characterized the spatial aptitude tests of Western psychologists as quick measures of "visual acuity, keenness of observation, and quick-wittedness" because subjects were asked to view artificial symbols or diagrams and evaluate interrelationships and patterns. These tests assess visual acuity, the ability to evaluate lines for size and position, and the ability to modify figures visually, only part of spatial reasoning and not connected with mathematical or other concept development or instruction. Yakimanskaya and her fellow Soviet researchers theorized levels of spatial thinking that, unlike the van Hieles' and Piagetian theories, were sensitive to individual differences and assumed that developmental differences were due to instructional differences (social learning theory). The Soviets described spatial thinking as "a multi-faceted, hierarchical whole, and essentially multi-functional" (p. 102).

Yakimanskaya's research team developed diagnostic problems that included a range of complexity levels; offered a view into problem-solving processes, not just solutions; were not dependent on specific curricula backgrounds; varied in graphic type; and were relatively brief in form. For example, one problem asked subjects to view a drawing of overlapping circle, triangle, and rectangle and to shade the intersection of the three figures. Another problem depicted four congruent right triangles and asked subjects to mentally create and then draw other figures that use all four triangles (triangle, rectangle, rhombus, trapezoid, hexagon, and non-rhombus, non-rectangular parallelogram).

These diagnostic problems were used in research with middle-school students to determine individual differences in spatial reasoning. Three groups of students emerged: a highly creative group that solved most of the problems (80–90%) quickly and with flexibility (3–4 minutes each), a second group that could handle many of the problems (60–70%) but less efficiently (5–6 minutes each) and with less creativity, and a third group that found most problems difficult and solved only 30–40 percent in 6 to 9 minutes each and were described as stubborn problem solvers with low independence. These three groups represented the researchers' three levels of spatial thinking—high, medium, and low. In this and subsequent studies, the researchers concluded that individual student differences can be observed in ability to create static and dynamic images and flexibility in creating and manipulating images.

Two general types of visuospatial assessments that inform mathematics instruction can be described as static and dynamic. **Static** assessments are those that are snapshots of a student's ability, typically using standard drawings of two- and three-dimensional objects. For example, a common assessment task is to show a student a picture of an object and ask the student to point to one of three pictures with the same object flipped or turned. **Dynamic** assessments attempt to capture processes, movement, and change through student interaction with objects, drawings, and concepts. For example, a student is shown a rectangle and asked to draw as many lines of symmetry for the rectangle as possible. In this task the researcher is able to detect the student's approach to the problem (such as paper folding), self-corrections, comments about the task, and duration of the activity. Mathematics skills are related to both static and dynamic tasks (Reuhkala, 2001), so both types of assessments may be needed. However, many studies incorporate only static assessments.

Some educators are concerned that students with spatial deficits (and related mathematics problems) are not identified as early as those with verbal deficits, sometimes not until the geometric concept demands of middle school. Concerned with the paucity of valid means for early identification, Cornoldi and his colleagues (2003) developed an 18-item screening measure for visuospatial learning disabilities. The *Shortened Visuospatial Questionnaire* (SVS) was developed for teachers to rate items such as comprehension of visuospatial relations, spatial orientation, skills in observing the environment, and dealing with novel objects. The purpose of this simple screening device is for earlier identification of children who may need further assessment for visuospatial deficits. Research with Italian and British children demonstrated validity for this purpose and appropriate reliability (.90 and .95) for teacher use.

Most diagnostic mathematics tools, such as the *KeyMath-R-NU* and *Stanford Diagnostic Mathematics Test 4*, include a subtest on geometry. These test items typically ask students to recognize shapes, apply formulas or theorems, and interpret diagrams. They do not assess spatial abilities such as imaging, making transformations, or manipulating images for problem solving. Evaluators administering these standardized instruments are not allowed to probe understanding or ask a student to continue developing a concept sampled too briefly. Because of the dearth of valid and reliable spatial assessments that can be linked to mathematics instruction, most researchers must create their own assessment devices, making research interpretation even more challenging.

Research with Students with Disabilities

Visuospatial deficits, or nonverbal learning disabilities, have been identified as a subtype of learning disabilities by a number of researchers (Gross-Tsur et al., 1995; Geary, 2003; Cornoldi et al., 1997; Rourke & Conway, 1997). Students with visuospatial disabilities (VSLD) demonstrate specific characteristics, including:

- difficulties processing nonverbal, nonlinguistic information
- stronger on verbal tasks on assessments than nonverbal or performance tasks

- social skills deficits, especially with attending to nonverbal communication and new situations; excessive verbalizations but with rote or meaningless content and literal interpretations
- mathematics deficits in problem solving, concept formation, visuospatial activities, and graphomotor tasks
- visuospatial working memory problems, but not with verbal memory

Performance of students with learning disabilities on geometric tasks has been studied since the mid 1970s. Students with LD typically can discriminate geometric shapes but perform lower than their peers on tasks requiring the reproduction of shapes and mental operations on complex spatial tasks (see, for example, Swanson, 1993).

Grobecker and De Lisi (2000) studied spatial-geometrical understanding in students with and without learning disabilities. Dynamic assessments in the study included anticipatory imagery tasks using pegboards and rubber bands and geometric figure drawing tasks, both with squares and diamonds. Students with LD were much fewer successful in both types of tasks and used more movements of pegs and less coordinated strategies overall. Both groups of students demonstrated the same (Piagetian) developmental trends, with the LD group demonstrating significant delay at each level.

Several current researchers are conducting systematic study of visuospatial working memory and its relationship to mathematics. Reuhkala (2001) studied the relationship between working memory capacity and visuospatial working memory (VSWM) with 62 ninth grade (15- to 16-year-old) Finnish students. The results from both static and dynamic tasks indicated a relationship between visuospatial ability, especially static VSWM and mental rotation capabilities, and overall mathematical skills. It was also found that mathematical skills in general were independent from phonological working memory and verbal central executive capacity. The author suggested that VSWM is the blackboard, the place where visuospatial operations needed in mathematics take place—an active processing system rather than a passive storage component. She also proposed that deficits in VSWM may lead to limited capacity for temporarily storing and processing visuospatial information while working problems, and that students with these deficits would need concrete supports as compensation.

Keeler and Swanson (2001) investigated the relationship between strategy knowledge, verbal working memory (WM) and visual-spatial WM in children with calculation-specific mathematics disabilities. Visual-spatial tasks in this research involved mapping and giving directions, from the second author's *Cognitive Processing Test*. "Stable strategy choices in the verbal domain and strategy expertise in the visual-spatial domain predicted mathematics performance" (p. 431). Both verbal and visual-spatial WM contributed significant, but independent, variance in mathematics ability. Implications for improving mathematics achievement in computation included improving students' knowledge base of effective strategies for mathematics in both verbal and spatial typologies.

There is growing evidence that students' spatial abilities can be improved with training and that younger students can work with concepts, such as projection, earlier than introduced in most textbooks if spatial experiences are guided (Yakimanskaya, 1991). However, very little research has been conducted on interventions with low achievers or students with disabilities. The next section provides recommendations for working with students with visuospatial deficits and related mathematics learning problems.

DEVELOPING SPATIAL ABILITIES ACROSS THE MATHEMATICS CURRICULUM

The NCTM curriculum standards (2000) emphasized geometry and spatial skills throughout the K–12 curriculum, with important applications for the process standards as well: connections among mathematics concepts, representations, problem solving, reasoning and proof, and communications. Across the curriculum, students should be exposed to **clear and specific language** for describing spatial concepts. For example, the terms *line*, *point*, and *plane* have very specific applications in Euclidian geometry. A line is not just any marking but "the set of points that move directly between two points" and continue infinitely in both directions. A line segment has two ending points. A ray has one ending point (Sidebotham, 2002). But the side of a three-dimensional shape is a special form of line called an *edge*, and edges and planes meet at special points called *vertices* (*vertex* is the singular). A line graph uses lines segments between points identified by coordinates.

Another guideline for developing spatial abilities across the curriculum is to use **good models**—hands-on objects, drawings, and computer simulations—for representing spatial concepts, describing terms and relationships, and demonstrating the results of operations on objects. Students should be encouraged to create their own models, at an age-appropriate level, and to describe and manipulate them. Manipulative use that is guided and connected to concepts has been demonstrated to benefit spatial concept learning at all grade and ability levels (Sowell, 1989). However, textbooks in the U.S. recommend their use for geometry only infrequently, and K–6 teachers report using manipulatives less than once a week or not at all. Teachers in Japan and Britain use manipulatives and other spatial models much more often (Clements & Battista, 1992).

Younger students can trace and cut out two-dimensional shapes that can also be turned and folded. They can use common containers with lids to represent three-dimensional shapes such as cubes and cylinders. Older students can construct two- and three-dimensional objects with increasingly sophisticated tools and precision. Students with fine motor problems may need to use computer models to represent shapes at their level of understanding. And computer modeling is excellent for demonstrating a range of spatial concepts once children are able to understand what a computer image represents. More in-depth information on manipulatives and computer applications is in Chapter 6.

Teachers at all grade levels should model cognitive imaging processes by employing **think-aloud techniques** (see Chapter 3). For example, if the teacher is demonstrating how to create and manipulate a mental image of a transformed triangle, he could describe aloud his own thoughts, "I am now holding the image of this triangle in my mind, like a picture inside a camera. I see the three sides of the triangle, and one angle is a 90-degree corner. Even if I turn it in my mental image, one angle is still that right angle. Now I am changing the triangle in my head so that none of the angles is a right

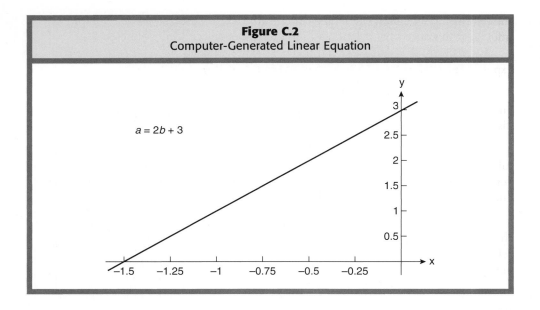

Figure C.2
Computer-Generated Linear Equation

$a = 2b + 3$

angle. Can you imagine that triangle also? I'm going to draw mine and I want you to draw what you think I was seeing in my head." Another teacher teaching algebraic equations might say, "Here is a graph of the equation $a = 2b + 3$ (show computer-generated image, as in Figure C.2). Where does the line cross the x-axis? The y-axis? Imagine how this graph would change if the equation were $a = b + 3$. Will the line have the same slope? Will it intersect at the same points? Let's find out if your mental image is correct."

Most textbooks promote rule, procedure, and definition instruction in geometry and other mathematics areas involving spatial sense such as measurement and graphing. This approach to instruction can cause dislike for these special mathematics topics, little concept understanding, and not much generalization. Perhaps more than any other domain, spatial sense requires interaction with models for understanding. The recommendations that follow for each grade span focus on active student engagement with objects and materials. These activities work best in teacher-guided instructional settings that employ explicit language, scaffolding, corrective feedback, individual accommodations, and planned generalization.

Promoting Spatial Development: K–2

Between kindergarten and grade 2, students should observe and describe two- and three-dimensional objects and their properties, manipulate these objects for applying spatial relationships, slides, flips, and turns. Young students should be able to create mental images of shapes. In reality, many children in the early grades are exposed to only simplistic geometric concepts (identifying circles and squares) that rarely harness their informal knowledge.

Lehrer, Jacobson, Kemeny, and Strom (1999) built on young children's informal experiences in four areas to develop spatial understanding:

■ Large-scale space activities such as walking, giving directions, using a compass, and map drawing (classroom and school) promote the concepts of position, direction, distance, and scale.

■ Drawing activities such as creating nets (two-dimensional patterns that can be folded into three-dimensional shapes, as in Figure C.3) help develop concepts of faces, vertices, and edges. Others, such as simple graph making, assist with connecting number and space concepts.

■ Physical experiences with shape and form, such as discussing attributes of specific shapes, lead to clearer mathematics language and understanding properties and their relationships. For example, discussing a possible definition of triangle may develop concepts such as symmetry, sum of angles, and types of triangles.

■ Early number activities that connect with measurement concepts, as with measuring length with children's feet, strips of paper, or personal units tape measures, develop concepts of length, equal units, partial units, and even proportional representations of measured objects.

Other recommendations for younger students to promote spatial skills include:

■ Gamelike activities with music or literature can promote the understanding of spatial terms such as over, under, around, between, behind, among, on, above, inside, and so forth.

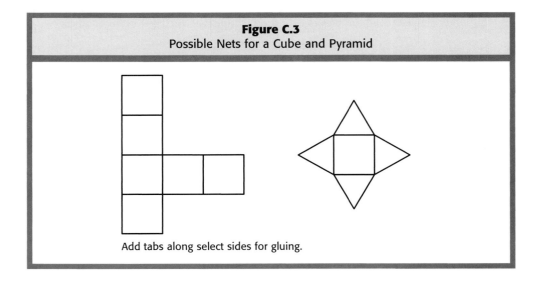

Figure C.3
Possible Nets for a Cube and Pyramid

Add tabs along select sides for gluing.

■ Seeking patterns in the environment, such as those in fabrics, architecture, nature, and art, can help children generalize their concepts of shapes.

■ Frequent interaction with solid and plane figures offers young children a more generalized sense of shape and the vocabulary for discussing shapes. Some activities include matching shapes to environmental models (triangle to the yield sign), cutting out shapes for designs, and cutting specific shapes into puzzles for reassembly (Rowan, 1990).

■ Guided activities with pattern blocks include making shapes, describing shapes, matching shapes, and even transforming shapes. Special grid paper (diagonal lines) is also useful for tracing shapes and covering areas with blocks.

■ The Quick Draw strategy (Wheatley, 1996) promotes imaging through training students to hold specific mental images in their working memory. A geometric drawing is shown to students on an overhead projector for 2–3 seconds, then students are asked to draw what they saw. A quick second look is provided. Finally, the drawing is shown for discussion about what students "saw" and how they attempted their drawings.

■ The Tangram Task (Wheatley & Cobb, 1991) involves briefly projecting for students a form and set of Tangrams creating that form. They are asked to fill the same form at their desks in the same pattern (see Figure C.4).

■ Liedtke (1995) recommended using a block collection (at least two each of many different types, painted the same color) to develop spatial concepts of perspective, characteristics of three-dimensional shapes, categorization schemes, connecting two-dimensional drawings (or overhead projector shadows) to three-dimensional objects, and creating sketches of objects.

■ Wooden proportional unit blocks (1:2:4), often used for building structures in kindergarten classrooms, can be used to develop spatial sense through activities such as creating other shapes using the blocks—rhombus, trapezoid, hexagon—and creating

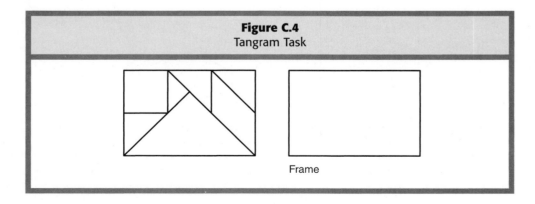

Figure C.4
Tangram Task

Frame

block patterns with the same area (called "surface covered" for younger children) as another pattern (Andrews, 1999).

Promoting Spatial Development: 3–5

In grades 3 to 5, students investigate more complex shapes and can classify by many properties and make more complex transformations. They develop facility with the coordinate grid for geometry and other applications. There is some evidence that elementary students actually perform spatial transformations more creatively and originally than older students (Yakimanskaya, 1991), possibly because older students have been taught restricted solution methods within narrow examples.

Activities that promote spatial development include:

■ Using dot paper to create shapes and patterns, even tessellations (a design that covers a plane with no gaps or overlaps). Dot paper can be created in many forms (rectangular array, isometric, hexagonal) and used throughout the grade levels to develop increasingly complex concepts: area, perimeter, congruence, symmetry, and angle (see for example Pandiscio, 2001).

■ Assisting students with new mathematics vocabulary by explicitly teaching morphemes and mnemonics. For example, the prefixes *milli-* and *centi-* mean thousandth and hundredth. A polygon has many (poly) sides, a quadrilateral has four (quad) sides. The sequence of metric measures can be recalled by KHDMDCM—King Henry Drinks Much Dark Chocolate Milk or other similar sentences created by students.

■ Exploring with Geoboards—activities such as stretching or shrinking shapes, calculating area and perimeter, and reproducing shapes with given attributes, transfering shapes from Geoboards onto dot paper, and playing re-creation games with Geoboards.

■ Folding paper can be adapted to any grade level. In one activity, the teacher folds a piece of paper (once or twice) and cuts off parts. While the paper is still folded, students are asked to draw what they imagine the paper will look like when unfolded (Wheatley & Reynolds, 1999). Another activity involves using Origami-type folding to create boxes of differing dimensions to compare dimensions and capacity (Higginson & Colgan, 2001). Many other paper folding activities can promote geometric concept understanding, problem solving, and accurate vocabulary use.

■ Creating nets for three-dimensional objects. Students can create all possible nets for a given object (e.g., eleven are possible for cubes) and match nets with faces of different colors to their corresponding objects (Leeson, 1994).

■ Combining interconnecting cubes or tiles to explore tetrominoes (shapes with four pieces), pentominoes (five pieces), or hexominoes (six pieces). Using pieces with different colors changes the number of possible combinations for patterns if color is considered a variable. Students should be encouraged to record their solutions on graph paper as a way of organizing and interpreting results (Olson, 2002).

Promoting Spatial Development: Middle Grades

In the middle grades, students' skills with classification and transformation of shapes should become more sophisticated with more drawing, construction, and transformation of objects; applying reasoning and mathematical arguments to problems; and making connections with numeric and algebraic concepts. However, half of middle school students have not developed the visualization and spatial reasoning skills to be prepared for high school topics.

Activities that can promote spatial sense in the middle grades include:

- Exploring patterns of geometric shapes such as the ones in Figure C.5. Triangles, squares, trapezoids, and other shapes with $\frac{1}{2}, \frac{1}{4}, \frac{1}{8}, \frac{1}{16}$, (and so forth) of the shape represented inside can link concepts of fractions, area, exponents, and two-dimensional models (Chávez & Reys, 2002).

- Creating nets of various dimensions and shapes can teach concepts such as least amount of surface area or greatest volume for real-world problems such as designing food packaging or architectural features. After creating nets, students can fold and glue them into their three-dimensional objects and check hypotheses about volume using rice.

- Constructing pyramids and prisms encourages students to explore more complex objects. Patterns or diagrams with bird's eye, worm's eye, and side views, along with rulers, compasses, card stock, scissors, and glue are needed for these activities (DeTemple & Miedema, 1997).

- Guiding students to "discover" formulas for areas of plane figures through Geoboard and grid paper activities (Rowan, 1990). For example, a parallelogram drawn

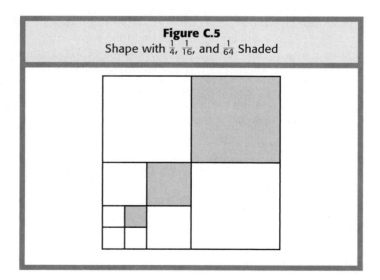

Figure C.5
Shape with $\frac{1}{4}, \frac{1}{16}$, and $\frac{1}{64}$ Shaded

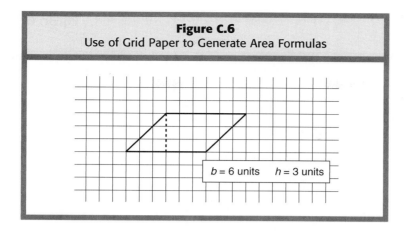

Figure C.6
Use of Grid Paper to Generate Area Formulas

$b = 6$ units $h = 3$ units

on grid paper can be cut and reassembled into a rectangle for counting the internal squares (see Figure C.6). Then students should be prompted to consider the roles of base and height of the rectangle and parallelogram in computing area.

Promoting Spatial Development: High School

In high school, students should develop deeper understandings of geometric ideas and conduct investigations of conjectures using many tools, including computer software. Geometric models are used for solving problems in other areas such as algebra and trigonometry. Unfortunately, many high school students still study geometry as a separate course, focused primarily on rote learning of construction and proof procedures and not connected with other areas of mathematics.

A note is needed here about the nature of high school geometric concepts. Euclidian geometry, often termed "school geometry," is axiomatic in nature. It is based on a set of five axioms that are generally believed true and don't require proof on which to build theorems, through logical arguments (Sidebotham, 2002). For example, one theorem is the *Angle Sum of a Triangle Theorem* that states that the three angles of a triangle add up to 180°. This theorem assumes specific notions about line, point, and angle.

There are other approaches to geometry, including analytic, transformational, and vector, that are important for college-bound students and are included in the 9–12 NCTM content standards (Clements & Battista, 1992). Analytic, or coordinate, geometry dates back to Descartes (Cartesian coordinates) and involves graphing on a plane with points identified with coordinates. This system allows geometric and algebraic problems to be treated with the methods of the other. Vector geometry extends coordinate plane concepts to represent magnitude and direction. It also involves both geometric and algebraic concepts. Transformational geometry is the study of how sets of points and their positions in space are changed by enlargements, reflections, rotations, and translations (Sidebotham, 2002).

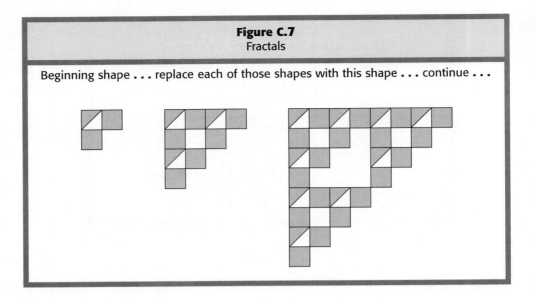

Figure C.7
Fractals

Beginning shape . . . replace each of those shapes with this shape . . . continue . . .

Some ideas for developing high-school level spatial concepts include:

■ Exploring the properties of fractals with square tiles and interlocking cubes (see Figure C.7). A big idea for fractals is the concept of *similarity*. When one plane figure is an enlargement of another plane figure, the two figures are similar (Sidebotham, 2002). These figures have the same shape, the angles are equal, and corresponding sides are in the same ratio. When one solid shape is an enlargement of another, the two objects are *similar shapes*. Fractals actually demonstrate self-similarity and these can be built (generated) in two- and three-dimensional models for better understanding. However, these representations will not demonstrate all properties of fractals, such as moving inward in the same pattern rather than creating larger and larger models (see full discussion in Coes, 1993).

■ Paper folding combined with drawing can be used to develop very sophisticated concepts such as parabola, ellipse, and hyperbola (Smith, 2003). For example, an ellipse is, in common terms, an oval. It has two axes of symmetry and the order of rotational symmetry is two (Sidebotham, 2002). A paper folding activity can be used to develop the concept of parabola by drawing a circle, a fixed point, and a random point within the circle. Fold the fixed point onto the random point and make a crease. Repeat foldings with other random points many times. A parabola emerges with several folds, an ellipse is formed within many folds, and selecting an outside fixed point for the same activity results in a hyperbola (see Smith, 2003 for details and proof procedures). An ellipse also can be drawn using two thumbtacks, a loop of string, and a pencil. The two thumbtacks represent the two axes. And, of course, all these representations can be produced using The Geometer's Sketchpad or other graphing software.

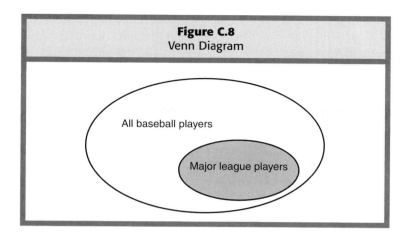

Figure C.8
Venn Diagram

All baseball players

Major league players

■ Using Venn diagrams (one type of Euler diagram) to explore types of reasoning—direct, indirect, and transitive—promotes experience with valid arguments (Van Dyke, 1995). For example, diagram the premise "all major-league baseball players use wooden bats" (see Figure C.8). Can either or both of the following conclusions be supported? All baseball players use wooden bats. Andruw Jones is a major league baseball player; therefore he uses a wooden bat. Convert statements to symbolic form $p \rightarrow q$: If p happens, then q will happen.

■ Using interactive computer applications illuminates the properties of polygons, platonic solids (faces are congruent regular polygons), other polyhedra, cylinders, cones, spheres, and other two- and three-dimensional geometric figures. Computer images can be rotated and manipulated in other ways, depending on the website or software used. More powerful applications allow students to enter variables or parameters into function tables to change figures' dimensions and attributes. Computers can also assist students with visualizing complex ideas such as proportionality, transformations, and symmetry.

INTEGRATION OF NUMBER AND SPATIAL SENSE

Measurement, like geometry, can involve one-, two-, or three-dimensional spatial reasoning. The earliest measurement activities with young children attempt to convey the concept of equal units of measure. One-dimensional measures (linear) can be made using the length of most any object—a shoe, block, paper clip, or book. Standard units of measure include metric and English units. With either system, students must grasp spatial concepts of repeating units and partial units, and numeric concepts of the zero position and counting units.

Three-dimensional units of measure are expressed in units cubed or volume. Two basic metric units are those for liquids—the liter and multiples or portions of a liter—and space—the cubic meter and its permutations. English units include the many, many measures of liquids (e.g., cup, gallon) and cubic units (e.g., cubic inch, cubic yard). Students need practice with marked containers and liquids or rice (to represent space) in order to develop visual comparisons of units.

Two-dimensional measure is typically via the Cartesian coordinate system—representations of positions on a plane and related concepts such as area and perimeter that depend on linear concepts as well. Spatial and numeric structuring can be connected through area-based activities such as work with rectangular arrays and grids, covering patterns with shapes to determine number of shapes needed to cover an irregular area, and predicting areas of regular and irregular shapes (Battista, 1999). Coordinate system and two-dimensional spatial concepts are also critical for graphing and mapping.

Another type of plane-surface measure is that of angle, performed with a protractor. Students with learning problems are often confused by the concept that an angle has a specific measure regardless of the length of the rays. They also have difficulty remembering which scale on the protractor to use and should be prompted to classify the angle by its appearance as acute or obtuse (and therefore less or more than 90°) prior to the measurement. The reflex angle can be computed by subtracting the angle measure from 360° or through measurement using a circular protractor.

Rational numbers are particularly spatial in their conceptualization. An essential big idea of rational numbers is the concept *parts per unit*, often a visual image for students. If the unit is one length of rope, then one-third would be a smaller section of the rope, smaller even than one-half. It would take three of the smaller pieces to be the same length as the original piece. If the unit comprises ten boxes in a "shipment," then half a shipment would be five boxes. Rational numbers—including fractions, decimal fractions, percents, proportions, and ratio—will be explored in depth in the next strand. The reader should keep in mind the integration of number and spatial sense for those concepts.

MULTICULTURAL CONNECTION

Mathematically significant spatial concepts are evident in the art and architecture of many cultures. Native Americans (Yup'ik, Hopi, and Navajo), Africans (Asante and Kuba), and natives of South America (Inca, Mayan), Europe (Celtic, Hungarian, Scandinavian), Asia, Austrialia, and the Pacific Islands incorporated traditional geometric patterns for weaving, pottery design, house decoration, and jewelry (see, for example, Zaslavsky, 1996). In the United States, quilts were first sewn by pioneer women to make use of every scrap of worn clothing (Krause, 2000). The designs for these quilts are extremely varied and have been handed down through generations. Consider the geometric properties of the quilt pattern "wheels" depicted in Figure C.9. How can the concepts of symmetry, rotation, and tessellations be developed by using quilt patterns? What other concepts can be developed?

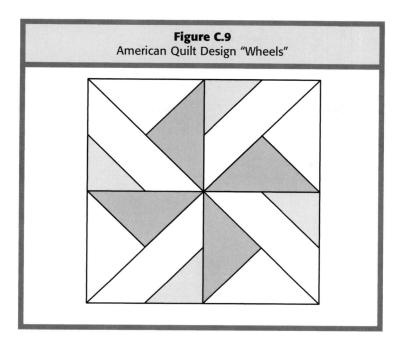

Figure C.9
American Quilt Design "Wheels"

RESOURCES

Clements, D. H., & Battista, M. T. (Eds.). (2001). *Logo and geometry*. Reston, VA: NCTM.

Cuoco, A. A. (Ed.). (2001). *The roles of representation in school mathematics*. Reston, VA: NCTM.

Del Grande, J. J., & Morrow, L. J. (1993). *Geometry and spatial sense*. Reston, VA: NCTM.

Jackiw, N. (1995). *The Geometer's Sketchpad*. Berkeley, CA: Key Curriculum Press. (Software)

NCTM *Navigating through Geometry* series (K–2, 3–5, 6–8, 9–12).

Olson, A. T. (1975). *Mathematics through paper folding*. Reston, VA: NCTM.

Strand D Rational Numbers

After studying this strand, the reader should be able to:

1. Describe the relationship among rational numbers—fractions, decimals, and percent— and the five types of rational number representations
2. Provide examples of proportional reasoning and probability
3. Describe the most common problems with rational number concepts
4. Discuss strategies for teaching rational number concepts

Henry is an eleven-year-old student with learning disabilities in reading and mathematics. His sixth-grade teacher at Maple Street Middle School is attempting to determine Henry's fraction concept understanding.

Mrs. Quaid: May I show you a picture of something and see if you know what it is. What is in that picture? [Shows a picture of a 6-pack of soda.]

Henry: I guess just soda pop cans or whatever.

Mrs. Quaid: Yes, soda pop cans, they are connected by those plastic things so you can carry them. They are called 6-packs. If you drank 2 of those, could you write me a fraction to show me how much you drank? Do you know how to write fractions?

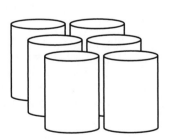

Henry: [Draws 6 lines on a piece of paper and marks through 2 of them.] Two-fourths?

Mrs. Quaid: Okay, can you write that as a fraction and explain it pointing to the cans?

Henry: [Writes $\frac{2}{4}$.] There are two here that I drank and four over there. ■ ● ▲

Rational number extensions beyond whole numbers, such as those of fractions and decimals, are often the first major conceptual challenges for students who have been working primarily with whole number concepts. Rational numbers are important for real-world applications and are essential for higher-level mathematics understanding. The concepts embedded within these constructs are complex and interconnected: proportion, ratio, equivalence, multiplicative reasoning, measure, decimal, percent, and rate. This strand will describe and illustrate the critical concepts related to rational numbers, offer common student misconceptions, and provide instructional strategies across the grade levels. Additional sources on these concepts are provided at the end of the strand. The reader should be aware that trained mathematicians still struggle to define terms and explain concepts related to rational numbers. Educators often were not provided adequate instruction in these concepts in their own K–12 experiences. Confusing terms or symbols are common in mathematics texts and journals. With more personal experience with rational numbers and observing the explorations of students and listening to their reasoning, educators can develop a stronger understanding that should continue to evolve and deepen.

RATIONAL NUMBERS

The diagram of the real number system in strand A (Figure A.1) illustrates the domain of rational numbers under which numbers are classified as integers (negative and positive whole numbers including zero) or non-integral numbers. Rational numbers are all numbers that can be expressed as $\frac{a}{b}$ where $b \neq 0$. Therefore 8 is a rational number because it can be expressed as $\frac{8}{1}$. The fractions $\frac{10}{15}$, $\frac{8}{12}$, and $\frac{4}{6}$ all represent the rational number $\frac{2}{3}$. These fractions are not separate rational numbers, they are all equivalent expressions of the same rational number. The rational number $\frac{1}{2}$ can be expressed in decimal form (termed *decimal fraction*, a number with no digits to the left of the decimal other than zero) as .5 or .50 or .500. A mixed decimal includes an integer and a decimal fraction as in 3.94. The rational number $\frac{1}{3}$ can be expressed as a repeating decimal fraction: $.33\overline{3}$. But decimal fractions that are not repeating or terminating (finite), such as π or $\sqrt{2}$, are irrational.

Rational numbers also can be expressed in percent form: 50%, 25.16%, or $33.3\overline{3}\%$. The word *percent* means *for each hundred*, so two decimal places are implied. The expression 50 percent means 50 per one hundred or $\frac{50}{100}$ or $\frac{5}{10}$ or .5. These equivalent forms all refer to the rational number $\frac{1}{2}$. A more precise definition proposed by Behr, Harel, Post, & Lesh (1992, p. 296) characterizes rational numbers as "elements of an infinite quotient field consisting of infinite equivalence classes, and the elements of the equivalence classes are fractions."

There is some agreement in the literature on five types of rational numbers (Behr, Harel, Post, & Lesh, 1992): part-whole comparisons, quotient, ratio, operator, and measure. Students often have trouble with rational number concepts because they have not had experience with applications of all five types or their experience was too abstract, not connected to models, real-world applications, or their informal mathematics understanding.

Part–Whole Comparison

Part-whole comparison is the comparison of one or more equal parts of a unit to the total number of equal parts. Part-whole comparisons use the familiar fraction notation with the part as numerator and whole as denominator. But they're not as simple as slices of pizza. The unit may be one object (continuous) such as one rectangle or one circle. In that case $\frac{3}{4}$ looks like

and $\frac{5}{4}$ looks like

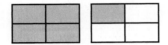

If the last diagram represented one unit rather than two, then the fraction for the part shaded would be $\frac{5}{8}$. The same diagram could be interpreted as $\frac{5}{4}$ or $\frac{5}{8}$, depending on the unit. Interpretation is relative to the information provided. When the unit comprises more than one object (discrete) as in sets, it is often easier to consider familiar units such as one group of children or a bag of clothespins. Discrete objects comprising one unit that come in familiar groups are called composite units, such as six-packs of soda or a dozen eggs. Students need practice with this unitizing or thinking about and visualizing a unit in different sized chunks (Lamon, 1999). The guiding question is, "What is the unit?"

Quotient

The quotient view of rational numbers includes part–whole comparisons (partitioning) and a representation of one share or part. The quotient is the division of the number of objects by the number of shares. The guiding question is, "How much is one share?" For example, eight children have four sticks of licorice. What part will each child receive? The answer is expressed as division: $\frac{4 \text{ sticks}}{8 \text{ children}}$ or $\frac{1}{2}$ stick for each child.

Ratio

Ratio is also a comparison but between two quantities. There is one teacher for each group of 20 children. This state has two registered cars for every three people. Some ratios compare part to part (five boys to six girls) and some compare part to whole (five boys in the group of eleven children). A special and powerful type of ratio is **rate,** comparing measures of different types such as $1.90 per gallon, 60 miles per hour, and

80 heartbeats per minute. In science, as depicted in Chapter 1 (Figure 1.7), some measures are actually ratios: speed, density, Hertz. To distinguish ratios, sometimes colon notation is used (3:2) and sometimes the compared measure is hidden in the notation (45 mph). It should be noted that ratios are not always rational (1: $\sqrt{2}$ and 5:0). Ratios may not be operated on in the same way as fractions. Students should consider the context of a problem before applying operations arbitrarily. Adding further to the confusion are the often careless uses of the terms ratio and rate in everyday language. A guiding question for ratios should be, "What type of measure does each term represent?"

Operator

The operator view of rational numbers is considering the rational number as a function or actively applied to or transforming something. Operators can enlarge, reduce, multiply, divide, increase, and decrease other objects. For example, applying $\frac{3}{4}$ to a garment's original price of $25 gives the process of taking $\frac{3}{4}$ of $25 or $18.75. How would we return the garment to its original price? By using the operator $\frac{4}{3}$, or the inverse, the operation becomes $\frac{4}{3}$ of $18.75, resulting in $25.00. (For readers who thought about adding $\frac{1}{4}$ of the amount, consider that these operators are *multiplicative*, not additive, and that the word *of* means multiply.)

Students who were taught that multiplication results in a larger number will be confused by the results of rational numbers as operators. Multiplying by a proper fraction will result in a smaller quantity; by an improper fraction, a larger quantity. Lamon (1999) proposed an exchange model for operators. The operator $\frac{2}{3}$ means that for every three items you give or put in, two will come back, or "two for three." The function machine concept can help students visualize the operator exchanging amounts. The guiding question for operator views of rational numbers is, "Am I being asked to take a fraction OF another quantity?" Students should have experiences with different types of fractions—proper, improper, and mixed forms—and recognize the results of multiplicative operators on these forms.

Measure

The measure concept of rational numbers is best visualized using a number line, but students should be exposed to other situations such as vertical and circular gauges. Between any two whole numbers along the line or arc are an infinite number of rational numbers. Figure D.1 illustrates the division between whole numbers 2 and 3 into four equal parts and into 16 equal parts. Students can compare the fractions $\frac{1}{4}$ and $\frac{1}{16}$ on parallel number lines. They can compare the measures of $\frac{4}{5}$ and $\frac{5}{7}$, often very difficult to sketch by hand using rectangles or circles. This measurement model of rational numbers is excellent for recognizing equivalent fractions, developing a sense of magnitude, and understanding the effects of addition and subtraction of fractions. This model also assists students with concepts of exactness and estimates. A guiding question for using measures is, "In this situation, can a number line be used to illustrate the relationship?"

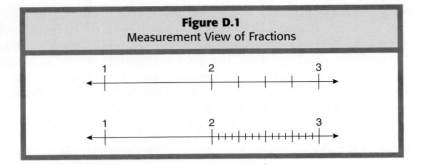

Figure D.1
Measurement View of Fractions

RELATED CONCEPTS

Concepts closely related to fractions, decimal fractions, percents, and ratios are those of equivalence, proportion, and probability. These concepts are critical foundations for algebra, data analysis, and higher-level problem solving.

Equivalence

Equivalence is a concept of sameness. One child has five pennies and another has a nickel. With experience, children understand that coins can have equivalent values regardless of number, appearance, or size. They understand that equivalent does not mean identical.

In mathematics, equivalence refers to a state of having the same value, magnitude, weight, force, or other comparative property. Some examples: $2 + 3 = 5$; 1 pound $= 16$ ounces; the area of square A is equivalent to the area of triangle C. Figure D.2 illustrates the importance of equivalence across the mathematics curriculum.

In set theory, *equal* and *equivalent* are distinct concepts. Equal sets contain the exact same elements; equivalent sets have the same total number of elements, but not the exact elements. In set theory, the = sign indicates equal sets with exactly the same members. For example, the set of children in Mrs. Bird's class = the set of children who attend art class with Mr. Philips. Equivalent sets are those whose members can be paired exactly using one-to-one correspondence. For example, a set of six pieces of fruit is equivalent to a set of six children, but the members are not exactly the same.

When young children are first introduced to formal mathematical notations (symbols) such as $2 + 3 = 5$ or

$$\begin{array}{r} 2 \\ + 3 \\ \hline 5 \end{array}$$

they tend to think of the parts as the "problem part" and the "answer part."

In the example above, the = sign or the horizontal line tells children "here comes the answer" rather than indicating equivalence when comparing sides of the equation. The equation $2 + 3 = 5$ means that the $2 + 3$ part is equivalent to the 5 part, so

Figure D.2
Equivalence across the Mathematics Curriculum

NCTM Strand	Illustrative Topics	Examples
Number and Operations	Arithmetic operations	$5 + 2 = 7$; $27 = 9 \times 3$
	Arithmetic properties	Identity property, inverse property, commutative property, property of 0
	Simplifying fractions	$\frac{5}{15} = \frac{1}{3}$; $\frac{6}{3} = 2$
	Converting between fractions, decimals, and percents	$\frac{1}{2} = \frac{50}{100} = .5 = 50\%$
	Exponents	$8.3 \times 10^{-4} = .00083$
	Negative Integers	$-5 - (-3) = -5 + 3$
Patterns, Functions, and Algebra	Algebraic properties of equality	Transitive (if $a = b$ and $b = c$, then $a = c$) Substitution (if $a = b$, then a may replace b or b may replace a)
	Solving equations and inequalities with one variable	$4x + 7 = 264$
	Factoring polynomials	$ca + cb = c(a + b)$
Geometry and Spatial Sense	Angles	Sum of angles of rectangle $= 360°$
	Symmetry	Reflection: divisible into two mirror images
	Formulas for 2- and 3-dimensional objects	Perimeter (sum of sides); Area (length $\times$ width variations)
Measurement	Time	60 minutes $=1$ hour
	Distance	1 foot $= .3048$ meter
	Volume	length $\times$ width $\times$ height $=$ cubic volume
	Currency	4 quarters $=1$ dollar
Data Analysis, Probability, and Statistics	Graphing	Different types of graphs can represent the same data.
	Least-squares regression line	$Y = .33x - 93.9$

Source: Standards reprinted with permission from *Principles and Standards for School Mathematics,* copyright 2000, by the National Council of Teachers of Mathematics (NCTM). All rights reserved. Standards are listed with permission of the NCTM, which does not endorse the content or validity of these alignments.

$5 = 2 + 3$ is also true and we can add one (or other amounts) to each part or subtract amounts from each part and maintain the equivalence: $5 + 1 = 2 + 3 + 1$ or $5 - 2 = 2 + 3 - 2$. These concepts and terms should be developed from the early grades with consistency as a foundation for more advanced algebraic experiences.

● ● ● ● ● ● ● ● ●
For solutions to the
problems presented in
this book, visit the
Companion Website at
www.ablongman.
com/gurganus1e.

● ● ● ● ● ● ● ● ●

Proportion

Proportion is one of the most useful concepts for mathematics problem solving and is based on the concept of ratio. As discussed in a previous section, a ratio is the comparison of one quantity with another using the same units by dividing. A proportion is the relationship of two ratios. A direct proportion is when two ratios are equal; inverse proportion involves one quantity increasing while the other decreases (Sidebotham, 2002). For example, 1 is to 2 as 3 is to 6, resulting in the proportion $\frac{1}{2} = \frac{3}{6}$. This direct relationship between elements in a proportion becomes particularly useful when one element is unknown. By applying the rules of mathematics, or properties and axioms, a student can solve for the unknown, regardless of its position within the proportion.

> We have six pizzas for our class of 24 students. How many pizzas would be needed for 30 students?

6 is (related) to 24 as the unknown is (related) to 30:

$$\frac{6}{24} = \frac{x}{30}$$

This problem can be set up with a different proportion:

6 is to the unknown as 24 is to 30: $\frac{6}{x} = \frac{24}{30}$

Proportional reasoning is more than setting up and solving a proportional equation. It is thinking about and comparing the relationships depicted in a variety of ways, through graphs, charts, and equations. It is a way to study and predict changes in the relationship. Some proportional relationships are simple and direct such as using one cup of water for every one-half cup of rice. You can reason how much water you would need with two cups of rice. Both quantities change in the same direction. An example of an inverse relationship: we have more workers today so the job will take less time. Proportional relationships also can be complex, with multiple variables changing in different ways.

Probability

Probability is closely related conceptually to proportional reasoning and ratio, yet has been treated as a separate domain in most textbooks. Probability refers to the chance of something happening and is useful for a wide range of applications, including many in science, social science, sports, and, of course, gambling. It is often paired with statistics because data sets are used with both domains and within statistics the characteristics of data sets intended to predict or generalize include confidence intervals (errors of measure) that represent the probability of a given event, view, or other situation.

Working with probability problems requires knowledge of the sample space (the set of all possible outcomes) or at least a good estimate of that value. The probability of an event is equal to the number of times something can occur divided by the number of events that could possibly occur. For example, the probability of selecting a red playing card is $\frac{26}{52}$ or $\frac{1}{2}$.

Odds, on the other hand, refer to the probability of one event divided by the probability of the opposite event. For example, the odds in favor of selecting a diamond from a deck of cards is $\frac{1}{4} \div \frac{3}{4} = (\frac{1}{4})(\frac{4}{3}) = \frac{4}{12} = \frac{1}{3}$. Concepts of probability and odds are best explored with hands-on experiments where students record findings in data charts.

COMMON PROBLEMS AND RECOMMENDATIONS FOR INSTRUCTION

The concepts of rational numbers, proportion, ratio, and equivalence are found primarily in the NCTM content standard "numbers and operations," but applications can be found in all the standards. Commonly used fractions, such as $\frac{1}{2}, \frac{1}{3}$, and $\frac{1}{4}$, are included in the PreK to grade 2 standards only briefly because of the developmental challenges of rational numbers. In grades 3 to 5, students' concepts of numbers are extended to include numbers less than 0 and fractional parts of the whole. By grade 5, students should be fairly fluent with using fraction, decimal, and percent forms of rational numbers: recognizing fractions, percents, or decimal forms as parts of wholes, as parts of a collection, as locations on a number line, and as divisions of whole numbers. They should be expressing fractions in simplest terms, adding and subtracting fractions and decimal numbers, and converting between fractions, decimals, and percents. By middle school, students are expected to work flexibly with whole numbers, fractions, percents, and decimals to compute, solve problems, make conversions to other number forms, and in applications within measurement, geometry, and data analysis. Many students with learning problems will not develop the connections among fractions, decimals, and percents or be able to solve related problems by fifth grade. Even with excellent instruction, these students may need more time and experiences to develop rational number concepts that are robust enough for algebraic and calculus concepts.

Common Problems

Rational numbers are among the most difficult concepts for students to understand and apply. For example, on the 2003 TIMMS study of mathematics performance, only 19 percent of fourth-graders could explain the commonalities of shaded diagrams representing $\frac{3}{6}, \frac{1}{2}$, and $\frac{5}{10}$ (U.S. Department of Education, 2004). On the 2003 Program for International Student Assessment (PISA) in mathematics literacy, 15-year-old students in the U.S. scored lower on each mathematics subscale than the international average of 29 industrialized countries (NCES, 2004). Only Italy, Portugal, Greece, Turkey, and Mexico had lower average scores. The mathematics category "quantity" involved operations with whole and rational numbers and magnitudes of numbers. One item in this category asked students to compute a monetary exchange rate. It was answered successfully by 67.8 percent of U.S. students and 74 percent of the whole sample. A second item asked about the relative changes in exchange rates (more complex proportional reasoning). U.S. students scored 37 percent, while the total average was 40 percent on this item.

Reasons even good students struggle with this area of mathematics vary considerably. Some researchers point to the complexity of the domain—rational numbers are not absolute; they represent relationships that are inherently complex (Hope & Owens, 1987; Baroody & Hume, 1991). Others explore the effects of the many underlying structures (number sense, spatial sense, multiplicative reasoning, proportional reasoning) and sub-constructs (measure, quotient, ratio, operator, part–whole) that challenge students' understanding of rational numbers (Kieren, 1988; Grobecker, 2000). Another often-identified factor is students' lack of access to quality instruction by teachers knowledgeable in rational number concepts and effective pedagogy (Boulet, 1998).

Research on specific difficulties with learning about rational numbers has yielded important insights that have direct implications for instruction. A few researchers noted students' confusion of algorithms and misapplication of algorithms (see, for example, Kelly, Gersten, & Carnine, 1990). However, these surface-level error patterns are symptomatic of a deeper issue—students lack a fundamental understanding of rational number concepts because of inadequate curriculum design and instructional practices (Baroody & Hume, 1991). Boulet (1998) offered a taxonomy of problems with understanding fraction concepts divided into four classes of difficulties: equipartition (viewing equal parts of different types of wholes), reconstitution (reversing the operation from parts to a whole), order (comparing sizes), and quantification (using symbols, language, and numbers to represent relationships). To understand learning problems with rational numbers, teachers must probe student understanding on a wide range of applications, not simply spot algorithm errors and re-teach rules by rote.

Instructional Strategies for Fraction Concepts

The most important factor for effective teaching about fractions is to provide models that are developmentally appropriate, represent concepts well, and provide clues about student understanding. Students should be able to manipulate the models and use them as references for later concepts. Models should show the wide range of problem types and be connected to student experience and real-world applications.

Often fractions are introduced in a very simplistic, limited way that confuses students and can actually create misconceptions about the properties involved. An example is the use of a pizza to show simple fractions. The basic idea is a sound one—use familiar materials to introduce new concepts. However, a circle is one of the hardest shapes to divide evenly—even with measurement tools. A critical understanding for parts of wholes is that each part is equivalent. Strips of paper and connecting cubes are more easily divided into even parts. Further, the pie example is too close conceptually to whole number ideas (you have 4 parts and eat 1 part, now you have 3 parts).

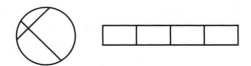

Basal textbooks typically present fractions as simple shaded areas of shapes—rectangles, circles, and triangles—in first- and second-grade books. Third-grade texts require students to compare fraction magnitude and begin adding and subtracting fractions. In late third grade or fourth grade, mixed fractions and operations with decimals are introduced. The concepts of ratio, percent, and probability aren't typically introduced until late fifth grade, after multiplication and division of all fraction forms.

In a review of three textbook series, Carnine, Jitendra, & Silbert (1997) found that big ideas related to fractions (underlying concepts) were rarely identified or integrated into instruction, content was introduced too rapidly and not interconnected, teaching demonstrations were vague, and review opportunities inadequate. Textbooks varied considerably in the integration of hands-on materials and depth of material in the teachers' guides. The authors noted that special education teachers, in particular, might not have the mathematics content expertise needed to modify and augment these limited materials. All teachers should analyze the sequence, methods, and depth of fraction instruction offered by adopted textbooks and make necessary modifications or use alternative materials (see Chapter 6).

Kalchman, Moss, and Case (2001) proposed an alternative sequence of instruction, citing the merging of spatial and numerical structures (senses) at about age nine or ten. During the first level of understanding, when whole-number concepts of counting and simple addition and subtraction are developing (ages three to five), children should be exposed to simple halving and doubling activities. During the second level (about age six), most children are able to represent problems both verbally and symbolically and should be able to make halves or doubles of other numbers ($\frac{1}{2}$, $\frac{1}{4}$, $\frac{1}{8}$ or 100%, 50%, 25%). At level three, about age seven, children should understand the basic relationship between fractions, decimals, and percents. By about ages nine to ten, children begin to develop a generalized understanding of the entire number system, and, depending on concurrent spatial development, can move fluidly among number representations and use a mental rational number line to solve problems. The authors proposed a fourth-grade sequence of instruction that begins with introduction to percents and computing with percents followed by an introduction to decimals using stopwatches, number lines, and games. Fractions were taught last with direct connections to percent and decimal concepts.

▲ ■ ▲ ● ▲ ■ ▲ ● ▲ ■ ▲ ● ▲ ■ ▲ ● ▲ ■ ▲ ● ▲ ■ ▲ ● ▲ ■ ▲

TRY THIS
Examine the rational number sequence of instruction in a local district textbook series.
▼ ■ ▼ ● ▼ ■ ▼ ● ▼ ■ ▼ ● ▼ ■ ▼ ● ▼ ■ ▼ ● ▼ ■ ▼ ● ▼ ■ ▼

Students should develop concepts of fractions using a variety of examples in both continuous quantities and as discrete quantities or sets (Baroody & Hume, 1991). Useful concrete materials for parts of sets include equal size and shape objects (cubes) and varying size and shape objects (buttons, plastic lids). There are twelve plastic lids on the table. Four are red. What fraction of the lids is red? Students should have experiences with continuous (paper strips, centimeter rods), transitional (egg cartons, interlocking cubes), and discrete (crayons, toy cars) materials for stronger concept development of both models of rational numbers (Behr, Wachsmuth, & Post, 1988). Development of subconstructs—part-of-whole, ratio, measure, quotient, and operator—can also be enhanced through hands-on manipulation of real-life or representational objects such as people, everyday objects, cooking supplies, number lines, rulers, and other measuring devices.

As teachers scaffold student understanding from concrete to representational, many students with learning problems will view diagrams of fractions as new concepts. Teachers should bridge student understanding by having them diagram actual concrete objects and verbally describe their drawings. "I drew this picture of the crayons on my desk—three are pink and two are blue. I can say that two-fifths of my crayons are blue. And three-fifths are pink."

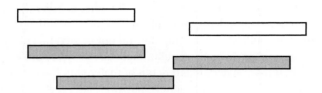

As students gain experience with drawings, they will be able to use more abstract representations, such as graph paper, to depict fractional parts.

By prompting students to use language to describe fractions and related concepts, students will more easily move to the fully symbolic format: $\frac{3}{5}$ is called three-fifths, which means that there are three equal parts out of five in all, or there are 3 crayons for 5 children, or we found that $\frac{3}{5}$ is the same number as $\frac{6}{10}$ which is $\frac{1}{10}$ more than $\frac{5}{10}$ or $\frac{1}{2}$. They begin using mathematical vocabulary such as numerator, denominator, common fraction, improper fraction, mixed number, equivalent, and simplified or reduced form. For many students this is like learning a foreign language, requiring many opportunities for oral expression and the direct connection of new vocabulary with concepts. Students often confuse number words such as ten, tens, and tenths; or have trouble changing word form, as from five to fifth.

The written form of fractions also can be confusing. For inexperienced students, the vertical fraction form, with a clear top and bottom and the division line between (—), may be clearer than a horizontal form with a diagonal line. The vertical format provides a more consistent representation for later operations using fractions such as multiplication, division, and even algebraic equations. But if state and district tests use both forms, students should be introduced to both.

$$\frac{2}{3} \quad \text{rather than} \quad 2/3$$

Another difficulty for many students is the concept that two expressions that look different mean the same amount. How can $\frac{6}{3}$ be the same as 2? How can $\frac{4}{12}$ be the same as $\frac{1}{3}$? And what about $2\frac{3}{4}$ and 2.75? To assist with these equivalent forms of number, teachers should use maps of the relationships such as fraction strips, graph paper, or number lines with fractions and decimals on opposing sides (see Figure D.3). Show students the patterns inherent in the decimal–fraction relationship. For fractions with tenths and fourths, try using dimes and quarters because most students have prior knowledge of their values in decimal form.

TRY THIS

Demonstrate the addition of $\frac{1}{2}$ and $\frac{1}{3}$ with paper fraction strips.

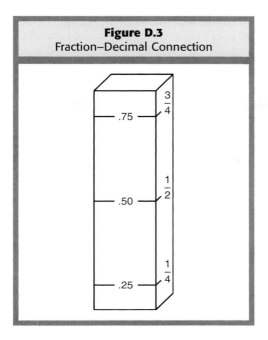

Figure D.3
Fraction–Decimal Connection

Students also confuse whole-number concepts taught in restricted ways with the broader multiplicative thinking required for rational number reasoning. For example, a restrictive view of multiplication is that products will be larger; division results in smaller quotients. Another is that zero is a placeholder with value when added to the end of a number. These perceptions will not apply to all rational numbers. Rational numbers are relative, not absolute, amounts. One-half of objects presented will depend on the unit in question. 150 percent of a wholesale price depends on the price. The mixed decimal 3.47 will not change with ten zeros added at the end because of their relative positions. Even after students with learning problems experience success with rational numbers, they sometimes experience "whole-number system" interference with their reasoning (Woodward, Baxter, & Robinson, 1999).

Here are some other instructional recommendations for fraction concepts:

■ Teach for concept understanding simultaneously with procedures. For example, students who don't understand why fractions must have the same denominator to perform addition and subtraction procedures but not multiplication and division will confuse procedures. The division rule "invert and multiply" makes no sense unless students spend a lot of time exploring their own procedures. Some students who really understand concepts are able to develop their own valid procedures.

■ Use real-life activities, especially for those very abstract concepts. For example, arrange students along a line parallel to a wall and ask them move $\frac{1}{2}$ the distance to the wall. Ask them to move another half and discuss that position as on a number line. Move another half distance toward the wall and keep repeating. Is it possible to find a final number of moves to reach the wall (concept of infinite rational numbers between 0 and 1)? Will an estimate be sufficient in this case?

■ Encourage students to use familiar fraction benchmarks ($\frac{1}{4}, \frac{1}{2}, \frac{3}{4}$) for problem solving, estimation, and magnitude comparisons.

■ Use a variety of teaching materials to promote concept generalization. Fractions aren't simply represented by sets of fraction circles. We can represent fractions with paper strips, graph paper, cubes, number lines, and so forth.

■ Provide practice not only in partitioning (into equal parts), but in reconstructing back to a whole. Use the term *whole* rather than *one* to prevent unit confusion (Brigham, Wilson, Jones, & Moisio, 1996).

■ Use virtual manipulatives with caution (see, for example, NCTM Illuminations or the National Library of Virtual Manipulatives). Use of these computer-world manipulations of virtual objects with students with learning problems seems promising but lacks a research base. Students need guided prompts and feedback to be successful with concept development using virtual or actual manipulatives.

■ Encourage estimation. For $\frac{3}{4} + \frac{1}{2}$, my answer will be more than 1 but less than 2. For $(\frac{1}{2})(\frac{5}{7})$ my answer will be only a half of $\frac{5}{7}$ between $\frac{2}{7}$ and $\frac{3}{7}$ on my mental number line.

■ Ask students to demonstrate fraction problems using manipulatives or other models, explaining their reasoning for other students in nonthreatening situations.

■ Allow a lot of time for fraction concept development between third and fifth or sixth grades. Students need to develop deeper concepts slower, not rush through rote procedures. Special and remedial educators' typical highly accelerated and economical mathematics procedures generally result in more time requirements for drill and practice, more errors, and low skill and concept transfer (Woodward, Baxter, & Robinson, 1999). Although students are faced with annual tests, these concepts do not develop in one year.

■ Connect fraction concepts with percents and decimals from their earliest introduction. Moving between different number representations is a form of "renaming." Begin with doubling and halving (50%, .50, $\frac{1}{2}$) across these number representations using familiar situations.

■ Many fraction problems ask students to express their results in simplest, lowest, or reduced terms (to rename the answer using the lowest numbers possible). Students need a lot of practice with equivalent fractions in activities such as matching or creating equivalent fraction games, parallel fraction lines, and finding the greatest common factor on hundreds charts. If we want to reduce $\frac{12}{16}$ to lowest terms, what is the greatest common factor of both 12 and 16? We can list or cover all the factors of both numbers and discover the greatest number is 4. Dividing both 12 and 16 by 4 results in $\frac{3}{4}$. Mastropieri and Scruggs (1994) offered a sequence of questions to guide attempts in reducing fractions. The first question was, "Can the denominator be divided by the numerator?" If that was not possible, students were encouraged to move through a sequence of questions based on divisibility rules beginning with 10, 5, and 3. (See the divisibility rules in strand B.)

■ Students need practice converting between mixed numbers and improper fractions, first through activities for understanding using number lines, objects, and diagrams, then through question prompts such as, "Is this fraction more or less than one?" Thought-provoking questions such as

"Why is $2\frac{3}{4}$ the same as $\frac{11}{4}$?"

can reinforce equivalence concepts.

■ By the end of middle school most students don't need objects to conceptualize rational number concepts; they use symbols. Students with learning problems may need object and picture references longer. But those prompts should be age-appropriate.

Strategies for Teaching Decimal Concepts and Calculations

As previously described, decimals are a way of naming fractions in a base-ten format with the decimal point indicating the position between whole number and fractional values. (Some countries use a comma instead of a decimal point.) While not all fractions can be converted into a precise decimal form, these representations of rational numbers are useful for measurement, calculators, and number magnitude comparisons. Teachers are sometimes so caught up in the challenges of teaching fractions and assume decimals are much easier to learn, they fail to notice the difficulties students encounter. The most common problems include not making the connection between fractions and decimals, applying whole-number concepts during procedures, and not understanding the role of the decimal symbol.

Here are some recommendations for instruction in decimal fractions:

■ Keep the big ideas of rational numbers in mind when planning instruction—multiplicative and proportional reasoning and equivalence.

■ Connect instruction in decimals to prior knowledge and experiences such as those with money, calculators, and fraction concepts.

■ Extend manipulatives used for place value and whole number concepts to decimals: base-ten blocks (Dienes blocks), place-value mats, graph paper, and number lines. These connections should show that decimals are part of the rational number system, not a new system of numbers.

■ Other good models for decimals are meter sticks, 10×10 grids, and computer-based manipulatives. A ruler with inches (fractions) on one side and centimeters (decimals) on the other is not a good representation because the units are different; therefore, the whole numbers are not aligned.

■ Clue students to focus on the tenths' place when comparing decimals. Use special highlighting or underlining to impress the importance of that perspective.

■ Don't assume that a mathematics textbook offers appropriate sequences, examples, or practice of decimal concepts and procedures. Critically review the total development of concepts across grade levels and modify or substitute as needed.

■ Encourage estimation before calculation. This tactic is especially helpful for multiplication and division procedures. For example, estimating 4.567×8.1789 will result in a product between 32 and 40, not 373 million!

■ Reinforce the interpretation of decimals across the curriculum, especially in science and social studies activities.

Strategies for Teaching Related Concepts

There is virtually no research on the instruction of related concepts such as percent, proportion, and probability with students with mathematics disabilities. Mathematical research that can assist teachers' understanding is that of cognitive psychology and mathematics education, specifically how concepts develop, misconceptions, and student differences in learning.

The most common misconception is that percent, proportion, and probability concepts are new and discrete number systems, not related to fractions, decimals, or each other. Another misconception, as with fractions and decimals, is that these concepts are simple. For example, many students readily understand benchmark percents such as 50 percent and 25 percent but have difficulty with the concepts underlying percent calculations (Dole, 2000). Dole (1999) found that 57 percent of eighth graders could calculate 4 percent of 75 but only 5 percent could solve a two-step word problem involving percents.

Limited research with average and above-average students (Lembke & Reys, 1994) found that above-average fifth graders without formal training in percents had informal knowledge about uses of percents in the real world and the concept of per 100, but most students viewed percents as amounts rather than ratios. Seventh graders also tended to view percents as amounts and had trouble using visual representations of percents. Seventh graders could use benchmarks to solve percent problems and had learned isolated rules but struggled to apply them in problems. Ninth graders viewed percents as easier than fractions and decimals and tended to apply a factor-factor-product strategy taught in an algebra course. Eleventh graders, who had not studied percents for two years, could apply percents to specific situations and use formulas taught in school. Even when they made errors, their answers were good approximations.

This limited research suggests that students can benefit from use of informal knowledge from the real world in understanding percent problems. They should also be encouraged to develop a solid concept of the "parts of 100" view of percents, benchmarks of percents for estimation and comparison, and visual models of total and percents. Formal instruction may have the effect of students' abandoning effective strategies; it should augment rather than replace informal learning.

Some researchers submit that percent procedures are best taught as proportional relationships, although proportional thinking takes a long time to develop (Parker & Leinhardt, 1995; Dole, 2000). Van de Walle (1998) identified the three most common percent problems as three versions of the following sample equation, each with a different unknown: 25% of 60 = 15. Dole (1999) offered a four-step process for solving these types of problems using proportional procedures: a) identify the elements, b) represent the percent situation as a proportion visually (dual-scale number line), c) translate the information into a proportion statement, and d) solve the equation. A percent problem reads, "A clothing store is offering 25% off the cost of any garment and Jerrod wants to buy a coat that costs $125. By how much would the cost be reduced?" The elements are the percentage reduction, the total cost and the unknown reduction amount. Visually, 125 is the total length of a number line and the percent reduction moves to a point down a mental number line by 25 percent. The reduction part will be less than the amount to be paid; both will be less than 125. A proportion statement would be $\frac{25}{100} = \frac{?}{125}$. Solving for the unknown would result in $100x = 125 \times 25$ or $x = 31.25$. The cost of a $125 coat would be reduced by $31.25, so the new price would be $93.75.

Dole found in further research with two mixed-ability groups of eighth graders that the proportional number line was a successful strategy for students to solve percent problems, especially when problems involved real-life examples (2000). The research results were not reported by ability level but the posttest scores averaged 66 and 76 percent as compared with 37 and 44 percent on pretests, indicating that although significant learning took place between pre- and posttests for the two groups, the instruction on concepts, rules, interpreting problems, equivalence, and representations (five teaching episodes over nine lessons) may not have been sufficient for some students.

Some teachers use both the proportional method and a three-case-equation method to teach students how to solve percent problems (Haubner, 1992). The equation method can also involve visual representations of percents but the equation would be drafted in either decimal or fraction form horizontally: 25% of 125 = x would read $.25 \times 125 = .31.25$ or $\frac{1}{4} \times 125 = 31.25$. The power in these methods for students with learning problems might be the visual models, as in Figure D.4.

Proportional reasoning is one of the most powerful and difficult mathematics tools. It has been called the capstone for elementary concepts and cornerstone of higher mathematics (Lesh, Post, & Behr, 1988). Lamon (1993) offered four problem types that involve proportional reasoning: well chunked (two quantities forming a rate such as miles per hour), part–part–whole (ratios of different subsets such as boys to girls), associated sets (unclear relationships such as children and crayons), and stretchers and shrinkers (one-to-one continuous mapping such as reducing a 5 × 7 photograph). Clinical interviews of sixth graders indicated that higher-level proportional reasoning was prompted by the concreteness of the problem representations, more easily used with associated sets and part–part–whole types. Lamon recommended beginning instruction with these types of proportions and using more representations for the more difficult types of chunking and stretching/shrinking.

Here are some other recommendations for developing proportional reasoning (Lamon, 1993; Billings, 2001; Chapin & Anderson, 2003):

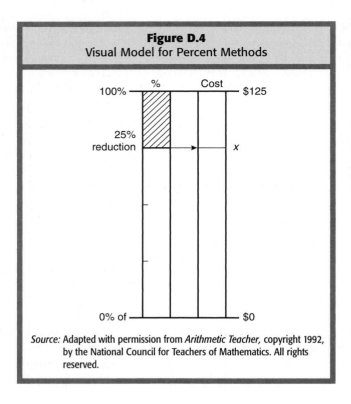

Figure D.4
Visual Model for Percent Methods

Source: Adapted with permission from *Arithmetic Teacher,* copyright 1992, by the National Council for Teachers of Mathematics. All rights reserved.

For solutions to the problems presented in this book, visit the Companion Website at www.ablongman. com/gurganus1e.

■ Pose problem situations that force students to see the difference between additive (absolute) and relative (proportional) perspectives. For example, the following problem could be solved from either perspective: *Jon and Libby bought three packs of paper from the school store and paid a total of $2. The class saw the paper and asked them to go back and buy 12 packs. How much did they pay for 12?*

■ Use nonnumeric problems to encourage reasoning. The following problem causes students to use proportional language and reasoning without having to compute. *Mary Jo and Caitlin decided to roller skate along the park path. One skates faster than the other but both started at the same time and maintained a constant speed. Mary Jo took longer to reach the end of the path. Who was skating faster? Explain why.*

■ Use arrows with the symbolic forms of proportion equations to show scalar and functional relationships (see Figure D.5).

■ As with fractions and whole number operations, use a variety of proportion problem types to deepen understanding. Allow time for concept development.

■ Use real-life situations as much as possible for percent, ratio, and proportion problems.

$$\times 4 \left(\frac{3}{12} = \frac{1.5}{6} \right) \times 4 \qquad \overset{\times .5}{\underset{\times .5}{\frac{3}{12} = \frac{1.5}{6}}}$$

MULTICULTURAL CONNECTION

A Chinese text, *Chiu Chang* (about first century C.E.), discussed a method for reducing fractions (Joseph, 1991). Begin with a common fraction and follow these steps:

■ If both numbers can be halved, then halve them.
■ Set the denominator below the numerator and subtract the smaller number from the larger number.
■ Continue this process until the common divisor (teng) is obtained.
■ Reduce the original fraction by dividing both numbers by teng.

For example, in the fraction $\frac{51}{85}$, the numbers cannot be halved.

51	51	17	17
85 subtract and get 34	34 subtract and get 17	34 subtract again	17

$51 \div 17 = 3$

$85 \div 17 = 5$ The simplified fraction is $\frac{3}{5}$.

An example with a fraction that can be halved:

$\frac{66}{330}$ halved would be $\frac{33}{165}$

33	33	33	66
165 subtract 33 is 132	132	99	66

$66 \div 66 = 1$

$330 \div 66 = 5$ The simplified fraction is $\frac{1}{5}$.

RESURCES

Barnett, C., Goldenstein, D., & Jackson, B. (Eds.). (1996). *Fractions, decimals, ratios, and percents: Hard to teach and hard to learn?* Portsmouth, NH: Heinemann.

Curcio, F. R., Bezuk, N. S., Armstrong, B. E., Artzt, A. F., Janzen, H., Klass, S. T., et al. (1989). *Understanding rational numbers and proportion: Addenda series, grades 5–8.* Reston, VA: NCTM.

Lamon, S. J. (1999). *Teaching fractions and ratios for understanding: Essential content knowledge and instructional strategies for teachers.* Mahwah, NJ: Lawrence Erlbaum Associates, Publishers.

Litwiller, B. (Ed.). (2002). *Making sense of fractions, ratios, and proportions: 2002 NCTM yearbook.* Reston, VA: NCTM.

National Library of Virtual Manipulatives, Utah State University. Web-based tools for visualizing fractions; comparing fractions, decimals and percents; and many other rational number concepts. Available at: http://matti.usu.edu/nlvm/nav/vlibrary.html.

NCTM Illuminations. Web-based tools such as Fraction Game, Fraction Pie, and Equivalent Fractions. Available at: http://illuminations.nctm.org/tools/index.aspx.

Textile Math: Multicultural explorations through patterns (grades K to 8). Wright Group www.wrightgroup.com. Activities involving logic, fractions, patterning, and measuring skills based on the textile designs from cultures around the world.

Strand E Functions

After studying this strand, the reader should be able to:

1. Provide examples of functional relationships, within and outside of mathematics
2. Trace a child's development of function concepts
3. Discuss common problems of students with learning problems in the areas of algebraic notation, simplifying expressions, solving equations, coordinate graphing, and solving linear functions
4. Use instructional methods that will promote concept development in functions and related areas

Sara is a new seventh-grade student at Maple Street Middle School. Ms Smith is assisting her mathematics teacher in conducting informal assessments of Sara's mathematics skills and concept knowledge.

Ms Smith: Sara, have you seen an equation like this one before? [2*x* + 5 = 11]. Can you solve this?

Sara: I think so. Two times five is ten so it should be 10, not 11.

Ms Smith: Why did you multiply to find that answer?

Sara: Because of the multiply sign right after the 2.

Ms Smith: OK, can you solve for what is missing in this problem? [7 = 15 + ?]

Sara: Well, the answer is seven, but it should be on the other side.

Ms Smith: Can you write what you mean by that?

Sara: [Writes 15 + ? = 7]. That's the way it should look.

Ms Smith: OK, can you solve for the question mark?

Sara: I think it is 22 but I'm not sure. I haven't had this kind of addition in a long time.

Function is a common word in the English language but is a big idea concept in mathematics, across the entire curriculum. Function, in its verb form, means to act or operate. The word originates from the Latin *fungi*, meaning to perform. The noun form is the action or performance. These meanings help us understand the mathematics use of the term. A mathematical function is the relationship where values of one term or magnitude depend on the values of another. It is a direct correspondence such that when an operation is applied to one it will also affect the other. For example, the price you pay for a tank full of gas depends on the cost of one gallon. If one gallon is $2.95, a 12-gallon tank will cost $35.40. But if the cost of a gallon increases to $3.05, then the tank will cost $36.60. A common misconception about functions is that they are simply algebraic equations. In fact, graphs, tables, words, diagrams, and formulas can represent functions.

Further, a function is a dynamic relationship, the action or the operation that causes a corresponding change. "The central idea of a function as a *process* is often overlooked" (Tall, 1992, p. 501). To convey this process concept, consider a computer analogy, the function keys. Press a key and whatever function is coded there will be applied to whatever is selected. While there are four types of relations in mathematics (correspondences), only two of these are functions: one-to-one and many-to-one (Sidebotham, 2002). An example of a one-to-one correspondence is the typical formula $y = f(x)$. For any one value of x, there is one value of y that is dependent on the value of x. An example situation for this relationship is the cyclist who can travel 1 mile in 3 minutes. For any distance, we can compute the approximate time, assuming traveling rates were consistent. An example of a many-to-one correspondence is the resulting cost of building materials where some wood costs $2 per foot, nails cost $4 per pound, and paint costs $5 per pint. If we need 100 feet of wood, $\frac{1}{2}$ pound of nails, and 2 pints of paint, then our project would cost $212. These functions can be represented with tables, diagrams, equations, or graphs so that solutions (dependent variable) can be identified for any given independent variable(s) (see Figure E.1).

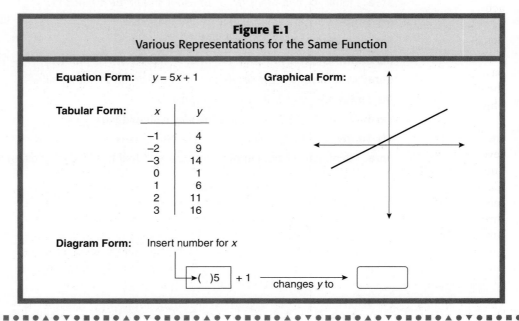

Figure E.1
Various Representations for the Same Function

Equation Form: $y = 5x + 1$

Graphical Form:

Tabular Form:

x	y
−1	4
−2	9
−3	14
0	1
1	6
2	11
3	16

Diagram Form: Insert number for x

( )5 + 1 — changes y to →

The function concept should be developed throughout the mathematics curriculum and is fundamental to algebraic thinking. Dubinsky asserted, "functions form the single most important idea in all mathematics, at least in terms of understanding the subject as well as for using it" (1993, p. 527). The function concept may serve as a unifying thread throughout the mathematics curriculum. This strand will explore the development of function concepts in children and adolescents, review the scope of the function concept in the K–12 mathematics curriculum, and address specific methods for developing these and related "big ideas" with students with learning problems.

DEVELOPMENT OF THE CONCEPT OF FUNCTION

The study of the cognitive development of function concepts in children was initiated by Piaget and his colleagues in the mid twentieth century and involved hundreds of children ages three to fourteen (Piaget, Grize, Szeminska, & Bang, 1968/1977). Before these studies, children younger than six were considered to have sensory-motor intelligence but no operational intelligence. Piaget defined functions as "univocal relations towards the right, i.e., as ordered pairs" (p. 3). This ordering of the pairs distinguishes a function from a relation. Given the ordered pair (x, y), the function assigns only one value (y) to that of x: $y = f(x)$. Piaget asserted that functions are the common source of operations and causal systems. Experimental tasks in this research included matching cards and making picture substitutions on grid charts of large and small flowers of red and blue color, tracing a route on a diagram of color-coded train tracks with numbered points of origin and destinations, covering two-colored cards with various shapes where multiple similarities and differences must be coordinated, comparing levels of liquid in various shaped containers, transforming the perimeter of squares using string and pegs, studying the relationship between the size of a wheel and the distance traveled, and several other gamelike activities that combined number and spatial relationships.

Piaget's conclusions included the view that a function essentially expresses a dependence, whether between properties of objects or between elements that are inherent in actions of the subject. The question raised from this conclusion is whether functions are basically physical or operatory (*static* or *dynamic*). Physical data are drawn directly from the objects and their positions and attributes, while operations depend on actions upon objects (termed *logico-mathematical*).

Elementary functions (also called *preoperatory functions* or *constitutive functions*), such as simple correspondences and groupings, precede operations that begin about age seven. Operations involve performing actions such as classifications, seriations (ordering), and correspondences between classes on objects or their representations or symbols. Causality (cause and effect) involves attributing operations to objects (which can themselves be operators). Moving from functions to a system of included classes occurs in three phases: introduction of equivalences (ages 5–6), then equivalences are formed as functions of actions (schemes), and finally the development of an operatory system of hierarchical grouping, with reversability (ages 8–9). For example, young children can be introduced to different models of equivalences such as five pennies are equivalent to one nickel, a team of nine girls is equivalent to a team of nine boys, and 10 is equivalent to

5 + 5 or 6 + 4 or 7 + 3. To develop the concept that equivalences are formed as functions of actions, the relationships among operations should be developed. Why is $3 + 3 + 3 + 3$ equivalent to 3×4? An operatory system with reversibility is developed through inverse operations such as 5×6 is equivalent to 30; what does that tell us about the factors of 30? Is 5×6 the same as $5 \times 2 \times 3$?

Hines, Klanderman, and Khoury (2001) summarized these levels of function conceptualization as (1) Learner notices no link between two variables, (2) Learner establishes underlying pattern in a recursive (forward and backward), sequential manner, and (3) Learner generalizes understanding of relationships to systematic covariation through verbal and symbolic means. These stages of function concept development are comparable with the van Hiele and SOLO stages for spatial development, discussed in strand C.

Piaget also proposed that related concepts such as variations of variations and proportionalities begin about age seven with simple comparisons of length but develop slowly through ages eleven or twelve to include more complex comparisons such as surface area and the ratio between different entities such as wheel size and distance. With more experience and generalization, older students engage in reflective abstraction, which allows for limitless generation of functions (there is always another function of a function, $n + 1$).

Kalchman, Moss, and Case (2001) hypothesized that the development of function concepts is similar in sequence (integration and elaboration of concepts with increased complexity) to those of whole and rational numbers (see discussion in strand D). In the first level, up through age nine or ten, children develop skills in iterative numerical calculations (number patterns) and spatial schema for representing quantities in bar graph form. In the second level, number and spatial abilities are combined to allow pairs of quantitative values to be represented in space, as with the Cartesian coordinate system. Students can map values and interpret patterns using the x and y axes, that can then be represented algebraically with expressions such as $y = 4x$, a functional relationship. The concept progression is from number pattern to analog representation (bar graph) to geometric representation (integrating number and space) to algebraic representation at the symbolic level. At level three, students begin to differentiate among families of functions (e.g., linear and nonlinear). The Cartesian plane expands to include four quadrants, representing the full scope of integer pairings. Finally, level four is where students relate linear and nonlinear terms and understand the properties of polynomials (the relationships of algebraic terms).

The researchers tested their function domain hypothesis through the application of a curriculum sequence with sixth, eighth, and eleventh graders. Even sixth graders were able to use relatively sophisticated strategies when reasoning about functions, but the older students, perhaps because of a combination of experience with advanced ideas and cognitive development, were able to deal with more challenging and complex problems. The curriculum sequence began with a "bridging context" or a real-life problem that allowed functions to be viewed graphically and computationally (e.g., a walkathon with changing rules of sponsorship for different participants). Students began with lessons on slope and the y-intercept, with data represented using tables, graphs of the tabular information, and then student-created linear equations for the same functions. Next, students were introduced to curved lines and negative slopes. Students then engaged in computer spreadsheet activities that included charting tools but were also required to record equations of their functions. Finally, students presented their functions to their peers, demonstrating various representations, so they would have to explain and clarify the functions for others.

There is virtually no research on function concept understanding or interventions for students with learning problems in mathematics. Recently researchers have begun to address specific aspects of algebra, graphing, and other secondary mathematics topics. Several studies have pointed to the difficulty students with learning disabilities encounter with algebraic notation (see, for example, Miles & Forcht, 1995; MacGregor & Price, 1999). Others fault insufficient pre-algebra concept development; lack of meaningful, problem-based algebra instruction; and inappropriate textbooks for low achievers in algebra (Witzel, Smith, & Brownell, 2001). A few studies have examined explicit instruction with the CRA sequence (instructional strategy framework for the research) on select topics but have not connected the contextual framework of functions. For example, Maccini and Hughes (2000) studied the effects of a CRA instructional sequence (using geometric concrete materials) combined with a problem-solving strategy to teach five high school students with learning disabilities to solve word problems with negative and positive integers. Witzel, Mercer, and Miller (2003) used a CRA sequence with more abstract concrete materials to teach transforming equations with single variables (i.e., solve for x) to groups of students (34 matched pairs) with mathematics disabilities. Ives and Hoy (2003) suggested that graphic organizers should be used to teach negative integer exponent concepts and solving three simultaneous linear equations with three variables to high school students with learning disabilities in upper-level mathematics courses studying algebraic systems. More research is needed that connects learner characteristics related to function concept development with corresponding instructional interventions in integrated curricula (number theory, algebra, geometry, graphing, measurement, and statistics), especially at the secondary level.

> **TRY THIS**
> Examine a mathematics textbook series for its introduction of function concepts and the sequence of instruction across grade levels.

FUNCTIONS ACROSS THE MATHEMATICS CURRICULUM

Function concepts should begin with the earliest mathematics experiences. Younger children should have systematic experiences with patterns, in verbal, numerical, and spatial forms. Classifying, ordering, predicting, and discussing patterns develop pre-operational function concepts. In the lower grades, children should begin to analyze recursive sequences (e.g., even numbers, Fibonacci sequence), often integrated with the study of numbers and operations, as discussed in strand A. In these initial experiences, "variables" are often used as constants, as substitutes for numbers as in the equation $4 + x = 7$. The concept of equivalence, and the equals symbol, is often viewed as an action prompt, rather than equivalent sides of an equation. The concept of change, essential for an understanding of functions, is developed through integrated science and mathematics activities, early graphing experiences, and discussions about events.

By middle school, students typically focus on linear functions and their representations, including work with negative integers, exponents, variables, and coefficients. Students gain experience with the manipulation of algebraic symbols, graphing technology, spreadsheets, and other tools for expressing and analyzing functional relationships. They create models in various forms (objects, diagrams, graphs, equations) that assist in understanding data or situations, making predictions, describing changes, and drawing conclusions. Some students in the middle grades move into nonlinear function contexts.

In high school, students should work with a range of function classes using multiple representations. Function classes include linear, quadratic, exponential, rational, absolute value, radical, periodic, logarithmic (inverse of exponential), and trigonometric, among others (Muschla & Muschla, 1995; NCTM, 2000; Heid, Zbiek, & Blume, 2004). Students should be engaged in activities for comparing classes of functions, such as studying the effects of parameter changes, exploring graphing software, manipulating equations, and predicting changes in equations and graphs. They should move flexibly among representations of functions—tabular, graphical, symbolic, and verbal—for understanding and solving problems. High school students should be engaged in modeling activities within more complex contexts such those of physical sciences, economics, social sciences, and geography. Their study also extends to the examination of algebraic systems (functions of functions) with additional solution tools such as matrices.

At all grade levels, the function concept should be extended into other content areas and real-life situations. Problems with embedded change, if–then situations, or other functional relationships can be found in science, health, social studies, current events, and even literature, art, and music. Tables and graphs are used in many contexts for understanding data and relationships such as with weather, sports, financial markets, and even children's weekly chores and allowances. It is also important that teachers understand function concepts from a K–12 perspective rather than applications for their grade level. The fourth-grade mathematics teacher who introduces negative integers should understand students' previous development of functional relationships and future applications of these concepts, such as with the Cartesian coordinate system and algebraic expressions. The eighth-grade algebra teacher should teach linear functions with the understanding that students have had previous experiences with symbols, tables, and graphs but will move on to other types of functions in later grades. The remedial or special education teacher should be seeking concept gaps in prior learning and building skills that lead to success in the general curriculum.

INSTRUCTIONAL METHODS FOR CHALLENGING CONCEPTS

The sections that follow explore some of the most critical foundational work for function concepts—algebraic notation and variables, simplifying expressions and solving one-variable equations, coordinate plane graphing, and linear functions—along with common learning problems and teaching strategies for these concepts across the K–12 curriculum.

It is beyond the scope of this text to explore nonlinear functions and algebraic systems, but these are briefly introduced in a final section. The material presented should provide a sound basis for further study. Recommended resources for these concepts and further study are found at the end of this strand.

Algebraic Notation

Unlike the alphabetic symbols for reading that represent phonemes, mathematics symbols represent concepts. To make matters more confusing, sometimes several symbols can represent the same concept, as with these examples for division:

$$\frac{7}{3}, 7 \div 3, 3\overline{)7}, \text{ and } 7/3$$

Sometimes the same symbol can have different meanings (semantics) based on the context (syntax). For example, consider the role of the number 2 in the following expressions: $2x$, x^2, $2 + x$, and x_2. Sometimes the insertion of symbols changes an expression (syntax), while other times it does not: $3y$ is the same as $3 \cdot y$ and the same as $3(y)$ and the same as $(3)(y)$, but not the same as $3 + y$, $3 - y$, or y^3. Some similar symbols have different meanings: the division ($\overline{)}$) and square root ($\sqrt{}$) symbols, the angle ($\angle$) and less than ($<$) symbols, and the ϵ (element of set) and Σ (the sum of) symbols. Further, punctuation symbols in English have different meanings in mathematics (e.g., : for ratio, ! for factorals, – for negative numbers or subtraction or not, [ ] for matrices). Chalouh and Herscovics (1998) identified "concatenation of symbols" as a common error, where students confuse place value concepts from arithmetic with symbolic notation. The value of the 4 in the following expressions may appear to mean the same to some students: 43, 4 1/3, $4x$, and $34x$.

The semantics and syntax of mathematical symbols also govern the interpretation of longer expressions, much like word meaning, morphemes, and grammatical rules govern the interpretation of sentences. For example, at first glance the following expressions seem to represent the same value:

$$(2 + 6)5 - 4^2 + \frac{5 + 4}{2} = A \qquad\qquad (2 + (6)(5) - 4^2) + \frac{5}{2} + \frac{4}{2} = B$$

But algebraic rules, called the order of operations, require the following sequence:

1. Simplifying within grouping symbols such as ( ), [ ], { }, —, and ||
2. Simplifying powers
3. Performing all multiplicative (multiplication and division) operations from left to right
4. Performing all additive (addition and subtraction) operations from left to right

Some students use the mnemonic device *Please Excuse My Dear Aunt Sally* to remember this sequence (parentheses, exponents, multiplication/division, addition/subtraction). Following the order of operations for the expressions above, the value for A is 19.5 and the value for B is 20.5.

Here are some recommendations regarding symbol and syntax instruction:

■ Post symbols on wall charts for easy reference. Students may even want to keep personal mathematics dictionaries with a section for symbols.

■ Ask students to read expressions that contain symbols and communicate their meaning. Include matching symbols with definitions on tests. Prompt students to "think in algebra" when working with algebraic notation.

■ Have students create "challenge equations" for each other to solve using the order of operations.

■ Use clear hand printing or an equation editor (with word processors) when preparing overhead transparencies, charts, and worksheets. X2 simply is not the same as x^2. Encourage students to use lined or grid paper to keep mathematics notation clear.

Variables are another source for confusion within algebraic and other notation systems. But not all letters within formulas and equations are variables. And in mathematics, some letters are from the English alphabet (from the Latin, Etruscan, and Greek, according to Omniglot, n.d.) while others (π, θ, α, etc.) are from the Greek alphabet. The symbols used to represent numbers with fixed values are called constants (Sidebotham, 2002). For example, in the following equations, A, L, W, R, and π represent constant values:

$$A = L \cdot W \qquad\qquad A = \pi R^2$$

Variables are symbols for changing values. Letters that represent variables are, by convention, in lower case form from the end of the alphabet, and most often x, y, z, t, and u. Frequently letters from the beginning of the alphabet (a, b, c) as well as capital letters (C, K, A) are used to represent constants. Sometimes specific letters are used with certain values, such as f and g for functions, x and y for ordered pairs, d for derivative, P for probability, m for slope, n for number, r for correlation coefficient or radius, t for time, d for distance, and i for $\sqrt{-1}$. It is good practice to avoid using letters whose shapes can be confused with other mathematical symbols (o, i, l, j, u, v, w) unless there is a specific use, as with set, velocity, or imaginary number. Within expressions and equations, variables are typically listed in alphabetical order (e.g., $x + 2y + z$).

One common problem for many students is viewing an algebraic statement as a literal sentence with direct word-to-symbol matching using the same syntax. The famous example is interpreting "Write an equation using the variables S and P to represent the following statement: There are six times as many students as professors at this university." The problem was posed by Clement (1982) to freshmen engineering students, with only 63 percent responding with the correct equation: S = 6P. Many students translated the sentence word-by-word into the algebraic notation: $6 \times S = P$, resulting in a lot of professors!

Here are some recommendations for teaching about variables:

■ Assist student in making the distinction between letters that represent constants and those that represent variables by making a habit of saying "the constant a" and "the variable x." Teach students to ask if the letter represents a constant or changeable value.

■ Teach students how to translate word problems into algebraic equations without the syntactic and semantic errors that are so common. Students may interpret some variables derived from word problems as labels rather than varying values. For example, if sodas cost s and cookies cost c, write an equation that gives the total cost t for 12 sodas and 36 cookies. ($t = 12s + 36c$) Ask students to describe the values of s and c (many will say 12 sodas and 36 cookies and view the variable as a label for the number as in arithmetic, rather than a changing value. Have students practice creating equations from word problems and vice versa.

■ Assist students making the transition from arithmetic and algebraic forms of equations. In the equation $x + 4 = 10$, x is a constant, not a variable. There is only one possible value for x. But in the algebraic equation $x + y = 10$, there are limitless values for the two variables, with a dependent (functional) relationship.

Monomials and **polynomials** are also fundamental concepts for understanding algebraic expressions and equations. Monomials are single terms, while polynomials have several terms, connected with addition or subtraction symbols. (Binomial has two terms and trinomial has three.) A term can be a real number, a variable, or the product of a real number and one or more variables. The following terms are all monomials:

$$4 \qquad 4x \qquad 4xy \qquad 4xyz \qquad 4x^2yz^3$$

The degree of a monomial is the sum of the exponents (the last monomial above has a degree of 5). Polynomials are the sum and/or difference of monomials and do not include negative exponents. Polynomials are usually arranged in descending or ascending order by the degree of each term. Similar terms (same variables and exponents) can be combined (added or subtracted).

Descending: $3x^2 + xy + 8$

Ascending: $4 + 3xy - z^3$

Addition of these polynomials results in $12 + 4xy + 3x^2 - z^3$

The word *coefficient* refers to the number that multiplies the variable(s) in a term. In the term $5x$, the coefficient is 5. In the term xy, the coefficient is 1. The multiplier coefficient can also be a fraction:

$\frac{2}{3}xy$, also written $\frac{2xy}{3}$

The most confusing concepts about monomials and polynomials are the words used (term, degree, coefficient), the use of a minus symbol or the plus symbol and a negative, and the rules for simplification of these expressions.

Here are some suggestions for teaching polynomial concepts:

■ Stress correct vocabulary use through word walls, charts, and frequent verbal communication of mathematics expressions. Make clear distinctions among words such as *expression* and *equation*, or the directions on many tests such as simplify, solve, transform, and interpret. Be aware of differences in mathematics vocabulary used by different textbooks. Send home vocabulary with definitions and examples so that parents can use the same terminology with their children.

■ Teach a line-drawing strategy for separating the terms in a polynomial for clear understanding of each symbol and for easier simplification (M. Del Mastro, personal communication, May 28, 2005). Some teachers even have students cut apart terms before each addition or subtraction symbol for rearranging (see Figure E.2).

■ Instead of teaching that the expression $2x-(-3)$ should be changed into $2x + (+3)$, where the negatives turn into positives, teach that the $-(-3)$ term is a negative-negative (double negative), therefore a positive $(+3)$.

■ Have students create long polynomials for rearranging and simplifying. Teach students the conventions of arrangement—that the terms are usually listed in order of degree of exponents for easier understanding and use.

Simplifying Algebraic Expressions and Solving Equations

A process that depends on understanding the concepts of algebraic notation is that of simplifying algebraic expressions. Simplification, including working with negative integers and using the order of operations, is required for solving algebraic equations, which also builds on the elementary concepts of equivalence and arithmetic properties. However, simplifying expressions and solving equations are not goals of mathematics learning; they become tools for solving problems.

In addition to the algebraic notations, order of operations, and arithmetic properties (commutative, associative, identify, inverse, zero, and distributive), students need experience with properties related to negative integers and exponents. Figure E.3 adds to the properties discussed in strand B (Figure B.1).

Figure E.3
Select Algebraic Properties

Property	Rule	Example
Property of -1	A negative number multiplied by a positive number yields a negative number.	$-1(4) = -4$
Properties of Opposites	Negative numbers multiplied yield positive numbers; a negative can be distributed.	$-(-6) = 6$ $-(2 + 3) = -2 + -3 = -5$
Properties of Equality	Performing the same operation to both sides of an equation does not change the equality.	If $a = b$, then $a + c = b + c$ and $a - c = b - c$ and $ac = bc$ With division, if $c \neq 0$, then $a/c = b/c$
Rules for Exponents	Multiplication, add the exponents	$x^2 \cdot x^3 = x^{2+3} = x^5$
	Division, subtract the exponents	$y^6/y^3 = y^{6-3} = y^3$
	Negative exponent is reciprocal	$z^{-3} = \frac{1}{z^3}$
	Powers of a Power	$(z^3)^4 = z^{12}$
	Exponent of 1	$3^1 = 3$
	Exponent of 0	$5^0 = 1$

Textbooks devote many pages to exercises in simplifying terms and solving one-variable equations. But early experiences with "keeping an equation in balance" should establish fundamental concepts for these skills. Elementary students should have experiences manipulating equations using properties of arithmetic. For example, in the identity equation $5 + 3 = 2 + 6$, students can add and subtract the same amounts from each side and keep the equation in balance. In the equation $8 - 6 + 4 = x - 2 + 5$, students can explore adding and subtracting different values and eventually end up with a value for x.

The following sequence for attacking an expression or equation is recommended in many textbooks:

1. Substitute an equivalent expression for any expression in the equation (sometimes combined with step 2 because it is a simplification of like terms). For $x = 9 - (-5)$, the number 14 can be substituted for the right side.

2. Simplify each side of the equation by combining similar terms, using the distributive property, and removing unnecessary parentheses, using the order of operations. For the expression: $2x + 4(3 + 7) - 5x$, the $3 + 7$ becomes 10, then the expression becomes $2x + 40 - 5x$ from multiplying, then $40 - 3x$ from combining like terms.

From this point *the order of operations is suspended* and a new order is followed. Basically, for an expression within an equation, follow the order of operations but to solve

Try to solve for *x* by isolating it on one side of the equation. Hints are provided.

a. $x - 3 = -8$ Hint: add 3 to both sides

b. $x + 5 = 2(6 + 2)$ Hint: distribute the 2 first, then add −5 to both sides

c. $-\frac{x}{4} = -10.5$ Hint: multiply −4 by both sides

d. $6x = -96$ Hint: divide both sides by 6 (or multiply by $\frac{1}{6}$)

e. $1 = (\frac{x}{12})5$ Hint: add −5 to both sides, then multiply by 12

f. $\frac{x + 2}{9} = -5$ Hint: multiply both sides by nine, then add −2

g. $(\frac{2x}{3}) + (\frac{x}{2}) = 7$ Hint: multiply both sides by 6 (distributive property applies on the left side), combine like terms, then divide by 7.

for one variable, start with additive combining. The purpose of solving is to "isolate the variable" on one side of the equation.

TRY THIS

Consider what actions should be applied to each side of the equations in Figure E.4 to result in a solution for *x*. Your mission here is to end up with the *x* on one side of the = and everything else, in simplest and neatest form, on the other.

3. Add (or subtract—add the reciprocal) the same real number to each side of the equation.

4. Multiply (or divide—multiply the reciprocal) the same nonzero real number to each side.

5. If the final transformation is a false statement $(3 = 5)$, then the equation has no solution $(\varnothing)$. If the final result is an equivalence $(x = x)$, then the equation is true for all real numbers.

Here are some recommendations for teaching equation solving and simplification:

■ Use a balance scale analogy for demonstrating the two sides of the equation. What's with the *x* that we have to get rid of using our rules for properties?

■ Use two-color chips or checkers to teach the properties of negative integers. Two yellow sides plus one red side will result in one red and one yellow canceling each other out (zero), so one yellow is left.

■ Use real-life data and formulas to introduce and create real equations for solving. The goal for learning these skills, after all, is to solve problems. Students can also create real-life problems for one-degree equations. For example, given the equation $c = 5 + 3x + 1.5z$, *c* is the cost of a party with $5 for the paper products, *x* the number of bags of chips at $3 per bag, and *z* the number of liters of soda at $1.50 per liter. If we think we'll need 5 bags of chips and 3 liters of soda, then our party will cost $24.50. Students can be prompted that linear equations deal with change so that money and time are good examples to use.

■ Use concrete objects, such as algebra tiles, Algeblocks, or Lab Gear (see Chapter 6), to model equations, but explore their representations and limits before using them with students. The red sides of algebra tiles represent negative values and help to reinforce reciprocal concepts. Each time these objects are used, it is critical that each shape be defined for the situation. Sometimes the small square represents a numerical value (1), and sometimes it represents a variable (y). Monitor whether these shifts in value are too confusing for some students. These manipulatives can also be placed on a Cartesian plane to make the geometric connection with algebraic expressions.

Coordinate Plane Graphing

The Cartesian coordinate system is named after René Descartes, who invented the grid system in the early seventeenth century, calling the x-axis the East axis (horizontal) and the y-axis the North axis (vertical) (Sidebotham, 2002). Points, two-dimensional figures, and some equations can be plotted on this four-quadrant plane (see Figure E.5). This concept of plotting points on a plane has been generalized to various mapping and graphing applications, such as using latitude and longitude in geography and constructing a line graph to depict census data or heart rates over time.

In the mathematics curriculum, formal point plotting in the first quadrant (both the x and y values are positive) is typically introduced in the fourth grade. However, kindergarten and first-grade students should be involved in data collection and the construction and interpretation of simple object, picture, and bar graphs of meaningful data. Students in grades 3 through 5 gain experience with line plots and graphs and begin exploring

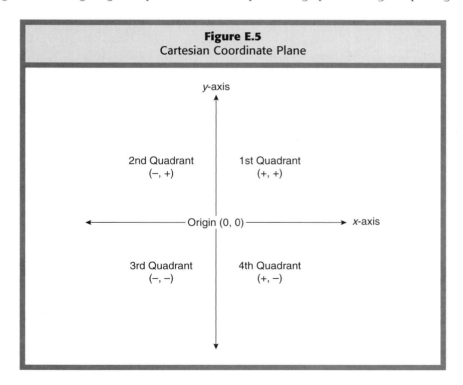

Figure E.5
Cartesian Coordinate Plane

y-axis

2nd Quadrant
(−, +)

1st Quadrant
(+, +)

Origin (0, 0) ——— x-axis

3rd Quadrant
(−, −)

4th Quadrant
(+, −)

integers less than 0 on the number line. Middle-school students should use four-quadrant graphs for representing data, geometric figures, and linear equations with some explorations into nonlinear equations. In high school, graphing applications include a range of function classes and vectors and extend learning to other coordinate systems such as spherical and polar. Coordinate graphing truly connects the mathematics curriculum—number theory (integers), operations (ratio and proportions), algebra (equation graphing), geometry (figure graphing), measurement (area and perimeter on a grid), and data analysis (depicting data in graph form). Graphing is a powerful tool for representing many mathematics concepts.

Here are some recommendations for teaching graphing skills:

■ Start with meaningful data graphed in more representational forms—such as picture and bar graphs. For example, first-graders could use actual buttons to create a graph of the number of buttons on each child's clothing. Second graders can create a bar graph depicting the length of each student's arm span.

■ Use graphing terminology, such as *origin* (0, 0), and *intercept, point,* and *line,* even with younger students.

■ When more challenging terms are introduced in the middle grades, mnemonic devices should be used to assist learning (e.g., "a" of *abscissa* comes before "o" of *ordinate* and "x" comes before "y." We always start with the abscissa or *x*-axis when graphing). Don't avoid these correct terms, teach and reinforce their use.

■ Teachers in the early grades should take care to use graphing conventions that will hold up throughout the grade levels. For example, number lines and graphs should have arrows at the ends of axes, depicting infinity. Number lines for students in the earlier grades should always have the zero position indicated (unless the number line depicts a sequence of integers where the zero could not be adequately indicated). Graphs may have differing units depicted (count by 2, count by 10, count by .5). The axes may use different scales, depending on the nature of values. For graphing functional relationships, the *x*-axis value should depict the independent variable and the *y*-axis value the dependent variable, connected to the equation form of $y = f(x)$. Time should always be depicted on the *x*-axis. Each axis should be labeled and the overall graph given a descriptive title. As students gain experience with various types of graphs, they should be asked to consider the type of data and the best type of graph and scale to represent those data.

■ Have students view a coordinate pair and state in which quadrant its point will fall before starting with the *x* value on the *x* line in a positive or negative direction. For example, the point $(-2, 3)$ will fall into the second quadrant.

■ Build flexible graphing skills by using a variety of materials and tools—computer spreadsheet software, graphing calculators, chalkboards, charts, and even the classroom floor. Graph paper with appropriate-sized grids should be available for student use, with the teacher modeling how to draw and mark off each axis. Graphs from newspapers and magazines should be collected for interpretation and display. Students with spatial deficits need more concrete, and perhaps longer, practice.

■ Have students predict graphs from equations or from changes in graphs. They can check results on a graphing calculator. For example, the graph for $y = 2x + 5$ will be a straight line with the line crossing the y-axis at 5. The graph for $y = 3x^2$ will be a parabola with an upwards turn from the origin. Teach students to rearrange and simplify equations into more standard formats before graphing.

■ The concept of slope (also called *gradient*) is another big idea for many areas of mathematics and can be linked to students' prior knowledge of a hillside, a skateboard ramp, a roofline, or a wheelchair ramp. The formula for a slope is expressed like a fraction: rise/run, with the common symbol m. A positive m is depicted with a line in the direction / (increasing from left to right) and a negative m in the direction \ (decreasing from left to right) (Sidebotham, 2002). With linear equations, the slope-intercept form of equations is $y = mx + b$, with b the y-intecept of the line, m the slope, and x and y are variables. In high school algebra, students will explore gradients of curves, which must change along the curve, so that tangents are used to find gradients at specific points along the curve.

■ Communication skills are critical for students to use when making the connections among representations, such as between data sets and graphs, tables and graphs, or graphs and equations. Students should describe and interpret graphs for others, using consistent terms. They should answer questions about their graphs such as, "What do the values on the x-axis mean?" "Where does this line intercept the y-axis?" "What would happen to this line if the equation were changed?" and "Is this a function?"

Linear Functions

Linear functions are relationships that, when graphed, form a straight line. Two variables (independent and dependent) are represented in the equation form, so the solution for one is always in terms of the other. If a value is known for x, the equation can be solved for y. If 0 is substituted for x, that is the point where the line will cross the y-axis, giving the value for y. Likewise, if 0 is substituted for y, the x-intercept is found. A linear function, in practical applications, represents a constant rate or change in one direction.

There are three conventional forms for writing linear equations (Muschla & Muschla, 1995):

■ Slope-intercept: $y = mx + b$ (m is the slope and b is the y-intercept)
■ Standard form: $Ax + By = C$ (A and B cannot be 0)
■ Point-slope form: $(y - y_1) = m(x - x_1)$ the point (x_1, y_1) lies on the line, m is the slope

Note that the degree of linear equations (greatest exponent used) is 1 and the independent variable (x) may not be the exponent (exponential function), in the denominator (rational function), or under the radical (radical function), as those functions produce

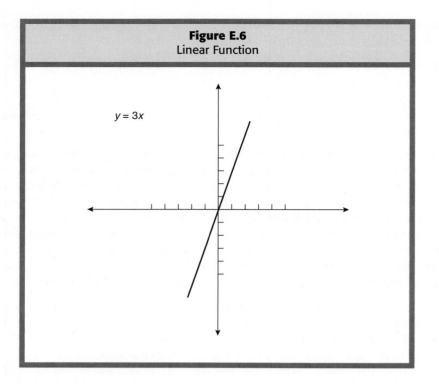

Figure E.6
Linear Function

$y = 3x$

nonlinear graphs. Figure E.6 depicts a linear function in graph form with the corresponding equations. Linear functions can be represented in many forms, including equations, graphs, tables, diagrams, and words.

Here are some recommendations for teaching about linear functions:

■ Provide meaningful and symbolic experiences with patterning with younger children. They should not only be asked to predict the next item in a pattern sequence but provide the controlling rule for the sequence (function). For example, in the number pattern 2, 5, 8, 11, ___, 17, the missing number is 14 and the controlling rule for the sequence is +3. In the picture sequence

the next element should be a ⬜ if the rule is a repeating *s s t t s s t t* (2*s* + 2*t* ...), or if the rule were 2*s*, 2*t*, 3*s*, 3*t* or to add 1 to the coefficient each time the term repeats. Patterning activities can range from simple to complex.

■ Begin with meaningful contexts (situations), not abstract definitions and rules. Definitions based on set theory are particularly obtuse for students engaged in initial learning. Research has demonstrated that rule-bound instruction at the symbolic level is related to student (and teacher) misunderstanding of overall function concepts, and problems with flexibility in moving among representations of the same function (Tall, 1992). Moreover, good problem contexts add meaning to how functions can be used in a variety of applications. Lobato and Ellis (2002) described the use of *Contemporary Mathematics in Context* (Coxford et al., 1998) for a 5-week unit on linear functions with thirty-six diverse high school students. The classroom teacher's lessons were videotaped for analyses, and incorporated a number of real-life situations (e.g., TV ratings, cost for soda machine, motion detector speed). Interestingly, as long as the discussion was about the situation, the teacher's questions were primarily functional and relational in nature, but when focus shifted to conventional representations, such as equations, the teacher's questions were focused more on methods and calculation. Interviews of seven high-performing students indicated that, even after a unit rich in situations, they interpreted linear equations as static, "storage containers" for inserting values rather than as a relationship between the x and y values, and they interpreted x as a label. Adopting a textbook that is situation-based, or beginning lessons with situations, is not enough to ensure concept understanding, even with higher-achieving students. Connections should be made across lessons and units.

■ Ensure that students understand that not all functions are linear, by introducing the concept of nonlinear functions, which will be developed into more distinct classes in later grades.

■ Use tables to facilitate student understanding of the relationships and patterns within functions. Use a realistic problem for which students can generate data into table form, such as testing physical models with mechanical devices, or exploring the effects of compounded interest in a bank account (Hines, Klanderman, & Khoury, 2001).

■ Use technology to display instant graphs and changes in graphs so that the characteristics of functions can be analyzed without the tedium of drafting and erasing. Model the use of graphing calculators using an overhead version. But take care to link graphs to equations (and original data) and teach students how to graph data manually. The graphing process helps students understand functions as relationships.

■ An introductory high school algebra course for all students could be designed around the concept of function, with variables representing changing quantities and a function being the relationship between two variables (Hodges, 2000; Heid, Zbiek, & Blume, 2004). This focus moves algebra from the abstract to meaningful, from static to dynamic, from rote and isolated to connected learning.

EXTENSIONS OF FUNCTIONS

Where next? The next function class is that of **quadratics,** easily spotted by an equation with the greatest exponent 2 (degree 2), or a graph of a parabola with a symmetrical axis at $x = -(\frac{b}{2a})$. Try graphing this quadratic equation to better understand the functional relationship between the x and y variables: $y = ax^2 + bx + c$. An example of a quadratic function in life is from volleyball. The equation $h = -4.9t2 + 3.82t + 1.7$, where h is the height of the serve (from a service position one meter behind the line) and t is time in seconds (Bellman et. al., 2004, p. 522). The graph is a parabola that looks like the track of the volleyball. Understanding these functions requires a solid foundation in the previous material in this strand.

Another extension of the foundations in this strand is solving two two-variable equations or three three-variable equations, often called **simultaneous equations** or systems of equations. Working with simultaneous equations is like viewing the intercept or relationship of two or three functions. The solution for a system of equations is any ordered pair in a system that makes all the equations true (common points on graph). Solution strategies include graphing (sometimes an estimation), manipulative models, substitution, elimination, multiplying matrices, or combinations of these approaches. An example of the application of linear systems is finding the break-even point in income and expense analyses for a business (Bellman et al., 2004, p. 363). For a publishing business, x is the number of newsletter copies and y is dollars in income or expenses. The equation $y = 0,9x + 600$ describes expenses for copies plus writing, while $y = 1.5x$ represents income at $1.50 per newsletter copy.

Ives and Hoy (2003) proposed a graphic organizer method for teaching students with learning disabilities to solve simultaneous equations. Using an example of three variable–three equation problems, the authors described a monetary problem, the teacher's prompting questions, and the graphic organizer strategy. The three equations are placed in the first cell of a three-by-two graphic organizer. Moving in a clockwise manner, the three equations can be reduced to two through substitutions and then to one, moving left to right across the top row of cells. Then moving right to left on the bottom row, the solutions for each of the three variables can be generated.

For solutions to the problems presented in this book, visit the Companion Website at www.ablongman.com/gurganus1e

TRY THIS

Solve for x, y, and z for the following simultaneous equations:

$$3x + 8y + z = 34; -3x - 3y + z = -11; 3x + y - 4z = -7$$

Ives and Hoy offered a number of generalizations for this strategy, including a two-equation modification, a four-equation proposition, and working with unequal coefficients, while discussing the limits of this approach for nonlinear systems. The evidence for the success of this approach was anecdotal, but this research was the first to move into making much higher mathematics concepts accessible for students with disabilities.

MULTICULTURAL CONNECTION

Functions are found everywhere in daily life, from interpersonal relationships to inflating a tire and baking bread. They are also relevant for leisure activities. People in most cultures enjoy board games and have developed quite a number of varieties. In most board

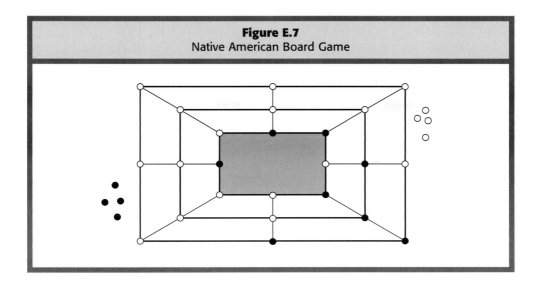

Figure E.7
Native American Board Game

games, a given move is a function of a previous move. Participants try to predict future moves to plan their next moves. Many board games around the world are based on three-in-a-row objects, including the common tic-tac-toe. For example, Native Americans of New Mexico played a "square game" called *pitarilla* (little stones) that is thought to have been adopted from the European Spanish (Culin, 1975), and most likely from Egypt originally but developed simultaneously in Asia (Zaslavsky, 1996). In most of these games, two players take turns moving objects along lines to specific points on the board, attempting to achieve three objects in a straight line while blocking the other player from getting three-in-a-row first (see Figure E.7). Each move becomes a function of the locations available on the board as a result of previous moves.

RESOURCES

Amdahl, K. (1995). *Algebra unplugged.* Broomfield, CO: Clearwater Publishing.

Curcio. F. R. (2001). *Developing data-graph comprehension in grades K–8* (2nd ed.). Reston, VA: NCTM.

Edwards, E. L., Jr. (Ed.). (1990). *Algebra for everyone.* Reston, VA: NCTM.

Fey, J. T., Cuoco, A., Kieran, C., McMullin, L., & Zbiek, R. M. (Eds.). (2003). *Computer algebra systems in secondary school mathematics.* Reston, VA: NCTM.

Moses, B. (Ed.). (1999). *Algebraic thinking, grades K–12: Readings from NCTM's school-based journals and other publications.* Reston, VA: NCTM.

NCTM Navigation Series: Navigating Through Algebra (PK–2, 3–5, 6–8, 9–12).

Appendix

Resources

0 to 99 Number Chart

1 to 100 Number Chart

100s Chart (Right to Left)

Place Value Mats

Fraction Strips

Number and Symbol Squares

Planning Matrix (Chapter 4)

Analysis of Word Problem Characteristics (Chapter 5)

Textbook Adaptation Checklist (Chapter 6)

Mathematics-Oriented Career Education Planning Chart (Chapter 7)

0 to 99 Number Chart

0	1	2	3	4	5	6	7	8	9
10	11	12	13	14	15	16	17	18	19
20	21	22	23	24	25	26	27	28	29
30	31	32	33	34	35	36	37	38	39
40	41	42	43	44	45	46	47	48	49
50	51	52	53	54	55	56	57	58	59
60	61	62	63	64	65	66	67	68	69
70	71	72	73	74	75	76	77	78	79
80	81	82	83	84	85	86	87	88	89
90	91	92	93	94	95	96	97	98	99

1 to 100 Number Chart

1	2	3	4	5	6	7	8	9	10
11	12	13	14	15	16	17	18	19	20
21	22	23	24	25	26	27	28	29	30
31	32	33	34	35	36	37	38	39	40
41	42	43	44	45	46	47	48	49	50
51	52	53	54	55	56	57	58	59	60
61	62	63	64	65	66	67	68	69	70
71	72	73	74	75	76	77	78	79	80
81	82	83	84	85	86	87	88	89	90
91	92	93	94	95	96	97	98	99	100

100s Chart (Right to Left)

10	9	8	7	6	5	4	3	2	1
20	19	18	17	16	15	14	13	12	11
30	29	28	27	26	25	24	23	22	21
40	39	38	37	36	35	34	33	32	31
50	49	48	47	46	45	44	43	42	41
60	59	58	57	56	55	54	53	52	51
70	69	68	67	66	65	64	63	62	61
80	79	78	77	76	75	74	73	72	71
90	89	88	87	86	85	84	83	82	81
100	99	98	97	96	95	94	93	92	91

Place Value Mats

thousands	hundreds	tens	ones

ones		tenths	hundredths	thousandths
	•			

Fraction Strips

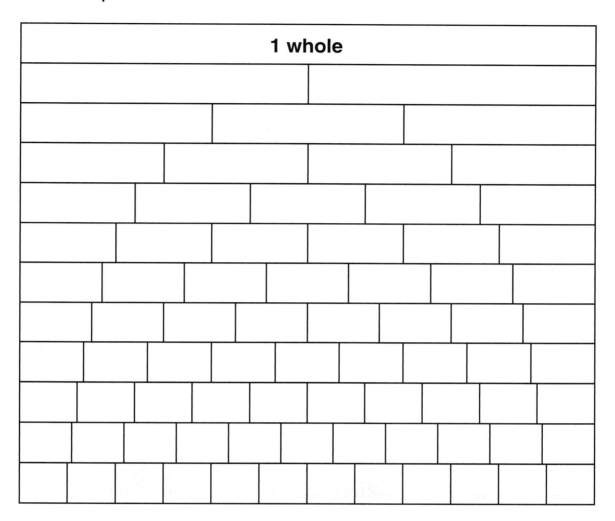

1 whole

Number and Symbol Squares

1	2	3	4	5	6
7	8	9	10	0	1
2	3	4	5	6	7
8	9	10	0	1	2
3	4	5	6	7	8
9	10	0	=	=	+
+	−	−	×	×	/
/	(	)	?	$	·

Planning Matrix (Chapter 4)

Topic:	
Level:	

Principles in Question Form	Brainstorming Lesson Content
1. What are the "big ideas" that provide underlying concepts and connections?	
2. What essential prior knowledge and skills do my students have?	
3. How can we promote positive attitudes in this unit?	
4. What problem-solving context would be appropriate?	
5. What sequence of instruction is needed?	
6. How explicit should the instruction be for this content?	
7. How can I provide variety within structure?	
8. What mathematics language is critical for understanding?	
9. What strategies would be helpful?	
10. How can I plan for transfer of learning?	

Analysis of Word Problem Characteristics (Chapter 5)

Word Problems:	Source:
1.	
2.	
3.	

	Problem 1	Problem 2	Problem 3
Math Content			
Problem Type			
Vocabulary			
Question	direct/indirect	direct/indirect	direct/indirect
Steps			
Information			
Strategies			

Textbook Adaptation Checklist (Chapter 6)

Topic: _____   Textbook: _____

1. Is this topic important, a key idea for future mathematics learning?
2. What is the primary instructional objective?
3. What prior knowledge (informal or formal) do students have about this topic?
4. What prior knowledge is essential for success with this objective?
5. What future skills will be developed based on this learning?
6. What vocabulary will be challenging?
7. What concepts will be confusing?
8. Are the examples appropriate for these students?
9. Is the sequence of instruction appropriate?
10. Is practice with new concepts sufficient?
11. Has judicious review been planned in future lessons?
12. Do extensions and applications in future lessons have concept fidelity?
Are adaptations required?   Yes   No
Other comments:

Mathematics-Oriented Career Education Planning Chart (Chapter 7)

Life Domain	Sub-domains	Mathematics Concepts and Skills—Examples
Personal	Health	
	Time Management	
	Goal Setting	
Interpersonal	Family Care and Relationships (including children/pets)	
	Social Relationships	
	Formal Relationships	
Home Life	Housing	
	Food	
	Clothing	
	Financial	
Leisure	Personal Activities	
	Group Activities	
	Vacations	
Employment/Education (specific to the position)	Job Skills Training	
	Salary and Benefits	
Community Living (specific to the community)	Transportation Accessing Services/Resources	
	Citizenship and Volunteering	

Mathematics Content Codes:
N = Numbers
F = Functions
M = Measurement
G = Geometry
D = Data Analysis

References

Adams, G., & Engelmann, S. (1996). *Research on Direct Instruction: 25 years beyond DISTAR.* Seattle, WA: Educational Achievement Systems.

Ambrose, R., Baek, J., & Carpenter, T. P. (2004). Children's invention of multidigit multiplication and division algorithms. In A. J. Baroody & A. Dowker (Eds.), *The development of arithmetic concepts and skills: Constructing adaptive expertise* (pp. 305–336). Mahwah, NJ: Erlbaum.

American Association for the Advancement of Science (2000). *Middle grades mathematics textbooks: A benchmarks-based evaluation.* Available: www.project2061.org/tools/textbook/matheval/intro.htm.

American Speech-Language-Hearing Association Ad Hoc Committee on Service Delivery to the Schools. (1993). Definitions of communication disorders and variations. *ASHA, 35* (Suppl. 10), 40–41.

Anderson, L. W., & Krathwohl, D. R. (Eds.). (2001). *A taxonomy for learning, teaching, and assessing. A revision of Bloom's Taxonomy of Educational Objectives.* New York: Longman.

Andrews, A. G. (1999). Solving geometric problems by using unit blocks. *Teaching Children Mathematics, 5,* 318–323.

Anthony, G. J., & Walshaw, M. A. (2004). Zero: A "none" number? *Teaching Children Mathematics, 11*(1), 38–42.

ARC Center (2003). *The ARC center tri-state student achievement study: Executive summary.* The K–12 Mathematics Curriculum Center. Available: www.comap.com/elementary/projects/arc.

Archbald, D. A., & Newmann, F. M. (1988). *Beyond standardized testing: Authentic academic achievement in the secondary school.* Reston, VA: National Association of Secondary School Principals.

Armstrong, T. (1994). *Multiple intelligences in the classroom.* Alexandria, VA: ASCD.

Arter, J., & McTighe, J. (2001). *Scoring rubrics in the classroom: Using performance criteria for assessing and improving student performance.* Thousand Oaks, CA: Corwin.

Ashlock, R. B. (2002). *Error patterns in computation: Using error patterns to improve instruction* (8th ed.) Upper Saddle River, NJ: Merrill Prentice-Hall.

Ashton, P. T., & Webb, R. B. (1986). *Making a difference: Teachers' sense of efficacy and student achievement.* White Plains, NY: Longman.

Atkinson, R. C., & Shiffrin, R. M. (1968). Human memory: A proposed system and its control processes. In K. W. Spence & J. T. Spence (Eds.), *The psychology of learning and motivation: Advances in research and theory* (Vol. 2, pp. 89–195). New York: Academic Press.

Ausubel, D. P., & Robinson, F. G. (1969). *School learning: An introduction to educational psychology.* New York: Holt, Rinehart, & Winston.

Badian, N. A. (1983). Dyscalculia and nonverbal disorders of learning. In H. R. Myklebust (Ed.), *Progress in learning disabilities* (Vol. 5, pp. 235–264). New York: Stratton.

Baker, J. M., & Zigmond, N. (1990). Are regular education classes equipped to accommodate students with learning disabilities? *Exceptional Children, 56,* 515–526.

Baker, R. W., & Hopwood, D. (Eds.). (1997). Egypt. *The New Encyclopaedia Britannica: Knowledge in Depth* (Vol. 18). Chicago: Encyclopaedia Britannica, Inc.

Ballheim, C. (2000, April). Reader reactions to the basics and other issues. *Dialogues.* Available: www.nctm.org/dialogues.

Ballheim, C. (2001, January). Reader responses (on content integration with mathematics). *Dialogues.* Available: www.nctm.org/dialogues/2001-01/20010105.htm.

Bandura, A. (1997). *Self-efficacy: The exercise of control.* New York: W. H. Freeman.

Barney, L. (1970, April). Your fingers can multiply! *Instructor,* 129–130.

Baroody, A. J. (1987). *Children's mathematical thinking: A developmental framework for preschool, primary, and special education teachers.* New York: Teachers College, Columbia University.

Baroody, A. J. (1990). How and when should place-value concepts and skills be taught? *Journal for Research in Mathematics Education, 21,* 281–286.

Baroody, A. J., & Ginsburg, H. P. (1986). The relationship between initial meaningful and mechanical knowledge of arithmetic. In J. Hiebert (Ed.), *Conceptual and procedural knowledge: The case of mathematics* (pp. 75–112). Hillsdale, NJ: Erlbaum.

Baroody, A. J., & Hume, J. (1991). Meaningful mathematics instruction: The case of fractions. *Remedial and Special Education, 12*(3), 54–68.

Bassarear, T. (1997). *Mathematics for elementary teachers.* Boston: Houghton Mifflin.

Bassok, M., Wu, L., & Olseth, K. L. (1995). Judging a book by its cover: Interpretative effects of content on problem-solving transfer. *Memory & Cognition, 23,* 354–367.

Battista, M. T. (1999). The importance of spatial structuring in geometric reasoning. *Teaching Children Mathematics, 6,* 170–177.

Bay, M., Staver, J. R., Bryan, T., & Hale, J. B. (1992). Science instruction for the mildly handicapped: Direct instruction versus discovery learning. *Journal of Research in Science Teaching, 29,* 555–570.

Behr, M. J., Harel, G., Post, T., & Lesh, R. (1992). Rational number, ratio, and proportion. In D. A. Grouws (Ed.), *Handbook of research on mathematics teaching and learning* (pp. 296–333). New York: Macmillan.

Behr, M. J., Wachsmuth, I., & Post, T. (1988). Rational number learning aids: Transfer from continuous models to discrete models. *Focus on Learning Problems in Mathematics, 10*(4), 1–18.

Bell, M., Bell, J., & Hartfield, R. (1993). *Everyday mathematics.* Evanston, IL: Everyday Learning.

Bellman, A. E., Bragg, S. C., Charles, R. I., Handlin, W. G., & Kennedy, D. (2004). *Prentice Hall mathematics: Algebra I.* Needham, MA: Prentice Hall.

Bentz, J. L., & Fuchs, L. S. (1996). Improving peers' helping behavior to students with learning disabilities during mathematics peer tutoring. *Learning Disability Quarterly, 19,* 202–215.

Bereiter, C., & Engelmann, S. (1966). *Teaching disadvantaged children in the preschool.* Englewood Cliffs, NJ: Prentice-Hall.

Berk, L. E., & Winsler, A. (1995). *Scaffolding children's learning: Vygotsky and early childhood education.* Washington, DC: NAEYC.

Berliner, D. C. (1989). The place of process-product research in developing the agenda for research on teacher thinking. In J. Lowyck & C. Clark (Eds.), *Teacher thinking and professional action* (pp. 3–21). Belgium: Leuven University Press.

Berra, Y. (1998). *The Yogi book.* New York: Workman.

Bhat, R., & Fletcher, A. (1995). *Pentominoes.* Available: www.andrews.edu/~calkins/math/pentos.htm.

Bidell, T. R., & Fischer, K. W. (1992). Beyond the stage debate. In R. J. Sternberg & C. A. Berg (Eds.), *Intellectual development* (pp. 100–140). Cambridge: Cambridge University Press.

Bidwell, J. K., & Clason, R. G. (1970). *Readings in the history of mathematics education.* Washington, DC: NCTM.

Bielinski, J., Ysseldyke, J. E., Bolt, S., Friedebach, M., & Friedebach, J. (2001). Prevalence of accommodations for students with disabilities participating in a statewide testing program. *Assessment for Effective Intervention, 26*(2), 17–20.

Biggs, J. B., & Collins, K. F. (1982). *Evaluating the quality of learning: The SOLO taxonomy.* New York: Academic Press.

Billings, E. M. H. (2001). Problems that encourage proportion sense. *Mathematics Teaching in the Middle School, 7,* 10–14.

Bitter, G. G., & Pierson, M. E. (2005). *Using technology in the classroom* (6th ed.). Boston: Allyn & Bacon.

Bloom, B. S. (1971). Mastery learning. In J. H. Block (Ed.), *Mastery learning: Theory and practice.* New York: Holt, Rinehart, & Winston.

Borkowski, J. G., & Burke, J. E. (1996). Theories, models, and measurements of executive functioning: An information processing perspective. In G. R. Lyon & N. A. Krasnegor (Eds.), *Attention, memory, and executive function* (pp. 235–262). Baltimore, MD: Brookes.

Bottge, B. A. (2001). Building ramps and hovercrafts—and improving math skills. *TEACHING Exceptional Children, 34*(1), 16–23.

Bottge, B. A., & Hasselbring, T. S. (1993). A comparison of two approaches for teaching complex, authentic mathematics problems to adolescents in remedial math classes. *Exceptional Children, 59,* 556–566.

Bottge, B. J., Gugerty, J. J., Serlin, R., & Moon, K. (2003). Block and traditional schedules: Effects on students with and without disabilities in high school. *NASSP Bulletin, 87*(636), 2–14.

Boudah, D. J., Lenz, B. K., Bulgren, J. A., Schumaker, J. B., & Deshler, D. D. (2000). Don't water down! Enhance content learning through the unit organizer routine. *Teaching Exceptional Children, 32*(3), 48–56.

Bouffard-Bouchard, T. (1990). Influence of self-efficacy on performance in a cognitive task. *Journal of Social Psychology, 130,* 353–363.

Boulet, G. (1998). Didactical implications of children's difficulties in learning the fraction concept. *Focus on Learning Problems in Mathematics, 20*(4), 19–34.

Bredekamp, S. (Ed.). (1987). *Developmentally appropriate practice in early childhood programs serving children from birth through age 8.* Washington, DC: National Association for the Education of Young Children.

Brigance, A. (1981). *BRIGANCE® Diagnostic Inventory of Essential Skills.* North Billerica, MA: Curriculum Associates.

Brigance, A. H., & Glascoe, F. P. (1999). *BRIGANCE® Diagnostic Comprehensive Inventory of Basic Skills, Revised.* North Billerica, MA: Curriculum Associates.

Brigham, F. J., Wilson, R., Jones, E., & Moisio, M. (1996). Best practices: Teaching decimals, fractions, and percents to students with learning disabilities. *LD Forum, 21*(3), 10–15.

Britton, E., Huntley, M. A., Jacobs, G., & Weinberg, A. S. (1999). *Connecting mathematics and science to workplace contexts: A guide to curriculum materials.* Thousand Oaks, CA: Corwin.

Broadbent, D. E. (1958). *Perception and communication.* London: Pergamon.

Broadbent, F. W. (1987). Lattice multiplication and division. *Arithmetic Teacher, 34*(5), 28–31.

Brolin, D. (1978, 1997). *Life centered career education: A competency based approach.* Arlington, VA: Council for Exceptional Children.

Brooks, J. G., & Brooks, M. G. (1993). *In search of understanding: The case for constructivist classrooms.* Alexandria, VA: ASCD.

Brown, B. L. (2002). School to work after the School to Work Opportunities Act. *ACVE.* Available at: www.cete.org/acve.

Brown, V. L., Cronin, M. E., & McEntire, E. (1994). *Test of Mathematical Abilities* (2nd ed.). Austin, TX: PRO-ED.

Bruer, J. T. (1998). Education and the brain: A bridge too far. *Educational Researcher, 26*(8), 4–16.

Bruner, J. S. (1960). *The process of education.* Cambridge, MA: Harvard University Press.

Bruner, J. S. (1966). *Toward a theory of instruction.* New York: Norton.

Bryant, B. R., & Maddox, T. (1996). Using alternative assessment techniques to plan and evaluate mathematics instruction. *LD Forum, 21*(2), 24–33.

Bugaj, S. J. (1998). Intensive scheduling and special education in secondary schools: Research and recommendations. *NASSP Bulletin, 82*(594), 33–39.

Bullock, J. (2000). *TouchMath: The alphabet of mathematics* (4th ed., revised and enlarged). Colorado Springs: Innovative Learning Concepts.

Bureau of Labor Statistics (2004–05). *Occupational Outlook Handbook.* Washington, DC: U.S. Department of Labor. Available at: www.bls.gov/oco.

Burger, W., & Shaughnessey, J. M. (1986). Characterizing the van Hiele levels of development in geometry. *Journal for Research in Mathematics, 17,* 31–48.

Campione, J. C., Brown, A. L., Ferrara, R. A., & Bryant, N. R. (1984). The zone of proximal development: Implications for individual differences and learning. In B. Rogoff & J. V. Wertsch (Eds.), *New directions for child development: Children's learning in the zone of proximal development* (pp. 77–91). San Francisco: Jossey-Bass.

Carbo, M. (1988). The evidence supporting reading styles: A response to Stahl. *Phi Delta Kappan, 70,* 323–327.

Carl D. Perkins Career and Technical Education Improvement Act of 2006.

Carnine, D. (1997). Instructional design in mathematics for students with learning disabilities. *Journal of Learning Disabilities, 30,* 130–141.

Carnine, D., & Gersten, R. (2000). The nature and roles of research in improving achievement in mathematics. *Journal for Research in Mathematics Education, 31,* 138–143.

Carnine, D., Jitendra, A. K., & Silbert, J. (1997). A descriptive analysis of mathematics curricular materials from a pedagogical perspective—A case study of fractions. *Remedial and Special Education, 18*(2), 66–81.

Carpenter, T. P., Franke, M. L., Jacobs, V., & Fennema, E. (1998). A longitudinal study of invention and understanding in children's multidigit addition and subtraction. *Journal for Research in Mathematics, 29,* 3–20.

Carroll, L. (1865/1981). *Alice in wonderland and through the looking glass.* New York: Putnam.

Case, L. P., Harris, K. R., & Graham, S. (1992). Improving the mathematical problem-solving skills of students with learning disabilities: Self-regulated strategy development. *The Journal of Special Education, 26,* 1–19.

Case, R. (1992). Neo-Piagetian theories of child development. In R. J. Sternberg & C. A. Berg (Eds.), *Intellectual development* (pp. 161–196). Cambridge: Cambridge University Press.

Cass, M., Cates, D., Smith, M., & Jackson, C. (2003). Effects of manipulative instruction on solving area and perimeter problems by students with learning disabilities. *Learning Disabilities Research & Practice, 18,* 112–120.

Cawley, J. F. (1985). Mathematics and vocational preparation for the learning disabled. In J. F. Cawley (Ed.), *Secondary school mathematics for the learning disabled* (pp. 201–233). Rockville, MD: Aspen.

Cawley, J., Parmar, R., Foley, T. E., Salmon, S., & Roy, S. (2001). Arithmetic performance of students: Implications for standards and programming. *Exceptional Children, 67,* 311–328.

Chalouh, L., & Herscovics, N. (1998). Teaching algebraic expressions in a meaningful way. In A. F. Coxford (Ed.), *The ideas of algebra, K–12* (1988 Yearbook) (pp. 33–42). Reston, VA: NCTM.

Chapin, S. H., & Anderson, N. C. (2003). Crossing the bridge to formal proportional reasoning. *Mathematics Teaching in the Middle School, 8,* 420–425.

Charles, R. I., & Lester, F. K. (2005). *Problem-solving experiences: Making sense of mathematics* (grades 3–8). Upper Saddle River, NJ: Prentice-Hall.

Chávez, Ó., & Reys, R. E. (2002). Do you see what I see? *Mathematics Teaching in the Middle School, 8,* 162–168.

Chou, H. (2003). Analysis—Amortization tables. *The Investment FAQ.* Available: http://invest-faq.com/articles/analy-loan-payments.html.

Clark, F. B., & Kamii, C. (1996). Identification of multiplicative thinking in children in grades 1–5. *Journal for Research in Mathematics Education, 27,* 41–51.

Cleland, J., Rillero, P., & Zambo, R. (2003). Effective prompts for quick writes in science and mathematics. *Electronic Journal of Literacy Through Science.* Available at: www.sjsu.edu/elementaryed/ejlts/archives/language_development/Joceland.htm.

Clement, J. (1982). Algebra word problem solutions: Thought processes underlying a common misconception. *Journal for Research in Mathematics Education, 13,* 16–30.

Clements, D. H., & Battista, M. T. (1992). Geometry and spatial reasoning. In D. A. Grouws (Ed.), *Handbook of research on mathematics teaching and learning* (pp. 420–464). New York: Macmillan.

Clements, D. H., Swaminathan, S., Hannibal, M. A. Z., & Samara, J. (1999). Young children's concepts of shape. *Journal for Research in Mathematics Education, 30,* 192–212.

Cobb, G. W., & Moore, D. S. (1997). Mathematics, statistics, and teaching. *The American Mathematical Monthly, 104,* 801–823.

Coes III, L. (1993). Building fractal models with manipulatives. *The Mathematics Teacher, 86,* 646–651.

Cohen, A. S., Gregg, N., & Deng, M. (2005). The role of extended time and item content on a high-stakes mathematics test. *Learning Disabilities Research & Practice, 20,* 225–233.

Cohen, S. R. (2003). *Figure it out: Thinking like a math problem solver* (grades 1–6). North Billerica, MA: Curriculum Associates.

Collins, J. L. (1982, March). *Self-efficacy and ability in achievement behavior.* Paper presented at the annual meeting of the American Educational Research Association, New York.

Columba, L., & Dolgos, K. A. (1995). Portfolio assessment in mathematics. *Reading Improvement, 32*(3), 174–176.

Connolly, A. J. (1998). *KeyMath-Revised* (Normative Update). Circle Pines, MN: American Guidance Services.

Conrad, P. (1991). *Pedro's journal: A voyage with Christopher Columbus, August 3, 1492–February 14, 1493.* New York: HarperCollins.

Consortium of National Arts Education Associations (1994). *The national standards for arts education.* Available at: http://artsedge.kennedy-center.org/teach/standards.

Cook, C. & Rasmussen, C. (1994). *Problem solving and critical thinking in mathematics: A K–8 professional development and interdisciplinary curriculum development project.* North Central Regional Educational Laboratory.

Cook, L., & Friend, M. (1995). Co-teaching: Guidelines for creating effective practices. *Focus on Exceptional Children, 28*(3), 1–16.

Cooper, G., & Sweller, J. (1987). Effects of schema acquisition and rule automation on mathematical problem-solving transfer. *Journal of Educational Psychology, 79*, 347–362.

Cornoldi, C., Venneri, A., Marconato, F., Molin, A., & Montinari, C. (2003). A rapid screening measure for the identification of visuospatial learning disability in schools. *Journal of Learning Disabilities, 36*, 299–306.

Council of Chief State School Officers (2002). *Key state education policies on PK–12 Education: 2002.* Washington, DC: Author.

Council of Chief State School Officers (2005). *Key state education policies on PK–12 Education: 2004.* Washington, DC: Author.

Countryman, J. (1992). *Writing to learn mathematics: Strategies that work.* Portsmouth, NH: Heinemann.

Coutinho, M., & Malouf, D. (1993). Performance assessment and children with disabilities: Issues and possibilities. *TEACHING Exceptional Children, 25*(4), 63–67.

Coxford, A. G., Fey, J. T., Hirsh, C. R., Schoen, H. L., Burrill, G., & Hart, E. W. (1998). *Contemporary mathematics in context: A unified approach, Course 1, Part A.* Chicago: Everyday Learning.

Crannell, A. (1994). How to grade 300 mathematical essays and survive to tell the tale. *PRIMUS, 4*(3), 193–201.

Cronin, M. E., & Patton, J. R. (1993). *Life skills instruction for all students with special needs: A practical guide for integrating real-life content into the curriculum.* Austin, TX: PRO-ED.

CTB Macmillan/McGraw-Hill. (2002). *California Achievement Tests* (6th). Author.

Culin, S. (1975). *Games of North American Indians.* New York: Dover Publications.

Davis, R. B., Maher, C. A., & Noddings, N. (Eds.). (1990). *Constructivist views on the teaching and learning of mathematics.* Reston, VA: National Council of Teachers of Mathematics.

Daw, N. (1995). *Visual development.* New York: Plenum.

de Lange, J. (1995). The invalidity of standardized testing for measuring mathematics achievement. In T. A. Romberg (Ed.), *Reform in school mathematics and authentic assessment.* Albany: SUNY Press.

Dehaene, S. (1997). The language of numbers. In *The Number Sense: How the Mind Creates Mathematics.* New York: Oxford University Press.

Dempster, F. N., & Farris, R. (1990). The spacing effect: Research and practice. *Journal of Research and Development in Education, 23*(2), 97–101.

Deno, S. L. (2003). Curriculum-based measures: Development and perspectives. *Assessment for Effective Instruction, 28*(3 & 4), 3–11.

Deno, S. L., & Fuchs, L. S. (1987). Developing curriculum-based measurement systems for data-based special education problem solving. *Focus on Exceptional Children, 19*(8), 1–16.

Derbyshire, J. (2004). *Prime obsession: Bernhard Riemann and the greatest unsolved problem in mathematics.* New York: Penguin.

Deschler, D. D., Alley, G., Warner, M., & Schumaker, J. (1981). Instructional practices for promoting skill acquisition and generalization in severely learning disabled adolescents. *Learning Disability Quarterly, 4*, 145–152.

Deshler, D. D., & Lenz, B. K. (1989). The strategies instructional approach. *International Journal of Disability, Development, and Education, 36*(3), 203–224.

Deshler, D. D., & Schumaker, J. (1986). Learning strategies: An instructional alternative for low-achieving adolescents. *Exceptional Children, 52*, 483–490.

DeTemple, D., & Miedema, A. (1997). Patterns and puzzles for pyramids and prisms. *The Mathematics Teacher, 90*, 370–374, 380–384.

Dickey, E., Brueningsen, C., Butsch, S. Chapman, C., Leiva, M., & Tunis, H. (1997). *Task force on integrated mathematics report to the board of directors.* Reston, VA: NCTM.

Dixon, R., & Carnine, D. (1994). Ideologies, practices, and their implications for special education. *The Journal of Special Education, 28*, 356–367.

Dole, S. (1999). Successful percent problem solving for year 8 students using the proportional number line method. In J. M. Truran & K. M. Truran (Eds.), *Making the difference. Proceedings of the annual conference of the mathematics education research group of Australasia Incorporated.*

Dole, S. (2000). Promoting percent as a proportion in eighth-grade mathematics. *School Science and Mathematics, 100*, 380–389.

Driscoll, M. P. (2005). *Psychology of learning for instruction* (3rd ed.). Boston: Allyn & Bacon.

Dubinsky, E. (1993). Computers in teaching and learning discrete mathematics and abstract algebra. In D. L. Ferguson (Ed.), *Advanced technologies in the teaching of mathematics and science* (pp. 525–583). New York: Springer-Verlag.

Duffy, G. G. (1987). Putting the teacher in control: Basal reading textbooks and instructional decision making. *Elementary School Journal, 87*, 357–366.

Dunn, C., & Rabren, K. (1996). Functional mathematics instruction to prepare students for adulthood. *LD Forum, 21*(3), 34–40.

Eiserman, W. D. (1988). Three types of peer tutoring: Effects on the attitudes of students with learning disabilities and their regular class peers. *Journal of Learning Disabilities, 21*, 223–229.

Elliott, S. N., Kratochwill, T. R., & McKevitt, B. C. (2001). Experimental analysis of the effects of testing accommodations on the scores of students with and without disabilities. *Journal of School Psychology, 39*, 3–24.

Elliott, S. N., Kratochwill, T. R., & Schulte, A. G. (1998). The assessment accommodation checklist: Who, what, where, when, why, and how. *TEACHING Exceptional Children, 31*(2), 10–14.

Engelmann, S., & Carnine, D. (1975). *DISTAR Arithmetic.* Columbus, OH: Science Research Associates.

Engelmann, S., & Carnine, D. (1982). *Corrective mathematics.* Columbus, OH: SRA/Macmillan/McGraw-Hill.

Engelmann, S., Carnine, D., Kelly, B., & Engelmann, O. (1996). *Connecting math concepts.* Columbus, OH: SRA/McGraw-Hill.

Engleman, S., & Carnine, D. (1982). *Theory of instruction: Principles and applications.* New York: Irvington.

English, L. D. (1997). Children's reasoning processes in classifying and solving computational word problems. In L. D. English (Ed.), *Mathematical reasoning: Analogies, metaphors, and images* (pp. 191–220). Mahwah, NJ: Erlbaum.

Enright, B. E. (1983). *ENRIGHT® Diagnostic Inventory of Basic Arithmetic Skills.* North Billerica, MA: Curriculum Associates, Inc.

Enright, B., & Beattie, J. (1989). Problem solving step by step in math. *Teaching Exceptional Children, 22*(1), 58–59.

Ericsson, K. A., & Simon, H. A. (1980). Verbal reports as data. *Psychological Review, 87*, 215–251.

Ericsson, K. A., & Simon, H. A. (1993). *Protocol analysis: Verbal reports as data* (Revised). Cambridge: MIT Press.

Evans, D. G. (1990). *Comparison of three instructional strategies for teaching borrowing in subtraction.* Doctoral dissertation. University of Oregon.

Everyday Learning Corporation (2002). *Everyday mathematics: The University of Chicago School Mathematics Project.* Chicago: Author.

Falkner, K. P., Levi, L., & Carpenter, T. P. (1999). Children's understanding of equality: A foundation for algebra. *Teaching Children Mathematics, 6*, 232–236.

Feldt, L. S., Forsyth, R. A., Ansley, T. N., & Alnot, S. D. (1996). *Iowa Tests of Basic Skills* (Forms K, L, M). Itasca, IL: Riverside.

Fitzmaurice-Hayes, A. (1984). Curriculum and instructional activities: Grades 2 through 4. In J. F. Cawley (Ed.), *Developmental teaching of mathematics for the learning disabled.* Rockville, MD: Aspen Systems.

Flavell, J. H. (1978). Metacognitive aspects of problem solving. In L. B. Resnick (Ed.), *The nature of intelligence* (pp. 231–235). Hillsdale, NJ: Erlbaum.

Fogarty, R. (1991). *The mindful school: How to integrate the curricula.* Palatine, IL: Skylight.

Foshay, R., & Ahmed, M. I. (2003). A practical process for reviewing and selecting educational software. Technical paper #8. Plato Learning, Inc. Available: www.plato.com/downloads/papers/paper_08.pdf.

Fosnot, C. T. (1996). Constructivism: A psychological theory of learning. In C. T. Fosnot (Ed.), *Constructivism: Theory, perspectives, and practice.* New York: Teachers College Press.

Freudenthal, H. (1973). *Mathematics as an educational task.* Dordrecht: Reidel.

Fuchs, D., Fuchs, L. S., Mathes, P. G., & Martinez, E. A. (2002). Preliminary evidence on the social standing of students with learning disabilities in PALS and No-PALS classrooms. *Learning Disabilities Research & Practice, 17*, 205–215.

Fuchs, L. S., & Deno, S. L. (1991). Paradigmatic distinctions between instructionally relevant measurement models. *Exceptional Children, 57*, 488–499.

Fuchs, L. S., & Fuchs, D. (2002). Mathematics problem-solving profiles of students with mathematics disabilities with and without comorbid reading disabilities. *Journal of Learning Disabilities, 35*, 563–573.

Fuchs, L. S., & Fuchs, D. (2003). Enhancing the mathematical problem solving of students with mathematics disabilities. In H. L. Swanson, K. R. Harris, & S. Graham (Eds.), *Handbook of learning disabilities* (pp. 306–322). New York: Guilford.

Fuchs, L. S., Bahr, C. M., & Rieth, H. J. (1989). Effects of goal structures and performance contingencies on mathematics performance of adolescents with learning disabilities. *Journal of Learning Disabilities, 22,* 554–560.

Fuchs, L. S., Fuchs, D., & Bishop, N. (1992). Instructional adaptation for students at risk for academic failure. *Journal of Educational Research, 86,* 70–84.

Fuchs, L. S., Fuchs, D., Eaton, S. B., Hamlet, C. L., & Karns, K. M. (2000). Supplementing teacher judgments of mathematics test accommodations with objective data sources. *School Psychology Review, 29,* 65–85.

Fuchs, L. S., Fuchs, D., Hamlett, C. L., Phillips, N. B., Karns, K., & Dutka, S. (1997). Enhancing students' helping behavior during peer-mediated instruction with conceptual mathematics explanations. *Elementary School Journal, 97,* 223–250.

Fuchs, L. S., Hamlett, C. L., & Fuchs, D. (1999). *Monitoring Basic Skills Progress* (2nd). Austin, TX: PRO-ED.

Fulkerson, E. (1963). Adding by tens. *The Arithmetic Teacher, 10,* 139–140.

Funckhouser, C. (1995). Developing number sense and basic computation skills in students with special needs. *School Science and Mathematics, 95,* 236–239.

Fuson, K. C. (1988). *Children's counting and concepts of number.* New York: Springer-Verlag.

Fuson, K. C. (1990). Conceptual structures for multiunit numbers: Implications for learning and teaching multidigit addition, subtraction, and place value. *Cognition and Instruction, 7,* 343–403.

Fuson, K. C. (1992). Research on whole number addition and subtraction. In D. A. Grouws (Ed.), *Handbook of research on mathematics teaching and learning* (pp. 243–275). New York: Macmillan.

Fuson, K. C., & Briars, D. J. (1990). Base-ten blocks as a first- and second-grade learning/teaching setting for multidigit addition and subtraction and place value concepts. *Journal for Research in Mathematics Education, 3,* 180–206.

Fuson, K. C., Richards, J. J., & Briars, D. J. (1982). The acquisition and elaboration of the number word sequence. In C. J. Brainerd (Ed.), *Progress in cognitive development: Vol. 1. Children's logical and mathematical cognition* (pp. 33–92). New York: Springer-Verlag.

Fuys, D., Geddes, D., & Tischler, R. (1988). The van Hiele model of thinking in geometry among adolescents. *Journal for Research in Mathematics Education* (Monograph Number 3). Reston, VA: NCTM.

Gagné, R. M. (1970). *The conditions of learning* (2nd ed.). New York: Holt, Rinehart, & Winston.

Gagné, R. M. (1985). *The conditions of learning* (4th ed.). New York: Holt, Rinehart, & Winston.

Gallagher, J. M., & Wansart, W. L. (1991). An assimilative base model of strategy–knowledge interactions. *Remedial and Special Education, 12*(3), 31–42.

Gardner, H. (1983). *Frames of mind: The theory of multiple intelligences.* New York: Basic Books.

Gardner, H. (1993). *Multiple intelligences: The theory in practice.* New York: Basic Books.

Gardner, H. (1999). Who owns intelligence? *The Atlantic Monthly, 283*(2), 67–76.

Garfield, J., & Ahlgren, A. (1988). Difficulties in learning basic concepts in probability and statistics: Implications for research. *Journal for Research in Mathematics Education, 19,* 44–63.

Gattegno, C. (1953). *Numbers in colour,* ATAM Bulletin, 2.

Geary, D. C. (1994). *Children's mathematical development: Research and practical implications.* Washington, DC: American Psychological Association.

Geary, D. C. (2003). Learning disabilities in arithmetic: Problem-solving differences and cognitive deficits. In H. L. Swanson, K. R. Harris, & S. Graham (Eds.), *Handbook of learning disabilities* (pp. 199–212). New York: Guilford.

Geary, D. C., Hamson, C. O., & Hoard, M. K. (2000). Numerical and arithmetical cognition: A longitudinal study of process and concept deficits in children with learning disability. *Journal of Experimental Child Psychology, 74,* 213–239.

Geary, D. C., & Hoard, M. K. (2001). Numerical and arithmetical deficits in learning-disabled children: Relation to dyscalculia and dyslexia. *Aphasiology, 15,* 635–647.

Gerber, M. M., Semmel, D. S., & Semmel, M. I. (1994). Computer-based dynamic assessment of multidigit multiplication. *Exceptional Children, 61,* 114–125.

Gersten, R., & Carnine, D. (1984). Direct instruction mathematics: A longitudinal evaluation of low-income elementary school students. *Elementary School Journal, 84,* 395–407.

Gersten, R., & Chard, D. (1999). Number sense: Rethinking arithmetic instruction for students with mathematical disabilities. *The Journal of Special Education, 33,* 18–28.

Gindis, B. (1995). The social/cultural implications of disability: Vygotsky's paradigm for special education. *Educational Psychology, 30*(2), 77–81.

Ginsburg, H. P. (1982). *Children's arithmetic: How they learn it and how you teach it* (rev ed.). Austin, TX: PRO-ED.

Ginsburg, H. P. (1997). *Entering the child's mind: The clinical interview in psychological research and practice.* Cambridge, UK: Cambridge University Press.

Ginsburg, H. P., & Baroody, A. J. (2003). *Test of Early Mathematics Ability* (3rd). Austin, TX: PRO-ED.

Glaser, R. (1966). Variables in discovery learning. In L. S. Shulman & E. R. Keislar (Eds.), *Learning by discovery: A critical appraisal.* Chicago: Rand McNally.

Goals 2000: Educate America Act of 1994, Pub. L. No. 103-227 (3/31/94) Stat. 108.

Goldenberg, E. P. (2000). Thinking (and talking) about technology in math classrooms. *Issues in Mathematics Education.* Education Development Center, Inc. Available at: www2.edc.org/mcc/pubs/default.asp.

Graham, S. (Ed.) (2005). Criteria for evidence-based practice in special education: Special issue. *Exceptional Children, 71,* 130–207.

Grauberg, E. (1998). *Elementary mathematics and language difficulties: A book for teachers, therapists and parents.* London: Whurr.

Gravemeijer, K. P. (1998). From a different perspective: Building on students' informal knowledge. In R. Lehrer & D. Chazan (Eds.), *Designing learning environments for developing understanding of geometry and space* (pp. 45–66). Mahwah, NJ: Erlbaum.

Graves, A., Landers, M. F., Lokerson, J., Luchow, J., & Horvath, M. (1993). The development of a competency list for teachers of students with learning disabilities. *Learning Disabilities Research & Practice, 8,* 188–199.

Gredler, M. E. (1997). *Learning and instruction: Theory into practice* (3rd ed.). Upper Saddle River, NJ: Merrill.

Greenwood, C. R., Delquadri, J., & Hall, R. V. (1984). Opportunity to respond and student academic performance. In W. L. Heward, T. E. Herron, J. Trap-Porter, & D. S. Hill (Eds.), *Focus on behavior analysis in education* (pp. 58–88). Columbus, OH: Merrill/Macmillan.

Greer, B. (1992). Multiplication and division as models of situations. In D. A. Grouws (Ed.), *Handbook of research on mathematics teaching and learning* (pp. 276–295). New York: Macmillan.

Grissmer, D., & Flanagan, A. (1998). *Exploring rapid achievement gains in North Carolina and Texas: Lessons from the states.* (ERIC No. ED425204)

Grobecker, B. (2000). Imagery and fractions in students classified as learning disabled. *Learning Disability Quarterly, 23,* 157–168.

Grobecker, B., & De Lisi, R. (2000). An investigation of spatial-geometrical understanding in students with learning disabilities. *Learning Disability Quarterly, 23,* 7–22.

Gross-Tsur, V., Manor, O., & Shalev, R. S. (1996). Developmental dyscalculia: Prevalence and demographic features. *Developmental Medicine and Child Neurology, 38,* 25–33.

Gross-Tsur, V., Shalev, R. S., Manor, O., & Amir, N. (1995). Developmental right hemisphere syndrome: Clinical spectrum of the nonverbal learning disability. *Journal of Learning Disabilities, 28,* 80–86.

Gurganus, S. (2004). 20 ways to promote number sense. *Intervention in School and Clinic, 40,* 55–58.

Gurganus, S., & Del Mastro, M. (1998). Mainstreaming kids with reading and writing problems: Special problems of the mathematics classroom. *Reading and Writing Quarterly, 14,* 117–125.

Gurganus, S., Janas, M., & Schmitt, L. (1995). Science instruction: What special education teachers need to know and what roles they need to play. *Teaching Exceptional Children, 27*(4), 7–9.

Gurganus, S. P. (2005). [Mathematical dispositions, content knowledge, and pedagogical understanding by special education teacher candidates.] Unpublished raw data.

Gurganus, S. P., & Shaw, A. N. (2005). [Diagnostic interviews about mathematics concepts with K–12 students with disabilities.] Unpublished raw data.

Guskey, T. R. (1997). *Implementing mastery learning* (2nd ed.). Belmont, CA: Wadsworth.

Gutek, G. L. (2004). *Philosophical and ideological voices in education.* Boston: Allyn & Bacon.

Gutiérrez, R. (2002). Beyond essentialism: The complexity of language in teaching mathematics to Latina/o students. *American Educational Research Journal, 39,* 1047–1088.

Harcourt Assessment, Inc. (2003). *Stanford Achievement Test* (10th). San Antonio, TX: Author.

Harcourt Brace Educational Measurement. (1996). *Stanford Diagnostic Mathematics Test* (4th). San Antonio, TX: Author.

Harcourt Educational Measurement. (2001). *Metropolitan Achievement Tests* (8th). Harcourt Assessment, Inc.

Harris, C. A., Miller, S. P., & Mercer, C. D. (1995). Teaching initial multiplication skills to students with disabilities in general education classrooms. *Learning Disabilities Research & Practice, 10,* 180–195.

Harris, K. R. (1982). Cognitive-behavior modification: Application with exceptional students. *Focus on Exceptional Children, 15*(2), 1–16.

Harris, K. R., & Graham, S. (1994). Constructivism: Principles, paradigms, and integration. *The Journal of Special Education, 28,* 233–247.

Harris, K. R., & Graham, S. (1996a). Constructivism and students with special needs: Issues in the classroom. *Learning Disability Research & Practice, 11*(3), 134–137.

Harris, K. R., & Graham, S. (1996b). *Making the writing process work: Strategies for composition and self-regulation.* Cambridge, MA: Brookline.

Hart, C. H., Burts, D. C., & Charlesworth, R. (Eds.). (1997). *Integrated curriculum and developmentally appropriate practice: Birth to age eight.* Albany: SUNY.

Haubner, M. A. (1992). Percents: Developing meaning through models. *Arithmetic Teacher, 40,* 232–234.

Havertape, J., & Kass, C. (1978). Examination of problem solving in learning disabled adolescents through verbalized self-instruction. *Learning Disability Quarterly, 1,* 94–100.

Haynes, M. C., & Jenkins, J. R. (1986). Reading instruction in special education resource rooms. *American Educational Research Journal, 23,* 161–190.

Heath, G. D. (2002). Using applets in teaching mathematics. *Mathematics and Computer Education, 36,* 43–52.

Heid, M. K., Zbiek, R. M., & Blume, G. W. (2004). Mathematical foundations for a functions-based approach to algebra. In R. N. Rubenstein & G. W. Bright (Eds.), *Perspectives on the teaching of mathematics: Sixty-sixth yearbook* (pp. 42–55). Reston, VA: NCTM.

Helton, S. M., & Micklo, S. J. (1997). *The elementary math teacher's book of lists.* West Nyack, NY: Center for Applied Research in Education.

Herman, J. L., Aschbacher, P. R., & Winters, L. (1992). *A practical guide to alternative assessment.* Alexandria, VA: ASCD.

Hiebert, J. (2003). What research says about the NCTM standards. In J. Kilpatrick, W. G. Martin, & D. Schifter (Eds.) *A research companion to principles and standards for school mathematics* (pp. 5–23). Reston, VA: NCTM.

Higginson, W., & Colgan, L. (2001). Algebraic thinking through origami. *Mathematics Teaching in the Middle School, 6,* 343–349.

Hines, E., Klanderman, D. B., & Khoury, H. (2001). The tabular mode: Not just another way to represent a function. *School Science and Mathematics, 101,* 362–371.

Hodges, K. (2000, April). Making high school algebra accessible to all. *Mathematics Education Dialogues, 8.*

Hodges, L. C., & Harvey, L. C. (2003). Evaluation of student learning in organic chemistry: Using the SOLO taxonomy. *Journal of Chemical Education, 80,* 785–787.

Hofmeister, A. M. (1993). Elitism and reform in school mathematics. *Remedial and Special Education, 14*(6), 8–13.

Hope, J. A., & Owens, D. T. (1987). An analysis of the difficulty of learning fractions. *Focus on Learning Problems in Mathematics, 9*(4), 25–40.

Houghton Mifflin (2002). *Mathematics: Grades K through 6.* Boston: Author.

Hresko. W. P., Schlieve, P. L., Herron, S. R., Swain, C., & Sherbenou, R. J. (2003). *Comprehensive Mathematical Abilities Test.* Austin, TX: PRO-ED.

Huff, D. (1999). *The complete how to figure it: Using math in everyday life.* New York: Norton.

Hutchings, B. (1976). Low-stress algorithms. In D. Nelson & R. E. Reys (Eds.), *Measurement in school mathematics* (pp. 218–239). Reston, VA: NCTM.

Hutchins, P. (1986). *The doorbell rang.* New York: Greenwillow Books.

Hutchinson, N. L. (1993). Effects of cognitive strategy instruction on algebra problem solving of adolescents with learning disabilities. *Learning Disability Quarterly, 16,* 34–63.

Huzita, H. (1992). Understanding geometry through origami axioms. *Proceedings of the First International Conference on Origami in Education and Therapy* (pp. 37–70), J. Smith (Ed.). British Origami Society.

Idol, L., Nevin, A., & Paolucci-Whitcomb, P. (1996). *Models of curriculum-based assessment: A blueprint for learning* (2nd ed.). Austin, TX: PRO-ED.

Individuals with Disabilities Education Act of 1997, 20 U.S.C.A. §1401 *et seq.*

Individuals with Disabilities Education Act of 2004, P.L. 108–446.

Ives, B., & Hoy, C. (2003). Graphic organizers applied to higher-level secondary mathematics. *Learning Disabilities Research & Practice, 18*, 36–51.

Jacobs, J. E., & Paris, S. G. (1987). Children's metacognition about reading: Issues in definition, measurement, and instruction. *Educational Psychologist, 22*, 255–278.

Jitendra, A. K. (2002). Teaching students math problem-solving through graphic representations. *Teaching Exceptional Children, 34*(4).

Jitendra, A. K. (in preparation). *Teaching word problem solving to students with learning disabilities.* Austin, TX: PRO-ED.

Jitendra, A., DiPipi, C. M., & Perron-Jones, N. (2002). An exploratory study of schema-based word-problem-solving instruction for middle school students with learning disabilities: An emphasis on conceptual and procedural understanding. *The Journal of Special Education, 36*, 23–38.

Jitendra, A. K., Griffin, C., McGoey, K., Gardill, C., Bhat, P., & Riley, T. (1998). Effects of mathematical word problem solving by students at risk or with mild disabilities. *Journal of Educational Research, 91*, 345–356.

Jitendra, A. K., & Hoff, K. E. (1995). *Schema-based instruction on word problem solving performance of students with learning disabilities.* East Lansing, MI: National Center for Research on Teacher Training (ERIC Document Reproduction Service No. ED 381 990).

Jitendra, A. K., & Hoff, K. E. (1996). The effects of schema-based instruction on the mathematical word-problem-solving performance of students with learning disabilities. *Journal of Learning Disabilities, 29*, 422–431.

Jitendra, A. K., Hoff, K., & Beck, M. M. (1999). Teaching middle school students with learning disabilities to solve word problems using a schema-based approach. *Remedial and Special Education, 20*(1), 50–64.

Jitendra, A. K., Kame'enui, E. J., & Carnine, D. W. (1994). An exploratory evaluation of dynamic assessment and the role of basals on comprehension of mathematical operations. *Education and Treatment of Children, 17*, 139–162.

Jitendra, A., & Nolet, V. (1995). Teaching how to use a check register: Procedures for instruction selection and design. *Intervention in School and Clinic, 31*, 28–33.

Jitendra, A. K., Sczesniak, E., & Deatline-Buchman, A. (2005). Validation of curriculum-based mathematical word problem solving tasks as indicators of mathematics proficiency for third graders. *School Psychology Review, 34*, 358–371.

Johnson, D. W., Johnson, R. T., & Maruyama, G. (1983). Interdependence and interpersonal attraction among heterogeneous and homogeneous individuals: A theoretical formulation and meta-analysis of the research. *Review of Educational Research, 53*, 5–54.

Johnson, E. S. (2000). The effects of accommodations on performance assessments. *Remedial and Special Education, 21*, 261–267.

Jones, E. D., Wilson, R., & Bhojwani, S. (1998). Mathematics instruction for secondary students with learning disabilities. In D. P. Rivera (Ed.), *Mathematics education for students with learning disabilities: Theory to practice* (pp. 155-176). Austin, TX: PRO-ED.

Jordan, L., Miller, M. D., & Mercer, C. D. (1999). The effects of concrete to semiconcrete to abstract instruction in the acquisition and retention of fraction concepts and skills. *Learning Disabilities: A Multidisciplinary Journal, 9*, 115–122.

Jordan, N. C., Levine, S. C., & Huttenlocher, J. (1995). Calculation abilities in young children with different patterns of cognitive functioning. *Journal of Learning Disabilities, 28*, 53–64.

Jordan, N. C., & Montani, T. O. (1997). Cognitive arithmetic and problem solving: A comparison of children with specific and general mathematics difficulties. *Journal of Learning Disabilities, 30*, 624–634.

Joseph, G. G. (1991). *The crest of the peacock: Non-European roots of mathematics.* London: Penguin.

Jovinelly, J. (2002). *Crafts of the ancient world* (series). New York: Rosen.

Jurdak, J., & Zein, R. A. (1998). The effect of journal writing on achievement and attitude toward mathematics. *School Science and Mathematics, 98*, 412–419.

Jurdak, M., & Shahin, I. (2001). Problem solving activity in the workplace and the school: The case of constructing solids. *Educational Studies in Mathematics, 47*, 297–315.

Kagan, D. M., & Tippins, D. J. (1991). Helping student teachers attend to student cues. *The Elementary School Journal, 91*, 343–356.

Kahl, S. R. (1992). *Alternative assessment in mathematics: Insights from Massachusetts, Maine, Vermont, and Kentucky.* (ERIC Document Reproduction Service No. ED 346 132).

Kalchman, M., Moss, J., & Case, R. (2001). Psychological models for the development of mathematical understanding: Rational numbers and functions. In S. M. Carver & D. Klahr (Eds.), *Cognition and instruction: Twenty-five years of progress* (pp. 1–38). Mahwah, NJ: Erlbaum.

Kame'enui, E. J., & Carnine, D. W. (1998). *Effective teaching strategies that accommodate diverse learners.* Des Moines, IA: Prentice-Hall.

Kame'enui, E. J., Carnine, D. W., Dixon, R. C., Simmons, D. C., & Coyne, M. D. (2002). *Effective teaching strategies that accommodate diverse learners* (2nd ed.). Upper Saddle River, NJ: Merrill Prentice-Hall.

Kamii, C. K. (1985). *Young children reinvent arithmetic.* New York: Teachers College Press.

Kaufman, A. S., & Kaufman, N. L. (2004). *Kaufman Test of Educational Achievement* (2nd ed., comprehensive form). Circle Pines, MN: American Guidance Service.

Kavale, K. A., & Forness, S. R. (1987). Substance over style: Assessing the efficacy of modality testing and teaching. *Exceptional Children, 54,* 228–239.

Kavale, K. A., Hirshoren, A., & Forness, S. R. (1998). Meta-analytic validation of the Dunn and Dunn model of learning-style preferences: A critique of what was Dunn. *Learning Disabilities Research & Practice, 13,* 75–80.

Kawasaki, T. (1989). On the relation between mountain-creases and valley-creases of a flat origami. In H. Huzita (Ed.), *Proceedings of the 1st International Meeting in Origami Science and Technology* (pp. 229–237). Ferrara, Italy.

Keeler, M. L., & Swanson, H. L. (2001). Does strategy knowledge influence working memory in children with mathematical disabilities? *Journal of Learning Disabilities, 34,* 418–434.

Kelly, B., Gersten, R., & Carnine, D. (1990). Student error patterns as a function of curriculum design: Teaching fractions to remedial high school students and high school students with learning disabilities. *Journal of Learning Disabilities, 23,* 23–29.

Kieren, T. E. (1988). Personal knowledge of rational numbers: Its intuitive and formal development. In J. Hiebert & M. Behr (Eds.), *Number concepts and operations in the middle grades* (pp. 162–181). Reston, VA: NCTM; Hillsdale, NJ: Erlbaum.

Kilpatrick, J., Swafford, J., & Findell, B. (Eds.). (2001). *Adding it up: Helping children learn mathematics.* Washington, DC: National Academy Press.

Kimmel, H., Deek, F. P., & O'Shea, M. (1999). Meeting the needs of diverse student populations: Comprehensive professional development in science, math, and technology for teachers of students with disabilities. *School Science and Mathematics, 99,* 241–249.

Knight, J. (2002). Crossing boundaries: What constructivists can teach intensive-explicit instructors and vice versa. *Focus on Exceptional Children, 35*(4), 1–16.

Knott, R. (2005). *Fibonacci numbers and the golden section in art, architecture, and music.* Available at: www.mcs.surrey.ac.uk/Personal/R.Knott/Fibonacci/fibInArt.html.

Koca, S. A., & Lee, H. J. (1998). *Portfolio assessment in mathematics education.* Columbus, OH: ERIC Clearinghouse for Science, Mathematics, and Environmental Education. (ERIC Digest No. ED 434 802).

Kon, J. H. (April 1994). *The thud at the classroom door: Teachers' curriculum decision making in response to a new textbook.* Paper presented at the annual meeting of the American Educational Research Association. New Orleans.

Kordaki, M., & Potari, D. (2002). The effect of area measurement tools on student strategies: The role of a computer microworld. *International Journal of Computers for Mathematical Learning, 7,* 65–100.

Koretz, D. (1994). *The evolution of a portfolio program: The impact and quality of the Vermont Portfolio Program in its second year* (1992–1993). (ERIC No. ED 379 301).

Kosslyn, S. M. (1980). *Image and mind.* Cambridge, MA: Harvard Press.

Krause, M. C. (2000). *Multicultural mathematics materials* (2nd ed.). Reston, VA: NCTM.

Kronick, D. (1990). Holism and empiricism as complementary paradigms. *Journal of Learning Disabilities, 23,* 5–8, 10.

Krulik, S. (Ed.). (1980). *Problem solving in school mathematics: Yearbook of the National Council of Teachers of Mathematics.* Reston, VA: NCTM.

Krutetskii, V. A. (1976). *The psychology of mathematical abilities in school children.* In J. Kilpatrick & I. Wirszup (Eds.). Chicago: University of Chicago Press.

Küchemann, D. (1978). Children's understanding of numerical variables. *Mathematics in School, 7*(4), 23–26.

Kuhn, D., & Phelps, E. (1982). The development of problem-solving strategies. In H. Reese & L. Lipsitt

(Eds.), *Advances in child development and behavior* (pp. 1–44). San Diego: Academic Press.

Kunzig, R. (1997, July). A head for numbers. *Discover*, *18*(7), 108–115.

Lajoie, S. P. (1995). A framework for authentic assessment in mathematics (pp. 19–37). In T. A. Romberg (Ed.), *Reform in school mathematics and authentic assessment*. Albany, NY: SUNY Press.

Lake, D. (2002). Critical social numeracy. *The Social Studies*, *93*(1), 4–10.

Lamb, M. E., Bornstein, M. H., & Teti, D. M. (2002). Origins of language in infancy. In *Development in infancy: An introduction* (4th ed.). Mahwah, NJ: Erlbaum.

Lamon, S. J. (1993). Ratio and proportion: Connecting content and children's thinking. *Journal for Research in Mathematics Education*, *24*, 41–61.

Lamon, S. J. (1999). *Teaching fractions and ratios for understanding: Essential content knowledge and instructional strategies for teachers*. Mahwah, NJ: Erlbaum.

Lang, F. K. (2001). What is a "good guess," anyway? Estimation in early childhood. *Teaching Children Mathematics*, *7*, 462–466.

Learning First Alliance (1998). *Every child mathematically proficient*. Washington, DC: Author.

Leeson, N. J. (1994). Improving students' sense of three-dimensional shapes. *Teaching Children Mathematics*, *1*, 8–11.

Lehrer, R., Jacobson, C., Kemeny, V., & Strom, D. (1999). Building on children's intuitions to develop mathematical understanding of space. In E. Fennema & T. A. Romberg (Eds.), *Mathematics Classrooms that Promote Understanding*. Mahwah, NJ: Erlbaum.

Lembke, L. O., & Reys, B. J. (1994). The development of, and interaction between, intuitive an school-taught ideas about percent. *Journal for Research in Mathematics Education*, *25*, 237–259.

Lenz, B. K., Bulgren, J. A., Schumaker, J. B., Deshler, D. D., & Boudah, D. A., (1994). *The unit organizer routine*. Lawrence, KS: Edge Enterprises.

Leon, J. A., & Pepe, H. J. (1983). Self-instructional training: Cognitive behavior modification for remediating arithmetic deficits. *Exceptional Children*, *50*, 54–60.

Lerner, J. (2000). *Learning disabilities: Theories, diagnosis, and teaching strategies*. (8th ed.). Boston: Houghton Mifflin.

Lesh, R., Post, T., & Behr, M. (1988). Proportional reasoning. In J. Hiebert & M. Behr (Eds.), *Number concepts and operations in the middle grades* (pp. 93–118). Reston, VA: NCTM.

Levin, I., & Druyan, S. (1993). When sociocognitive transaction among peers fails: The case of misconceptions in science. *Child Development*, *63*, 1571–1591.

Levy, F., & Murnane, R. J. (2004). Education and the changing job market. *Educational Leadership*, *62*(2), 80–83.

Liedtke, W. W. (1995). Developing spatial abilities in the early grades. *Teaching Children Mathematics*, *2*, 12–18.

Lloyd, J. W., Forness, S. R., & Kavale, K. A. (1998). Some methods are more effective than others. *Intervention in School and Clinic*, *33*, 195–200.

Lobato, J., & Ellis, A. B. (2002). The teacher's role in supporting students' connections between realistic situations and conventional symbol systems. *Mathematics Education Research Journal*, *14*, 99–120.

Lott, J. W. (2003). The time has come for Pre-K–5 mathematics specialists. *NCTM News Bulletin*, *40*(1), 3.

Lowenthal, B. (1987). Interviewing to diagnose math errors. *Academic Therapy*, *23*, 213–217.

Loyd, R. J., & Brolin, D. (1997). *LCCE modified curriculum for individuals with moderate disabilities*. Arlington, VA: Council for Exceptional Children.

Lubienski, S. T., & Shelley, M. C., II. (April 2003). *A closer look at U.S. mathematics instruction and achievement: Examinations of race and SES in a decade of NAEP data*. Paper presented at the annual meeting of the American Educational Research Association, Chicago.

Lucangeli, D., Coi, G., & Bosco, P. (1997). Metacognitive awareness in good and poor math problem solvers. *Learning Disabilities Research & Practice*, *12*, 209–212.

Maccini, P., & Hughes, C. A. (2000). Effects of a problem-solving strategy on the introductory algebra performance of secondary students with learning disabilities. *Learning Disabilities Research & Practice*, *15*, 10–21.

MacGregor, M., & Price, E. (1999). An exploration of language proficiency and algebra learning. *Journal for Research in Mathematics Education*, *30*, 449–467.

Mahy, M. (1987). *17 kings and 42 elephants*. New York: Dial Books for Young Readers.

Mandler, G., & Shebo, B. J. (1982). Subitizing: An analysis of its component processes. *Journal of Experimental Psychology: General, 111,* 1–21.

Markwardt, F. C., Jr. (1998). *Peabody Individual Achievement Test* (Revised-Normative Update). Circle Pines, MN: American Guidance Service.

Marsh, L. G., & Cooke, N. L. (1996). The effects of using manipulatives in teaching math problem solving to students with learning disabilities, *Learning Disabilities Research & Practice, 11,* 58–65.

Marshall, S. P. (1995). *Schemas in problem solving.* New York: Cambridge University Press.

Martin, R. (1998). *Science for all children: Methods for constructing understanding.* Boston: Allyn & Bacon.

Martinez, J. G. R., & Martinez, N. C. (1996). *Math without fear: A guide for preventing math anxiety in children.* Boston: Allyn & Bacon.

Marzola, E. S. (1987). Using manipulatives in mathematics instruction. *Journal of Reading, Writing, and Learning Disabilities International, 3,* 9–20.

Mastropieri, M. A., & Scruggs, T. E. (1994). *Effective instruction for special education.* (2nd ed.). Austin, TX: PRO-ED.

Mather, N., & Roberts, R. (1994). Learning disabilities: A field in danger of extinction? *Learning Disabilities Research & Practice, 9,* 49–58.

Mayer, R. E. (1981). Frequency norms and structural analysis of algebraic story problems into families, categories, and templates. *Instructional Science, 10,* 135–175.

Mayer, R. E. (2004). Should there be a three-strikes rule against pure discovery learning?: The case for guided methods of instruction. *American Psychologist, 59,* 14–19.

McGraw-Hill (2002). *Mathematics.* New York: McGraw-Hill.

McKnight, C. C., et al. (1987). *The underachieving curriculum: Assessing U.S. school mathematics from an international perspective. A national report on the second international mathematics study.* Champaign, IL: Stipes.

Meichenbaum, D. (1977). *Cognitive behavior modification: An integrated approach.* New York: Plenum.

Mercer, C. D., Harris, C. A., & Miller, S. P. (1993). Reforming reforms in mathematics. *Remedial and Special Education, 14*(6), 14–19.

Mercer, C. D., Jordan, L., & Miller, S. P. (1996). Constructivistic math instruction for diverse learners. *Learning Disability Research and Practice, 11*(3), 147–156.

Mercer, C. D., & Mercer, A. R. (2005). *Teaching students with learning problems* (6th ed.) Upper Saddle River, NJ: Merrill Prentice-Hall.

Mercer, C. D., & Miller, S. P. (1991–1994). *Strategic math series* (A series of seven manuals: Addition Facts 0 to 9; Subtraction Facts 0 to 9; Place Value: Discovering Tens and Ones: Addition Facts 10 to 18; Subtraction Facts 10 to 18; Multiplication Facts 0 to 81; Division Facts 0 to 81). Lawrence, KS; Edge Enterprises.

Mercer, C. D., & Miller, S. P. (1992). Teaching students with learning problems in math to acquire, understand, and apply basic math facts. *Remedial and Special Education, 13*(3), 19–35, 61.

Mercer, C. D., & Pullen, P. C. (2005). *Students with learning disabilities* (6th ed.). Upper Saddle River, NJ: Merrill.

Meyer, C. A. (1992). What's the difference between authentic and performance assessment? *Educational Leadership, 49*(8), 39–40.

Miles, D. D., & Forcht, J. P. (1995). Mathematics strategies for secondary students with learning disabilities or mathematics deficiencies: A cognitive approach. *Intervention in School and Clinic, 31*(2), 91–96.

Miller, D., Brown, A., & Robinson, L. (2002). Widgets on the Web: Using computer-based learning tools. *TEACHING Exceptional Children, 35*(2), 24–28.

Miller, S. P., & Mercer, C. D. (1993). Using a graduated word problem sequence to promote problem-solving skills. *Learning Disabilities Research & Practice, 8,* 169–174.

Miller, S. P., & Mercer, C. D. (1997). New Products: Teaching math computation and problem solving: A program that works. *Intervention in School and Clinic, 32*(3), 185–189, 192.

Miura, I. T., & Okamoto, Y. (2003). Language supports for mathematics understanding and performance. In A. J. Baroody & A. Dowker (Eds.), *The development of arithmetic concepts and skills: Constructing adaptive expertise* (pp. 229–242). Mahwah, NJ: Erlbaum.

Mix, K. S., Huttenlocher, J., & Levine, S. C. (2002). *Quantitative development in infancy and early childhood.* New York: Oxford University Press.

Montague, M. (1992). The effects of cognitive and metacognitive strategy instruction on the mathematical problem solving of middle school students with learning disabilities. *Journal of Learning Disabilities, 25,* 230–248.

Montague, M. (1996). Assessing mathematical problem solving. *Learning Disabilities Research & Practice, 11,* 238–248.

Montague, M. (1997). Cognitive strategy instruction in mathematics for students with learning disabilities. *Journal of Learning Disabilities, 30,* 164–177.

Montague, M. (2003). *Solve It! A practical approach to teaching mathematical problem solving skills.* Reston, VA: Exceptional Innovations.

Montague, M., & Applegate, B. (1993). Mathematical problem-solving characteristics of middle school students with learning disabilities. *The Journal of Special Education, 27,* 175–201.

Montague, M., & Applegate, B. (1993). Middle school students' mathematical problem solving: An analysis of think-aloud protocols. *Learning Disability Quarterly, 16,* 19–32.

Montague, M., Applegate, B., & Marquard, K. (1993). Cognitive strategy instruction and mathematical problem-solving performance of students with learning disabilities. *Learning Disabilities Research & Practice, 8,* 223–232.

Montague, M., & Bos, C. S. (1986). The effect of cognitive strategy training on verbal math problem solving performance of learning disabled adolescents. *Journal of Learning Disabilities, 19,* 26–33.

Montague, M., & Bos, C. S. (1990). Cognitive and metacognitive characteristics of eighth-grade students' mathematical problem solving. *Learning and Individual Differences, 2,* 109–127.

Montague, M., Warger, C., & Morgan, T. H. (2000). Solve it! Strategy instruction to improve mathematical problem solving. *Learning Disabilities Research & Practice, 15,* 110–116.

Montessori, M. (1912). *The Montessori method.* New York: Frederick A. Stokes Company.

Morgan, C. (1998). *Writing mathematically: The discourse of investigation.* (Studies in Mathematics Education Series: 9). London: Falmer Press.

Moshman, D. (1982). Exogenous, endogenous, and dialectical constructivism. *Developmental Review, 2,* 371–384.

Murnane, R. J., & Levy, F. (1996). *Teaching the new basic skills.* New York: The Free Press.

Muschla, J. A., & Muschla, G. R. (1995). *The math teacher's book of lists.* Englewood Cliffs, NJ: Prentice Hall.

Myller, R. (1962). *How big is a foot?* New York: Dell Publishing.

Nadeau, I. (2002). *Food chains in a meadow habitat.* New York: Rosen.

NAEYC and NCTM (2002). Early childhood mathematics: Promoting good beginnings. A joint position statement of the NAEYC and the NCTM. Available: www.naeyc.org/resources/position_statements/psmath.htm.

National Academy of Sciences (1997). *Preparing for the 21st century: The education imperative.* Washington, DC: The National Academies Press.

National Center for Educational Outcomes (2005). *Special topic area: Accommodations for students with disabilities.* University of Minnesota. Available: http://education.umn.edu/NCEO.

National Center for Educational Statistics (2003). *National assessment of educational progress: Mathematics study 2003.* Available: http://nces.ed.gov/nationsreportcard.

National Center for Education Statistics (2003). *Overview and Inventory of state education reforms: 1990 to 2000.* Washington, DC: U.S. Department of Education.

National Center for Educational Statistics (2004). *Highlights from the trends in international mathematics and science study (TIMMSS) 2003.* Washington, DC: U.S. Department of Education.

National Center for Education Statistics (2004). *International outcomes of learning in mathematics literacy and problem solving: PISA 2003 results from the U.S. perspective.* Washington, DC: U.S. Department of Education.

National Commission on Excellence in Education (1983). *A nation at risk: The imperative for educational reform.* Washington, DC: U.S. Government Printing Office.

National Council for the Social Studies (1994). *Expectations of excellence: Curriculum standards for social studies.* Silver Spring, MD: Author.

National Council of Teachers of Mathematics (1989). *Curriculum and evaluation standards for school mathematics.* Reston, VA: Author.

National Council of Teachers of Mathematics (1989, 2000). *Principles and standards for school mathematics.* Reston, VA: Author.

National Council of Teachers of Mathematics (1991). *Professional standards for teaching mathematics.* Reston, VA: Author.

National Council of Teachers of Mathematics (1995). *Assessment standards for school mathematics*. Reston, VA: Author.

National Council of Teachers of Mathematics (1998). *Mathematics for second language learners*. Available at: www.nctm.org/about/position_statements/position_statement_06.htm.

National Council of Teachers of Mathematics (2003). *A research companion to principles and standards for school mathematics*. J. Kilpatrick, W. G. Martin, & D. Schifter (Eds.). Reston, VA: Author.

National Joint Committee on Learning Disabilities (2005). Responsiveness to intervention and learning disabilities. *Learning Disability Quarterly*, 28, 249–260.

National Research Council (1995). *Mathematical preparation of the technical work force: Report of a workshop*. Washington, DC: National Academies Press.

National Research Council, Mathematical Sciences Education Board (1989). *Everybody counts: A report to the nation on the future of mathematics education*. Washington, DC: National Academies Press.

National Research Council, Mathematical Sciences Education Board (1990). *Reshaping school mathematics: A philosophy and framework for curriculum*. Washington, DC: National Academies Press.

National Research Council, Mathematical Sciences Education Board (1998). *High school mathematics at work: Essays and examples for the education of all students*. Washington, DC: National Academies Press.

Newcomer, P. L. (2001). *Diagnostic Achievement Battery* (3rd). Austin, TX: PRO-ED.

Newcomer, P. L., & Bryant, B. R. (1993). *Diagnostic Achievement Test for Adolescents* (2nd). Austin, TX: PRO-ED.

No Child Left Behind Act of 2001. P. L. 107-110. 34 C.F.R. § 200 et. seq.

Northwest Regional Educational Laboratory (2000). *NWREL mathematics problem-solving scoring guide*. Available at: www.nwrel.org/msec/mpm/ scoregrid.html.

Nunes, T., Schliemann, A. D., & Carraher, D. W. (1993). *Street mathematics and school mathematics*. Cambridge, UK: Cambridge Press.

O'Connor, J. J., & Robertson, E. F. (2003). *Mathematics and art: Perspective*. MacTutor History of Mathematics. Available at: www-history.mcs.st-andrews.ac.uk.

O'Connor, J. J., & Robertson, E. G. (2000). *An overview of Egyptian mathematics*. MacTutor History of Mathematics. Available: www-history.mcs.st-andrews.ac.uk.

Oberlin, L. (1982). How to teach children to hate mathematics. *School Science and Mathematics*, 82, 261.

Odom, S. L., Brantlinger, E., Gersten, R., Horner, R. H., Thompson, B., & Harris, K. R. (2005). Research in special education: Scientific methods and evidence-based practices. *Exceptional Children*, 71, 137–148.

Ogle, D. S. (1986). K-W-L group instructional strategy. In A. S. Palincsar, D. S. Ogle, B. F. Jones, & E. G. Carr (Eds.), *Teaching reading as thinking* (Teleconference Resource Guide, pp. 11–17). Alexandria, VA: ASCD.

Olson, J., & Platt, J. (1992). *Teaching children and adolescents with special needs*. New York: Merrill/Macmillan.

Olson, M. (2002). Responses to the coloring tetras with two colors problems. *Teaching Children Mathematics*, 8, 277–279.

Omniglot (n.d.). *A guide to written language*. Available: http://omniglot.com.

Organization for Economic Co-operation and Development. (2004). *Learning for tomorrow's world: First results from PISA 2003*. Available: www.oecd.org.

Orkwis, R., & McLane, K. (1998). *A curriculum every student can use: Design principles for student access*. ERIC/OSEP Topical Brief. ERIC Clearinghouse on Disabilities and Gifted Education. Reston, VA: Council for Exceptional Children.

Ostad, S. A. (1998). Developmental differences in solving simple arithmetic word problems and simple number-fact problems: A comparison of mathematically normal and mathematically disabled children. *Mathematical Cognition*, 4, 1–19.

Pandiscio, E. A., (2001). Problem solving in middle-level geometry. *The Clearing House*, 75(2), 99–103.

Papert, S. (1980). *Mindstorms: Children, computers, and powerful ideas*. New York: Basic Books.

Parker, F. (1993). *Turning points: Books and reports that reflected and shaped U.S. education, 1749–1990s*. (ERIC Document Reproduction Service No. ED 369 695).

Parker, M., & Leinhardt, G. (1995). Percent: A privileged proportion. *Review of Educational Research*, 65, 421–481.

Parmar, R. S., Cawley, J. F., & Frazita, R. R. (1996). Word problem-solving by students with and without mild disabilities. *Exceptional Children*, 62, 415–429.

Parsons, J. L., Marchand-Martella, N. E., Waldron-Soler, K., Martella, R. C., & Lignugaris/Kraft, B. (2004). Effects of a high school-based peer-delivered Corrective Mathematics program. *Journal of Direct Instruction*, 4, 95–103.

PBS-Nova (1997). *Pyramids*. Available: www.pbs.org/wgbh/nova/pyramid.

Pearson, E. S. (1986). Summing it all up: Pre-1900 algorithms. *The Arithmetic Teacher, 33*(7), 38–41.

Peck, R. (2000). *A year down under*. Dial.

Pegg, J., & Davey, G. (1998). Interpreting student understanding in geometry: A synthesis of two models. In R. Lehrer & D. Chazan (Eds.), *Designing learning environments for developing understanding of geometry and space* (pp. 109–135). Mahwah, NJ: Erlbaum.

Pemberton, J. B., & Smith, D. D. (1994). *An analysis of teacher-time during the school day: A study comparing five special education service delivery models available to students with disabilities.* Paper presented at the Symposium on Inclusive Education, Cambridge University, England.

Peterson, S. K., Mercer, C. D., & O'Shea, L. (1988). Teaching learning disabled students place value using concrete to abstract sequence. *Learning Disability Research & Practice, 4,* 52–56.

Piaget, J. (1952). *The origins of intelligence in children.* New York: International Universities Press.

Piaget, J., Grize, J., Szeminska, A., & Bang, V. (1977). *Epistemology and psychology of functions.* Boston: Dordrecht-Holland (first published in 1968).

Piaget, J., & Inhelder, B. (1948/1956). *The child's conception of space.* London: Routledge and Kegan Paul.

Piaget, J., & Inhelder, B. (1969). *The psychology of the child.* New York: Basic Books.

Piaget, J., Inhelder, B., & Szeminsak, A. (1948/1960). *The child's conception of geometry.* London: Routledge and Kegan Paul.

Picciotto, H. (n.d.). *Algebra manipulatives: Comparison and history.* Available at: www.picciotto.org/math-ed/manipulatives/alg-manip.html.

Pintrich, P. R., & De Groot, E. V. (1990). Motivational and self-regulated learning components of classroom academic performance. *Journal of Educational Psychology, 82,* 33–40.

Pólya, G. (1945). *How to solve it: A new aspect of mathematical method.* Princeton, NJ: Princeton Press.

Poplin, M. S. (1988). Holistic/constructivist principles of the teaching/learning process: Implications for the field of learning disabilities. *Journal of Learning Disabilities, 21,* 401–416.

Pound, L. (1999). *Supporting mathematical development in the early years.* Philadelphia, PA: Open University Press.

Prawat, R. S., & Floden, R. E. (1994). Philosophical perspectives on constructivist views of learning. *Educational Psychologist, 29*(1), 37–48.

Project 2061 (2000). *Comparing middle grades mathematics textbooks.* American Association for the Advancement of Science. Available: www.project2061.org.

RAND Mathematics Study Panel (2003). *Mathematics proficiency for all students: Toward a strategic research and development program in mathematics education.* Santa Monica, CA: RAND.

Randolph, T. D., & Sherman, H. J. (2001). Alternative algorithms: Increasing options, reducing errors. *Teaching Children Mathematics, 7,* 480–484.

Rasmussen, M. J. (2002). PSST!! Pass it on . . . Lessons from the field. *Journal of School Improvement, 3*(2).

Reed, S. K. (1999). *Word problems: Research and curriculum reform.* Mahwah, NJ: Erlbaum.

Reid, D. K., Kurkjian, C., & Carruthers, S. S. (1994). Special education teachers interpret constructivist teaching. *Remedial and Special Education, 15,* 267–280.

Reid, D. K., & Stone, C. A. (1991). Why is cognitive instruction effective? Underlying learning mechanisms. *Remedial and Special Education, 12*(3), 8–19.

Reisman, F. K. (1977). *Diagnostic teaching of elementary school mathematics: Methods and content.* Chicago: Rand McNally.

Reschley, D. J. (1997). Functional assessment and special education decision making. In L. M. McDonnell, M. J. McLaughlin, & P. Morison (Eds.), *Educating one and all: Students with disabilities and standards-based reform.* Washington, DC: National Academy Press.

Resnick, L. B. (1987). *Education and learning to think.* Washington, DC: National Academy Press.

Resnick, L. B., & Omanson, S. F. (1987). Learning to understand arithmetic. In R. Glaser (Ed.), *Advances in instructional psychology* (Vol. 3, pp. 41–95). Hillsdale, NJ: Erlbaum.

Reuhkala, M. (2001). Mathematical skills in ninth-graders: Relationship with visuo-spatial abilities and working memory. *Educational Psychology, 21,* 387–399.

Riley, M. S., Greeno, J. G., & Heller, J. I. (1983). Development of children's problem-solving ability in arithmetic. In H. Ginsburg (Ed.), *The development of mathematical thinking* (pp. 153–196). New York: Academic Press.

Rivera, D. M., & Smith, D. D. (1997). *Teaching students with learning and behavior problems.* Boston: Allyn & Bacon.

Rivera, D. P., Smith, R. G., Goodwin, M. W., & Bryant, B. R. (1998). Mathematical word problem solving: A synthesis of intervention research for students with learning disabilities. *Advances in Learning and Behavioral Disabilities, 12,* 245–285.

Romberg, T. A. (1993). NCTM's standards: A rallying flag for mathematics teachers. *Educational Leadership, 50*(5), 36–41.

Romberg, T. A., & Wilson, L. D. (1995). A framework for authentic assessment in mathematics. In T. A. Romberg (Ed.), *Reform in school mathematics and authentic assessment.* Albany: SUNY Press.

Romberg, T. A., Zarinnia, E. A., & Collis, K. F. (1990). A new world view of assessment in mathematics. In G. Kulm (Ed.), *Assessing higher-order thinking in mathematics.* Washington, DC: American Association for the Advancement of Science.

Rosenshine, B. V. (1986). Synthesis of research on explicit teaching. *Educational Leadership, 43*(7), 60–69.

Rossman, A. J., & Chance, B. L. (1999). Teaching the reasoning of statistical inference: A "top ten" list. *The College Mathematics Journal, 30,* 297–305.

Rourke, B., & Conway, J. (1997). Disabilities of arithmetic and mathematical reasoning: Perspectives from neurology and neuropsychology. *Journal of Learning Disabilities, 30,* 34–36.

Rowan, T. E. (1990). The geometry standards in K–8 mathematics. *Arithmetic Teacher, 37*(6), 24–28.

Rubenstein, R. N. (2000). Word origins: Building communication connections. *Mathematics Teaching in the Middle School, 5,* 493–498.

Rubenstein, R. N., & Thompson, D. R. (2002). Understanding and supporting children's mathematical vocabulary development. *Teaching Children Mathematics, 9*(2), 107–112.

Russell, R. L., & Ginsburg, H. P. (1984). Cognitive analysis of children's mathematics difficulties. *Cognition and Instruction, 1,* 217–244.

Saloman, G., & Perkins, D. N. (1989). Rocky roads to transfer: Rethinking mechanisms of a neglected phenomenon. *Educational Psychologist, 24,* 113–142.

Salvia, J., & Ysseldyke, J. E. (2001). *Assessment* (8th ed.). Boston: Houghton Mifflin.

Santos, K. E., & Rettig, M. D. (1999). Going on the block: Meeting the needs of students with disabilities in high schools with block scheduling. *Teaching Exceptional Children, 31*(3), 54–59.

Scheid, K. (1993). *Helping students become strategic learners: Guidelines for teaching.* Cambridge, MA: Brookline.

Schloss, P. J., & Kobza, S. A. (1997). The use of peer tutoring for the acquisition of functional math skills among students with moderate retardation. *Education & Treatment of Children, 20,* 189–208.

Schoenfeld, A. H. (1987). Pólya, problem solving, and education. *Mathematics Magazine, 60*(5), 283–291.

Schoenfeld, A. H. (1992). Learning to think mathematically: Problem solving, metacognition, and sense making in mathematics. In D. A. Grouws (Ed.), *Handbook of research on mathematics teaching and learning* (pp. 334–370). New York: Macmillan.

School-to-Work Opportunities Act of 1994, P.L. 103-239.

Schunk, D. H. (1989). Self-efficacy and cognitive skill learning. In C. Ames & R. Ames (Eds.), *Research on motivation in education.* Vol. 3, *Goals and cognitions* (pp. 13–44). San Diego: Academic Press.

Schwartz, J. L. (1988). Intensive quantity and referent transforming arithmetic operations. In J. Hiebert & M. Behr (Eds.), *Number concepts and operations in the middle grades* (Vol. 2, pp. 41–52). Reston, VA: NCTM.

Scott, K. (1993). Multisensory mathematics for children with mild disabilities. *Exceptionality, 4*(2), 97–111.

Scruggs, T. E., Mastropieri, M. A., & Richter, L. (1985). Peer tutoring with behaviorally disordered students: Social and academic benefits. *Behavioral Disorders, 12*(11), 36–44.

Seo, K., & Ginsburg, H. P. (2003). "You've got to carefully read the math sentence . . .": Classroom context and children's interpretations of the equals sign. In A. J. Baroody & A. Dowker (Eds.), *The development of arithmetic concepts and skills: Constructing adaptive expertise.* (pp. 161–188). Mahwah, NJ: Erlbaum.

Seo, K., & Ginsburg, H. P. (2004). What is developmentally appropriate in early childhood mathematics education: Lessons from new research. In D. H. Clements & J. Sarama (Eds.), *Engaging young children in mathematics: Standards for early childhood* mathematics education (pp. 91–104). Mahwah, NJ: Erlbaum.

Shiah, R-L., Mastropieri, M. A., Scruggs, T. E., & Fulk, B. J. M. (1994–5). The effects of computer-assisted instruction on the mathematical problem solving of students with learning disabilities. *Exceptionality, 5*(3), 131–161.

Shulman, L. S., & Keislar, E. R. (Eds.). (1966). *Learning by discovery: A critical appraisal.* Chicago: Rand McNally.

Sidebotham, T. H. (2002). *The A to Z of mathematics: A basic guide.* New York: John Wiley & Sons.

Siegler, R. (2003). Implications of cognitive science research for mathematics education. In J. Kilpatrick, W. G. Martin, & D. Schifter (Eds.), *A research companion to principles and standards for school mathematics* (pp. 289–303). Reston, VA: NCTM.

Simon, R., & Hanrahan, J. (2004). An evaluation of the TouchMath method for teaching addition to students with learning disabilities in mathematics, *European Journal of Special Needs Education, 19,* 191–209.

Singh, S. (1977). *Fermat's enigma: The epic quest to solve the world's greatest mathematical problem.* New York: Walker.

Skinner, B. F. (1963). Operant behavior. *American Psychologist, 18,* 503–515.

Slavin, R. E. (1984). Students motivating students to excel: Cooperative incentives, cooperative tasks, and student achievement. *The Elementary School Journal, 85,* 53–63.

Slavin, R. E. (1995). *Cooperative learning: Theory, research, and practice.* Boston: Allyn & Bacon.

Slavin, R. E. (2003). *Educational psychology: Theory and practice* (7th ed.). Boston: Allyn & Bacon.

Smith, S. G. (2003). Paper folding and conic sections. *Mathematics Teacher, 96,* 202–207.

Snider, V. E. (1992). Learning styles and learning to read: A critique. *Remedial and Special Education, 13*(1), 6–18.

Snider, V. E., & Crawford, D. B. (1996). Action research: Implementing Connecting Math Concepts. *Effective School Practices, 15*(2), 17–26.

Sophian, C. (1998). A developmental perspective on children's counting. In C. Donlan (Ed.), *The development of mathematical skills* (pp. 27–46). New York: Psychology Press.

South Carolina Department of Education (2005). *South Carolina social studies curriculum standards.* Columbia, SC: Author.

Sowder, J. T. (1988). Mental computation and number comparison: Their roles in the development of number sense and computational estimation. In J. Hiebert & M. Behr (Eds.), *Number concepts and operations in the middle grades* (pp. 182–197). Hillsdale, NJ: Erlbaum.

Sowell, E. J. (1989). Effects of manipulative materials in mathematics instruction. *Journal for Research in Mathematics Education, 20,* 498–505.

Sprenger, M. (1999). *Learning and memory: The brain in action.* Alexandria, VA: ASCD.

Starkey, P., & Gelman, R. (1982). The development of addition and subtraction abilities prior to formal schooling in arithmetic. In T. P. Carpenter, J. M. Moser, & T. A. Romberg (Eds.), *Addition and subtraction: A cognitive perspective.* (pp. 99–116). Hillsdale, NJ: Erlbaum.

Stein, M., Kinder, D., Silbert, J., & Carnine, D. (2006). *Designing effective mathematics instruction: A direct instruction approach* (4th ed.). Upper Saddle River, NJ: Merrill.

Steinberg, A., Cushman, K., & Riordan, R. (1999). *Schooling for the real world.* San Francisco: Jossey-Bass.

Stenmark, J. K. (Ed.) (2002). *Mathematics assessment: Myths, models, good questions, and practical suggestions.* Reston, VA: NCTM.

Stern, C. (1949). *Children discover arithmetic: An introduction to structural arithmetic.* New York: Harper & Brothers.

Stiff, L. V., & Curcio, F. R. (Eds.). (1999). *Developing mathematical reasoning in grades K–12: 1999 Yearbook.* Reston, VA: NCTM.

Stipek, D., Givvin, K. B., Salmon, J. M., & MacGyvers, V. L. (1998). Can a teacher intervention improve classroom practices and student motivation in mathematics? *Journal of Experimental Education, 66,* 319–337.

Swanson, H. L., & Sáez, L. (2003). Memory difficulties in children and adults with learning disabilities. In H. L. Swanson, K. R. Harris, & S. Graham (Eds.), *Handbook of learning disabilities* (pp. 182–198). New York: Guilford.

Swanson, H. L. (1993). An information processing analysis of learning disabled children's problem solving. *American Educational Research Journal, 30,* 861–893.

Swanson, H. L. (1994). The role of working memory and dynamic assessment in the classification of children with learning disabilities. *Learning Disabilities Research & Practice, 9,* 190–202.

Swanson, H. L., Hoskyn, M., Sachee-Lee, C., & O'Shaughnessy, T. (1997). *Intervention research for students with learning disabilities: A meta-analysis of treatment outcomes.* Washington, DC: U.S. Department of Education.

Sylwester, R. (1995). *A celebration of neurons: An educator's guide to the human brain.* Alexandria, VA: ASCD.

Tahta, D. (2004, January). An account of the first decade of AT(A)M. *Mathematics Teaching.* Available: www.atm.org.uk/about/first-decade.html.

Tall, D. (1992). The transition to advanced mathematical thinking: Functions, limits, infinity, and proof. In D. A. Grouws (Ed.), *Handbook of research on mathematics teaching and learning* (pp. 495–511). New York: Macmillan.

Technology-Related Assistance for Individuals with Disabilities Act, 1988. (P.L. 100-407).

Test, D. W., Howell, A., Burkhart, K., & Beroth, T. (1993). The one-more-than technique as a strategy for counting money for individuals with moderate mental retardation. *Education and Training in Mental Retardation, 28,* 232–241.

Thayer, J., & Giebelhaus, C. R. (2001). Integrating writing to improve math achievement. *Mid-Western Educational Researcher, 14*(2), 11–16.

The American Heritage Book of English Usage (1996). Word choice: New uses, common confusion, and constraints. *The American heritage book of English usage. A practical and authoritative guide to contemporary English.* Boston: Houghton Mifflin.

The Psychological Corporation. (2001). *Wechsler Individual Achievement Test* (2nd). San Antonio, TX: Author.

The University of Chicago School Mathematics Project (2001). *Everyday Mathematics.* Chicago: Everyday Learning.

Thompson, D. R., & Rubenstein, R. N. (2000). Learning mathematics vocabulary: Potential pitfalls and instructional strategies. *Mathematics Teacher, 93,* 568–574.

Thompson, P. (1992). *Blocks microworld.* University of California, San Diego.

Thompson, S. J., & Thurlow, M. L. (2000). *State alternate assessments: Status as IDEA alternate assessment requirements take effect.* (Synthesis Report 35). Minneapolis, MN: University of Minnesota, National Center on Educational Outcomes. Available at: http://education.umn.edu/NCEO/OnlinePubs/Synthesis35.html.

Thurlow, M. L., Elliott, J. L., & Ysseldyke, J. E. (1998). *Testing students with disabilities: Practical strategies for complying with district and state requirements.* Thousand Oaks, CA: Corwin.

Thurlow, M. L., Lazarus, S., Thompson, S., & Robey, J. (2002). *2001 state policies on assessment participation and accommodations.* (Synthesis Report 46). Minneapolis, MN: University of Minnesota, National Center on Educational Outcomes. Available at: http://education.umn.edu/NCEO/OnlinePubs/Synthesis46.html.

Timmerman, M. A. (2003). Perceptions of professional growth: A mathematics teacher educator in transition. *School Science and Mathematics, 103,* 155–167.

Tindal, G., & Fuchs, L. S. (1999). *A summary of research on test change: An empirical basis for defining accommodations.* Lexington: University of Kentucky, Mid-South Regional Resource Center.

Tompert, A. (1990). *Grandfather Tang's story.* New York: Crown.

Tompkins, P. (1978) *Secrets of the great pyramid.* New York: Harper & Row.

Tout, N. (2005). *Calculator timeline.* Available at: www.vintagecalculators.com/html/calculator_time-line.html.

Tralli, R., Colombo, B., Deshler, D. D., & Schumaker, J. B. (1996). The strategies intervention model: A model for supported inclusion at the secondary level. *Remedial and Special Education, 17,* 204–216.

Travers, K. J., & McKnight, C. C. (1985). Mathematics achievement in U.S. schools: Preliminary findings from the second IEA mathematics study. *Phi Delta Kappan, 66*(6), 407–413.

Trent, S. C., Artiles, A. J., & Englert, C. S. (1998). From deficit thinking to social constructivism: A review of theory, research, and practice in special education. *Review of Research in Education, 23,* 277–307.

Tucker, J. A. (1985). Curriculum-based assessment: An introduction. *Exceptional Children, 52,* 199–204.

Tyler, R. W. (1949). *Basic principles of curriculum and instruction.* Chicago: University of Chicago Press.

U.S. Congress, Office of Technology Assessment (February, 1992). *Testing in American schools: Asking the right questions.* OTA-SET-519. Washington, DC: U.S. Government Printing Office (ED 340770).

U.S. Department of Education (2004). *National Assessment of Educational Progress, 2003 Mathematics Assessments.* Washington, DC: Author.

U.S. Department of Education (14 August 2006). 34 CFR Parts 300 and 304, Assistance to States for the Education of Children with Disabilites, Final Rule. *Federal Register, 71*(156), 46752–46845.

University College London (2002). What is ancient Egyptian art? *Digital Egypt.* Available: www.digitalegypt.ucl.ac.uk.

Usiskin, Z. (2003). The integration of the school mathematics curriculum in the United States: History and meaning. In S. A. McGraw (Ed.), *Integrated mathematics: Choices and challenges* (pp. 13–31). Reston, VA: NCTM.

Van Biersel, S. S. (2004). *Fossil fuel sources, usage and alternatives: What are the options?* Yale-New Haven Teachers Institute Curriculum Project. Available at: www.yale.edu/ynhti/curriculum/units.

Van de Walle, J. A. (1998). *Elementary and middle school mathematics: Teaching developmentally* (3rd ed.). New York: Longman.

Van Dyke, F. (1995). A visual approach to deductive reasoning. *Mathematics Teacher, 88,* 481–487.

van Garderen, D., & Montague, M. (2003). Visual-spatial representations and mathematical problem solving. *Learning Disabilities Research & Practice, 18,* 246–254.

van Hiele, P. M. (1959/1985). The child's thought and geometry. In D. Fuys, D. Geddes, & R. Tishler (Eds.), *English translation of selected writings of Dina van Hiele-Geldof and Pierre M. van Hiele* (pp. 243–252). Brooklyn, NY: Brooklyn College School of Education.

Varelas, M., & Becker, J. (1997). Children's developing understanding of place value: Semiotic aspects. *Cognition and Instruction, 15,* 265–286.

Vaughn, S., & Fuchs, L. S. (Eds.). (2003). Redefining learning disabilities as inadequate response to instruction (Special issue). *Learning Disabilities Research & Practice, 18*(3).

Vaughn, S., Gersten, R., & Chard, D. J. (2000). The underlying message in LD intervention research: Findings from research syntheses. *Exceptional Children, 67,* 99–114.

Vergnaud, G. (1988). Multiplicative structures. In J. Hiebert & M. Behr (Eds.). *Number concepts and operations in the middle grades* (pp. 141–161). Reston, VA: NCTM; Hillsdale, NJ: Erlbaum.

von Glasersfeld, E. (1991). Introduction: Aspects of constructivism. In C. T. Fosnot (Ed.). *Constructivism: Theory, perspectives, and practice* (pp. 3–7). New York: Teachers College Press.

Vygotsky, L. S. (1924/1979). Consciousness as a problem in the psychology of behavior. *Soviet Psychology, 17*(4), 3–35.

Vygotsky, L. S. (1934/1986). *Thought and language.* Cambridge, MA: MIT Press.

Watson, J. B. (1920). Is thinking merely the action of language mechanisms? *British Journal of Psychology, 11,* 87–104.

Weiner, B. (1985). An attributional theory of achievement, motivation, and emotion. *Psychological Review, 92,* 548–573.

Weller, D., R., & McLeskey, J. (2000). Block scheduling and inclusion in a high school. *Remedial and Special Education, 21,* 209–218.

Wendler, C., Zeller, K., & Allspach, J. (April 2003). *The impact of calculator performance and use on performance on a mathematics reasoning test.* Paper presented at the annual meeting of the American Educational Research Association, Chicago IL.

What Works Clearinghouse (2005). *The middle school math topic report.* Available: www.whatworks.ed.gov.

Wheatley, G. (1996). *Quick draw: Developing spatial sense in mathematics.* Tallahassee, FL: Mathematics Learning.

Wheatley, G., & Cobb, P. (1991). Analysis of young children's spatial constructions. In L. Steffe (Ed.), *International perspectives on transforming early childhood mathematics education.* Hillsdale, NJ: Erlbaum.

Wheatley, G. H. (1991). Constructivist perspectives on math and science learning. *Science Education, 75*(1), 9–21.

Wheatley, G. H. (1998). Imagery and mathematics learning. *Focus on Learning Problems in Mathematics, 20,* 65–77.

Wheatley, G. H., & Reynolds, A. M. (1999). "Image Maker": Developing spatial sense. *Teaching Children Mathematics, 5,* 374–378.

Wiggins, G. (1998). An exchange of views on "semantics, psychometrics, and assessment reform: A close look at 'authentic' assessments" (Letter to editor). *Educational Researcher, 27*(6), 20–21.

Wiley, D. A. (Ed.). (2001). *Instructional use of learning objects: Online version.* Available at: http://reusabililty.org/read.

Willingham, D. T. (2004). *Reframing the mind.* Hoover Institution. Available at: www.educationnext.org/20043/18.html.

Wilson, C. L., & Sindelar, P. T. (1991). Direct instruction in math word problems: Students with learning disabilities. *Exceptional Children, 57,* 512–519.

Wilson, L. D., & Blank, R. K. (1999). *Improving mathematics education using results from NAEP and TIMSS.* Washington, DC: Council of Chief State School Officers.

Wilson, L. D., & Kenney, P. A. (2003). Classroom and large-scale assessment. In J. Kilpatrick, W. G. Martin, & D. Schifter (Eds.) *A research companion to principles and standards for school mathematics* (pp. 53–67). Reston, VA: NCTM

Wilson, M. (1995). Assessment nets: An alternative approach to assessment in mathematics achievement (pp. 236–259). In T. A. Romberg (Ed.), *Reform in school mathematics and authentic assessment.* Albany: SUNY Press.

Wilson, R. (1987). Direct observation of academic learning time. *TEACHING Exceptional Children, 19*(2), 13–17.

Wirtz, R. (1974). *Drill and practice at the problem-solving level.* Washington, DC: Curriculum Development Associates.

Witzel, B., Smith, S. W., & Brownell, M. T. (2001). How can I help students with learning disabilities in algebra? *Intervention in School and Clinic, 37,* 101–104.

Witzel, B. S., Mercer, C. D., & Miller, M. D. (2003). Teaching algebra to students with learning difficulties: An investigation of an explicit instruction model. *Learning Disabilities Research & Practice, 18,* 121–131.

Wolfram, S. (2002). *A new kind of science.* Champaign, IL: Wolfram Media.

Woodcock, R. W., McGrew, K. S., & Mather, N. (2001). *Woodcock-Johnson Tests of Achievement* (3rd). Itasca, IL: Riverside Publishing.

Woodward, J., & Baxter, J. (1997). The effects of an innovative approach to mathematics on academically low-achieving students in inclusive settings. *Exceptional Children, 63,* 373–388.

Woodward, J., Baxter, J., & Robinson, R. (1999). Rules and reasons: Decimal instruction for academically low achieving students. *Learning Disabilities Research & Practice, 14,* 15–21.

Woodward, J., Monroe, K., & Baxter, J. (2001). Enhancing student achievement on performance assessments in mathematics. *Learning Disabilities Quarterly, 24,* 33–46.

World Wide Web Consortium (W3C). *About the World Wide Web.* Available at: www.w3.org/WWW.

Xin, Y. P., & Jitendra, A. K. (1999). The effects of instruction in solving mathematical word problems for students with learning problems: A meta-analysis. *The Journal of Special Education, 32,* 207–225.

Xin, Y. P., Jitendra, A. K., & Deatline-Buchman, A. (2005). Effects of mathematical word problem-solving instruction on middle school students with learning problems. *The Journal of Special Education, 39*(3), 181–192.

Xu, F., & Spelke, E. S. (2000). Large number discrimination in 6-month-old infants. *Cognition, 74,* B1–B11.

Yakimanskaya, I. S. (1991). The development of spatial thinking in schoolchildren. In P. S. Wilson & E. J. Davis (Eds.), R. H. Silverman (Trans.), *Soviet Studies in Mathematics Education* (Volume 3). Reston, VA: NCTM.

Yell, M. L., & Drasgow, E. (2005). *No child left behind: A guide for professionals.* Upper Saddle River, NJ: Pearson.

Zaslavsky, C. (1996). *The multicultural math classroom: Bringing in the world.* Portsmouth, NH: Heinemann.

Zawaiza, T. B., & Gerber, M. M. (1993). Effects of explicit instruction on community college students with learning disabilities. *Learning Disability Quarterly, 16,* 64–79.

Zigmond, N. (2003). Searching for the most effective service delivery model for students with learning disabilities. In H. L. Swanson, K. R. Harris, & S. Graham (Eds.), *Handbook of learning disabilities* (pp. 110–122). New York: Guilford.

Zimmerman, W., & Cunningham, S. (Eds.) (1991). *Visualization in teaching and learning mathematics.* Mathematical Association of America.

Index

Inductive argument, 21
Informal mathematics knowledge,
    34–36, 98–99, 292–293
Information processing theory, 43–44
Instruction
    collaboration for, 134–137
    competency areas for, 95
    effective, 121–122
    planning and delivering, 112–126
    presenting new concepts, 102
    principles of, 96–112
    sequence of, 102–104
    student-centered curriculum for,
        126–134
Integers, 185, 250
International Education Software (IES)
    Math Education and Technology
    website, 205
Interrelated learning theories, 45–48

Judicious review, 112

Key-Math Revised (program), 70
K–12 Mathematics Curriculum Center,
    205

Labeling, 31
Lab Gear model, 197
Language
    of mathematics, 105–109, 115,
        255–256
    myths about, 99
    problem areas in, 106
    teacher modeling of, 256
    written, 215–219
Language development, 33
    problems in, 36, 54–55
Language disabilities, 33–34
Learning
    brain development and, 30–31
    cognitive structure development and,
        33–34
    concept and skill development and,
        31–32, 39
    constructivism and, 51
    early milestones in, 29–30
    habits of, 56
    informal knowledge and, 34–36
    obstacles to, 209
    precursors of, 29–36
Learning objects, 203
Learning problems. *See also*
    Mathematics disabilities
    characteristics of, 54–57
    identification of, 61
    signs of, 36
    students with. *See* Students with
        learning problems

Learning styles approach, 47–48
Learning theories, 41–48
    behaviorist, 42
    cognitive, 43–44
    interrelated, 45–48
    about mathematics disabilities, 53–57
    socio-cultural, 44–45
Leisure activities, 233, 235
Lesson planning matrix, 113, 117, 355
Lessons
    content types, 118–119
    grouping students for, 119–121
    instructional techniques for, 121–122
    planning for, 118–122
    techniques for, 121–122
    types of, 126
    variety in, 104–105, 106
Life Centered Career Education
    (LCCE) curriculum, 227–228
Life skills, 229–237
    task analysis for, 236
Linear functions, 64, 343–345
Literature, mathematics and, 219–220
Loans, 233
LOGO Foundation, 205

Magic squares, 252, 253
Maintenance, 111
Manipulatives, 188–197
    commercial, 193–197
    creating materials, 189–193
    edible, 192
    safety issues with, 192–193
    virtual, 202–203
Mastery measures, 73, 76–77
Mathematics
    applied, 237–238
    art and, 221–224
    attitudes toward, 2–3, 7–8
    in career education, 225–229
    connection with science, 211–213
    cross-curricular integration of,
        209–225
    language of, 105–109, 256–257
    in life skills, 229–237
    literature and, 219–220
    as tool for social studies, 213–215
    transition planning and, 238–242
    writing in, 215–219
Mathematics disabilities, 53–57
    characteristics of, 54–57
    types of, 53–54
Mathematics instruction. *See* Instruction
Mathematics learning. *See* Learning
Mathematizing, 89
Math Forum @ Drexel, 205
Measure, 313
Measurement, 21–22

manipulatives for, 191–192
    subjects, tools and units in, 21
Memory
    development of, 33
    problems with, 55
    types of, 44
Mental representations, 34
Metacognitive processes, 46, 161
    problems in, 56
Middle level assessment, 88
Mobiles, 223
Möbius strips, 222–223
Modeling, 122
Modes of representation, 102–103
Money
    for teaching place value, 261–262
    using, 231–231
Monitoring Basic Skills Progress
    (program), 70
Monomials, 337
Motivation, 100
Motor skills, problems in, 56
Multi-digit computation, 278–288
    addition and subtraction, 279–281
    alternative algorithms for, 283–288
    multiplication and division, 281–283
Multiple intelligences theory, 46–47
Multiplication
    alternative algorithms for, 286
    of multi-digit numbers, 281–281
    of single-digit numbers, 275–278
    strategies for, 276–277, 283

National Association for the Education
    of Young Children (NAEYC), 36,
    37, 39
National Council of Teachers of
    Mathematics (NCTM), 204
National Council of Teachers of
    Mathematics (NCTM) standards,
    10–22
    assessment and, 64–66
    content standards, 17–22
    influence on textbook content, 14
    problem solving, 140
    process standards, 15–16
National Library of Virtual
    Manipulatives, 204–205
A Nation at Risk, 9–10
Negative teacher behaviors, 2
Nets, geometric, 301, 303
Newspapers, 204
No Child Left Behind Act,
    23, 24, 63
Norm-referenced tests, 67
Number games, 252
Number lines, 252–253
Numbers, 17

Spatial sense (*cont.*)
   lack of emphasis on, 292
   manipulatives for, 191–192
   in mathematics curriculum, 292,
      299–307
   in middle grades, 304–305
   in other cultures, 208, 238
   in students with disabilities, 297–299
   terminology describing, 290
   van Hiele levels of thinking about,
      294–295
Standardized tests, 23–24
   accommodations for students with
      learning problems in, 23, 24,
      63–64, 142
   criterion-referenced, 67
   format of, 24
   group-administered, 67, 69
   high-stakes, 23–24
   individually administered, 68–69,
      70–71
   modifications for, 23
   norm-referenced, 67
   problem solving in, 141–142
Standards. *See* NCTM standards
Static assessment, 297
Statistical analysis packages, 201
Statistics, 22
Strategic Math Series (program), 148,
   175–176
Strategies
   for addition and subtraction, 280
   for assessment, 86–89
   computational, 109
   conspicuous, 112
   for decimal concepts, 323–324
   for fractional concepts, 318–323
   for multiplication and division,
      276–277, 283
   power of, 109–111
   for problem solving, 150–162
Strategies Intervention Model (SIM), 110
Students with learning problems
   adapting textbooks for, 184–187
   assessment for, 60–61, 71–88
   attitude of, 6–8, 99–100
   constructivist approach to teaching,
      51–52
   curricula for, 174–187
   encouraging, 8–9
   high-stakes testing and, 23–24

as problem solvers, 145–146
   research on, 145–146
   spatial sense in, 297–299
   standards and, 11, 12, 14
   transition services for, 240
Subitizing, 34
Subtraction
   alternative algorithms for, 285
   of multi-digit numbers, 279–281
   of single-digit numbers, 268–273
   strategies for, 280–285

Table of specifications, 85–86
Tangrams, 196
Tangram Task, 302
Teachers
   attitude of, 3–6
   changing roles of, 25–26
   competency areas for, 95
   training of, 26
Technology
   assistive, 173
   calculators, 198–199
   computer environments, 202–204
   software, 200–202
   web, 202
Ten frame, 260–261
Testing. *See* Standardized tests
Test of Early Mathematics Ability
   (TEMA-3), 70
Test of Mathematical Abilities (TOMA-
   2), 71
Textbooks, 95
   adaptation checklist for, 356
   adapting for special populations,
      184–187
   adoption criteria for, 180–182
   influence of standards on, 14
Theorems, 20
Think-aloud techniques, 82–83, 299
Time, telling, 231
TouchMath, 178–179
Transfer-of-learning strategies, 111–112,
   149
Transition planning, 238–242
Trapezoids, 35

Underlying concepts, 96–97, 127, 245
Unit blocks, proportional, 302
Unit cubes, 194
Unit Organizer Routine, 127–128

Unit planning, 127–132
   content organizer for, 127–128
   correlation coefficients, 116–118
   for elementary school, 129
   equivalent fractions, 112–116
   for high school, 132–134
   for middle school, 129–131
   problem-based, 131
   thematic, 129–130
   for wide range of skill levels, 132
Universal design, 172–174
University of Virginia Center for
   Technology and Teacher
   Education, 205

Validity, 62
van Hiele levels of geometric thinking,
   294–295
Variables, notation for, 336
Varied practice, 104–105, 106
Venn diagrams, 307
Virtual manipulatives, 202–203
Visualization, of numbers, 251
Visuospatial disabilities, 53
Vygotsky, Lev, 44–45

What Works Clearinghouse, 180–181
Whole-number relationships
   multi-digit computation, 278–288
   properties, 269
   single-digit operations, 267–278
Wisconsin Online Resource Center, 205
Word problems. *See also* Problem
   solving
   carrying out plan for, 161–162
   characteristics of, 165
   developing plan for, 153–161
   in high-stakes testing, 141–142
   review of, 162
   routine versus nonroutine, 147, 150
   steps in solving, 146–150
   types of, 150
   understanding, 150–153
   use of visual imagery with, 145–146
   writing for, 218
Writing, in mathematics, 215–219
   conventions of, 218–219
World Wide Web, software on, 202

Zero, teaching concept of, 255
Zone of proximal development, 45